REC-
ONCILIATION

**ESSAYS ON AUSTRALIAN
RECONCILIATION**

ESSAYS ON AUSTRALIAN
RECONCILIATION

REC-
ONCILIATION

EDITED BY
MICHELLE GRATTAN

Black Inc is an imprint of Bookman Press Pty. Ltd.
227 Collins Street
Melbourne Victoria 3000
Australia
61 3 9654 2000

All rights reserved.
No part of this publication may be reproduced, stored in a retrieval system, or transmitted in any form or by any means electronic, mechanical, photocopying, recording or otherwise without the prior consent of the publishers.

Copyright to this collection © Michelle Grattan 2000
Copyright in the individual stories is retained by the authors.

National Library of Australia
Cataloguing-in-Publication entry

Grattan, Michelle.
Reconciliation: essays on reconciliation in Australia.

ISBN 1 86395 186 5

1. Aborigines, Australian - Government relations. 2. Social justice - Australia. 2. Aborigines, Australian - Social conditions. 4. Aborigines, Australian - Treatment. 5. Australia - Race relations. I. Title.

305.89915

Permission to re-print lyrics from 'Special Treatment' by Paul Kelly and 'Treaty' by Yothu Yindu kindly granted by Mushroom Music.

Permission to re-print lyrics from 'Thou Shalt Not Steal' by Kev Carmody kindly granted by Larrikin Music.

Permission to re-print lyrics from 'Blackfella Whitefella' written by Neil Murray/George Rurrambu kindly granted by Rondor Music Australia.

'The Dawn is at Hand' and 'Aboriginal Charter of Rights' by Oodgeroo of the tribe Noonuccal from *My People*, 3e, The Jacaranda Press, 1990. Reproduced by permission of John Wiley & Sons Australia.

Michelle Grattan has been chief political correspondent of the *Sydney Morning Herald* and head of its Canberra bureau since 1999. She joined the *Age* in 1970 after tutoring in politics at Monash University, and was posted to Canberra in 1971. From 1976 to 1993 she was the *Age's* chief political correspondent, heading its Canberra bureau, before editing the *Canberra Times* in 1993-95. She returned to the *Age* as political editor in 1995 and was a political columnist with the *Australian Financial Review* in 1996-98. She co-authored *Can Ministers Cope?* (with Patrick Weller) and *Managing Government* (with Fred Gruen). Her writing on journalism includes the monograph *Editorial Independence: An Outdated Concept?* Michelle holds the honorary appointment of adjunct professor in journalism at the University of Queensland.

Table of Contents

Oodgeroo   1
Aboriginal Charter of Rights

Michelle Grattan   3
Introduction

Sir William Deane   9
Australia Day 2000 Message

Aden Ridgeway   12
An Impasse or a Relationship in the Making?

Evelyn Scott   18
A Personal Reconciliation Journey

Frank Brennan   25
Reconciling our Differences

Newspoll, Saulwick & Muller and Hugh Mackay   33
Public Opinion on Reconciliation

Henry Reynolds   53
A Crossroads of Conscience

Paul Keating   60
The Redfern Park Speech

Linda Burney   65
Not Just a Challenge, an Opportunity

Colin Tatz   74
The Dark Side of Sport

John Howard   88
Practical Reconciliation

Paul D. Wand   97
Aboriginal Communities & Mineral Resources: The Rio Tinto Experience

Rick Farley   105
What's the Alternative?

Mary Darkie   113
This is My Life

Boori Monty Pryor   116
Breaking the Cycle

Robert Milliken   121
A New Confidence

Robert Manne   129
The Stolen Generations

Aban Contractor   140
Forgive Us Our Trespasses

Lillian Holt   146
Reflections on Race and Reconciliation

Tim Costello   152
An Opening to New Seasons

Drusilla Modjeska   158
A Bitter Wind

Noel Pearson 165
Aboriginal Disadvantage

Kim Beazley 176
Unfinished Business

Peter Garrett 182
A Humbug-free Zone

Djon Mundine 191
Negotiating Co-existence

Hannah McGlade 195
Doubtful Island

Melissa Castan 202
Reconciliation, Law and the Constitution

Pera Wells 210
Does Australia Have a Human Rights Diplomacy?

Petro Georgiou 217
Justice for All as Long as You're White

Peter Jull 220
Embracing New Voices: Reconciliation in Canada

Geoff Clark 228
Not Much Progress

P.P. McGuinness 235
Reconciliation is a Two-way Street

Inga Clendinnen 242
True Stories and What We Make of Them

Bain Attwood 254
The Burden of the Past in the Present

Christopher Pearson 260
The Need for Scepticism

Patrick Dodson 264
Lingiari: Until the Chains are Broken

Raimond Gaita 275
Guilt, Shame and Collective Responsibility

Lowitja O' Donoghue 288
A Journey of Healing or a Road to Nowhere?

Gustav Nossal 297
Symbolism and Substance in the Surge Towards Reconciliation

Council for Aboriginal Reconciliation 305
Draft Declaration of Reconciliation

Oodgeroo 307
The Dawn is at Hand

Notes on Contributors 309

Indigenous Issues on the Net: A List of Websites 315

Aboriginal Charter of Rights
Oodgeroo, from the tribe Noonuccal

We want hope, not racialism,
Brotherhood, not ostracism,
Black advance, not white ascendance;
Make us equals, not dependants.
We need help, not exploitation,
We want freedom, not frustration;
Not control, but self-reliance,
Independence, not compliance,
Not rebuff, but education,
Self-respect, not resignation.
Free us from a mean subjection,
From a bureaucrat Protection.
Let's forget the old-time slavers:
Give us fellowship, not favours;
Encouragement, not prohibitions,
Homes, not settlements and missions.
We need love, not overlordship,
Grip of hand, not whip-hand wardship;
Opportunity that places
White and black on equal basis.
You dishearten, not defend us,
Circumscribe, who should befriend us.
Give us welcome, not aversion,

Give us choice, not cold coercion,
Status, not discrimination,
Human rights, not segregation.
You the law, like Roman Pontius,
Make us proud, not colour-conscious;
Give the deal you still deny us,
Give goodwill, not bigot bias;
Give ambition, not prevention,
Confidence, not condescension;
Give incentive, not restriction,
Give us Christ, not crucifixion.
Though baptised and blessed and Bibled
We are still tabooed and libelled.
You devout Salvation-sellers,
Make us neighbours, not fringe-dwellers;
Make us mates, not poor relations,
Citizens, not serfs on stations.
Must we native Old Australians
In our land rank as aliens?
Banish bans and conquer caste,
Then we'll win our own at last.

Introduction
Michelle Grattan

The origins of this book lie in the early 1970s when, as a junior reporter arriving in Canberra, Aboriginal affairs became part of my beat. It would turn into an enduring interest.

A few years before, the Holt government had gained Commonwealth power at a 1967 referendum to make policy for Aborigines. Politically, the land rights cause was stirring. In its 1972 Australia Day statement on policy for Aborigines, the McMahon government promised funding to buy land outside reserves, but it refused to grant land rights on reserves based on traditional association. That day, Aboriginal protesters set up their tent embassy outside Parliament House, including a minister for 'Caucasian affairs'. Surely one of the most savvy and potent protests in Australia's history, the 'tent city' captured imagination at home and abroad, as several times it was pulled down in dramatic physical clashes, only to be re-erected with dogged determination.

Almost three decades later, in 2000, there was a repeat of the perennial media speculation that the Howard government might move the tent embassy, now an historical tourist attraction outside the 'old' Parliament House. All those years on, the embassy could still niggle at a Liberal government's sense of order, a metaphor perhaps for the unfinished business that Aboriginal affairs policy represents.

The years between have been simultaneously encouraging and disappointing. Legislative gains and landmark legal victories in the Mabo and Wik High Court cases have secured extensive land rights. Part of the cost, though, was an ugly backlash that partly fuelled the One Nation party. Progress has been made in education and health. Aborigines remain, however, among the most severely disadvantaged Australians on almost every measure. The emergence of a prosperous and successful Aboriginal middle class cannot offset the fact of the vast number of underprivileged blacks who are struggling, economically and socially. Two Aborigines became senators (the late Neville Bonner, a Liberal, and Aden Ridgeway, an Australian Democrat) and an elected Aboriginal body oversees much federal administration. Still, many Aborigines feel disempowered. The whole nation has become aware of the stolen generation of part-Aboriginal children forcibly separated from their families. But dealing with the legacy is unfinished business, made harder because the Howard government plays down its significance, denying the separated children amount to a generation and describing the phrase 'stolen generation' as rhetorical. The cognoscenti debate and dispute 'black armband' and 'white out'/ 'white-wash' versions of history, while the relationship and responsibilities of current generations to those past are unresolved.

In 1972 the then Liberal government failed to understand the symbolic importance of land to the people who, the High Court would later rule, had owned it before white settlement. In 2000 there is a similar blind spot as prime minister John Howard declines to say sorry on behalf of the nation for past misdeeds of the 'invaders' or 'settlers', according to which vocabulary one prefers (both are accurate). We reporters recorded in 1972 that the nation's treatment of its first people, highlighted by the tent embassy, was an international embarrassment. In 2000, the lack of an apology and Canberra's failure to override the mandatory sentencing systems of the Northern Territory and Western Australia drew sharp condemnation in a report from the United Nations Committee on the Elimination of Racial Discrimination, provoking the government to fury.

There have been many milestones and special moments down the years. For me, one of the latter was 20 January 1973 when I heard Aboriginal affairs minister Gordon Bryant tell a meeting of Gurindjis at Wattie Creek they would be given ownership of their tribal lands—a claim they had been pressing after they walked off Vestey's Wave Hill station in a strike over pay and conditions in 1966. Listening to these people, the primal importance of the land could not fail to move. I reported then:

> About 70 Gurindji men gathered in an open bough hut in the sweltering heat at Wattie Creek to hear Mr Bryant... One by one the Gurindji men came to the centre of the hut and in soft voices told of their feelings for the land. Mick Gunginan from Victoria River Downs, his legs shaking with nervousness, said: 'I want to get back my land. I want to get it back badly.' Lupgna Giari ('Captain Major') told them: 'We'll own the station—and we'll have to look after it properly. We've got to look after ourselves when we get the land, and try to make a living with cattle. I think we can handle it.' Gurindji leader Vincent Lingiari, who has travelled throughout

Australia to get support for the land claims, sat silently in a chair, his hat pulled far down over his eyes. He said later: 'I feel very good about the decision. When I was first in the strike Vestey tried to push me back to Wave Hill. I told him no. I said this was my father's land and my grandfather's land.'

Lingiari (who lived to see his people get their land) and Torres Strait Islander Eddie Mabo (who led the successful bid for local ownership of Mer Island, only to die of cancer several months before the High Court decision) are among the heroes of the land rights and wider indigenous causes. These heroes include non-Aborigines such as 'Nugget' Coombs, that remarkable Australian who cajoled and confronted governments of both persuasions on behalf of the nation's indigenous people.

Coombs, with his great blend of economic and social policy interests, came to Aboriginal affairs late and nearly by chance. Prime minister Holt and his department head John Bunting had asked him, in the wake of the 1967 referendum, to advise about possible organisational structures to put in place. He recommended a small Council for Aboriginal Affairs, which Holt then invited him to head. 'I had had no previous professional or administrative experience with Aborigines', Coombs wrote later, apart from as a young teacher living in a Western Australia country town when he saw 'how prejudice and fear can drive otherwise kindly people to behave towards their more unfortunate compatriots with cruelty and derision... I think that, like most Australians of my generation, I accepted the prevailing dogma that Aborigines were doomed to become extinct and believed that, apart from behaving towards those we encountered with common humanity, there was nothing that we could usefully do.' A little over a decade after he threw himself into the fray, Coombs was promoting the idea of an Aboriginal treaty.

Lingiari, Mabo and Coombs are all dead, but their influence remains to inspire indigenous and non-indigenous alike as they face today's challenges.

Of these, reconciliation is perhaps the most ambitious and elusive. The degree to which it is attained will declare much about Australians as a people. Yet who's to say at what point—if ever—substantial reconciliation will have been achieved or how much must be done before progress can be claimed? This is not something that can be precisely measured by the number of houses built, the proportion of Aboriginal children finishing school, or improvements in infant mortality rates. It vitally involves material progress, but also intrinsically matters of the spirit. It is about attitudes, white and black, as well as the tangibles. Non-Aboriginal cynics tarnish hopes by saying gestures will always be followed by indigenous demands for more. Black sceptics incline to an all-or-nothing approach. Between the extremes, Aboriginal and non-Aboriginal pragmatists and idealists accept this is a journey of nearly endless length.

There are, however, inns along the way. Reconciliation is a road down which the nation's original citizens, and those who came after, are walking, bound together as members of the great Australian tribe, but still trying to get into step.

Gus Nossal, deputy chair of the Council for Aboriginal Recognition, has reminded us reconciliation has two sides: the symbolic and the action-oriented.

> The symbolic side is enormously important. There must be a respect for indigenous cultural identity and spiritual beliefs; an acknowledgement of the tragic history since white settlement, including dispossession from land and family, loss of identity, heritage, culture and language, and poor treatment by a variety of institutions; and a recognition of indigenous rights stemming from the unique status of Aborigines and Torres Strait Islanders as the first Australians, the original occupants and custodians of this land. Equally, action plans leading to greater social justice for indigenous Australians are essential. There must be a renewed effort to address the serious disadvantages of indigenous people in all key sectors, including health, education, housing, employment and community justice. There also must be a commitment to work towards the fuller participation of indigenous people in the economic, political, cultural and social life of the nation.

The quest has become a political obstacle course. After a confrontation at the 1997 Reconciliation Convention, in his 1998 election victory speech victory John Howard vowed 'to commit myself very genuinely to the cause of true reconciliation with the Aboriginal people of Australia by the centenary of federation.' He added, 'We may differ and debate about the best way of achieving reconciliation, but I think all Australians are united in a determination to achieve it.' By early 2000 Howard, unwilling to make the national apology that many regard as essential, was regretting his commitment to a timetable. The 'differences' were overwhelming the 'determination'. 'True reconciliation' had become 'practical reconciliation.'

When Australia federated a century ago the Aborigines were not even on the fringes of the debate. They were seen as a fast disappearing race with little relevance to future politics. In contrast, the position and plight of Aborigines are at the centre of things as we come to the centenary of federation. Looking back over the century, Aboriginal affairs has been one of the most difficult, traumatic areas of public policy in this country. Atrocities have been committed against the continent's original people, driven by greed, fear or, sometimes, honourable motives now often considered misguided. The nation's policy has swung between assimilationism and brands of self-determination and self-management. Aboriginal leaders have divided among themselves about the way forward.

Even the decade-long formal reconciliation process, run by the Council for Aboriginal Reconciliation and now reaching an end, albeit not a final outcome, arose out of a failure to agree on grander gestures. Earlier talk of a 'compact' or even a treaty had floundered. The council, set up under legislation in 1991 with bipartisan support, was a fall-back, with judgement day—the council under a sunset clause goes out of existence at the end of 2000—a long way off. To politicians, a decade is an eternity. And indeed, neither of the leaders there when the act was passed, prime minister Bob Hawke, and opposition leader John Hewson, is still in politics.

For the new council however, this was the beginning of an extraordinary journey. At the first meeting, council members, in a bonding session, sat round the table on a Saturday afternoon introducing themselves. Television personality Ray Martin, an inaugural member who is still on the council, recalls:

> The whitefellas told stories of how they got on the council. The blackfellas told their stories, and they were without exception stolen generation or affected by the stolen generation. Their stories were enough to make you cry. They were tales of truth—of deprivation, death, discrimination—simple down-to-earth talk, matter-of-fact, a total absence of whingeing. All the whitefellas walked away shocked—we thought, if only the rest of Australia could hear this.

And indeed, reconciliation must be a matter for the people as well as the leaders. The opinion polling done for the council in 2000 shows that the Australian public is willing to accept it is important (eight out of ten people agree it is) but when the talk becomes specific—like embracing an apology, or acknowledging Aboriginal disadvantage—the nation has a long way to go. However, the news from the ground appears more encouraging. The council's consultations have found that a lot of communities seem to be taking the cause to their hearts. In contrast to what happens in the world of white and black stakeholders, there is less politics at the grass roots. As for indigenous people specifically, qualitative research done for the council in March/April 2000 found a widespread sense of dispossession, but a willingness to forgive the past nevertheless. Indigenous views about an apology were mixed: some thought it important; others felt it didn't mean anything, especially if not given sincerely.

While it is vital the politicians provide impetus, the political static suggests the reconciliation movement may at the moment have to rely heavily on people power. That could mean results do not appear as dramatic as might be wished; then, grand national markers are perhaps inevitably imperfect. Hopefully that will not stop the march—and ultimately the real test must be at the local and personal level anyway. A friend recently told me of an experience he had a few years ago at an evening sharing songs with a group of Adnyamathanha people in the Flinders Ranges. After he sang a song he'd written about the country, one of the Aborigines walked around the camp fire, put his hand on the white man's shoulder, and said, 'This is your country too.' As Aden Ridgeway says, reconciliation is about the merging of two versions of the past, bringing together 'two perspectives of one history.'

Talking is the tool of reconciliation. At the political level, even when big differences over history and policies remain, face-to-face dialogue can be a clearing house for tension, as John Howard and the ATSIC commissioners found during a frank and sometimes emotional dinner at the Lodge recently.

The essays in this collection span a wide range of views of the reconciliation process, from those who doubt its efficacy, through to passionate advocates and most positions between. They contain also some moving stories of personal journeys of struggle, achievement and faith, including that from council chairwoman Evelyn Scott; she takes hope from the young people committed to the cause, who have 'a vision of an Australia free of bigotry and racism.' The stolen generation comes up time and again: Robert Manne's historical account is galvanising and shocking.

As well as pieces prepared for this book, some articles and speeches have been adapted or reproduced. For instance, Noel Pearson's 1999 lecture to the Brisbane Institute is much quoted but hard to find in its detail; similarly, Paul Keating's Redfern address. We have also included two parts of the new research commissioned by the council, as well as a long-term overview of public opinion by Hugh Mackay—important source material for those seeking to promote reconciliation or to assess what is being done. There is also a list of useful websites.

Both John Howard and Kim Beazley have contributed, as has Aden Ridgeway, who has a foot in both parliamentary and Aboriginal politics, and Geoff Clark, who holds the most senior position in indigenous politics, as the first elected chair of ATSIC.

Business, the entertainment industry, the arts and sport all have distinctive roles in reconciliation. Paul Wand's contribution presents the new and more positive face of business that has been emerging in the last few years. As we approach the Olympics, Colin Tatz's observations about sport are timely if confronting. Peter Garrett records the power of song to touch the heart and capture the issues; Djon Mundine writes of art, where Aboriginal culture has impacted perhaps most directly on the wider community, and paints a disturbing picture.

My thanks to contributors who gave generously of their time in face of what one described as 'brutal' deadlines; to Bookman's Nadine Davidoff whose ideas and contacts greatly widened the book's scope and authors' list, and whose untiring effort and commitment to the just-in-time principle made the impossible possible; and to researcher Pera Wells, a contributor herself, who helped shape the book as well as looking after much detail.

13 April, 2000

Australia Day Message 2000
Sir William Deane

This Year 2000 Australia Day is a time to look back at the past and forward to the future. Back at our origins, our achievements, our successes and our failures. Forward to the challenges which lie ahead—including the critical challenge of preventing and healing harmful divisions within our society.

There are three strands of our Australian identity upon which we should particularly rely in facing that critical challenge.

The first is the national ethos of mutual acceptance and respect which binds us Australians together notwithstanding our diverse origins. That multicultural inclusiveness sustains our nation.

The second of these strands is what I think of as 'the spirit of Anzac'. It takes us all the way back to the early hours of that day, almost 85 years ago, when the boats carrying the first 1,500 young Australians were moving through darkness towards the Gallipoli shore. Last Anzac Day, at the deeply moving dawn service at Gallipoli, I tried to explain what that spirit means to us Australians: 'Courage and endurance, and duty, and love of country, and mateship, and good humour and the survival of a sense of self-worth and decency in the face of dreadful odds'.

It also means mutual dependence. It is, as our great historian Manning Clark wrote, 'something too deep for words'. It inspires our nation.

Even at this moment, that spirit is being demonstrated by our fellow Australians who are serving—in our defence force, in police forces or in aid organisations—in hazardous peacekeeping and humanitarian operations in East Timor, in Bougainville and many other foreign places.

The third strand is the generosity and the sense of fair play that are so common between Australians.

During the almost four years that I have been governor-general, my wife, Helen, and I have been overwhelmed by the generosity of the countless Australians who work—or give—to help those who are living below the poverty line or are in need of assistance. In times of national tragedy, we have been equally impressed by the willingness of ordinary Australians to stretch out the hand of assistance and comfort. That spirit of generosity is the great healing force of our nation.

We Australians enjoy tremendous natural advantages. Our country is among the most beautiful and resource-rich on the globe. Currently, we are experiencing sustained economic growth. Yet the divisions among us—between the haves and the have-nots and even the city and the country—give cause for concern. And while criticism and disagreement are hallmarks of true democracy, there is a real danger that an unjustifiable degree of distrust or denigration will damage our democratic institutions or discourage people from serving in them.

The three strands of our history and identity which I have mentioned—our multicultural inclusiveness, the spirit of Anzac and the generosity of ordinary Australians—will enable each of us, in our own way, to help heal those divisions and avoid that danger in the days ahead. They will also help us realise a vision which I think we all share for our country: of Australians coming and staying together and supporting one another, in changing and often difficult times.

In the coming months, there are at least two national events which will be of true significance in that regard.

In May, we will all have an opportunity to seek national consensus on the draft document which the Council for Aboriginal Reconciliation will present after years of work. With goodwill on all sides, we can reach that consensus. If we do, it will reflect the real progress which we have made in recent years. And, while there will still be much further to go, we will have reached an important milestone in the journey towards true and lasting reconciliation.

And then, in June, the Olympic Torch will arrive at Uluru—to commence its journey around Australia in the lead up to the Sydney Olympics. That journey will provide a wonderful opportunity for all Australians to come together in the months leading up to what should be a great world celebration of our nation and its people. Each of us, in our own way, can help make certain that it is.

The young Bendigo poet of federation, William Gay, died some three years before his plea that Australians 'rise, united… And be one people' was fulfilled by the establishment of our nation on 1 January 1901. William Gay also wrote:

From all division let our land be free,
For God has made her one: complete she lies
Within the unbroken circle of the skies,
And round her indivisible the sea
Breaks on her single shore.

As we approach the centenary of our federation, my wish is that the prayer that our land be free of harmful division is also fulfilled. If it is, then the future will be one of untold promise, not only for our country but for all Australians.

An Impasse or a Relationship in the Making?
Aden Ridgeway

When we travel we remember a journey by simple postcards and the indulgent 'down-time' away from the doldrums of work and daily life. It is almost ritualistic that photographs ought to capture the moment; a prized possession for posterity's sake to tell a future grandchild of a past experience—of another place, other people and another time. All is now long past and everything is only ever remembered as a fleeting moment in the sparkling eye of youth now gone.

And so for me!

Earlier this year, I was in Davos, Switzerland, attending the World Economic Forum. While there, I was profoundly struck by comments of the world-renowned author and philosopher, Umberto Eco, when he said, 'If we lose our memory, we have no soul.'

What he had in mind when he said this is that history and tradition can inform or imprison societies. Memory and tradition are vital ingredients of our sense of people and place, and blood and belonging.

I have been a silent critic that not enough politicians tell 'stories' and even more tell 'tales'. Telling a story is necessary if we are to see ourselves as the sum of what is remembered and recorded about our past; and tradition, custom and belief must be practised because they contain those things of long-standing value.

The advent of globalisation has placed new pressures upon retaining value in society and, if not managed properly, has dire consequences for indigenous Australians. More generally, Australians have a lot to worry about if the new technology revolution means learning more and forgetting faster.

The art of storytelling is at the centre of reconciliation, and reconciliation is at the heart of Australian society. The twenty-first century gives us an opportunity to reflect on the past, to think about the Australia we learnt about at school, and confront what is often an uncomfortable and unfamiliar past.

Many Australians have lost the ability to tell a story and find it even more difficult to accept some 'home-grown' truths particularly as told by indigenous storytellers, peacemakers, healers and bridge-builders.

The idea of reconciliation was borne out of an all-denominational understanding of peace, love and friendship. The road to reconciliation in Australia, however, remains blocked and blurred by the failure to honestly and openly confront stories of lived experiences.

When we take the time to go beyond a superficial social analysis of our history, we may compare ourselves to other people and other places, whether that be South Africa, Northern Ireland, the USA, France or Germany. In each of these cases, and in many others, national identity has been shaped by the traumatic forces of violence and conflict.

Whatever the point of comparison, it is generally assumed that our country has not been defined by widespread war and violence. We have lived far from the rest of the world, isolated from societal trends and without disturbance from neighbouring countries. It is however, true to speak of Australia being less than perfect in its dealings with Aborigines and Torres Strait Islanders. For many indigenous people, it has been an era in which we can rightly say that it has been a most 'bloody and violent period' characterised by war, slavery, conflict and civil unrest. A violence has been done to the Aboriginal mind and personality.

It is understandable then, that there exists a fabric of commonality for people who have been denied recognition, disempowered and denied the human ability to practise and maintain cultural personality. As a consequence, it is not surprising that the people of the oldest living culture on the globe have resisted the idea of full Australian socialisation.

It is easy to describe the end of the twentieth century as a time when many first-world nations saw sense in the need to reconcile with themselves and with each other. Time makes little difference to the quest for reconciliation. This is evidently shown by acts of reconciliation between France and Germany following World War Two; the quest to achieve peace and reconciliation in Northern Ireland; and in 1996, a quiet, but significant reconciliation march by Christians who sought forgiveness from Moslems for acts of atrocity committed by the Crusaders, 900 years ago.

Even for the nations that Australia can identify with: the USA apologised to African Americans for slavery; and the most historic to date, the apology given in the Israeli parliament (Knesset) in February 2000 by president Rau of Germany to the Jewish people and particularly Holocaust survivors. Acts of reconciliation are not extraordinary events. They are just made difficult by men with false ideals and even more difficult by others who can never forgive. It is not surprising, therefore, that when president Rau addressed the Knesset pleading for forgiveness for the Holocaust, several members walked out.

Australian people are also finding the idea of an apology and reconciliation difficult but generally would agree that Aborigines and Torres Strait Islanders have been treated badly in the past. However, some suggest that reconciliation is a conspiracy between the 'Aboriginal industry' and the major parties to defraud the Australian people. This sentiment resonates well with middle-class Australians who feel that the beneficiaries of globally influenced economic change are indigenous people due to perceived special treatment from Australian governments.

The reality, of course, is the misperception that declining economic fortunes, a growing sense of loss of community, and shrinking 'white privilege', can easily be blamed on perceived increasing 'black privilege'. The real story is not that indigenous people have deviated from the idea of 'Australian fairness' or 'a fair go' but that Australia has left indigenous people behind and we are on a journey of 'catch-up' and 'culturally more'.

'Culturally more', also ought not be interpreted as separateness but the means and rights of reconstructing cultural personality. It is in essence, not to have extraordinary rights but to feel normal in a culturally diverse Australian nation and where possible, engage in visible reconstruction of cultural personality and society.

Reconciliation will never be perfect, but it should seek to provide a foundation from which a new relationship can be made and from which we can better understand the perspective of the other side.

In my recent travels, I have sought to take the Australian nation on a journey to confront a new truth and be challenged about our shared past.

As Australians we can be proud that our history has been much different, but we cannot accept credit if false pride blinds us to the necessity of dealing with unfinished business and recognising the damage caused to the personality of indigenous Australians.

Many Australians choose to view the past in a singular way, but history should inform us that the stories of the past are not there to imply guilt; rather they are instructions of the things we must avoid repeating in the future. We must also understand that if we are to view the past differently or without blinkers, it is okay to view the same events in different ways so long as there is a shared conclusion that sometimes good intentions produce enormous harm.

Perhaps as a complete act of blind faith, if reconciliation is to potentially succeed, it may require the sort of apology given recently by

Germany to Jewish people without guilt and without passing the sins of the past to our next generation. In Australia, it is clear that following an act of confrontation with the past, the basic conditions of indigenous Australians to restore cultural personality must be met in balance with the interests of other Australians. There is nothing more than this that I would wish may happen but the gap between indigenous and non-indigenous views on a common past are so great that this renders reconciliation as a fragile Australian imperative.

Notably, there has been a call that the national day of celebration on 26 January should be moved to a more inclusive date in which all Australians can proudly celebrate. I do not agree with this idea. If each of us is the sum of what is remembered and told about our past then there is nothing un-Australian in the idea of one part of the nation celebrating 'settlement' and another celebrating 'survival'. These two notions do not exist exclusive of each other but are the celebration of a single Australia Day, commemorated from different perspectives about the same past.

Last year, I joined with the prime minister of the Australian parliament to call upon the nation to support a Motion of Reconciliation. That motion read as follows:

That the parliament:

(a) reaffirms its whole-hearted commitment to the cause of reconciliation between indigenous and non-indigenous Australians as an important national priority for all Australians;

(b) recognising the achievements of the Australian nation, commits to work together to strengthen the bonds that unite us, to respect and appreciate our differences, and to build a fair and prosperous future in which we can all share;

(c) reaffirms the central importance of practical measures leading to practical results that address the profound economic and social disadvantage which continues to be experienced by many indigenous Australians;

(d) recognises the importance of understanding the shared history of indigenous and non-indigenous Australians and the need to acknowledge openly the wrongs and injustices of Australia's past;

(e) acknowledges that the mistreatment of many indigenous Australians over a significant period represents the most blemished chapter in our national history;

(f) expresses its deep and sincere regret that indigenous Australians suffered injustices under the practices of past generations, and for the hurt and trauma that many indigenous people continue to feel as a consequence of those practices; and

(g) believes that we, having achieved so much as a nation, can now move forward together for the benefit of all Australians.

I gave my support to the motion because what I thought was most needed at the time, was a way of galvanising the stories of the stolen generations to bring about a national cathartic confrontation with the past in order to transform ourselves and deal with the unfinished business.

The motion has not been entirely welcomed nor has it been completely rejected and I hold high hope that this is but a small step in a long and difficult path to reconciliation.

We are a community of shared remembering and if we confront the truth, we can claim ownership of a common story and draw a line between the past and the future, which all Australians can walk.

A nation, however, cannot be told how it ought to reconcile. It must come from within through the acceptance of truth and the need for justice. Today, the delivery of justice will not be an easy one because it requires a policy response from government of 'positive engagement and constructive partnership'.

Reconciliation will also require a change in attitudes and views to provide the right conditions in which the Aboriginal mind and personality can thrive. If achieved, reconciliation can become a crucial factor in giving the gift of national social cohesion.

Ultimately its outcome should produce a new social compact promoting 'rights and responsibilities' balanced against the needs of the wider community, industry and government. In this vein, I believe that there is an increasing need to engage the governments of the day in constructive dialogue, and to make the Aboriginal and Torres Strait Islander ways of life more normal to other Australians.

It will demand that Australia's first peoples must become shareholders in the nation but importantly, that more and more people become involved in making decisions about things that affect their lives. In essence, it will be about achieving mutually beneficial understanding and narrowing the gap of difference without indigenous people feeling further marginalised in Australian society.

Perhaps to make some points on these comments, our ongoing conversation after the year 2000 will need to be more about being hard on the issues while being soft on the personalities involved. Invariably, future talks must never be about 'giving in' or 'giving too much away' but about seeking creative gains and finding solutions to a 200-year impasse.

Our goal is to guarantee a future meeting of young black and white Australians where their talks on reconciliation are not marked by reconciling future actions with our past positions. It is our duty to change the conditions of the future by the decisions we make now.

Overall, it must mean behaving 'fairly' and protecting ourself against those who would be 'unfair' in their dealings. This is what I have sought to do throughout my life—mostly with success and sometimes with no success at all.

At the same time, it will be difficult to achieve all things that are wanted. I suspect, though, that globalisation will make land rights aplenty as more and more people re-locate to metropolitan centres and larger rural towns. Many may think that if existing places become ghost towns, the only people to be left behind will be the Aborigines—what then the fate of the oldest surviving people on the earth? This is another story waiting to be told.

Finally, an Australian never challenged by reconciliation is one who never knows the truth of the past and will never know the meaning of the future. I hope you, who have read my words, will tell your stories and listen to the meaning others may find in them.

A Personal Reconciliation Journey
Evelyn Scott

A lot of people have been referring to the year 2000 as the year for reconciliation and I hope that they are right. But reconciliation will take a lot longer than this year to come into fruition. It will take the commitment of many Australian governments, corporations, community organisations, institutions and individuals. I believe reconciliation will be a reality, but we have much to overcome. Indeed, we are not nearing the end of the reconciliation process—I believe we are at a new beginning.

The Council for Aboriginal Reconciliation has made great progress towards increasing community awareness and establishing a process of reconciliation. Since the council's inception, reconciliation has been a focus for many Australians and a priority of governments.

We recognise that the council will cease to exist under its legislation on 1 January 2001 and that there is still much work to be done. For that reason, we are working towards the establishment of an independent foundation, Reconciliation Australia, to help continue the reconciliation process beyond the council's life.

The foundation will rely heavily upon the People's Movement for Reconciliation consisting of individuals, local, regional and state community groups working towards reconciliation.

In May, the council will hold a major national event called Corroboree 2000 at the Sydney Opera House. At that event, we hand over our final proposal for a national document of reconciliation after years of consultation with the Australian community. From the feedback we have collated to date, 76 percent of Australians who responded individually to the draft document strongly agreed that a document would improve relations between Aboriginal and Torres Strait Islander peoples and the wider Australian community.

When council hands over its final proposal, it will be a reconciliation document which has the support of thousands of Australians. At that time, I will not feel like my work is done. Nor will I feel that reconciliation is achieved in this country.

The way I see it, we are starting a new era for reconciliation; one that has moved on and changed from the agenda of the 1967 referendum days, but which retains the same fundamental bottom line—equality, respect and social justice for indigenous peoples. In this essay, I would like to share some personal insights which have informed and inspired my life and work for indigenous rights and reconciliation.

• • •

On New Year's Eve 1999, my sister and I sat at her place in Bambaroo, near Ingham in Queensland and we got to talking about the new millennium. We talked about the end of the council's term, and I reflected on where I have come from, as the eldest daughter and the second child of a family of 13 children.

My grandfather was a South Sea Islander, stolen at the age of 19, shackled to a ball and chain and brought as a slave to Australia. He was sent over with the Kanakas to clear land in northern Queensland for the sugar industry. I often wish he and my parents were alive to see the changes I have seen. As the granddaughter of a slave, I think I have done alright.

I was brought up in Ingham, northern Queensland on a diet of respect and honesty—and I am grateful for that. My parents always taught me to be proud of who and what I am. My father was one of the first black men to take a white teacher to court and win.

Teachers in those days used to use lawyer canes to discipline students. On one particular day when my brother was clowning in class, the teacher only had a skipping rope which he belted across my brother's back. My father, who had been taught by that teacher years before, believed in discipline but he objected to the fact that the teacher had kept my brother in class during lunchtime, which was not allowed. The doctor who tended to my brother's welts suggested that action needed to be taken. This was in October 1949, when the White Australia Policy was still in full swing. Lots of people tried to discourage my father from taking the teacher to court, saying that we had no hope and that we would never win. When my father came out of the courtroom after winning the case, one of the first people to shake his hand was the teacher's son. I learned a lot from my dad's way of challenging and questioning authority.

After dad won the case, he took us all out of that school and transferred us to another. The new school didn't have a seventh grade, so I was to stay at home to help my mother look after my younger brothers and sisters until I was 21.

My first job outside the home was as a housemaid in a boarding house. I hated that job. There was a vacancy for a domestic at the Ayr Base Hospital, and even though my relatives told me not to apply, I did, and went to become the first black employee in the domestic section at that hospital in 1957. Working there opened the door for other indigenous staff to be employed at the hospital and it contributed to my confidence and development. I became the Australian Workers' Union representative at the hospital, gaining an understanding of our rights as workers and being encouraged to ask questions and to challenge long-held beliefs.

The first time I really started to speak out against racism was in my late twenties and had supportive friends in the trade union movement. Without a formal education, my training came from my life experiences. In the late 1950s, I was introduced to the Federal Council for the Advancement of Aborigines and Torres Strait Islanders (FCAATSI) by its chairman, Joe McGinness, who later became my mentor for life. Joe used to give me material when he was campaigning for the '67 referendum. His attitude was, 'If it's broken—fix it!' and he always had the energy and belief to see his vision through. A Janala man from the Northern Territory, I believe Joe was the most inspirational and respected indigenous leader in the country at that time. I don't believe he has received the full acknowledgement that he deserves for his role in the struggle for justice and equality for our people. His attitude was that it is human instinct to improve a bad situation, and it was his practical approach that I admired.

It was a great honour to be involved in the 1967 referendum campaign and to work with such a dedicated group of indigenous and non-indigenous Australians. That was an important part of this nation's history and a great step forward for reconciliation.

The indigenous members of FCAATSI always met on the Good Friday before the Easter weekend annual meeting to set the agenda. We always had traditional people from all over Australia at those meetings, and I remember one particular indigenous-only meeting when there was a change of government policy about Aboriginal affairs. The leader of the Northern Territory delegation was interpreting the change of policy to his people and he simply said: 'It's like this: same horse, different saddlecloth'. I am pleased to say that I believe things have changed since those days. Looking back over the last 30 years of governments dealing with indigenous affairs, there have been significant changes in policies and methods of forming those policies, though remote communities would understandably find that hard to believe. The creation of the Department of Aboriginal Affairs in the states was one important change, as was the setting up of our own representative body, ATSIC. However, there remains more to be done.

The first time I experienced blatant racism was when I was 28 and I was not allowed to try on the wedding dress that I wanted. In those days, Aboriginal people weren't to be seen shopping in such places—the assumption being that we couldn't afford such dresses. I ended up getting married in a dress I didn't really like. At the time, I had become so used to the racism that I was resigned to it and said nothing. That happened in 1963. I cut that wedding dress up when my two eldest girls were two and three and made them little white outing dresses.

I was married to a Scotsman, and in the sixties, a multi-racial relationship was not accepted easily by either the black or white communities. It was his unequivocal support during my life with him that made it possible for me to pursue activism. He would always look after the kids when I had to go away to the FCAATSI conference every Easter in Canberra. I lost him when I had five children under eleven, and I returned to the workforce with the help of my sisters. I wanted the best education I could get for my children, and I worked hard to make sure I gave them the best I could.

Part of wanting the best for my children involved fighting for and promoting indigenous rights. I want a better Australia, free of racism, where my children have more opportunities than I ever did as a child. That is where reconciliation fits into the picture. I do not believe we could go forward as a nation without it.

Racism is alive and well in Australia today—but it is usually in a more subtle, insidious form than in the days of my youth. It's when you go into a shop and get ignored because you're black; it's when you go to rent a house and are rejected time and again because you're black; it's when hotels and businesses check your credit card but don't check the card of the white person next to you. It's also when a taxi driver refuses you a ride because you're black. This kind of discrimination continues to happen to me in my role as chairperson of the council, and it continues to upset and anger me.

Of course, there are the more overt expressions of racism today too, such as the Pauline Hanson One Nation phenomenon. The simplistic, misinformed policies and comments by her party are not only a danger in themselves. The attention they generate in the media and the passions they stir up in Australians who are blinded by ignorance and fear give rise to other dangers. When a large proportion of Australians don't understand and fear indigenous issues, it becomes easy for mainstream politicians, focused on the short-term political mood, to be tempted to imitate the popular catch-cries of racism in a bid to win seats or preference votes. This acceptance of racism can be overt—as shown by Ms Hanson's rhetoric—or disguised as pseudo-intellectual and 'practical' policies by others who suggest a degree of sympathy with those concerns. I believe it is the quieter, more 'accepted' racism which, if it continues unquestioned, is more harmful. Ignorance has a lot to answer for as the breeding ground of fear, prejudice and misunderstanding. It's one of the great joys of the reconciliation process that two of its central themes are overcoming ignorance and promoting cross-cultural understanding.

Since my early days, I have seen great changes in this country. It's mainly people's attitudes which have changed. During the council's recent consultations about the draft document for reconciliation, I have seen people who are aggressive at the start of meetings who then change as they learn new things about Aboriginal people and the process of reconciliation. I talked to many people in towns across Australia who hadn't met an Aboriginal person before. It is vital that we share with those people the reasons why reconciliation is so important to our reputation as a nation and as a fair and honest people. Reconciliation must have practical as well as spiritual outcomes if it is to appeal to all Australians, and that is why the council has made its Strategies to Advance Reconciliation such a major part of its final document.

There are some very practical examples of reconciliation in action that have inspired me during my time with the council. One such example is that of the mining sector. Twenty years ago, mining companies did their best to ignore indigenous peoples. Indigenous people were exploited, sacred sites were unthinkingly desecrated or destroyed, indigenous cultural and personal sensitivities were ignored or even mocked.

Those practices created trauma, resentment, mistrust and in some cases, resistance among Aboriginal peoples. Over time, this ongoing lack of understanding and consultation meant that in many cases each side was reacting to stereotyped images of the other, and not the real thing.

Today, some mining companies employ senior level Aboriginal staff, consult and form partnerships with Aboriginal communities. These partnerships are formed for the benefit of both parties, and are a fundamental part of the reconciliation process.

Australia's ethnic communities have been firm supporters of the reconciliation process, sharing reconciliation's rejection of racism and search for equality. Ethnic communities know about the politics of division which thrives on fear and ignorance. They have worked very closely with the council over its nine years to share understanding of indigenous cultures through their networks and have always supported the struggle for indigenous rights. Of course, Australia's ethnic communities have shared the burden of racism carried by indigenous people, though in a different form.

The attacks on people of minority or indigenous backgrounds in Australia has lead many people to fear for our future and to question whether reconciliation is possible. I am not one of those who despair, and nor are the members of the Council for Aboriginal Reconciliation.

We believe there is enough support for reconciliation in the Australian people and enough willingness to learn about the indigenous contribution to the heritage and the identity of Australia in our education systems to see through the necessary changes. Australians have a new readiness to explore and address the complex causes of the social and economic disadvantages still suffered by so many Aboriginal and Torres Strait Islander people. We see more awareness and commitment in the People's Movement for Reconciliation, pushing our formal political institutions towards the practical and symbolic steps that need to be taken to make sure we never turn back from the path to reconciliation.

Above all, my greatest hope lies with the young people I have met, read about and seen in action promoting reconciliation. I have great faith in young Australians and their ability to effect change. The Students who Action Reconciliation Seriously (STARS) network is a shining example of young activists who aren't waiting until they're older and in positions of power to make a difference. I admire that. They have a vision of an Australia free of bigotry and racism and they are seeing it out. Young indigenous and non-indigenous people are organising their own conferences, staging performances, increasing awareness among their peers and their families. I am confident that these young talents will see through our hopes and visions for a better Australia.

I believe reconciliation is about getting win-win outcomes. If that means we progress slowly—so be it. It could take decades to achieve true reconciliation, but we have come a long way since 1967.

I feel that I've made a small contribution to reconciliation and to the advancement of Aboriginal and Torres Strait Islander peoples in my lifetime. When you are dedicated to a cause such as this, it is your whole life. I didn't spend the time with my children that I should have, but I will make up for that when I hand in my chairperson's title at the end of this year. I will still be interested in what develops in reconciliation and indigenous affairs, but it will be from the sideline, and I am happy to move over for the younger generation to take over.

When the council walks away at the end of this year, I think we can say that it raised people's awareness about working together to make this a country to be proud of. I think Australia is the best country in the world, but until we recognise and address the rights of indigenous people, we cannot stand proud as a nation.

Aboriginal peoples are the first peoples of this country. Our rights stem from that fact. I know what it means to have my rights ignored and disrespected. So do thousands of Aboriginal and Torres Strait Islander peoples. The wider Australian community needs to understand that for many indigenous peoples, recognition and respect for our rights forms the basis of a meaningful reconciliation process. We also need action by governments to ensure our rights are upheld.

I believe we need a united indigenous leadership to allow our leaders to lead and to give us the power to find the solutions we want.

I think we should look at forming partnerships with governments not only to improve our people's situation, but to empower all people in the communities across Australia. Only then will we see the council's vision of a united Australia which respects this land of ours, values the Aboriginal and Torres Strait Islander heritage, and provides justice and equity for all.

Reconciling our Differences
Frank Brennan

I am a fifth generation Australian out of Ireland. I was raised and educated in Queensland before moving south and then travelling extensively as a lawyer and priest espousing Aboriginal rights and reconciliation. Here are some of the highlights in my journey of reconciliation followed by some reflections for the future.

Two weeks after I started secondary school in Toowoomba, Queensland, decimal currency was introduced. In my mind I can still hear the song from the advertisement for 'the 14th of February 1966'. Of course, the change had immediate practical impact on my life every time I went to the school tuck shop. A year later was the 1967 referendum which focused on Aboriginal rights. I have no memory of that referendum. It had no immediate practical impact on my life. As far as I know, there were no Aborigines at my school. As far as I know, I had never met an Aborigine. I definitely had no Aboriginal friends. I cannot recall any advertisement about the campaign. I cannot remember any teacher having mentioned the matter. In all of this, I was not the only one. My classmates were all the same as me. Aborigines were out of sight and out of mind.

In 1971, I entered the big world of university. There was a lot of political activity. Draft dodgers were objecting to conscription and many students were demonstrating against Australian involvement in the Vietnam War. The colourful Sir Joh Bjelke-Petersen went one step further than his southern colleagues and declared a state of emergency for the playing of the last Springbok Rugby Test in Brisbane. I was a first year law student perplexed about the relationship between law, politics and power on the one hand and race and sport on the other. Often there would be rowdy forums held on campus during lunch time. Aboriginal leaders like Len Watson, Dennis Walker and Cheryl Buchanan would come and decry the situation on Aboriginal reserves where people were still 'living under the Act'. I did not take a lot of notice, but I wondered if their stories could possibly be true. Were there really separate laws for Aborigines? That year, for the first time, an Australian court looked at the issue of Aboriginal land rights and said no rights could have survived the assertion of British sovereignty on the Australian continent. In 1972, one law student (known to be a Communist!) asked if he could write his assignment for property law on Aboriginal land rights. He was told that he could not because there was no such thing.

My later years at university were during the Whitlam government which promised land rights for Aborigines in the Northern Territory. The Aboriginal legal service was established in Brisbane. I went in one day a week as a volunteer, regularly meeting Aborigines in the office and in the courts. Gradually I came to realise that all was not well and that the present situation of many disadvantaged Aborigines in trouble with 'the law' was determined by a dreadful history whereby 'the law' was used as an instrument of oppression and neglect. Law, politics and power impacted on the lives of these people whose opportunities as Australians were nothing like mine, and largely because they were Aborigines.

By 1981, I was heavily involved in the law and politics of Aboriginal rights. As a barrister, I appeared in court for an Aboriginal man who had killed his partner. They both lived on the Weipa Aboriginal reserve in north Queensland. The homicide rate on Queensland reserves was the highest recorded amongst any group in the world. The court heard that one did not have to be mad or bad to be a member of such a community; one had only to be Aboriginal. This man and his partner were both shaped and destroyed by life in such a community. The accused had been subjected to all sorts of testing in the preparation of the case. Using standard intelligence tests, the psychologists had concluded that he was borderline defective. But using a culture fair test, a professor of psychology placed him in the top ten percent of the population. I remember asking the professor in the witness box whether it was possible that the man in the dock was the most intelligent person in the courtroom. He said it was not improbable. What had we done as a society, as a nation, to create such a situation?

Law, policies and government programs were one thing. But what about personal relationships, knowledge of our shared history, hearing the stories, and going forward together? Over the next couple of decades, I devoted myself to working for better laws and policies. I established contacts, working relationships and friendships with many Aborigines. I also had my fair share of disagreements and misunderstandings. I could see that change to 'the law' was not enough. Mind you, there were big legal and political developments including Mabo, Wik, land rights, native title legislation, heritage protection legislation, ATSIC, land funds, Abstudy, Aboriginal hostels and programs for better health, education and community government. A better life for all Australians, including Aborigines, could not be dictated or mandated by Canberra or Brisbane, Sydney or Perth. We had to find a way of owning the past, drawing the line and moving forward, shaping a better future. For me, this is what reconciliation is all about. I have never been too hung up on the word. Like all buzz words, it can be used dangerously in the political process. In the wrong hands, reconciliation can be used to paper over the differences, pretending the worst is all behind us, acting as if there is now a level playing field, and silencing the advocates for justice who might be upsetting the existing power and resource sharing arrangements. In the right hands, reconciliation is a useful concept because its preconditions are recognition, respect and justice, allowing us to work together, building trust, even when faced with intractable problems which require compromise and understanding from both sides.

In 1985, I attended a meeting of Aborigines living in a fringe camp at Mantaka on the outskirts of Kuranda by the Barron River in north Queensland. The Aborigines had lived on a reserve which was run by a church and which had since closed. Some of the people moved to government housing in Cairns but they did not like it much and the neighbours liked it even less. Eventually they ended up as fringe dwellers on land they regarded as their traditional country. They were seeking land title and money for houses from governments in Brisbane and Canberra. At the end of the meeting, the convenor pointed across the river and said, 'See that house: that is Mr X's weekender. They don't come very often but when they do they come by helicopter. See that helipad on the roof. It cost $3/4 million.' That was almost twice the amount they were seeking for basic permanent housing.

I have often told this story in schools. Especially in the better-off schools, there are many questions: Why don't the Aborigines build their own houses if they want them? What are they complaining about? If the white man didn't come, they wouldn't even have a water supply. If it weren't for Mr X paying his taxes, there would be no money to pay these people welfare. After many years, I gave up trying to answer these questions or to refute these comments. In response, I ask only one question: Which side of the river are you standing on as you ask your questions?

There is never any doubt about which side of the river people are standing on. Can you see that there are just as many questions that can be asked from the other side of the river? They are just as unanswerable.

They are likely to make you just as upset and powerless and confused. Reconciliation is about being able to stand on either side of the river. It is also about being able to assist with the bridge building needed so that others can move more readily from one side of the river to the other.

I well recall my first visit to Bourke in western New South Wales. I was asked to come because there were race problems even in the primary school playground. I arrived at the school, and was asked, 'Are you a blow-in?' I was then introduced to the school staff, including the Aboriginal teacher aides. The person introducing me listed my qualifications and credentials but omitted the main one—that I was a blow-in. I then introduced myself, admitting upfront that I was a blow-in. I had never been to Bourke before. I might never come again. I knew little about life in Bourke except that it was difficult and it did not matter whether you were black or white, an adult walking down the main street at night or a child in the school playground by day. Race relations were poor. Everyone's quality of life was affected. We Australians are very good at passing the buck. We could blame Canberra or Sydney or history. But the buck has to stop here and now. The blow-ins cannot solve the problems. We have to accept joint responsibility for our local situation. This is another key aspect of reconciliation.

That night at a community meeting, some local Aborigines told the story of their history in the area. A white cotton farmer was very moved, observing that his family had lived in the area for many generations but that he 'had no idea' that these things went on. Telling and hearing the stories is often the beginning of true reconciliation.

During the Wik debate, I stumbled in late to a meeting of angry pastoralists, one of whom told me that I should return to my city church and say my prayers. At first I was upset but then I realised this man had done me a great service. Wik, like many of the issues in reconciliation, requires the people most affected—Aborigines, pastoralists and miners—to get together and appreciate each other's positions. But the issues are so complex that they cannot be solved by only the stakeholders coming together. There is a place for honest brokers, blow-ins, and facilitators so that bridges of understanding can be built and so that all players can appreciate the limits of principled compromise.

I was privileged to be one of the participants at the 1997 Reconciliation Convention. At that time, the prime minister's past speech writer, Christopher Pearson, offered this observation of me in the *Australian Financial Review*: 'Parliamentarians aside, Fr Frank Brennan seems to have been the individual most responsible for lumbering the body politic with reconciliation as a shibboleth'. I was supposed to be insulted, but I was flattered. In the Old Testament Book of Judges when there was war between Ephraim and Gilead, the men of Gilead were able to weed out the Ephraimite fugitives wanting to cross the River Jordan by asking them to pronounce the word 'Shibboleth'. Unable to pronounce it correctly, they would give themselves away, saying 'Sibboleth', whereupon they would be seized and slaughtered. If the Scripture were to be believed, 42,000 Ephraimites perished by failing this test of pronunciation. In recent times, the Australian test has been saying the word, 'sorry'. According to Christopher Pearson, I am the type who 'Give him an inch and he'll eat your ruler.' I remain unashamedly an ambassador for reconciliation but it must be more than a word; it must be an empowering principle of our social relations. So too must any word of apology.

At that Reconciliation Convention, the mining company CRA (now Rio Tinto) featured in the reconciliation awards. The Aboriginal Training and Liaison Unit of Hamersley Iron won a prize. One of the local women, Jill Churnside spoke of the 'ups and downs of my people' and 'the tremendous satisfaction of both learning and trying to do business together'. The Daiwul Gidja Culture Group Aboriginal Corporation of the Warmun Community connected with the Argyle Mine was shortlisted for an award in the Culture/Land Category. A year before, CRA formally expressed regret to Aboriginal Australians for the company's failures. The company's vice-president had told a national conference of Aboriginal leaders:

> For most of the time of iron ore mining and infrastructure development in the Pilbara, the local Aboriginal people were ignored. There is a large scar on the site of the barramundi dreaming at Argyle—there is a similar scar on the spirit of the women of the area. In the light of CRA's present position on Aboriginal relations—a position that I believe will endure—I feel that it is appropriate to express regret to Aboriginal people in general and the communities of Cape York, the Pilbara and the eastern Kimberley region in particular.

With the politics of apologies, we need to remember that the words are cheap unless we have a commitment to righting the wrongs. The ongoing effects of past injustices are still enormous. Though policies have changed, indigenous children are still seven times more likely than other Australian children to be in substitute care and five times more likely to be subject to abuse and neglect notifications. Though all governments now accept that such children are best cared for in an indigenous cultural environment, the mantra of self-determination can be a convenient excuse for other Australians to withhold resources and professional care. Let's remember that the stable Aboriginal family is likely to have seven times the demands of any other stable family in assisting their own with the nurture of children in need of substitute care. If only they could be assured the equality which is the dream of so many of Ms Hanson's supporters.

In 1997, we celebrated the thirtieth anniversary of the 1967 referendum which promised so much for indigenous Australians. One of the great campaigners was the Pacific Islander, Faith Bandler. She recalled that an Aboriginal woman Pearl Gibbs said to her in the 1960s: 'You mightn't be one of us, but you won't be free until we are.' That group of '67 lived and worked equality and it came to be. They achieved the formal legal equality so as to overcome adverse special treatment. We, the inheritors of their achievements, must live and work reconciliation and it will come to be. Our aim must be the equality of opportunity for all and the special recognition of the place of indigenous Australians in the life of the nation.

Pat Dodson, as chairperson of the Council for Aboriginal Reconciliation, said at the 1997 Reconciliation Convention, 'It is a fact that indigenous people and many other minority groups feel threatened and endangered. Some Aboriginal parents are even afraid to send their kids to school. Is this justice, equality and a fair go for all?' The political issues of the moment will change from year to year. But gone are the days when these issues can be resolved by the whitefellas giving Aborigines the answers and the leftovers. We have to work on these things together.

There has been big change in the Australian mindset about Aboriginal issues. When the Mabo decision was given in 1992, mining magnates claimed it was a radical decision which would destabilise the country. By the time of the 1997 Reconciliation Convention, Campbell Anderson, chairman of the Minerals Council of Australia, was able to say:

> I see the division or differences that need to be reconciled as being fundamentally the lack of respect for the different values held to be important as between Aboriginal and non-Aboriginal people. I remain concerned about the ultimate economic implications of Mabo, but now as we approach the fifth anniversary of the decision, I am convinced it will be remembered as a turning point in changing community perceptions and in bringing indigenous and non-indigenous people together to work towards reconciliation. Without the Mabo decision, I question whether the Council for Aboriginal Reconciliation could have achieved the community interest in the Australian Reconciliation Convention.

Mabo was an inevitable decision and is here to stay. John Howard as prime minister has told parliament: 'The substance of that decision, now with the passage of time, seems completely unexceptionable to me. It appears to have been based on a good deal of logic and fairness and proper principle.' That view is shared by both sides of the political chamber and by most lawyers at home and abroad. Mabo was surely right and in accordance with contemporary Australian values. Respect for property and the principle of non-discrimination might even be thought to be 'the vibe of the Constitution' to quote *The Castle*.

Moving beyond the law and politics of land rights, Australia's first couple of reconciliation, Sir William and Lady Deane, have provided us with two convenient tests for reaching the goal of reconciliation. At the 1997 Reconciliation Convention, Lady Deane said: 'What indigenous women want for their families and communities is very much the same as what I want for my own family and for those who are close to me.' Sir William Deane added: 'We will not achieve true reconciliation unless and until...the future prospects of an Aboriginal baby are comparable with those of a non-Aboriginal one.'

Rather than awaiting government action, we can all make a contribution to the reconciliation process. Our apology and commitment to action could take this form: 'We who are recent migrants and descendants of migrants who have come to this land, thank you, the indigenous peoples of Australia for your tolerance of us, our cultures and aspirations. And we apologise for the hurt done to you, your ancestors and your lands by our ancestors and by our presence and actions in this land over the last 212 years.' Together with indigenous Australians we might then say: 'Committed to walking together in this land, we commit ourselves to reconciliation, building better relationships, so that we can constitute a united Australia, respecting the land, valuing Aboriginal and Torres Strait Islander heritage, and providing justice and equity for all.'

We need to transform the words of reconciliation and apology into the commitment to an Australia whose history works no further racially discriminatory injustices compounded by the uncomprehending, populist notions of the present ideology. Reflecting on the experience of others whose life experience is so different from my own, I hear the Aboriginal cry for recognition and justice across the cultural divide as a reminder, 'You mightn't be one of us, but you won't be free until we are.' If that means eating the ruler when you are given an inch, so be it. Native title, reconciliation, apology and stolen children are not present day ideological constructs. They are shared attempts to understand the past, transforming its effects into a secure, hope-filled future for all Australians.

At the end of the 1997 Constitutional Convention, Pat Dodson read a 'Call to the Nation' which concluded: 'We commit ourselves to leave this gathering determined to work with all those prepared to join us in this movement. We call on all Australians not to stand on the sidelines but to demonstrate a commitment to reconciliation by becoming personally involved in reconciliation activities in their neighbourhood, their communities, and their workplace.'

As reconcilers, we can go and do something about it, with hope. The last thing we want is another shibboleth lumbering the body politic—whether the word of the moment be extinguishment, equality, native title, reconciliation or just that plain simple word, 'sorry'. Reconciliation remains a call to action on both sides of the river. Both banks are constitutive of modern Australia. Reconciliation is coming home to who we are, where we are and where we are from as a modern nation. The Council for Aboriginal Reconciliation's Corroboree 2000 and the proposed draft document of reconciliation provide the next formal step in our national commitment to honouring the personal and local commitments to walk together. It will be more than a word game only if the words match our desire. Accepting that Australia in the past was a radically unreconciled society and believing that most Australians want to be part of a justly reconciled society in the future, I regard reconciliation as a noble present activity for any Australian. I am happy to be aboard.

Public Opinion on Reconciliation: Snap Shot, Close Focus, Long Lens
Newspoll, Saulwick & Muller and Hugh Mackay

In 1999–2000 the Council for Aboriginal Reconciliation commissioned research on Australians' attitudes to indigenous people and to reconciliation. Newspoll did the national quantitative survey. Irving Saulwick and Denis Muller undertook the detailed qualitative work. The findings follow in the next two pieces. Hugh Mackay's contribution, prepared specifically for this book, examines material gathered over a longer timeframe.

The Newspoll Survey

Australians want reconciliation but they are not anxious to do anything that could carry an imputation that they, or their generation, are to blame for what happened to Australia's first peoples. That is the message from a Newspoll survey of 1,300 people nationwide done for the Council for Aboriginal Reconciliation in early 2000.

The findings highlighted the contradictions in the nation's thinking about Aborigines. People accepted they had been badly treated in the past but were much more reluctant to acknowledge present disadvantage. They saw the need for assistance, but had trouble fitting this with a notion of 'equality'.

More than eight in ten agreed Aborigines were treated harshly and unfairly in the past; about six out of ten thought the nation should formally acknowledge Aborigines as Australia's original owners and that the continent was occupied without their consent.

But only 41 percent thought of Aborigines as a disadvantaged group; 52 percent did not. Nevertheless, on the specific of living conditions, 52 percent said Aborigines were generally worse off than other Australians.

More than seven in ten people accepted a need for government programs to help reduce Aboriginal disadvantage. This goes hand in hand with about 60 percent saying Aborigines received too much special government assistance and about 70 percent believing Aborigines did not do enough to help themselves. About eight in ten people supported the proposition that, 'The nation should help Aboriginal people become more financially independent and self-reliant'.

The researchers concluded: 'If it is a statistical fact that Aboriginal and Torres Strait Islander people are the poorest, unhealthiest, least employed, worst housed and most imprisoned Australians, but only half the community believes Aboriginal people are generally worse off than other Australians (and only around 30 percent believe they are 'a lot' worse off), then there is a significant gap between the facts and what many people believe about the position of Aboriginal people.'

When the link between the past and the present was explored, the survey found that 'more people are inclined to say Aboriginal people have themselves to blame for any disadvantage they may experience, as opposed to putting the blame on past mistreatment'. However the researchers pointed out that this finding should be tempered: 'the premise "past injustice = cause of disadvantage" is a very complex one...Perhaps the most appropriate way to view the finding is that either because of the complexity of the premise, or other attitudes, a majority of Australians do not believe there is a link between current disadvantage and the past'.

On the key question of an apology, 40 percent agreed and 57 percent disagreed with the statement that, 'On behalf of the community, governments should apologise to Aboriginal people for what's happened in the past'. About six in ten felt 'Australians today weren't responsible for what happened in the past, so today's governments should not have to apologise for it'. Almost eight in ten agreed that, 'Everyone should stop talking about the way Aboriginal people were treated in the past, and just get on with the future'.

So although a majority are in agreement with the notion of formally recognising the past, the majority are not prepared to apologise for it— 'why should we, we didn't do it'. It is also apparent that, as found in the qualitative research, there is a desire in the community for a sense of closure or resolution, and to get on with the future. Flowing from this, a little over 80 percent of people feel the reconciliation process is important, and 37 percent believe it is very important. 'When it comes to motivation for this belief, the researchers identified a spectrum ranging from 'righting the wrongs' to 'getting on with it'.

In principle, 57 percent agreed and 37 percent disagreed that a reconciliation document might help relations between Aborigines and the wider community. But only 28 percent favoured giving the document legal status.

A sub-sample of 280 of the 1,300 were given the draft declaration. The overall reaction of a large majority (74 percent) was more positive than negative. One quarter supported all the contents; 49 percent supported most of the declaration, with some reservations or concerns; 26 percent said they tended not to support most or all the contents. The sections most liked were those that focused 'on unity, sharing or equality, as opposed to a focus on some acknowledgement or recognition of Aboriginal and Torres Strait Islander people'. The most likely difficulty with the declaration was the apology. Although more people liked than disliked paragraphs two (referring to Aborigines as original owners and custodians) and five (acknowledging the land was colonised without consent), these paragraphs followed the apology as problem areas for people.

Respondents' overall reactions to the declaration indicate that for many, the words evoke a positive sentiment to which they warm. There are paragraphs which tap into the glue that binds people together—regardless of their feelings about the more controversial issues. This glue includes the notions of equality, unity and a desire for resolution and moving forward.

However beneath this there are undoubtedly problems. Even among the largest segment who say they support most of the contents but have reservations or concerns, a significant proportion find sticking points concerning the apology, original ownership or colonisation without consent.

Attitudes to Reconciliation among Non-indigenous Australians: Saulwick & Muller

The qualitative study conducted for the Council for Aboriginal Reconciliation by Irving Saulwick and Associates and Denis Muller and Associates consisted of a series of 14 focus group discussions conducted throughout Australia from 7 December 1999 to 13 January 2000, and 23 depth interviews with leading citizens in 'high contact' areas during the same time.

Each focus group contained some eight to ten people, drawn from areas of high and low contact between indigenous and non-indigenous Australians. Respondents came from a range of socio-economic backgrounds, and from various age groups. Respondents were told that they were being invited to discuss 'Australian society' in very broad terms. They were not told in advance about the actual nature and purpose of the research.

Spontaneously, every group identified the plight of Aboriginal Australians as a tragedy and a major failing of Australian society since white settlement. The following is a summary of the main themes that came through.

There is a widespread feeling throughout Australia that Aborigines have been badly treated in the past. At the same time, there is little recognition of the effect this may have had on present-day Aboriginal citizens.

There is a willingness to treat Aboriginal Australians like any other Australians provided they are prepared to accept 'our' values and play by 'our' rules.

There is impatience with, and lack of understanding of, Aborigines who will not conform to general community norms, and in particular with those in rural areas who live on welfare on the fringe of small towns. Those living in cities are thought not to be representative of all Aborigines and, indeed, not to be 'real' Aborigines, particularly if they have some white forebears. Indeed many of these people are accused of claiming Aboriginality in order to gain the welfare benefits which flow from this status. They are seen as more demanding, and somehow less 'genuine' than Aborigines living in remote areas.

There is also a widespread view that many Aborigines now look to welfare and other support systems and are not prepared to help themselves. The many who do work and who do not seek welfare are not seen. While most people support the concept of a safety net, they see Aborigines as exploiting the welfare system which they are paying for.

Aboriginal interest in land rights is not understood by most Australians. Many believe that it has a pecuniary base. Many also believe that to accede to it would be to accept double standards—one rule for Aborigines and one for others. Non-Aboriginal Australians do not want this. They have accepted the concept of multiculturalism—one nation, one people.

Most also have become convinced that to offer an apology for past treatment could lead to further claims for compensation. They do not want this either.

Most see reconciliation as an Aboriginal issue, not as an issue for all Australians. It is similar to the way multiculturalism was seen in the past—as an issue for 'new' Australians, as distinct from how it is seen now—as describing Australian society as a whole. One requirement is to move the concept of reconciliation from a narrow one to a broad one.

Many who have thought about it, even minimally, tend to confuse reconciliation with issues such as Mabo, land rights, and compensation. This makes them nervous.

The Council for Aboriginal Reconciliation is not widely known among ordinary citizens.

In the study, respondents were shown a draft declaration of reconciliation which had been written by the council. Their reactions varied. A few liked it in its entirety. Most did not. Many saw it as divisive, backward-looking, based only on the Aboriginal perspective, requiring a series of concessions from non-Aboriginal Australians without any corresponding 'give' by Aboriginal people, and a high-risk document which would probably be used as the basis for claims for land and monetary compensation.

It was also seen as coming from an elite group of people who probably had little idea of how ordinary people lived and thought.

When asked what should be done with any such document, people responded by saying that it needed to be 'owned' by the people, but at the same time they did not want to see it rejected and the cause of reconciliation damaged.

Summary of main findings from the focus groups

There is little overt prejudice directed towards Aborigines or to other minority groups in Australia on the basis of race alone. Although there is often a lack of understanding of the lives, beliefs and attitudes of minority groups within the Australian community, and at times a feeling that separateness is undesirable, there is tolerance of the idea of difference. This tolerance is bounded by the egalitarian ideal that we are, or should be, one people—one nation. It is also bounded by the inability of many citizens to imagine that other people might have fundamentally different ways of looking at life than the way they do, or that other people may want fundamentally different things from life than those offered by the dominant culture. The dominant culture defines the norm, and most people accept it without too much questioning.

It is agreed universally that the position of the Aborigines in Australia today is a tragedy. There is widespread agreement that Aborigines were badly treated by the early white settlers. Many people find it hard to face up to this. Some, particularly those who are defensive on this point, argue that there was bad behaviour on both sides—that both settlers and Aborigines behaved badly towards each other. There are few who are inclined to see one side as the invaders and the other as the invaded. Nor are there many who wish to accept any responsibility for what happened in what most see as far-off days.

Some say that what happened was wrong. Others say that those who did take the land or in other ways disrupt Aboriginal society did not know it was wrong. Some say that those who created the missions or took the children did these things with the best intentions. Some say that some good was done. Most say, with some vehemence, that one cannot judge past actions by today's standards. The vast majority say that they personally were not involved and certainly should not be expected to accept personal responsibility for what happened, or feel the need to apologise or have anyone else apologise for them. Among the descendants of postwar non-British immigrants this feeling was very strongly expressed.

Behind many of these statements appears to lie an intolerance or a lack of empathy; there also appears to be a widespread inability or a disinclination to attempt to look at the matter from an Aboriginal perspective or from the perspective of the disinherited. It could be argued that there are shades of racism in this, although to argue whether this is racism or not appears to us not to be greatly productive. It is as though people do not have the imagination to look at the world through the eyes of a victim. After listening carefully to our respondents, we believe the wellsprings of their attitudes are to be found in the following factors:

> It is too painful or too threatening to take on the mantle, even in one's imagination, of the victim.

> It is too confronting to accept that we have produced a splendid and democratic society which does have a serious flaw.

> The thought that it is the collective 'we' who are to blame is too difficult to accept. This is one area where we subconsciously know that we cannot attribute the blame to our leaders whom we usually delight in criticising and lampooning.

> The fact that our education and our folk culture have largely written out these matters means that some of us do not understand the background, some of us do not want to, and some of us are given licence to disregard it.

> The problem, despite the fact that some attention has been paid to it in the last couple of decades, is so difficult to resolve, so persistent, that many of us don't want to hear about it.

> There are too many legal and financial risks involved in facing up to the realities.

There is a widespread feeling that the Aboriginal culture has been seriously damaged, that it cannot be restored to its pre-settlement condition and that there is no good in pretending that it can be. There is little understanding of the possible psychological or social effects on a people of the undermining of their culture by a dominant culture. Thus there is little tolerance for any anti-social or apparently aberrant behaviour of Aboriginal people which might arise because of their position in society or because of what they have experienced.

People argue that there are few 'real' Aboriginal people left. Some define 'real' as people with 50 percent or more Aboriginal lineage who live in a tribal and usually remote environment. They see many of these people as retaining a tribal culture, and believe that if they wish to continue in their traditional ways (separate from, and outside of, white society and not dependent on it) they should be free to do so.

People tend to see people with less than 50 percent Aboriginal lineage as not 'real' Aborigines. They claim that many of these people have been brought up on welfare (many for two or three generations), that they expect it, that they do nothing to help themselves, and that they do not take responsibility for themselves. Even non-Aboriginal people who have grown up with Aboriginal people and have friends among them whom they like and admire, when they talk about Aboriginal people tend to concentrate on the stereotypes described above. People generally see these Aboriginal people as living off society and they resent this. This resentment is based on a number of platforms: the feeling that their taxes are going to support people who will not help themselves; the feeling that Aboriginal people are getting special privileges which others are not, despite the fact that the others are not well off; and the feeling that Aborigines, or people who choose to call themselves Aborigines, are abusing the system.

People argue that Australia is a free and democratic society in which all people should be treated equally. They argue that Aborigines, and those who call themselves Aborigines, at the moment get better treatment: they get special money; they are treated, even if they are drunk in a park, better than non-Aborigines are treated.

In this context people see the treatment of Aborigines as offending against the egalitarian ethic. They also claim that, because it does not encourage Aborigines to take responsibility for themselves, it does not encourage the development of Aboriginal self-respect.

Aboriginal demands on land, or the possibility of such demands, worry people. The worry seems to arise from a number of sources: people on rural properties think that their tenure may be disturbed; many do not know of the definition of identification with the land which the courts have made, and feel insecure as a consequence of their ignorance; some feel that excessive demands are, or will be, made which have little basis but which will nonetheless be pursued; many feel that Aboriginal leaders will make claims so that they will be in a position to negotiate on mineral royalties from the land claimed.

Again there is a feeling that here is an example of people being treated as special. People argue that they have had to work hard to buy their land and feel that all other people should have to do the same.

As a result of this cluster of attitudes, many people say that all Australians should come together as one people and that there should be no apologies, and Aboriginal people should not continue to receive special help—as they believe that this is both unfair and tends to perpetuate a culture of dependency.

People's reasons for not wanting an apology were threefold. First they said, 'We did not do it' and second, that the past was past and that reconciliation was about the present and the future. The further concern was that such an apology might lead to further substantial claims for compensation in one form or another. People are prepared to acknowledge the past without apologising for it. They do not want to be lectured to or made to feel guilty or have imposed on them some contrived set of norms. In their pragmatic way they say, 'Let's get on with it'.

Although this is the majority view, it is certainly not universally held. Some feel that an apology would help the healing process. Some feel that each 'side' should apologise to the other.

Attitudes to the draft document for reconciliation are wide-ranging.

There are those who look past the words and say that they like the sentiments. Others say that the document is divisive, or that it is biased in favour of the Aboriginal and Torres Strait Islander communities. Some say that it opens the door to further land and other claims, and are not inclined to accept it because of this. Some of a more pragmatic bent found the language overblown in places. Still others questioned assertions about spirituality and interrelationships which they felt were not necessarily universally shared.

In addition to the draft declaration, respondents were also shown a document which outlined four strategies designed to advance the cause of reconciliation. One concerned economic independence, the second concerned disadvantage in such areas as health and education, the third concerned Aboriginal rights and responsibilities, and the fourth concerned ways of continuing the reconciliation processes. Attitudes to the strategies were also wide ranging. However, the majority view is that while economic independence is a worthy objective, it may not be achieved because of lack of education and related problems among the recipients, and thus the scheme may degenerate to further 'hand-outs' to which they object. The other strategies raise similar problems: in most cases the yardstick used is: 'Does this represent special and preferred treatment? If it does, I don't support it—partly because it is not fair, and partly because it has been tried in the past and has failed.'

People had given little thought to reconciliation, and few knew anything about the process or about the council. Only one or two had heard about a document of reconciliation, and they knew nothing about its contents.

They did not want to see the document used in any way which risked demonstrating a lack of support for reconciliation. Thus they were worried about it being put to a vote in parliament or at a referendum. A few were opposed to giving it any legal standing on the grounds that it was impossible to say what the legal consequences might be, particularly with respect to land rights.

On the other hand, people wanted it given some kind of meaningful status. They were content to have it available in public places to be signed by individuals or organisations (provided it was satisfactorily worded). But many wanted something more. Endorsement by the parliaments—short of legislative enactment—was regarded positively on condition that sufficient political groundwork was done to ensure unanimous or near unanimous endorsement and provided it did not become a spring-board for further claims of privileges.

People say that no amount of official action will provide a complete solution. Official action can contribute to a climate but in the end it will be what is done by ordinary people in their day to day lives which will be the measure of reconciliation. Many say that this may take generations.

Summary of main findings from the interviews with community leaders

Attitudes of community leaders tend to be more positive than those of the general public. They recognise that Aboriginal people have suffered disadvantage and that some initiatives to help them overcome this legacy could be useful. They tend not to carry with them the resentment which is found in the general community towards programs designed to assist the Aboriginal people. They seem more able to bring empathy and generosity to the issues involved. There were one or two notable exceptions and these were to be found among the elected local government officials.

Community leaders, by virtue of their position, have been forced to think more deeply about these matters and to look for ways to advance the cause of reconciliation.

Unlike ordinary people, they do have some knowledge about the process of reconciliation and about the council. Many had heard of a document of reconciliation, and some had seen it before.

In common with ordinary citizens, they did not want to see the document used in any way which would risk demonstrating a lack of support for reconciliation. Thus they were worried about it being put to a vote in parliament or at a referendum. A few were opposed to giving it any legal standing on the grounds that it was impossible to say what the legal consequences might be, particularly with respect to land rights.

The Police
The police are practical people. They have to be. They have been given the tasks of ensuring that people obey the law, of maintaining civil order and—in their own words—doing society's dirty work. Because they are accountable for these tasks in a highly political operating environment they have had to think hard about how to meet them in ways which conform with community expectations and standards. When, in the past, they have failed to do this, they have been severely censured.

Their work with individual Aborigines and with the Aboriginal community is especially sensitive and operationally demanding. Of course many Aborigines are law-abiding citizens and are not seen by the police. But in some places, particularly in northern Australia, the police and some elements of the Aboriginal community are in constant contact. The reasons are many, and we do not wish to canvass them here. What we want to emphasise is that we have been impressed by what we have heard from senior officers during this study. These officers were not only committed to the concept of reconciliation, but were introducing, often in difficult circumstances, and at times despite the views of people in the non-Aboriginal community, partnership programs with Aboriginal people both inside and outside the force which they saw as reconciliation in practice. They were, in their language, 'walking the walk'.

We found a nice combination of realism and concern. The police were realistic about the need to keep the peace in circumstances where an element of the Aboriginal community acted in anti-social and self-destructive ways, and so provoked outrage in the wider community. They were concerned to try to treat Aboriginal offenders fairly, humanely and sensitively wherever possible, while fending off pressure from the wider community to take a more punitive approach.

We heard of examples where the force was learning from its Aboriginal members, and was attempting to employ them in ways which were consistent with, or were not antithetical to, their own culture.

One of the stereotypes of policing in Australia is that in high-contact areas, the police take a brutal and uncompromising approach to Aborigines. We do not know whether this stereotype is justified or not. However, we do say that the evidence from our discussions with senior officers in three states and the Northern Territory suggests it is unjustified. If the policies espoused by these officers are in fact practised on the ground, then we believe that the way these police in outback Australia are handling Aboriginal–non Aboriginal relations may form one important model for reconciliation throughout the nation.

It was put to us by a number of other community leaders in each of the towns where we conducted in-depth interviews, that the police were doing a good job in extremely difficult circumstances. Success can be hard to quantify. However, in the Northern Territory the police quoted statistics indicating a drop in youth suicide in one Aboriginal community where a special program of policing, involving Aboriginal and non-Aboriginal officers, had been introduced in consultation with that community.

The police live on the ground. Some of the police to whom we spoke knew a lot about the Aboriginal people in their area. For example, they could talk about tribal groups in their area and about tribal rivalries. They knew and listened to the elders. The elders, in turn, listened to them. Over time they were beginning to build real mutual respect. This in turn was leading to other examples of cooperation, such as where local Aboriginal auxiliary police were working to good effect in their own communities.

Some people in our group discussions complained that Aboriginal people were treated more leniently than were non-Aborigines. They thought this unfair. The police, while in no way being soft hearted, believed that at times, particularly where alcohol was involved, different practices were appropriate.

We also learned that considerable resources and time were being devoted to the training of Aboriginal liaison officers, even though the attrition rate, due among other things to burnout, was high.

In Kalgoorlie a new position of liaison officer to communicate with the three or four local clans, was being considered.

Local Government

Our discussions suggest that the attitude of local government is very much influenced by the opinions of the mayor, who often seems to devote much, if not all his or her working time, to the post.

We heard some mayors who were attempting to deal with the Aboriginal citizens with sensitivity and great tolerance. Some had been in the area for a long time and had developed deep friendships with people in the Aboriginal community and probably had earned their respect. We spoke with others who were highly critical of local Aboriginal behaviour and who seemed not to wish to understand the reasons for this behaviour. In their view, anyone who offended against community norms should pay the price.

Townsville, in particular, gave us grounds for concern. This was the one high-contact centre where the mayor did not see us, despite repeated attempts to make an appointment. A council 'cultural attache' was offered to us, but we declined. People in the Townsville focus group and others to whom we spoke told us of a recent incident in which the council had unleashed dogs on Aboriginal 'parkies'—people who lived rough in the city parks. We should add that this remains hearsay since we were not able to raise it with the mayor.

The councils of all the mayors we spoke to were involved in one initiative or another to manage the local 'Aboriginal problem'. In some cases this meant creating special camping sites on the edge of town where Aboriginal people from the out-stations could gather and live without arousing the enmity of townspeople. Many had initiated or taken part in local reconciliation meetings or public ceremonies. They were familiar with the council and some had seen the draft document of reconciliation.

Others were going out of their way to promote the positive aspects of the town's Aboriginal heritage, partly to improve the position of the local Aboriginal community and partly to promote the tourist trade.

Chambers of Commerce

The chambers of commerce saw themselves as the representatives of the local business community, and in particular the local traders. Anything which enhanced their position was good; anything which acted negatively on them was bad.

Some did have contact with the local Aboriginal community. For example, the Jarwon Association (who manage the Katherine Gorge tourist site and who had other commercial ventures) had recently joined the local chamber, and in time would sit on their executive.

But in the main the chambers showed little interest in, and a good deal of antagonism to, those members of the Aboriginal community who spent time sitting around the town. One gained the impression that local traders thought that their presence was not good for business.

The chambers spoke of few initiatives designed to foster employment among local Aborigines, nor of other initiatives to assist them. The one program on which we saw any literature was in the Northern Territory. One leading chamber member to whom we spoke in north Queensland was personally involved in working with Aboriginal people and was deeply committed to this work. Another expressed personal feelings of concern for the position of Aborigines in her community, but had no idea what, if anything, could be done about it.

Industry

From our limited experience we may suggest that industry does see itself participating, in a practical way, in reconciliation.

Mt Iza Mines runs special employment induction courses for potential Aboriginal employees. Management is committed to this program, despite the fact that few will offer for work and some of those who do will not stay for the long term. Management believes it is contributing to skill enhancement which may assist the individuals involved in the long term.

MIM also run special classes for all employees to give them a better understanding of people in the Aboriginal community.

Kalgoorlie Consolidated Gold Mines also has taken initiatives to build up employment opportunities for Aborigines. In addition to employing a small number of Aborigines on staff, it has followed up approaches from Aboriginal communities who have sought to enter into commercial relationships with the company for the provision of environmental restoration services and other contract work. Little has come of this, however. We were told that even though there had been many meetings at which the Aboriginal communities had confirmed their interest, they had not taken the next necessary steps, such as providing a quotation.

The mine management indicated that it was prepared to assist in every possible way to ensure that the Aboriginal communities got the work, but that in the end it had to operate on the basis of proper management and financial principles.

The Gwydir Cotton Growers' Association is excited about the employment initiatives it has taken and the success it has achieved. It works closely with members of the Aboriginal community.

In each case the commitment and enthusiasm of the executive in charge was the critical factor. Without their commitment on the ground—which was plainly evident to us—even activities which had proven useful could fade away.

Vox Populi—Hugh Mackay

The voice of the people is the lifeblood of democracy. But in a parliamentary democracy like Australia, there are good reasons to be grateful for the tension that often exists between public opinion and political leadership.

Indeed, were public policy the mere puppet of public opinion, we would pay unrealistically low taxes, treat the poor and disadvantaged even more harshly than we do now, be hidebound by draconian legislation that responded to every new wave of community concern, and, quite possibly, still be administering the death penalty.

Public opinion is a lumbering, cumbersome creature that needs to be twitched into life by the energy of men and women of vision. Left to ourselves, we citizens might never rise to the noble heights of which we are capable. We need education and enlightenment. Sometimes, we need to borrow the inspiration of someone else's dream.

That's certainly the case when it comes to the question of Aboriginal reconciliation. The recent history of public opinion on this subject offers little encouragement to those who want to see the reconciliation process on the community's 'must-do' agenda, and even less to those who hoped that an upsurge of community support would create irresistible pressure on the federal government to hasten the process.

Back in November 1993, a Newspoll survey found that when people were asked to rate each of 12 issues according to their importance, only 32 percent rated Aboriginal and native title issues as 'very important'. Six years later, in January 2000, the figure was 30 percent. With only two exceptions (in May and September 1998, when immigration was rated 'very important' by even fewer people), Aboriginal and native title issues have consistently bumped along on the bottom of the list of issues investigated by Newspoll.

That situation was reflected in a series of six public opinion surveys conducted by Donovan Research, from November 1991 to May 1995, focusing on the specific question of reconciliation. Respondents were asked: *From what you expect, know or have heard, are you in favour of, against, or have no feelings either way about a process for Aboriginal reconciliation?* Those responding 'in favour' or 'against' were asked: *Is that strongly in favour/against or somewhat in favour/against?*

Those 'strongly in favour' comprised 22 percent of respondents in 1991 and again in 1995, though the number of strong supporters rose to a peak of 28 percent in September 1993. The total number of supporters (including those both strongly and somewhat in favour of reconciliation) hovered around 50 percent throughout the run of six surveys.

There was a flurry of excitement and controversy in May 1996 when, on the basis of research conducted for the Aboriginal Council of Reconciliation by Brian Sweeney and Associates, it appeared there had been a dramatic increase in support for reconciliation, up from 22 percent in May 1995 to 48 percent in May 1996.

Such an increase would have been almost unprecedented in public opinion research but, on closer inspection, it became clear that the surge was an artefact created by a change in the research method rather than a genuine shift in community attitudes. The wording of the question had been significantly altered from the Donovan surveys, and a series of questions preceding the reconciliation question established a supportive context that was absent from the Donovan questionnaire. (For a comprehensive analysis of the technical differences between the two surveys that created the different results, see Robert J. Donovan, 'Increased Support for Aboriginal Reconciliation: Fact or Artefact?' in *Australasian Journal of Market Research*, Vol 6, No 1, January 1998.)

Beneath the stark figures of quantitative polling, the evidence of diagnostic, qualitative research has suggested that although Australians' attitudes toward Aboriginal issues are gradually becoming more positive, there is still enough negativity and indifference in the community to comfort those who believe that an apology for past injustices is neither necessary nor appropriate.

To anyone committed to the reconciliation process, the lingering hostility towards Aborigines clearly signals a need for strong, passionate leadership on the subject of reconciliation (and, indeed, of native title). It also suggests that the prejudice—revealed most starkly in offensive jokes—is merely an attempt to conceal a deep reservoir of shame about white Australians' treatment of Aborigines since the beginning of European settlement.

Among the large majority of Australians who are *not* strongly committed to Aboriginal reconciliation, three attitudes prevail: Aborigines are so low-status as to be beneath serious consideration; Aborigines have become a drain on the community's resources (especially via welfare); Aborigines are an uncomfortable reminder of Australians' failure to address some of our most pressing social problems.

These attitudes have emerged in a series of qualitative research projects, conducted between 1986 and 1998, as part of a continuous program of social research published as *The Mackay Report*.

In May 1986, *The Mackay Report: Class and Status* noted that Aborigines were repeatedly identified as 'the quintessence of the Australian lower class'. Indeed, it was clear from that research—and from a replication of the same study in March 1998—that indigenous people were not really included in any consideration of social class and status by white Australians: they were either off the bottom of the scale, or in a separate category altogether. Respondents in 1986 were quoted as saying such things as:

> The park is full of boongs and they are full of plonk, and they are all living on our money.

> There's no doubt Abos are the bottom of the lower class in our society.

The 1998 report on *Class and Status* detected some softening of language in discussion of Aborigines, but reached similar conclusions about the white community's perception of their status. Notwithstanding a growing awareness of the need for reconciliation, Aborigines were typically assumed to lack any social standing, to suffer from a kind of social dysfunctionality, and to be associated with the 'lower-class' stigma attaching to alcohol abuse and crimes of violence.

There were signs of more positive attitudes emerging between 1986 and 1998, but these seemed largely to be driven by the achievements of exceptional, high-profile Aborigines—notably Cathy Freeman, Noel Pearson and a number of artists and musicians—who had achieved celebrity status (and, in Australia in 1998, being seen as a celebrity was enough to lift you out of any status trough). In response to a new-found respect for certain individual Aborigines, some 'white' Australians were encouraged to claim Aboriginal blood among their own ancestors. As one respondent put it:

> I had a great-grandmother who was a Maori. In those days, you couldn't admit to being Aboriginal, so you had to be a Maori. Whether or not you can be proud of your ancestry has changed over the last ten or 15 years. When I was a kid, it was shameful if you had convict or Aboriginal blood.

Still, even in 1998, many of the most scathing prejudices of 1986 were still present:

> The Aborigines are in a class of their own, and they can't get out of it. They have equal rights, but they are still pretty well downtrodden.

Another 1986 Mackay Report, *Contemporary Social Issues*, included a passing mention of Aborigines in discussing community attitudes to abuse of the welfare system. Here, Aborigines were lumped in with particular migrant groups who were widely regarded at the time as being the recipients of undue generosity at the hands of the Department of Social Security:

> Of course, if you really want to get preferential treatment in this country, you have to be black. Aborigines get all sorts of hand-

outs through the system which are not available to white people. Aborigines I know of got a grant for potato farming. They ate the seed potatoes and the tractor is still sitting there.

Aborigines are good customers—you always get paid because they can just go to the government and get a handout if they are short of money.

It was characteristic of the group discussions from which those comments were taken that other people, hearing such claims, were inclined to believe them and to incorporate them into a series of prejudices about Aboriginal people: they are treated too generously; they can 'rip off the system' with impunity; they are fundamentally unreliable and irresponsible, at least by the standards white Australians claim to set for themselves.

By July 1995, *The Mackay Report: Society Now* was detecting greater complexity in attitudes towards Aborigines. While the old prejudices were still evident, they were sometimes tempered by a more rueful, reflective concern about white Australians' failure to understand—let alone solve—the problems facing Aboriginal people: 'While Australians have taken some pride in their hospitable attitude towards immigrants, they continue to feel perplexed about their apparent failure to come to terms with "the Aboriginal problem".'

That report detected signs of shame mingled with feelings of resentment and hostility; it also noted that prejudices against Aborigines were generally expressed more strongly than prejudices directed towards any immigrant group, including Asians. If such vehement expression of prejudice against an oppressed minority is itself a sign of repressed guilt, then some Australians have at least been prepared to approach the articulation of that possibility:

We've done a lot of terrible things to the Aborigines. We seem to have more time for the other people that come here than for our own Aborigines.

The Aboriginal problem is something that has got to be looked at. It's being badly handled by the government, and by the Aborigines themselves. We thought if we threw more and more money at it, it would ultimately fix itself. But the problem keeps on coming back. I think it will be with us forever.

We need to work out a better deal for Aborigines. They are getting a raw deal, but how do we arrest their problems?

But such ruminations have not always been well received. Some Australians, in 1995, were as resistant as ever to the idea of a more compassionate, more tolerant attitude to Aborigines based on recognition of their poor treatment at the hands of our European-settler forebears:

> We're supposed to hang our heads in shame for the last 200 years. I have a bit of trouble with that. Are our kids going to be ashamed of the white culture because they've been taught to be?
>
> Why should Aborigines have more free dental care than me and my children? It's discrimination!

The introduction of greater complexity into white Australians' attitudes to Aborigines was no guarantee of ultimate support for the process of reconciliation. But, by July 1997, the slow evolution of attitudes towards Aborigines had reached the point where *The Mackay Report: Mind & Mood* was including those attitudes among the factors leading many Australians to feel rather embarrassed about the state of Australian society: 'There is a sense,' the report said, 'of failing to fulfil our promise, and of having failed even to articulate our goals. One source of that embarrassment is our continued failure to come to terms with the Aboriginal question and to reach some form of reconciliation which is satisfactory to both white and black Australians.'

The 1997 report identified three factors contributing to Australians' embarrassment over the apparent intractability of the Aboriginal problem: first, white Australians' inability to imagine what it must be like to be an Aborigine in contemporary Australia; second, an admitted failure to comprehend Aborigines' aspirations and goals; third, a sense of confusion about the implications—and the ultimate relevance—of High Court decisions in Mabo and Wik.

Those two decisions, and their legislative consequences, had put the question of native title firmly on the community's agenda, but the underlying sense of confusion and uneasiness—fuelled by some politicians' suggestions that new native title legislation could lead to successful claims being made over suburban backyards—made people impatient to move on to other issues. John Howard was undoubtedly right when he said, in 1997, that most people simply wanted the native title debate 'off the agenda'. (The fact that they might have *wanted* it off the agenda was not, of course, sufficient reason to remove it.)

Confusion about native title was most vividly expressed in the tension between a desire to 'do the right thing' and the lurking suspicion (fuelled by the rhetoric of Pauline Hanson and her One Nation Party) that Aborigines might somehow be exploiting the economic resources of Australian society.

For some of the respondents in our 1997 study, even that tension was perceived as disgraceful: they believed Australia's record of dealing with Aboriginal people had been so appalling that the charge of 'genocide' (surfacing in the mass media at that time) did not seem too harsh. They also believed that Aborigines required special treatment and that, since they were so obviously an underprivileged and disadvantaged group, they should receive more generous and compassionate treatment than other members of our society.

> I'm appalled at the government's performance over Wik. It's so cold-blooded and it's a despicable way they've acted. The major beneficiaries of the ten-point plan will be the major corporations and the big pastoral companies. There's no consideration of the Aborigines' view and what's best for the country in the long term. They've used fear tactics about how the Aborigines would act, and yet Aborigines have shown they can negotiate with the big mining companies.

> Taking Aboriginal children from their parents is unforgivable, whichever way you look at it. Of course we were trying to wipe out Aboriginal culture. Why else did we do it? It might have been considered reasonable at the time, but there's no way we could think of it as reasonable today. We mightn't have done that kind of thing ourselves, but we are part of the society that did it. I'm a believer in shared responsibility.

At the other extreme, the 1997 report quoted people who were scathingly and unashamedly racist in their dismissive attitude towards Aborigines. In their view, Aborigines should simply integrate themselves into white society or be left to fend for themselves (and, presumably, to die out as quickly as possible).

> Where does all the money go we give them? I'll tell you where it goes. You go out 15 kilometres from Cairns where beautiful houses were built for them and within three months they had to pull them all down again because they had kicked everything about and burnt everything.

> We think they need extra help to catch up, but what if they don't want to get anywhere? Aboriginal children are given free shoes. What about the poor white children? Don't they get any help?

> Our local high school was closed down by the government because they said it would cost too much to repair. A few days later they gave it to the Aborigines and they have a special bus to pick them up. Now they're asking the white kids to go back, because they want to fill the school. I'm not racist, but it's the grants and crap like that that annoy me.

Between the extremes of support and contempt for Aborigines, the more typical response, in 1997, was tentative, perplexed and rather confused. People caught in the grip of their own uncertainty were theoretically open to the possibility of inspired leadership on the subject, but they were also vulnerable to the temptation to sink back into the comfort of prejudice and cynicism—and there has been no shortage of cynics to regale them with tales of 'fake' Aboriginality and of land disputes that seemed to be more about hard, cold cash than about religious or cultural connection to the land in question:

> How legitimate are the Aborigines about their land claims...are they only after dollars and cents? Look how immediately they sold off that land on the NSW north coast.

> Our Aborigines have been infiltrated by a lot of overseas people—trashy white people. The government might have taken their land, but we bought our land—we had nothing to do with it.

> The thing is, minority groups, like Aborigines, have the power at the moment: they're the ones getting the benefits, not the majority. That's very sad, because it means we're not equal and we should be—regardless of race, colour or whatever.

That last comment—typical of many made in the 1997 study—captures the confusion which many Australians still feel about Aboriginal issues in general, and reconciliation in particular. As soon as people begin talking about the concept of 'equal treatment' or about the idea that 'we are all members of one society', they can easily lose sight of ugly historical realities that have created injustice, inequality and disadvantage. From there, it is a short step to feeling outraged by the idea that Aborigines might be receiving special (for which read 'unwarranted') treatment.

Yet, in spite of lingering widespread prejudice, and in spite of the evidence of a great uncertainty about how to address Aboriginal issues, the 1997 report noted that 'white Australians are becoming better informed about Aboriginal issues, and the graphic telling of stolen children stories brings the issue of collective guilt (and collective embarrassment) much closer to home'.

The big change, between 1995 and 1997, was that Australians were moving towards the conviction that something more creative, more enlightened and more effective needed to be done, if the Aboriginal problem—however it might be defined—were ever to be solved. Even the most intransigent bigots seemed willing to acknowledge that the problem needed to be addressed, and the emerging support for Aboriginal reconciliation was part of a gnawing sense that, worldwide, the claims of indigenous people are being taken more seriously.

> If we extinguish native title, we'll lose too much credibility overseas.

> We've done the wrong thing by them all along, and we're doing the wrong thing in terms of fixing it up, too.

• • •

On the night of his 1998 re-election as prime minister, John Howard committed himself to 'very genuine' reconciliation with the Aboriginal people. There is therefore some bad news for the federal government in the Newspoll survey published on 31 January 2000. Once again,

Aboriginal issues ranked at the bottom of the 13 issues listed (the list having been expanded from 12 to 13 since May 1999, with the addition of education—now consistently ranked as the most important of all the issues).

But the disturbing thing, from the federal government's point of view, is that when respondents were asked who was best equipped to handle Aboriginal issues, only 24 percent cited the Coalition.

There are at least three possible interpretations of this result.

The first—rather gloomy—possibility is that the community's own lack of passion on the subject of reconciliation makes the question of who is best equipped to handle Aboriginal issues a matter of indifference.

Second, it might reflect a belief that the Coalition, in office, has failed to make significant improvements in Aboriginal health and welfare, and that during the Howard government's term of office, tensions between some prominent Aboriginal leaders and the government have heightened.

The most likely explanation, though, is that the prime minister's refusal to make a formal apology to Aborigines is regarded as a stumbling block in the path of reconciliation. There is some hard evidence to support this interpretation: a survey conducted by AC Nielsen in 1997 (after the release of the report by the Human Rights and Equal Opportunity Commission on the stolen generations) found that 65 percent of Australians supported a formal parliamentary apology being made to Aborigines. Perhaps we're not so indifferent after all.

A Crossroads of Conscience
Henry Reynolds

I am a convert to the process of reconciliation—a quite recent convert.

Initially I felt some doubt about the project. There were a number of reasons for this. The term 'Aboriginal reconciliation' was concerning. It suggested that it was the indigenous people who had to take the initiative and lead the way. Reconciliation was, after all, a word with several meanings. It might mean that indigenous and settler Australians should be reconciled. It could equally mean that Aborigines should reconcile themselves with their loss of land, with injustice and poverty. I was also not sure what was expected of white Australians. Did reconciliation require anything of them beyond having to come to terms with a few home truths about the past which had long been hidden away in the cupboard of forgotten things?

I was also suspicious about the timing of the process—the long lead time of ten years which may have been seen to be a convenient way to delay any serious discussion of a treaty which prime minister Hawke had committed himself to—if only transiently—at the Barunga Festival in June 1988.

Some of my unease remains, especially when it comes to the role of government. The Howard government inherited the idea and the institution and clearly felt obliged to give lip service to the process. But there has never been much enthusiasm there or much idea about the potential for significant change. The prime minister, Mr Howard, has resolutely resisted any discussion of a treaty and appears to see reconciliation as being about improving service delivery. It is a narrow, unimaginative and essentially assimilationist view. Mr Howard has also adamantly refused to give the apology which many Australians—black and white alike—see as an essential component of reconciliation. And yet the government will presumably want to have some agreed form of words in the months prior to the Olympic Games and the intense international media focus they will bring. The danger is that the reconciliation movement will split with one section willing to find some compromise form of words acceptable to the prime minister and another section strenuously opposing it and marching off in the opposite direction.

But I am a convert as I have already mentioned—a convert to the popular movement. I should explain why.

In the last 18 months I have spoken to many audiences all over Australia. From as far south as Hobart to as far north as Darwin, and in South Australia and all the other states except Western Australia. Almost everywhere I have been, no matter how large or small the community, whether the meeting was at lunchtime or at night, on almost every occasion I was impressed by the size of the audience. But there was something else about the audiences and that was their deep concern, their intensity, their obvious concentration on the subject, their clear sense that this was an important thing they were involved in. The significant thing is that the reconciliation process has spread widely right across Australia. It is no longer just a movement of educated middle-class people. It is no longer just an urban movement. There are reconciliation groups all over the country.

These groups are doing many interesting things. They are meeting together with local indigenous people. The degree of indigenous participation varies widely, but in some places it is very substantial. In communities right across Australia, there are people meeting, thinking, researching, talking and coming up quite often with extremely interesting and creative proposals to try and reach reconciliation there in their own communities.

If reconciliation is to achieve anything, it has to happen at both the local and the national level, and I think that probably the local level in the long run is the most important. Even if the process at the national level doesn't lead to anything of great consequence, the local movement will go on, because I am certain that those hundreds and thousands of people who turn out to meetings are determined that something will happen now, in their lifetime.

Quite a lot of those talks I gave related to a book I published in 1998 called *This Whispering in Our Hearts*. It is about the humanitarians going right back to the 1820s. Many readers were extremely interested and even inspired by the story of all of those people in the past who stood up and demanded changes to what was happening around them—people who were not willing simply to go along with the rhetoric of colonisation, with the easy moral justification of colonisation and settlement. These people were often isolated from one another. Sometimes they may have had no idea that there were other people who thought like them in other districts of Australia. And they often had no idea there was a history of this sort of concern. And yet all over the country there were individuals who made themselves unpopular, who were boycotted for standing up and saying, 'No this is wrong, we should not go on like this'.

My readers felt moved by the fact that there was a history which went right back to the 1820s. On the other hand they were deeply depressed that all this activity, all of these fine speeches, all of this powerful rhetoric, all these letters to newspapers and petitions to parliament, in the end had not changed all that much. In fact (while you'd have to change some of the wording because it was a bit archaic) you could take some of the letters written to the newspapers in the 1820s in Hobart and Launceston and Sydney and present them to a contemporary newspaper and readers would think they were talking about today.

As well as a sense of continuity, there was a feeling that since these people have been trying to change things for so long, we must now make a difference.

It is that feeling, which I sense in audiences all around Australia, which converted me to be a supporter of reconciliation. It is a powerful social movement, and for the first time since 1967 it has given white Australians a means and an instrument to get involved in the cause.

In some places it has been very much a multi-racial movement, and sometimes in quite unlikely places. In the north Queensland city of Mackay the local council, led by the mayor, committed itself to a great deal of expenditure to have a reconciliation convention. It was an enormous success and involved not only the indigenous community (and Mackay also has a very large population of Pacific Islanders)—the whole community became involved.

Wollongong had a very successful convention late in 1999 with the local government deeply involved. But there are also other extraordinary things happening involving local government.

The Redlands Shire between Brisbane and the Gold Coast is not the place you would pick for doing new things about relations between white and indigenous Australians. But the local council has negotiated an extremely progressive land use/native title agreement with the Aboriginal community on Stradbroke Island which is a model of its kind that could be adopted profitably all over Australia.

However, much of the progress in recent times has not come from government. It has come from the courts.

There is no doubt in my mind that the Mabo case was a judicial revolution and the consequences of that case will go on affecting Australia for a long time to come.

In the judicial battles that have followed Mabo, there have been gains and losses—but nonetheless we can now list the important developments.

The significant thing that Mabo did, irreversibly, was to say that all indigenous people were once the owners of Australia—the owners and the possessors of the land. Some people, like the Meriam of Murray Island, were still the owners and possessors of their country, but other people once were land owners. They were once land owners and they lost their land, but that is a significantly different situation to being regarded as people who never owned anything.

Once native title was established, then many of those things which protect property owners swung into action, though not all of them. It is a form of title which discriminates, but nonetheless there have been significant advances—for instance, in the Croker Island case, which extended native title out into the seas. There is the decision relating to the far north west of Western Australia, around the Ord River, where the content of native title was significantly expanded—although the Western Australian government is appealing. There was a decision just recently that native title continued to exist on significant areas in and around Alice Springs. There is the Yanner case about fishing and hunting rights, finding that they continue unless they have been extinguished.

There have, of course, been defeats—and often it is the people who have suffered most who are most likely to be defeated. The Yorta Yorta people lost their case but that is now under appeal and it is quite possible that they will win the appeal. Although the process is slow and cumbersome it rolls on. In the Yanner case dealing with hunting and fishing rights, two of John Howard's appointed judges sided with the 5:2 majority which recognised the continuation of hunting and fishing rights.

There is, of course, much more that could be achieved—the sorts of things that are being done in New Zealand now, and were done in the US in a previous generation. That is, to have some process by which people could go to the court and establish where and how they lost their title and whether or not they should be compensated. The Waitangi Tribunal in NZ is doing this and the Indian Claims Commission in the US was doing it for 30 years between 1946 and 1975. So there are significant areas where we could push the issue of previous and prior land ownership and start talking about some form of recognition at least, if not compensation and reparation.

There is something else that is obviously missing from the Australian debate. We are talking about reconciliation, which is about mutual understanding, mutual agreement about history. We've obviously had significant debate and discussion about land ownership. What has been absent from the Australian discussion is the question of government and the constitutional role and position of indigenous people. Despite the fact we have recently had a significant national debate about the Constitution for the new century there has been very little thought about the political or constitutional position of indigenous people.

This is where Australia differs significantly from Canada and the US. In those two countries which, in so many ways are similar to Australia, treaties were signed between government and indigenous people. The Canadian government has restarted that process—following a 1972 Supreme Court case about native title which was an exactly comparable case to Mabo. It related to British Columbia, where there had been no treaties and where indigenous property rights were treated in the same way as in Australia; that is, they didn't exist. This was true also of the whole north of Canada, the north-west territories and the Yukon, that vast area north of latitude 60°.

In 1972 the Supreme Court recognised that native title existed in British Columbia, and so the Canadian governments realised that it would almost certainly be found to exist also across the north. So they began a process of what is essentially modern treaty making. It was initiated by the question of unresolved issues in relation to land—the question of native title—but it didn't just deal with native title, because in their process of coming to settlement (and this is still going on) they negotiated about much more than land. They negotiated about control of resources, about service delivery, resource development and environmental controls. But they also negotiated about government and about the position of indigenous people in the Canadian Constitution.

This led to the development of the theory that there was in Canada among indigenous people an inherent right to self-government. That is, native title existed because the land had belonged to the Indians before the Europeans arrived. In a similar way, it was argued, because these indigenous societies once governed themselves and had their own laws they also inherited a right to self-government within the Canadian federation.

The most significant and mature example of this development was the recent establishment of Nunavut, a province of the Inuit or Eskimo people in the Eastern Arctic. This represents a new level of government in Canada, and in a similar way the new treaties in British Columbia are about government. The Nisga'a people of British Columbia are going to have very large powers of government over their home territories in the northern part of the province.

This is something we really have not talked much about in Australia. The most significant discussion of this question was produced by a Queensland taskforce of indigenous people set up to look at the government of all the Queensland Aboriginal and Torres Strait Islander communities.

Members travelled across Queensland, talked in every community, and came up with a proposition that was not just something they had taken to the communities. It was more what they brought back. The opinion of those communities was that they should be given the go-ahead to develop their own constitutions and run their own affairs, particularly in relation to many of those things that are now delivered by state government. The proposition was that each community should be encouraged and helped to develop, over a period of time, their own written constitution and that they should be able to take control over the internal development of their community and in particular have control of things like education. But each community should decide which services it would take control of and which it would continue to receive from government.

Clearly this desire for self-government is powerfully present. It's most often expressed by the Torres Strait Islanders, who have for a long time been demanding autonomy of the sort there is in the external territories like Norfolk Island. This is an area that we have in many ways let slip, as though it isn't important. After all, this is what is meant by self-determination in respect of indigenous people. This is an idea which has been talked about in Australia, but we have not got much beyond self-management, and the present government has endeavoured in international discussions to try and get self-determination taken out of the evolving Draft Declaration of the Rights of Indigenous People.

The right of all people to self-determination is enshrined in the principal international covenants and declarations including the Universal Declaration of Human Rights and the Covenant on Civil and Political Rights. There are endless arguments as to what is meant by 'people', but it is an idea which cannot be deflected. It is an idea which will become more and more important, and international events recently have put Australia in a somewhat strange position in relation to self-determination. This is, we have had almost all our viable fighting forces in East Timor under a UN mandate protecting the right of the East Timorese to self-determination.

If it is such an important principle that we commit so much to this issue just over the Arafura Sea from Australia, how can we possibly say 'but this isn't significant within Australia'? This brings us to the question of Australia's standing internationally.

At present our close neighbours are scrutinising Australia. Unfortunately, a thoroughly honourable commitment to East Timor rekindled ideas of white dominance, of the old imperialism. It reawakens those suspicions about Australia, which was for so long in this century committed to 'white Australia'. There is no doubt in my mind what the critics of Australia will look at first and foremost—and that is whether our commitment to human rights, which we trumpet around the world, is actually carried out in Australia, or whether we are hypocritical. These societies in most cases, and Indonesia most notably so, spent much of the time of their existence in the twentieth century fighting against colonisation and then working through the process of decolonisation. It won't be surprising if they look at Australia and say: 'You have still got a colonial situation in your country.'

This touches on a problem that has perplexed me for some time, that is our inability to look at ourselves as outsiders see us. I was very much reminded of this in respect of the document which the Australian government put out a short time ago called *In the National Interest*. It was a White Paper about foreign policy, but above all it talked about the domestic foundations of foreign policy. It was clearly developed as an answer to the Hanson phenomenon.

In that document Tim Fischer and Alexander Downer said that above all else, Australia was committed to human rights, and of those, the thing that matters most to us was the question of racial discrimination. Yet at much the same time that Tim Fischer was putting his signature to the document, he was going around the country calling for 'bucketloads of extinguishment'. That is, he was advocating the forced expropriation of the property of indigenous Australians by legislation in a way that would have been unthinkable had this been addressed to any other recognisable minority in the country. And yet, it was as though this had no relationship to the question of racial discrimination.

Tim Fischer, after all, is a person who has travelled more in Asia than almost any of his contemporaries. He came out very early and attacked Pauline Hanson far more vigorously than did John Howard. But the same person can adopt policies in Australia which outsiders necessarily see as racially discriminatory, and this is exactly why Australia was taken to task by the CERD Committee, the committee that oversees the Convention on the Elimination of Racial Discrimination.

And while on the one hand Australia answered the UN's call to defend self-determination in East Timor at great expense to ourselves, the government of Australia simply rejected the CERD Committee report and wouldn't allow the members of the committee to come to Australia. So it seems to me that Australia, particularly since East Timor, has to be even more careful and more scrupulous and more determined to deal fairly and justly within Australia. And to root out the remaining examples of racial discrimination in our own midst, otherwise everything we say overseas will be seen as not just lacking substance, but above all it will be seen as the mouthings of a hypocrite.

Reconciliation matters within Australia. It also has an international dimension. Australia has a responsibility to the world for the survival of indigenous cultures. That is the consequence of colonising a country occupied by other people, and that is a task that the world will expect us to carry out. They will see it, many of them, as the need to bring into Australia the decolonisation that swept the world in the 1950s and the 1960s. That is the task for the next generation of reformers. That must be the next goal for reconciliation.

The Redfern Park Speech
Paul Keating

This will be a year (1992) of great significance for Australia. It comes at a time when we have committed ourselves to succeeding in the test which so far we have always failed. Because, in truth, we cannot confidently say that we have succeeded as we would like to have succeeded if we have not managed to extend opportunity and care, dignity and hope to the indigenous people of Australia—the Aboriginal and Torres Strait Island people.

This is a fundamental test of our social goals and our national will: our ability to say to ourselves and the rest of the world that Australia is a first rate social democracy, that we are what we should be—truly the land of the fair go and the better chance. There is no more basic test of how seriously we mean these things. It is a test of our self-knowledge. Of how well we know the land we live in. How well we know our history. How well we recognise the fact that, complex as our contemporary identity is, it cannot be separated from Aboriginal Australia. How well we know what Aboriginal Australians know about Australia.

Redfern is a good place to contemplate these things. Just a mile or two from the place where the first European settlers landed, in too many ways it tells us that their failure to bring much more than devastation and demoralisation to Aboriginal Australia continues to be our failure.

More I think than most Australians recognise, the plight of Aboriginal Australians affects us all. In Redfern it might be tempting to think that the reality Aboriginal Australians face is somehow contained here, and that the rest of us are insulated from it. But of course, while all the dilemmas may exist here, they are far from contained. We know the same dilemmas and more are faced all over Australia.

This is perhaps the point of this Year of the World's Indigenous People: to bring the dispossessed out of the shadows, to recognise that they are part of us, and that we cannot give indigenous Australians up without giving up many of our own most deeply held values, much of our own identity—and our own humanity.

Nowhere in the world, I would venture, is the message more stark than in Australia. We simply cannot sweep injustice aside. Even if our own conscience allowed us to, I am sure, that in due course, the world and the people of our region would not. There should be no mistake about this—our success in resolving these issues will have a significant bearing on our standing in the world.

However intractable the problems may seem, we cannot resign ourselves to failure—any more than we can hide behind the contemporary version of Social Darwinism which says that to reach back for the poor and dispossessed is to risk being dragged down. That seems to me not only morally indefensible, but bad history.

We non-Aboriginal Australians should perhaps remind ourselves that Australia once reached out for us. Didn't Australia provide opportunity and care for the dispossessed Irish? The poor of Britain? The refugees from war and famine and persecution in the countries of Europe and Asia? Isn't it reasonable to say that if we can build a prosperous and remarkably harmonious multicultural society in Australia, surely we can find just solutions to the problems which beset the first Australians—the people to whom the most injustice has been done?

And, as I say, the starting point might be to recognise that the problem starts with us non-Aboriginal Australians.

It begins, I think, with the act of recognition. Recognition that it was we who did the dispossessing. We took the traditional lands and smashed the traditional way of life. We brought the disasters. The alcohol. We committed the murders. We took the children from their mothers. We practised discrimination and exclusion. It was our ignorance and our prejudice. And our failure to imagine these things being done to us.

With some noble exceptions, we failed to make the most basic human response and enter into their hearts and minds. We failed to ask—how would I feel if this were done to me? As a consequence, we failed to see that what we were doing degraded all of us.

If we needed a reminder of this, we received it this year. The report of the Royal Commission into Aboriginal Deaths in Custody showed with devastating clarity that the past lives on in inequality, racism and injustice in the prejudice and ignorance of non-Aboriginal Australians, and in the demoralisation and desperation, the fractured identity, of so many Aborigines and Torres Strait Islanders.

For all this, I do not believe that the report should fill us with guilt. Down the years, there has been no shortage of guilt, but it has not produced the responses we need. Guilt is not a very constructive emotion. I think what we need to do is open our hearts a bit. All of us.

Perhaps when we recognise what we have in common we will see the things which must be done—the practical things. There is something of this in the creation of the Council for Aboriginal Reconciliation. The council's mission is to forge a new partnership built on justice and equity and an appreciation of the heritage of Australia's indigenous people.

In the abstract those terms are meaningless. We have to give meaning to 'justice' and 'equity'—and, as I have said several times this year, we will only give them meaning when we commit ourselves to achieving concrete results. If we improve the living conditions in one town, they will improve in another. And another. If we raise the standard of health by 20 percent one year, it will be raised more the next. If we open one door others will follow.

When we see improvement, when we see more dignity, more confidence, more happiness—we will know we are going to win. We need these practical building blocks of change.

The Mabo judgement should be seen as one of these. By doing away with the bizarre conceit that this continent had no owners prior to the settlement of Europeans, Mabo establishes a fundamental truth and lays the basis for justice. It will be much easier to work from that basis than has ever been the case in the past. For this reason alone we should ignore the isolated outbreaks of hysteria and hostility of the past few months.

Mabo is an historic decision. We can make it an historic turning point, the basis of a new relationship between indigenous and non-Aboriginal Australians. The message should be that there is nothing to fear or to lose in the recognition of historical truth, or the extension of social justice, or the deepening of Australian social democracy to include indigenous Australians. There is everything to gain.

Even the unhappy past speaks for this. Where Aboriginal Australians have been included in the life of Australia they have made remarkable contributions. Economic contributions, particularly in the pastoral and agricultural industry. They are there in the frontier and exploration history of Australia. They are there in the wars. In sport, to an extraordinary degree. In literature and art and music. In all these things they have shaped our knowledge of this continent and of ourselves. They have shaped our identity. They are there in the Australian legend. We should never forget—they helped build this nation.

And if we have a sense of justice, as well as common sense, we will forge a new partnership. As I said, it might help us if we non-Aboriginal Australians imagined ourselves dispossessed of land we have lived on for 50,000 years—and then imagined ouselves told that it had never been ours. Imagine if ours was the oldest culture in the world and we were told that it was worthless. Imagine if we had resisted this settlement, suffered and died in the defence of our land, and then were told in history books that we had given up without a fight. Imagine if non-Aboriginal Australians had served their country in peace and war and were then ignored in history books. Imagine if our feats on sporting fields had inspired admiration and patriotism and yet did nothing to diminish prejudice. Imagine if our spiritual life was denied and ridiculed. Imagine if we had suffered the injustice and then were blamed for it.

It seems to me that if we can imagine the injustice then we can imagine its opposite. And we can have justice. I say that for two reasons: I say it because I believe that the great things about Australian social democracy reflect a fundamental belief in justice. And I say it because in so many other areas we have proved our capacity over the years to go on extending the realms of participating, opportunity and care.

Just as Australians living in the relatively narrow and insular Australia of the 1960s imagined a culturally diverse, worldly and open Australia, and in a generation turned the idea into reality, so we can turn the goals of reconciliation into reality.

There are very good signs that the process has begun. The creation of the Reconciliation Council is evidence itself. The establishment of ATSIC—the Aboriginal and Torres Strait Islander Commission—is also evidence. The council is the product of imagination and goodwill. ATSIC emerges from the vision of indigenous self-determination and self-management. The vision has already become the reality of almost 800 elected Aboriginal regional councillors and commissioners determining priorities and developing their own programs.

All over Australia, Aboriginal and Torres Strait Islander communities are taking charge of their own lives. And assistance with the problems which chronically beset them is at last being made available in ways developed by the communities themselves.

If these things offer hope, so does the fact that this generation of Australians is better informed about Aboriginal culture and achievement, and about the injustice that has been done, than any generation before. We are beginning to more generally appreciate the depth and the diversity of Aboriginal and Torres Strait Islander cultures. From their music and art and dance we are beginning to recognise how much richer our national life and identity will be for the participation of Aborigines and Torres Strait Islanders. We are beginning to learn what the indigenous people have known for many thousands of years—how to live with our physical environment. Ever so gradually we are learning how to see Australia through Aboriginal eyes, beginning to recognise the wisdom contained in their epic story. I think we are beginning to see how much we owe the indigenous Australians and how much we have lost by living so apart.

I said we non-indigenous Australians should try to imagine the Aboriginal view. It can't be too hard. Someone imagined this event today, and it is now a marvellous reality and a great reason for hope.

There is one thing today we cannot imagine. We cannot imagine that the descendants of people whose genius and resilience maintained a culture here through 50,000 years or more, through cataclysmic changes to the climate and environment, and who then survived two centuries of dispossession and abuse, will be denied their place in the modern Australian nation. We cannot imagine that. We cannot imagine that we will fail. And with the spirit that is here today I am confident that we won't.

I am confident that we will succeed in this decade.

Not Just a Challenge, an Opportunity
Linda Burney

As Patrick Dodson, founding chair of the Council for Aboriginal Reconciliation, told the National Press Club three years ago, we have to ask ourselves, what Australians want to be:

> Together, indigenous and other Australians are called on to choose the path we now take. Our choices will determine the future shape of our nation…Will it be a nation which lives in harmony because it has healed the wounds of its past with generosity of spirit and wisdom of intellect? Or will it be a nation where the wounds created by dispossession and injustice still fester, and where the same old conflicts still linger, because the imperative of reconciliation did not inform crucial decisions?

At the Australian Reconciliation Convention, 'Renewing the Nation', in 1997 Dr Faith Bandler echoed this message:

> In this climate of callousness, where moves to dismantle structures of democracy are heavily overshadowing us, our task now is to use our voices, our energy, our will and our talents to mobilise the forces for good. I am sure we can demolish these forces of destruction under the banner of justice for all….But we must act today, because tomorrow it may be too late.

These two quotes embrace the themes I want to explore. Firstly, Patrick puts in front of us the choice and decision we must take about the future shape of our nation. Then Faith puts in front of us the urgency and the bravery required to take that decision.

We have the chance, and it may be our last chance for quite some time, to go forward into the new millennium in the vision of the Council for Aboriginal Reconciliation:

> A united Australia which respects this land of ours;
> Values the Aboriginal and Torres Strait Islander heritage;
> And provides justice and equity for all.

Today is about the future. But in an Aboriginal world-view the past, the present and the future are interconnected, like everything in Aboriginal culture. For this reason, I want to take another look at Australian history in terms of the attitudes and values and the frames of reference which have made Australians what we are—both indigenous and other Australians. Firstly, some of these mindsets have survived into the present. Secondly, history for Aboriginal people is not something dead and gone. It is a living, breathing burden that we carry every day of our lives—the more so when wounds have been re-opened by the stolen generations inquiry.

The invasion and colonisation of this country is not 200 years ago as the 1988 bicentennial encouraged many people to think. Some massacres are within living memory. All over the country stories are handed down in family tradition. And over the last decade there have been the most graphic possible reminders, the Royal Commission into Aboriginal Deaths in Custody and the stolen generations inquiry.

There is a school of thought that says the physical landscape has shaped in a major way who and what we are as Australians—the garden of Eden, the unforgiving land, the sunburnt country, the land of sweeping plains, etc. The same landscape is dotted with signposts of horror and guilt—Slaughterhouse Creek, Poison Swamp Creek, Murdering Flat, Blackfellow's Leap, Myall Creek, Coniston and all the others. We need to think about what has this done to the collective psyche of mainstream Australia.

As Paul Keating said at Redfern Park in 1992, Australians need to think how they would feel if this happened to them, to know where we are coming from:

> ...it might help if we non-Aboriginal Australians imagined ourselves dispossessed of land we had lived on for 50,000 years—and then imagined ourselves told it had never been ours. Imagine if ours was the oldest culture in the world and we were told it was worthless. Imagine if we had resisted this settlement, suffered and died in the defence of our land, and then were told in history books that we had given up without a fight. Imagine if non-Aboriginal Australians had served their country in peace and war and were then ignored in history books. Imagine if our feats on

the sporting field had inspired admiration and patriotism and yet did nothing to diminish prejudice. Imagine if our spiritual life was denied and ridiculed. Imagine if we had suffered the injustice and then were blamed for it.

It is not about guilt, but it has to be about shame. If there are things in Australian history we can all be proud of, there are also things we all should be ashamed of. As the governor-general said in 1996:

> ...true reconciliation...is not achievable in the absence of acknowledgement by the nation of the wrongfulness of the past dispossession, oppression and degradation of the Aboriginal peoples...Where there is no room for national pride or national shame about the past, there can be no national soul.

A fundamental issue is that the indigenous people of this country were not recognised as citizens for almost 70 years after federation, and that, even after that recognition, there is a real difference between having rights on paper and being able to exercise and enjoy those rights.

One hundred years ago Aboriginal people were excluded from the debates about federation, then mentioned just twice in the 1901 Constitution, both times to be excluded—from the census and from the law-making powers of the Commonwealth. The first act of the new parliament was the Immigration Restriction Act, which enacted the White Australia Policy. Aboriginal people were excluded from employment by the post office, which meant the public service, from pensions and maternity allowances, from enlistment in the armed forces from 1909 up to 1951; the list goes on.

At the first Native Welfare Conference of federal and state ministers and officials responsible for Aboriginal affairs in 1937, the WA chief protector, A.O. Neville, said:

> The different states are creating institutions for the welfare of the native race, and, as a result of this policy, the native race is increasing. What is to be the limit? Are we going to have a population of 1,000,000 blacks in the Commonwealth, or are we going to merge them into our white community and eventually forget that there were ever any aborigines (sic) in Australia?

That conference inaugurated the 'new policy' of assimilation to make Aboriginal people eventually the same as other Australians. Aboriginal people could in effect have citizen rights only by becoming, over time, less Aboriginal. When exemption certificates were introduced for supposedly more 'advanced' Aboriginal people, they could be revoked if people continued to associate with family. This policy actually denied to Aboriginal people the right to be a citizen of this country. But the point of course was that we were not citizens at that time.

White Australia

White Australia was the reason for this exclusion of Aboriginal people. Australia was based on the most fundamental denial of rights. Captain Cook's claiming of Australia as Crown land on the basis of the legal fiction of *terra nullius*—land belonging to no one—denied the property rights, the humanity and even the existence of Aboriginal people. The White Australia Policy then defined Australia as white. Generations of Australians grew up with that white-European frame of reference.

This is why reconciliation is a matter of generational change and education is the key. We have to change the frame of reference of Australians so that Aboriginal issues are no more out there on the margins, at the fringes of consciousness, but at the heart of debate. We achieve this by making Aboriginal Australia integral to the education of all students, a natural part of the socialisation of all Australians.

What is reconciliation?

Broadly speaking, reconciliation is about recognition, rights and reform. It is recognition of Aboriginal and Torres Strait Islander peoples as the original peoples of this land, and it is recognising the Aboriginal history of this land, both the long Aboriginal history before the invasion, and the shared history since. Reconciliation is recognising the rights that flow from being the first peoples, as well as our rights as Australian citizens in common with all other citizens. It is about reforming systems to address the disadvantages suffered by indigenous peoples and, as I have said, it is about changing the frame of reference of all Australians to include Aboriginal Australia.

There are many issues of recognition. As Professor Mary Kalantzis said at the Australian Reconciliation Convention:

> The call for inclusion and recognition is not one that stems from charity or the heart. It is a call for accounting properly for contributions genuinely made. Constitutional reform that allows for an inclusive sense of belonging is a critical part of renewal and reconciliation.

One of the most contentious issues of recognition is the Aboriginal dead of the frontier wars. Almost 20 years ago in 1981 Henry Reynolds wrote:

> How, then, do we deal with the Aboriginal dead? White Australians frequently say 'all that' should be forgotten. But it will not be. It cannot be. Black memories are too deeply, too recently scarred. And forgetfulness is a strange prescription coming from a community which has revered the fallen warrior and emblazoned the phrase 'Lest we Forget' on monuments throughout the land.

Another issue is recognition of the rights of Aboriginal and Torres Strait Islander peoples as first peoples. As Mick Dodson wrote, there must be:

> ...recognition and understanding by the Australian nation-state of our distinctive status as first peoples. This must be the starting point.

An acceptable preamble to the Australian Constitution must include recognition of indigenous custodianship of the land, as the 1998 Constitutional Convention recommended. There must be an apology for the stolen generations and for all the impacts of invasion on Aboriginal peoples across the country. As Malcolm Fraser wrote:

> ...An apology above all is recognition that something wrong was done and we regret that it happened. It is perhaps the most important thing we can do which is within our power to address matters of the spirit. There will never be reconciliation with Aboriginal people and other Australians unless we understand that there are both material and spiritual issues involved.

Social justice

The most fundamental prerequisite is social justice. Aboriginal people have always said there can be no reconciliation without justice—and that means social justice. Social justice is not something abstract, but what happens to people on the ground, well defined by Mick Dodson in his first annual report as Aboriginal and Torres Strait Islander social justice commissioner:

> Social justice must always be considered from a perspective which is grounded in the daily lives of indigenous Australians. Social justice is what faces you in the morning. It is awakening in a house with an adequate water supply, cooking facilities and sanitation. It is the ability to nourish your children and send them to a school where their education not only equips them for employment but reinforces their knowledge and appreciation of their cultural inheritance. It is the prospect of genuine employment and good health: a life of choices and opportunity, free from discrimination.

Social justice means dealing with issues of the so-called 'level playing field' and claims that 'blacks get too much', when in fact on every social indicator indigenous people are still the most disadvantaged of all Australians. There is still a hangover from colonial times, bitter resistance in some quarters to any special provision for indigenous people. But the point is that treating people 'equally' when they are not equal to start with only institutionalises inequality.

One particularly important issue which relates both to recognition and to social justice is racism. Australians need to recognise the undeniable fact that racism exists in this country—at times from both sides of the racial divide. At the same time freedom from racism is fundamental to social justice. And the absence of racism is essential to real equal citizenship.

Reconciliation demands action, not just words on paper. There are levels of responsibility from the national down to the local, and from the local level up. The Commonwealth has a particular responsibility to provide leadership and must also take the lead role in facilitating constitutional reform to guarantee social justice. State and territory and local governments are responsible for delivering most of the services to which all citizens are entitled, and as such the main role is theirs. Sectors such as education, and both union and employer groups, have their responsibilities. But we have to be aware that none of these agencies will fulfil their responsibilities unless reconciliation becomes a people's imperative. It is the humble actions of individuals that add up to the collective will which governments cannot ignore.

The prime minister has pledged his government to achieving reconciliation in terms of addressing health, education and employment outcomes, but needs to understand also the importance of matters of the spirit, such as an apology and recognition of Aboriginal Australia. The eyes of the world will be on Australia in the lead-up to the 2000 Olympics. At the same time the centenary of the Australian nation-state makes Australians think about what Australia is. The reconciliation debate, in changing the mindset of Australians, can make a critical contribution to this nation being able to define for ourselves what is Australia, who are Australians and what is Australian citizenship.

Citizenship

Clearly citizenship is about rights and obligations. Most people agree on what citizen rights are, but defining what are the obligations each citizen owes and to whom is more complex and demands a greater level of consensus and shared vision. In the Aboriginal world-view all rights are inextricably linked to obligations, part of a reciprocal network of rights and obligations in all relationships.

It seems to me that citizenship in the civic sense must be about participation in the life of the community, as a full member of that society. That means citizenship has to be about belonging. There needs to be both knowledge and awareness of the political and social systems involved and there needs to be a level of shared faith in those systems. The greatest problem of contemporary society is alienation—and no one has more reason to be alienated than Aboriginal people. What is needed is a sense of belonging for all citizens.

Citizenship should unite all Australians; it should be something we are all proud to be part of. It is a matter of shared values and identity. There has been a lot of focus on differences among Australians. We need to focus more on what we have in common, what might unite us as Australians. The debate on reconciliation is central to and can be an essential resource for the wider debate on what is Australia and who are Australians—a tool to define all of us honestly.

Talking of identity brings us to the 'real Australian' question, one of the main themes of intellectual debate in this country. This search for the 'real Australian' has always been a white Australian preoccupation. It has never been an issue for Aboriginal people. We grow up learning exactly who we are and the relationships that make up our identity. I want to suggest that the real reason why Australian identity has always been such a problem for other Australians is simply because the Aboriginal element has been left out.

I want to suggest now some of the issues and the heritage and identity that Australians share. First, I want to quote the words of Lady Deane, wife of the governor-general and an inspirational leader in her own right, speaking at the Reconciliation Convention:

> What indigenous women want for their families and communities—good health, effective education, a minimum standard of housing, safety, self-respect, a sense of place and purpose—is very much what I want for my own family and those who are close to me....They aspire, like all women, to full equality of opportunity, to be treated with respect and protected from exploitation and violence and to have the diversity of their roles and responsibilities recognised and valued.

To reinforce what Lady Deane has said, we have seen in the last few years an army of other Australians across the country supporting our struggle.

Sharing our history means honouring Australians who have stood up for Aboriginal rights over the years. Recognising how many other Australians have always wanted to belong to this land, for example, most white Australian art has always been basically about land. Recognising also the people who are sometimes called 'white blackfellows'—other Australians who lived with Aboriginal people over the years, learning to belong to the land, assimilating Aboriginal values and ways of seeing.

Many of the so-called 'typical Aussie' characteristics come equally from Aboriginal society, and some cannot really be properly explained any other way; for example the well-known Australian egalitarianism comes equally from Aboriginal society in the first place.

Sharing our heritage means recognising what Aboriginal Australia has contributed to Australia: war service, the outback cattle industry, sports stars, and more recently art. Also a sense of the power of the Dreaming in Australian arts; a vividness in Australian language largely based on image and metaphor, eg. flash talk, big smoke, sit down money; elements of the Aussie sense of humour.

Is it really coincidence that mainstream Australian culture, film, art literature, flowered at the same time Australians began to recognise Aboriginal people as part of Australia, and to break down the silly racist lie of white Australia?

Think about the way Aboriginal symbols have been used to identify Australia, the boomerang being the most obvious example, as in the Sydney 2000 logo. Many people call this cultural appropriation—and some of it is. But appropriation can also be seen as cultural homage—no one takes something unless they value it. And it can be seen as white Australians recognising that Australia is Aboriginal, and trying to belong to the land.

These are some examples of how all Australians have a shared heritage, and how we can focus on what unites us. This is critical if we are to reach the kind of consensus that is fundamental not only to reconciliation, but also to a shared citizenship where beliefs and values, rights and obligations are recognised and shared.

Reconciliation is about partnerships

Much of achieving reconciliation depends on partnerships between indigenous and other Australian agencies and individuals at sectoral, local and national levels to change systems and mindsets. There are hundreds of such initiatives across the country. These three I think show what can be done:

Teaching the teachers
A partnership of the University of New South Wales and the NSW Aboriginal Education Consultative Group (AECG) developed resources to empower all teachers to teach Aboriginal studies to all students.

Camilla Cowley and Gunggari people
In south-west Queensland, Camilla Cowley and her family and the local Gunggari people sat down and negotiated a land-use agreement which must also be signed by any purchaser of the property in the future.

Joint management of Uluru Kata Tjuta National Park
The key to the success of Uluru Kata Tjuta National Park is the cooperation between the traditional owners and the National Parks and Wildlife Service, sharing knowledge and expertise in managing their shared environment.

Finally, I want to suggest how Aboriginal ways of relating can help all Australians to develop a shared and inclusive citizenship. Aboriginal world-views are about community, identity and belonging.

First and foremost, the Aboriginal idea of belonging to the land and being responsible for country is critical. More than anything else it is the land that has divided us in the past and should unite us now. More Australians are learning to love and to respect the land, rather than seeing it as a quarry, beginning to get used to the idea that individuals do not own land but are custodians for all people. And Aboriginal people can teach other Australians how to look after this country.

The second philosophical contribution is the local identity of Aboriginal people. This relates to the idea of belonging not just to the land in general, but to a particular place, or 'country' as we call it. This belonging grows a sense of community and common goals. This local identity can be an antidote to globalism, which tends to deny all group identity, to make people feel powerless and encourage them to focus on self.

Our sense of community, based on belonging to the land, but also on the multiple and complex relationships of our extended families, with their reciprocal rights and obligations, may be a corrective to the individualism and selfishness of much mainstream Australian life now. It is this wider sense of family belonging that has been lost in much modern life, especially in the cities where most Australians live. This is something we can teach other Australians. As the Aboriginal mother says in *Bringing Them Home*, the video of the stolen generations inquiry, 'We're family people. We're family people.'

The Dark Side of Sport
Colin Tatz

Reconciliation is a strange word

We approach this new century with the belief (or the hope) that with time, experience and growth, it should be much better than the last one. We look back on virulent nationalism, wholesale genocide and legions of the dead. We deplore the bitter memories and past conflicts between clans, tribes, factions, ethnicities and nations which resulted in recent catastrophes in Bosnia, Serbia, Kosovo, Somalia, Rwanda, Burundi, South Africa, Sudan, the Middle East, Greece, Turkey, Spain, Indonesia, East Timor... We condemn the on-going violent politics—of remembering—so explicit in, for example, Irish politics and the Zulu Inkatha movement; and we preach, instead, a politics of reconciliation and peace—of forgetting.

Former president Nelson Mandela and archbishop Desmond Tutu are celebrated as the arch reconciliators of our time, as Christians in the widest and best sense of forgiveness. East Germany said 'sorry' to the Jews minutes before reunification, and Poland followed suit. By 1999 the Vatican had invested a decade preparing a ten-page apology for its 'tepid' response to, and during, the Holocaust. 'One cannot dwell constantly on memories and resentments', intoned François Mitterand in 1994. Haunted by memories of his labours for Vichy and his friendship with the infamous secretary-general of the Vichy Police, René Bousquet, Mitterand found the flowers to half-atone for the deportation of so much of French Jewry.

As the year 2000 begins, dozens of prominent Australians believe we should stop 'hounding' Latvian Arajs Kommando member, Konrad Kalejs: even if he was involved in the murder of 30,000 Jews and Gypsies, he is, after all, 86, 'and we should all move on'.

Reconciliation appeals as a sane approach, ethical and moral. The word seems to resonate a merciful Christ rather than an unforgiving Jehovah. It offers hope, harmony and 'humane-ness'. It suggests an end to enmity and a settling of differences. We have a somewhat battered Aboriginal Reconciliation Council; a week in May set aside as National Reconciliation Week; and a rather tattered concept, constantly invoked as a magic mantra to ward off contentious legislation, talk of double-dissolution 'race elections', 'vexed' land claims, and the like. When such problems 'get in the way of reconciliation', they should be removed rather than addressed. The prime minister, for example, suggests that any Aboriginal demonstration or protest at the Olympic Games will 'diminish' the public's concerns for or about Aborigines. Ergo, they shouldn't demonstrate or embarrass 'us'.

Reconciliation is never defined: it is simply parroted, leaving assumptions to struggle for meaning and purpose or, rather, meaning and purpose to struggle amid assumptions. Reconciliation is a strange word, with undefined implications. Who has to be brought to a state of acquiescence, friendliness, agreement and harmony? Why? And how?

Reconciliation began as a non-Aboriginal concept—the invention of Robert Tickner, Labor's Aboriginal affairs minister, at the start of the last decade. It was to be a program lasting ten years, aimed at improving race relations, increasing understanding of Aboriginal and Islander culture, history and the causes of their continued disadvantage in health, housing, education and employment. It means different things to different people. For prime minister John Howard and Aboriginal affairs minister John Herron, it appears to mean more money for better health, education, housing and employment (even while they provide less). For many proponents and believers, it means a moratorium—each party desisting from causing injury to the other. For some, it is a walking together, a talking together, towards anything that simply has to be better than the past or present. For others, reconciliation can only mean the national Australian government bringing itself to use the 'sorry' word for the forcible removal of children, to articulate atonement and find a means of restitution or reparation for these practices. For the majority, reconciliation signifies or symbolises a new deal, a fresh start, a 'moving on'—much in the manner of the 1967 referendum—but without the faintest idea of how to achieve it. For all Aboriginal organisations, there can be no reconciliation until the matter of the stolen generations is addressed, then redressed, legally and politically. One suspects that the ambiguities could be convenient for governments: since no one defines the term with any precision, specific programs don't have to be devised, let alone implemented.

Sir Gustav Nossal sees reconciliation as 'a movement in people's hearts, a public movement'. Yes, it is. In its way, it is a strong social movement—but one clearly in need of an Aboriginal or Islander leadership (from someone like Noel Pearson or Peter Yu or one of the Dodson brothers) to turn it into a political one. If leaderless, and without the appearance of, literally, movement towards political goals, it will wither.

Sir Gustav says he's optimistic and sees little signs here and there. He is confident that the reconciliation document will contain both sufficient aspirational (and inspirational) words and hard-edged policies and strategies to effect real change. I wish I could share his and his council's optimism. I, too, am (emotionally) optimistic: how else could one engage in Aboriginal affairs daily for 40 years? But part of me is highly pessimistic (intellectually), and with good reason.

In 1967 there was both illusion and self-delusion by high-powered and informed people—including Doug Nicholls, Charlie Perkins, Stan Davey, Doris Blackburn, Gordon Bryant, Don Dunstan, Jack Horner, Faith Bandler and Bill Wentworth—that this was the era of the 'new deal', the fresh start, of 'citizenship rights'. Inherently flawed, it was none of these things—merely a concurrent Commonwealth power to legislate and the counting of Aborigines and Islanders in the census. Apart from a failed national land rights act, the native title law, the now emasculated Wik law, some heritage and environmental matters, the Commonwealth has backed off 'control' of Aboriginal policy. Each of the states that surrendered administration to the Commonwealth in the early 1970s has re-created Aboriginal affairs administrations. It took nearly 30 years for the census people, in 1996, to get it (reasonably) 'right'. That referendum was, indeed, a movement in people's hearts: nearly 90 percent of Australia's voters felt, or thought they felt, positive. In the end, it delivered nothing.

Some high-powered and informed people—Charles Rowley, Nugget Coombs, Diane Barwick and poet Judith Wright—promoted the idea of a treaty in the early 1980s. There was strong backing from the public, but when Aborigines presented the Makarrata, their treaty that embodied a detailed (and expensive) invoice to the nation, the matter died.

The Royal Commission into Aboriginal Deaths in Custody was one of the two most important inquiries of the 118 investigations of Aboriginal matters in the twentieth century. Supported widely by political leaders, the press, the churches, by eminent men and women across the nation, it produced—under the heading 'Towards Reconciliation'—339 very specific, hard-edged recommendations in 1991. The commission's findings were aired abroad, attracting notice and criticism—for a while. Yet, by 2000, no more than 20 percent of the specific items have been addressed or attended to. The rate and the number of deaths by suicide, both inside and outside of custody, have increased since the Royal Commission.

Of equal significance was *Bringing Them Home*, the inquiry that examined, in minute detail, the forcible removal of children from one group to another, defined by the United Nations Convention as an act of genocide. It carried the weight of Sir Ronald Wilson, Mick Dodson and a host of church organisations which admitted complicity. The report, and its publicity, was the catalyst which produced 'the movement in people's hearts', coming as it did on top of the appalling ill-health reports that disfigure both lives and our comfortable television screens; the Mabo debate and legislation; the Wik decision and its manifestly unfair dilution; the continuing deaths in custody; the ever-present furores over racial vilification on the football fields; the reports of ever-increasing youth suicide; the truculence and intransigence of Howard and Herron about any form of apology, or even acknowledgement, that child removals were injurious.

Will the reconciliation document have a better fate? It should have. But I have learned, over four decades, an indelible reality here, in South Africa, New Zealand, Israel, Canada, and the United States—that the greatest obstacle to change in 'native administration' is bureaucratic indifference, and often enough, hostile indifference. To illustrate this attitude, let me commend John Howard for his particular role in an Aboriginal issue.

A few years ago he sent the army into some Northern Territory communities to establish and help operate sanitation systems. It worked. But we all lost sight of the crucial issue: why the army? Simply because the civil infrastructure, covering dozens of agencies, had neither the interest nor the will—in peacetime—to provide an essential service which they would never dare fail to provide in any white community. That is hostile indifference.

There is a gulf between Aborigines and non-Aborigines. No other people, in Maureen Watson's words, have been so 'wedded, enslaved, whitewashed and saved'. Very few minorities have suffered anything like the duration and extent of the gun and the whip, the neck chains and the rape, the exile to remoteness, the break-up of families, the forcible removal of children, the indefinite periods of legal wardship and minority status, the levels of want, poverty, deprivation and exclusion—even as of now. For the vast majority of Aborigines and Islanders, the past is not a foreign country. What governments concede Aborigines may have endured in the past, they are still enduring—namely, wholesale imprisonments, removal of children to institutions of various kinds, gross ill-health, appalling environmental conditions, unemployability, increasing illiteracy, family breakdown, internal violence, and almost unbelievable levels of youth suicide. Neither in theory nor in practice does, or can, the concept of reconciliation, as variously interpreted, address these issues.

Can sport address them?
There is a universal notion, exaggerated in Australia, that sport connects people who are not connected either by history, community, culture, gender, race, class or status. Sport is seen as the transcender, the unifier and the healer of difference.

Australia's victory in the America's Cup in 1983 is the exemplar. Described by the (then) prime minister Bob Hawke as 'Australia's greatest sporting achievement', the euphoria and rhetoric that day seemed to have created a 'one Australia'. A mere decade later, the only common memory is the winning boat's connection with its disgraced owner and entrepreneur. (Even then, memory is short. Alan Bond's malfeasance is forgotten amid the 'news' that his oil painting of Aboriginal footballer Peter Matera was sold to a Perth brothel-keeper for $28,000; and, despite her dislike of the work—or of Bond, or Matera—she won't part with it for less than half-a-million.)

Sport, we like to believe, enables, or even ensures, that divergent communities, classes, cultures, ethnicities, religions and races become one under the banner of loyalty to the 'nation'. Thus, the success of its soccer team enabled postwar Hungary, then living under crushing Soviet communism, to hold up its united head: the Magyars thrashed England 6–3 at Wembley in 1953, uniting the nation as never before, albeit fleetingly. Here, Cathy Freeman's second 400m title in the World Championships came close—as close as Lionel Rose's world bantamweight title in 1968—to 'bleaching' or transcending all racial differences.

Does sport really have these magical qualities for Aborigines and Islanders? Does it heal? In a land obsessed with sport, we don't expect to see or find racism there. The nation's rulers and writers are besotted with 'the level playing field', now the appropriate and sophisticated metaphor in place of the 'old-fashioned' 'land of the fair go'. Is there a dark side of Australian sport that needs forgetting, or forgiving? Is there some behaviour they should desist from? What, in short, has been the Aboriginal and Islander sporting experience?

Racism in word
'Australia used to be racist, but it isn't any more'; 'unlike South Africa, our racism wasn't intentional or malevolent but accidental or (hopefully) benevolent'; 'there may have been racism in sport, but there isn't any now'; 'in any event, the 1967 referendum gave Aborigines "equal rights"'. These myths are, regrettably, widespread.

There are, of course, gradations of racism. At one end there is racial prejudice, expressed verbally, often not acted upon. At the other is overt racism, acted upon by individuals and by institutions, the latter much more serious, harmful and, as Aboriginal history shows, even fatal.

Racial vilification in sport has reached some appalling depths. As world heavyweight champion, Tommy Burns was determined not to fight a black man but couldn't refuse £15,000 to fight 'the Black Menace', American Jack Johnson, in Sydney on Boxing Day, 1908. Every Australian, the collective clergy and the collective press, hated Johnson with a seething, hysterical hatred. The epitome of evil, 'the Fear of Dark' had come to white Australia. The public and the press saw the contest either as the possible end of white privilege or as the venue for putting all blacks in their place—the ultimate contest for white supremacy. Johnson physically and verbally humiliated Burns, a defeat the Australian public took very badly indeed.

In the 1890s Frank Ivory played two rugby union matches for Queensland against New South Wales. 'The half-caste from Maryborough' was given a torrid time by the Sydney crowd, because of his colour. A century later sections at Lang Park stadium still rave on about 'coons'. Several senior *Age* journalists over the years have reported how well-dressed, well-educated ladies in the members' stand at the Melbourne Cricket Ground scream, 'kill the black f...g c...t' and/or 'go sniff your petrol' to Chris Lewis, the Krakouers and McAdams of Australian football fame.

Not much changes: Ivory in the 1880s and the Ella brothers in the 1980s. In the rugby union Test against Scotland in July 1982, the Brisbane crowd booed and abused every move of Mark and Glen because they'd been chosen ahead of Queenslanders Roger Gould and Paul McLean. The Ellas felt they were playing Queensland, not Scotland. While this was said to be a classic case of state chauvinism, there is no doubt the Ellas' black presence figured in the crowd's emotions.

Mark talks of one or two disappointments in his career: one was this Ballymore 'debacle', which the press called 'an unbelievable and shameful act'. His other bitterness was the loss of his successful Australian captaincy. There is no doubt that Mark wasn't considered by one or two power-brokers—to wit Alan Jones—to 'have class enough' to make the dinner speeches.

Two racist insults were a turning point, and a spur, in the career of Evonne Goolagong. The first, at age 16, when one of her defeated opponents in Sydney referred to her as a 'nigger'; the second was in the 1980 Wimbledon final: a senior Victorian politician said he hoped she 'wouldn't go walkabout like some old boong'. The last word was hers: 'All tennis players lose concentration, but since I'm an Aborigine it's brought up constantly—except when I'm winning!'

Glenn James, qualified teacher and Vietnam war veteran, was the first black 'man in white': his great achievements were umpiring the 1982 and 1984 Australian football grand finals at the MCG, when he was subjected to gross racial vilification from fans and players. Lawyer Greg Lyons pointed to the particularly racist aspects of the abuse and the obscenities:

> He is [considered] a boong and a Sambo long before he is an umpire...one has the feeling that James will have to excel as an umpire—that he will have to be better than most white umpires—before he can hope to win acceptance as a football umpire who just happens to be an Aborigine.

In 1993 Collingwood Football Club president, Allan McAlister, told the television world that as long as 'they' behaved themselves like white folks off the field, they would be admired and respected; it would be better, he said, if Aborigines behaved themselves 'like human beings'. Following a 1993 match won by St Kilda against Collingwood, the *Sydney Morning Herald* commented:

> The Collingwood cheer-squad had decided to remind Nicky Winmar, an Aborigine...that he was one of them rather than one of us, and they did so in the manner for which they are justly notorious...after the final siren he gave the 'Pie cheer squad as good as he had received, lifting his jumper and pointing to his skin...Winmar has never been more eloquent or effective for his cause or his colour than he was in that moment.

What has changed is press (and public) reaction to such protests. Ten years earlier, Winmar would have been pilloried for his political (or 'cheeky') gesture.

In my research and writing about Aborigines in sport, I am constantly offered well-meant, racist comments about sportspeople. Typical are: 'Joey Smith is only a half'; 'Molly Brown isn't even an eighth'; 'Harry Jones is a not really'; 'Charlie White hasn't even got a splash'; and 'Barry Cable is as black as a snowflake'. Harmless? Perhaps—unless you are Smith, Brown, Jones or Cable.

Racism in deed—individuals
Deed is, for the most part, more deadly than word. Racism is not simply having prejudiced beliefs about others: it is the belief that we are entitled to act on the basis of such beliefs. Some 10,000 Aborigines were slaughtered between 1824 and 1908. Only when the massacres reached such great numbers was Archibald Meston appointed royal commissioner, in 1896. His report led to that strangely titled statute *The Aboriginals Protection and Restriction of the Sale of Opium Act 1897*. Mid-slaughter, the Aborigines at Deebing Creek, near Ipswich, were playing excellent cricket against white teams, and the colonial under-secretary sent two bats to the mission 'as a present to the aborigines, in appreciation of their excellent behaviour and smart turnout while in Brisbane'. Cricket featured in Aboriginal lives at this time.

The second protector, Dr W.E. Roth, removed many Aborigines from Ipswich to north Queensland. They were 'malcontents' who 'spoke English well and were cheeky enough for anything: they had evidently been too much engaged in competition with Europeans in the way of cricket matches etc, and had been treated socially far above their natural station in life'. Alec Henry, who took 21 wickets in seven Shield games for Queensland, and who was considered by the English visitors 'the fastest trundler in the world', was removed for 'loafing, malingering and defying authority' and died at remote Yarrabah, aged 29.

Jack Marsh, undoubtedly Australia's greatest fast bowler at the turn of the last century, took 34 wickets in six Shield games for New South Wales. Considered a certainty to tour with Joe Darling's team to England, he was omitted because M.A. Noble felt he 'didn't have class enough' to play for Australia. Cricketers L.O.S. Poidevin and Warren Bardsley had no doubt that class meant colour. Marsh was kicked to death in a street in Orange in 1916. Charged with manslaughter, not murder, the two assailants were acquitted without the jury leaving the box. Judge Bevan's opinion from the bench was that Marsh probably deserved his ending!

Genocide is not simply biological killing: it includes the forced removal of children from one group to another—a practice still operating in some parts of Australia in the 1990s. All protectors felt that 'half-caste' children should be saved by removal, forcible removal, into the mainstream. Chief protector C.F. Gale in Western Australia quoted one of his travelling protectors in his annual report: 'I would not hesitate for one moment to separate any half-caste from its Aboriginal mother, no mater how frantic her momentary grief might be at the time. They soon forget their offspring.'

And so began the wholesale removal of children, often by force. In Victoria all half-castes under 34 had to leave missions and settlements, irrespective of marriage, parent-child or sibling relationships. In this way Cummeragunja (Cummera) and Coranderrk missions lost at least half their male populations, their leaders, tillers of the soil, their cricketers and professional runners. Nancy Cato, the biographer of Daniel Matthews, founder of Cummera, wrote: 'Aborigines had discovered that their prowess in sport, particularly in cricket and running, gave them a passport to the white man's world, even to his respect and friendship'. Matthews tried to withhold such passports. The Aborigines were defiant. The entire mission workforce of 140, based on a 48-hour working week, earned a total of $1,164 in the year 1928; while Cummera's Doug Nicholls won the Warracknabeal Gift in the following year, taking 12 seconds to run 120 yards and earn $220! Aborigines ran faster for a simple reason: they were hungrier and needier.

Removal and institutionalisation are not distant memories. Several of the recent great Australian footballers from the west—including Maurice Rioli, Graham ('Polly') Farmer, Billy Dempsey, Ted ('Square') Kilmurray and Syd Jackson—had such beginnings; many spent decades searching for their biological parents, for origins and identity. Jackson was removed at the age of two—he found his mother when he was 37. Removal, and the resultant large-scale trafficking in adoptions, continued until about 20 years ago.

The deeds are endless, especially in Queensland. In 1903 the Queensland Amateur Athletic Association tried to disbar all Aborigines, firstly, because they lacked moral character, then because they had insufficient intelligence, and finally, because they couldn't resist white vice. When all these 'criteria' failed, they deemed them all professionals. In the boom period of professional running, the names of every Aboriginal runner carried separate initials—an 'a', or 'h.c.' or 'c.p.'—to avoid 'misleading the public'. Misled about what: their running ability, or their social, legal or racial standing as Aborigines, half-castes or coloured persons?

In the 1910s, a local Dalby citizen successfully applied to the protector for Jerry Jerome's removal from the list of controlled Aborigines—on the grounds that this most Aboriginal of men wasn't an Aborigine! Jerome was thus 'free' to become the first Aboriginal holder of an Australian boxing title, the middleweight championship in 1912. In the late 1920s, the great Aboriginal axeman, Leo Appo from Tweed Heads, was advised to enter Royal Easter Show competitions as a 'New Zealander', thereby enabling readier access to contests. Percy Hobson won the high jump for Australia at the 1962 Commonwealth Games, but had to agree to omit his Aboriginality. In the 1980s, lawn bowls champion Bob Appo was often introduced by his hosts as a Sri Lankan, a status they felt more acceptable, or credible. An esteemed jockey won a Melbourne Cup in 1973, but steadfastly denied his Aboriginality until his death: that was one handicap, Frankie Reys argued, that he could do without in a racist industry. (His widow has given me permission to make his name and origins public.)

Frank Fisher from Cherbourg (Qld), a contemporary of cricketer Eddie Gilbert, played rugby league for Wide Bay against the visiting English team in 1936. The legendary Englishman, Gus Risman, wrote to Fisher saying he was the best player he had seen on the tour and invited him to join an English club. The Aboriginal authorities refused, stating that one star from Cherbourg (Gilbert) was enough! Fisher was Cathy Freeman's grandfather. With this background, it was no surprise that the politically aware Cathy paraded the Aboriginal flag after winning both the 200m and the 400m at the XVth Commonwealth Games in Victoria, Canada in August 1994. Those who deplored her 'un-Australian' behaviour have no understanding of Aboriginal history.

Eddie Gilbert was 'a dynamic Aboriginal fast bowler who at his prime ranked second only to Bradman among Queensland fans'. In December 1931, off a run of only four or five paces, he bowled Bradman for a duck—after a five-ball spell of which Sir Donald wrote:

> He sent down in that period the fastest 'bowling' I can remember ...one delivery knocked the bat out of my hand and I unhesitatingly class this short burst faster than anything seen from Larwood or anyone else.

In that December game he also took 4 for 74 off 21 overs, in an innings in which the great Stan McCabe scored 229 not out. For his 23 first-class matches for Queensland, the Aboriginal protector wouldn't pay his expenses but 'gave his permission' for Gilbert to travel (but not in 'white' motor-cars) and to play. He was always chaperoned to matches, in case he made contact with white ladies!

Gilbert's career ended in 1936 with this remarkable letter from the secretary of the Queensland Cricket Association, addressed not to Gilbert but to the chief protector:

> At the meeting of my Executive Committee held last evening, the matter of Eddie Gilbert was fully discussed, and as it was considered unlikely that he would be chosen for any representative team this season, it was decided with your concurrence, to arrange for Gilbert to return to the settlement [Cherbourg] next week...With regard to the cricketing clothes bought for Gilbert, it is asked that arrangements be made for these to be laundered at the Association's expense, and delivery of the laundered clothes to be made to this Office.

There is more. All of Elley Bennett's earnings as Australian feather and bantamweight champion went to the Queensland Aboriginal Affairs department. Ron Richards—who epitomises the tragedy of Aboriginal boxers—was exempt from the Aboriginal Act because his father was exempt, but Ron was persuaded to apply for 'control', in his best interests. Given the sadness of Richards's life story, such protection did nothing for him.

Early on, the Cummera man who was to become Pastor Sir Douglas Nicholls, KCVO, OBE, KStJ, and governor of South Australia in 1976, discovered that the only way 'to crack the white world' was to do better than the white man. In 1929 he won the Nyah Gift and then the Warracknabeal, second only to Stawell in importance. Trying out for Carlton FC, he was rejected: because of his colour, they said, he 'smelled'. For five years he played Association rules football for Northcote, and then came the glory years with Fitzroy.

In the 1950s and 1960s it wasn't much different. In South Australia, Wally McArthur was a brilliant junior who ran well at the national championships in Hobart. Wally gave up amateur athletics, alleging that his colour was against him. Instead he went to England and played 165 rugby league games for four senior English sides. Percy Hobson's choice was to be a non-Aboriginal Aborigine for the Commonwealth Games.

Before 1960 only six Aborigines had made it into senior Australian football; only five had come through to first-division rugby league in New South Wales.

Racism in deed—teams

Exclusion of Aboriginal teams is another black mark in the land of the level playing field. In the early 1950s, federal government policy was moving towards 'emancipation' of the 'half-castes' in the Northern Territory. Many traditional Aborigines from Bathurst and Melville Islands were working for the armed services in Darwin on three-month stints. The Catholic bishop suggested that while in town, Australian football might be a good thing for the men. However, the Aboriginal Half-Caste Progress Association wasn't keen on too much association with those still destined to be controlled and the town authorities weren't all that anxious to have 'more blackfellas in town'. The two joined forces to delay the birth of St Marys, the team which eventually came to dominate the game up north.

Narwan rugby league team in Armidale had similar origins in the mid-1970s. Tired of sitting on reserve benches, Aboriginal kids, aided by Father Dave Perrett, managed to establish Narwan amid some furious opposition from the citizens in the city they call 'the Athens of the North'.

In Australian football—once described to me by Aboriginal soccer player John Moriarty as 'a colonial bastion with colonial attitudes'—there are some appalling case studies. For most of the 1980s, the Fitzroy All-Stars in Melbourne were denied entry into more senior leagues on the spurious grounds of too many teams, distance of travel, and the like. In 1987, the Purnim Bears from Framlingham settlement (Victoria) won the Mt Noorat League grand final. The league then voted, four to three, to expel the competition premiers. The only reason given was that the league had the right to make such decisions.

In May 1993, the Coomealla team from Dareton, just across the Murray River in New South Wales, was banned from the Millewa League. The league's president said players often failed to appear before the tribunal, their play was 'unduly rough' and their language had led to complaints from other clubs and their supporters. However, no one, it seems, is upset by the language of the MCG's ladies and gentlemen.

The NSW Aboriginal Knockout, the world's biggest rugby league competition (with over 50 teams), has always been in strife with the municipal administrations and with police—despite only one year of 'troubles'. The 1989 carnival was held in Walgett, a town of about 2,300 people. Police fears of an 'invasion' by 5000 Aborigines reached such paranoia that the chief superintendent of the region sought ministerial intervention to have the event moved or cancelled. In the end, the special task forces and tactical response people were called in to await armageddon. There were five arrests in the entire period!

One can almost sense reader irritation with all this history. Surely, I hear, we have 'moved on', at least since the 1980s. The tradition of this competition, which began in 1971, is that the winning team hosts the following year's tournament. Wellington won in 1998—yet that town's council imposed such impossible conditions on the organisers that the competition was forced to move to Dubbo in 1999. There can be no doubt that the council used every device possible to avoid having 'the black hordes' in their town.

In 2000 the famous Moree Boomerangs remain excluded from the region's rugby league competition. Wilcannia, possibly the most destitute and forlorn Aboriginal community in New South Wales, and for whom rugby league was a salvation, have no one to play against, and sport has ceased for them. In 2000, white teams refuse to play the Aboriginal team in Bourke, despite the local police commander offering to pay expenses and to police the grounds. For these communities, football was and is not *a* but *the* raison d'etre. Without it, such life as there is loses all meaning, and the health consequences are disastrous.

Opposition to all-black teams, including a league team in the rugby league Winfield Cup, persists. The expressed reason is that assimilation is the right way to go, that segregation is akin to South African apartheid. The real reason, as we know from the Aboriginal experience at Lake Tyers in Victoria and Cowra in NSW, is that teams don't want to lose the services of their black players, many of them keys to their success.

'Moving on'

When is 'on', and how far in time does one have to 'move' from 'on' before we can say that we have 'moved on'?

Modern Australia is a racist society. Fortunately, amid the Olympic 2000 bid, there were no Chinese researchers to examine our record on human rights. We are lucky that people tend to see human rights or, rather, inhuman rights, solely in terms of such episodic massacres as at Tiananmen Square or Sharpeville and Boipotong in South Africa. 'Happily', at Olympic bid time, no one abroad was documenting life expectancy, infant mortality, homelessness, illiteracy, rates of incarceration, deaths in custody, suicides, self-mutilation, homicides, deaths from non-natural causes.

However, one 'sporting' example might have been of interest. The Rovers Football Club had some notable Australian football successes in the far west of South Australia, Ceduna way. Visiting in 1989, I was shown a photo of the 1958 premiership side. Would I like to meet Keith Willoughby? Why Willoughby? I asked. Because he was the only surviving member of the 18! This meant that 17 of 18 men didn't make it to 50, perhaps 55. There is no genetic predisposition to want to die at those ages.

In 1993 the visiting International Olympic Committee told protesting Aboriginal delegations it wasn't interested in abysmal social conditions, only in sports discrimination. Regrettably, the Redfern Legal Service and others didn't discuss the 'sporting' conditions at Toomelah, Mornington Island, Hopevale, Kalumburu, Mowanjum, Yalata, Wilcannia, Kintore, Gingie Reserve in Walgett (among many others). These conditions portray not only state and national neglect, total social and human breakdown, but also, in the great illusion of sporting brotherhood, demonstrate that certain words simply don't exist in the Aboriginal vocabulary or experience: words like track, oval, turf, pool, change-room, gym, gloves, weights, sauna, trainer, coach, physio, manager, bus, travel, comp, and trophy. Their sports facilities are, for the most part, non-existent and where they do play in remote communities, their sports costs are infinitely greater. If sports costs were considered a tax, then Aborigines pay the highest taxes in the country.

There is virtually no recognition of any of this. There is little effort to provide any kind of playing fields, let alone level them; there is little done to ensure, or to insist, that there be access to competition. National and state sports policies are devoted essentially to elite sport, to finding winners, more Cathy Freemans and Nova Peris-Kneebones. It is likely that 12 or 13 Aborigines/Islanders will represent Australia at the Sydney Olympics: an outstanding achievement given the obstacles, but illusion nevertheless—as illusory as Michael Jordan, Michael Johnson and Tiger Woods bringing all Afro-Americans into the national brother- and sisterhood.

Sport creates the illusion of national unity, that all is well with the world. Embracing Cathy Freeman, appropriating her achievements, makes everyone feel good: Cathy laughing, Cathy running, Cathy the embodiment of youth and health and optimism tells us we have 'no problems'. We look at some facets of the recent past and the present and see, or think we see, an era and a spirit of equality. Lionel Rose's homecoming as world bantamweight champion in 1968 was stunning. From the airport to town hall some 200,000 people—more than the Beatles attracted—shouted 'Good on ya, Lionel! You beaut little Aussie!' His colour disappeared, momentarily. The adulation and joy of Evonne Goolagong-Cawley, with her two Wimbledon crowns, remains in our memory. So too does the recollection of the immortal Graham 'Polly' Farmer, one of the greatest Australian footballers of the century; of Mark Ella, veteran of 26 Tests in the silvertail sport of rugby union, with nine matches as captain; of 'Artie' Beetson, rated as one of the greatest forwards ever to play rugby league, a man with a profound influence on the game; of Danny Morseu's 27 basketball internationals for Australia; of 'Darby' McCarthy's unique breakthrough in big time horseracing; of Mal Meninga, the man who has more records than any other league player, with 45 Test appearances and 23 captaincies; or Laurie Daley with his startling performances in 34 matches for Australia.

Sport, more so than art or music, has been the passport to some respect from non-Aboriginal Australia. It has given Aborigines a sense of worth and pride. Success, however, has not lessened the harsh experience. The odds have been monumental: a different legal status, geographic isolation, severe administrative control, poverty, extreme prejudice, ill-health, low life expectancy, an almost total absence of facilities—and the talents and training of their opponents. Sport has shown Aborigines that using and selling their bodies is still the only way they can compete on equal terms with an often hostile, certainly indifferent, mainstream society—but, and this is the dreadful catch-22 of sport, only momentarily!

Practical Reconciliation
John Howard

The process of national reconciliation between indigenous and non-indigenous Australians is an important challenge we face as a nation entering its second century. It is also important for Australians that it succeed.

On the eve of the centenary of our federation, we look forward to celebrating the nature of the Australian achievement and its future possibilities.

At such a time it is also right that we openly acknowledge the mistaken attitudes and practices of the past that brought dislocation, distress and a sense of alienation to many indigenous Australians. And it is right that we address in a practical and effective way the ongoing consequences of these aspects of our history.

Reconciliation is about attitudes and acceptance just as it is about policies and programs. It calls for goodwill and a preparedness on all sides to move on some issues to what is common ground for all of us.

All aspects of our history as a nation—our triumphs as well as our mistakes—should be acknowledged and understood in an unvarnished way. Our achievements as a nation have been great. But we have also made mistakes that have caused great pain and hardship for many fellow Australians. We need to confront both dimensions of our national story.

Reconciliation is a process of facing up to the realities of our past as well as understanding the needs of the present and the priorities of the future. We cannot change what has happened in our history but we can ameliorate the legacy of those events and practices that proved deeply damaging. We can share a common resolve that the mistakes of the past will not be repeated.

National reconciliation calls for more than recognition of the damaging impact on people's lives of the mistaken practices of the past. It also calls for a clear focus on the future. It calls for practical policy-making that effectively addresses current indigenous disadvantage particularly in areas such as employment, health, education and housing.

At the heart of the reconciliation process is the challenge to all of us of owning and valuing a shared history, a shared heritage and a shared future.

True reconciliation cannot be legislated or mandated. It involves a process that is genuinely community-based. Its success lies in the attitudes and the openness of Australian individuals and in the commitment of our democratic and community organisations.

The task of national leadership in these circumstances is not to impose a process and outcome on the community. The challenge is to communicate clearly the objectives of the reconciliation process, why reconciliation is in the national interest and the respective roles of government, indigenous Australians and the wider community in the process.

Success in this process will ultimately be measured not simply by the effectiveness of government policies and programs but more by the extent to which Australians develop a genuine personal commitment to reconciliation so that it is a unifying experience for our country.

From its earliest days in office, this government has been publicly committed to the reconciliation process in Australia. In launching Aboriginal Reconciliation Week in May 1996, I said that reconciliation is a remarkable word that seeks to bring people together, not in a judgmental sense, but by drawing upon their better aspirations, addressing present inadequacies and future hopes rather than focusing completely on past failures and past wrongs.

Australia is a unique society with people drawn from many parts of the world united behind a commitment to a common future. My vision is of all Australians working together under one set of laws to which all are accountable and from which all are entitled to an equal dispensation of justice.

Objectives of reconciliation

It is this vision of Australia that has inspired our commitment to reconciliation, much of which was outlined in my address to the Australian Reconciliation Convention in May 1997. I said at that time that three fundamental objectives lie at the heart of the reconciliation process.

The first is a shared commitment to raise the living standards and to broaden the opportunities available to indigenous Australians as part of a wider commitment to providing equality of opportunity to all Australians.

Consistently I have maintained that the cornerstone of the reconciliation process should be a renewed national focus on the substantive causes of Aboriginal and Torres Strait Islander disadvantage. Through practical measures, to which I will return, the government has focused its efforts on the areas of indigenous health, education, housing and employment.

A second objective of reconciliation is a realistic acknowledgement of the inter-related histories of the various elements of Australian society. The purpose of making such an acknowledgement is not to apportion blame and guilt for past wrongs, but to build support for a practical program of action that will remove the enduring legacies of disadvantage.

At the same time, there is also a need to acknowledge openly that the treatment accorded to many indigenous Australians over a significant period of European settlement represents the most blemished chapter in our history.

As I stated at the Reconciliation Convention in 1997, I feel deep personal sorrow for those of my fellow Australians who suffered injustices under the practices of past generations towards indigenous people. Equally, I am sorry for the hurt and trauma many people may continue to feel as a consequence of those practices.

However, I do not believe it is accurate or fair to portray Australia's history since 1788 as little more than a disgraceful record of imperialism, exploitation and racism. Such a portrayal is a gross distortion and deliberately neglects the overall story of great Australian achievement that is there in our history to be told.

Australians of this generation should not be required to accept guilt and blame for past actions and policies over which they had no control. But we do have an obligation and responsibility to overcome their legacies for our fellow Australians.

A third objective of the reconciliation process is a mutual acceptance of the importance of working together to respect and appreciate our differences and to ensure that they do not prevent us from sharing the future.

We all have rights and obligations as Australians. They include the right to individual self-fulfilment and cultural freedom without discrimination and intimidation as well as the right of all Australians to dignity and self-respect. We cannot share a common destiny if these rights are available to some Australians, but not all. Likewise, we cannot share a common destiny without an overriding and unifying commitment to Australian institutions.

In meeting these challenges the reconciliation process must focus on the future in a positive and principled way. Specific strategies need to be devised, specific priorities need to be identified and specific practical programs need to be agreed and implemented.

I have always maintained that governments and leaders alone cannot make reconciliation happen simply through legislation, decrees, declarations or rhetoric. To be effective, the reconciliation process must involve and inspire all Australians.

It is self-evident that true reconciliation must come from the hearts and minds of the Australian people, in the respect they have for differences, in the attitudes they encourage in their children, and in their recognition of the common destiny we share as Australians.

Practical reconciliation

The government has always stressed that practical measures to address the profound economic and social disadvantage of many indigenous Australians are at the heart of a successful reconciliation process.

As a starting point, the government quarantined indigenous housing, health, education and employment from budget cuts over the last four years. These programs now account for 70 percent of the $2.2 billion in special Aboriginal programs supported by the federal government.

Health

A high priority of the government has been indigenous health where Commonwealth spending has increased by 51 percent since 1996 and will have increased by 62 percent in real terms by 2002–3.

Such a tangible commitment is intended to build on the substantial improvement in Aboriginal health over the past 20 years where indigenous infant mortality has fallen from 20 times the non-indigenous rate to just twice the rate.

There is also further evidence of improved indigenous health where, on specific measures, the prevalence of trachoma has substantially fallen overall and male death rates from cardiovascular disease, lung cancer, injury and homicide have also been declining since the mid-1980s.

A milestone was achieved in August 1997 when Commonwealth, state and territory health ministers agreed to a set of 58 national performance indicators and key targets for indigenous health. Targets now include a 20 percent reduction over ten years in both the overall death rate and the rate in comparison with other members of the population.

Since coming to office, federal government resources have been allocated for 36 new indigenous health services in rural and remote Australia, eye and ear programs, a respiratory illness and influenza immunisation program, AIDS prevention initiatives and for improved diagnostic technology to reduce the prevalence of sexually transmitted diseases.

Housing and infrastructure

In the early 1970s up to 20 percent of Aboriginal families lived in improvised dwellings. Assisted by a re-allocation of spending priorities so that indigenous housing now accounts for 20 percent of the federal government's total spending on public and community housing, the proportion of indigenous families living in improvised dwellings has fallen to below three percent.

There has been a similar improvement in overcrowding which has been reduced from 4.4 indigenous persons per household 15 years ago to 3.7 persons today.

Likewise, the proportion of indigenous families who own their own home has increased from around one in four in the early 1970s to around one in three today.

In our joint program with the Australian army, remote Aboriginal communities are now benefiting from the construction of many capital works such as the provision of water, sewerage, power systems, roads, airstrips, as well as the construction and upgrade of community housing.

An additional benefit of this program has been the way in which construction skills and maintenance responsibilities have been passed on to community members.

This and other government housing programs are now providing 1000 new homes to indigenous Australians each year.

Education

The government is working to redress low levels of literacy and numeracy amongst Aboriginal children which are a factor in them being only half as likely as other children to complete secondary school.

In spite of this statistic there have been improvements in education outcomes amongst indigenous people over the past generation: the proportion of indigenous adults who have never attended school has fallen from 14 percent in the mid 1970s to three percent today; the proportion of indigenous children who complete secondary schooling has increased fourfold since the mid 1970s, from 8.6 percent to 33 percent; the proportion of indigenous people with post-secondary school qualifications has doubled in the last decade; and indigenous higher education enrolments have tripled over the same period.

Further improvements are sought under existing programs where indigenous education agreements have been reached with schools specifying targets in key areas such as literacy, numeracy and school attendance rates. Other schemes are providing tutorial assistance, encouraging greater parental involvement and offering career guidance.

Efforts will also be made to further bridge the gap in literacy levels between indigenous and other Australian students by encouraging better teaching practices and a more relevant curriculum for indigenous students.

Already we can point to improvements such as an increase in the number of indigenous students in higher education from under 7,000 in 1996 to over 8,000 in 1999.

Vocational education and training (VET) outcomes have also significantly improved in recent years. Ten years ago, there were an estimated 15,000 indigenous VET students in 1990. By 1998 that number had risen to nearly 45,000 students—almost three percent of the total student body and well above the Aboriginal and Torres Strait Islander population share of two percent.

There was also a record number of about 5,200 indigenous traineeship commencements during 1997–98, an increase from only 817 in 1994/95.

In 1998 there were approximately 2,000 commencements by Aboriginal and Torres Strait Islanders through Commonwealth New Apprenticeship Centres. In 1999 this rose to over 4,000.

Employment

Lasting and fulfilling employment is fundamental to an improvement in indigenous living standards. There is a positive outlook with the proportion of indigenous Australians in vocational training increasing six-fold in a decade and the number employed in professional occupations increasing from 14.2 percent to 22 percent in the ten years to 1996.

However, the unemployment rate for indigenous Australians remains unsatisfactorily high at around three times the national average.

There are several government programs to redress this problem. About one quarter of indigenous Australians in the labour force are now involved in Community Development Employment Projects, the indigenous equivalent of Work for the Dole.

These projects aim to provide work skills recognised in the mainstream employment market and offer training opportunities, a work ethic and greater self-esteem for participants.

In the 1999 federal budget the government also announced a new indigenous employment policy providing a strong emphasis on private sector employment and effectively doubling funding available for such indigenous-specific programs.

This policy includes several important new initiatives. New wage assistance for employers is providing incentives to help disadvantaged indigenous job seekers to find long-term jobs either through the Job Network or through their own efforts using an eligibility card.

Under the CEO's for Indigenous Employment Project, major national companies are being supported to generate more jobs in the private sector. Companies, such as those in the mining sector, that undertake employment of indigenous people are being offered flexible funding assistance under this program.

The new Voluntary Service to Indigenous Communities Foundation is aimed at offering assistance to indigenous communities seeking volunteers from the wider community with professional and technical skills, as well as mentoring.

The government also offers support for the development and expansion of indigenous businesses under an Indigenous Small Business Fund. This fund helps indigenous people to start businesses, obtain access to further business capital and supports them with skills development programs, advisory services and market development opportunities. It builds on other programs such as the Business Development Program which has helped provide seed funding and low interest loans.

In each case the aim is to assist indigenous Australians to achieve economic independence.

Other progress
Over the last four years the government has taken other several important steps towards reconciliation.

In May 1997 the parliament supported a resolution to recognise the 30th anniversary of the referendum that amended section 51 (xxvi) of the Constitution.

The 1967 referendum, which received the support of 90 percent of the Australian people, gave the Commonwealth parliament the power to make laws for Aboriginal and Torres Strait Islander people.

In marking this anniversary, I reaffirmed the government's belief that the proper basis of reconciliation is to recognise the truth about the past, remain proud about what this country has achieved and resolve as Australians to unite together to work towards a better and more cooperative future.

In December 1997 the government unveiled a $63 million package of initiatives in response to the *Bringing Them Home* report aimed at addressing family separation and its consequences. Measures included a national network of family linkup and counselling services to reunite separated families; a Commonwealth government records identification project to enable indigenous people to find historical information about themselves and their families; a national oral history project to record peoples' stories of separation; and programs to preserve and develop indigenous culture and language.

The re-election of the government in October 1998 provided an opportunity to recommit my government to the cause of reconciliation. On election night I said that I wanted to commit myself very genuinely to the cause of true reconciliation with the Aboriginal people of Australia.

Building on this undertaking, perhaps the most important statement of our commitment was contained in the Motion of Reconciliation considered by the parliament in August 1999.

The motion which repeated many of our themes about reconciliation stated: That this House:

(a) reaffirms its wholehearted commitment to the cause of reconciliation between indigenous and non-indigenous Australians as an important national priority for Australians;

(b) recognising the achievements of the Australian nation commits to work together to strengthen the bonds that unite us, to respect and appreciate our differences and to build a fair and prosperous future in which we can all share;

(c) reaffirms the central importance of practical measures leading to practical results that address the profound economic and social disadvantage which continues to be experienced by many indigenous Australians;

(d) recognises the importance of understanding the shared history of indigenous and non-indigenous Australians and the need to acknowledge openly the wrongs and injustices of Australia's past;

(e) acknowledges that the mistreatment of many indigenous Australians over a significant period represents the most blemished chapter in our international history;

(f) expresses its deep and sincere regret that indigenous Australians suffered injustices under the practices of past generations, and for the hurt and trauma that many indigenous people continue to feel as a consequence of those practices; and

(g) believes that we, having achieved so much as a nation, can now move forward together for the benefit of all Australians.

The purpose of the motion was to generically express the regret that the people of Australia feel for past practices and the continuing consequences of them.

The motion was an historic statement of recognition and empathy—recognition of the scale of past wrongs and of the need to overcome their enduring legacies, and empathy with the aspiration of all Australians to build a common future in which we can all fairly share.

In moving the motion I said that to apply retrospectively the standards of today in relation to the behaviour of some who were very sincere in their actions does them immense injustice, but that does not mean that we ought not to express a sincere regret for what has occurred.

Conclusion

It remains the case that an important dimension of building a stronger Australian society in the period ahead relates to the success of the national reconciliation process among indigenous and non-indigenous Australians.

However, meeting the challenge of reconciliation is an often slow and sometimes difficult process. Real progress is being made but can take significant time. Patience, perseverance and goodwill on all sides will be needed. So too will a sense of realism about what can be achieved over a given period of time. Too often on public policy issues, artificial time deadlines imposed on sensitive processes can have quite counter-productive effects.

The government remains strongly of the view that the cornerstone of the reconciliation process will continue to be practical and effective measures which address the legacy of profound economic and social disadvantage which many indigenous Australians continue to experience.

Our hope for the period ahead is that all parties in the national reconciliation process will build constructively on what has been achieved in the recent past; that we will focus on what unites us as Australians rather than what divides us; that we will respect and appreciate our differences and not make demands on each other which cannot be realised; and that together we will build a future in which we can all share fairly as united Australians.

Aboriginal Communities and Mineral Resources: The Rio Tinto Experience
Paul D. Wand

In September 1998, I addressed the Second World Conference on Remedies to Racial and Ethnic Economic Inequality in Adelaide, South Australia. As the only speaker from a global mining company, I found myself characterised as being opposed to the aspirations of many indigenous people.

For many of my audience, it was an article of faith that multi-national resource companies were a threat to the economic, political and spiritual wellbeing of indigenous communities. It was also obvious that Australia was seen as a particularly egregious example of the power imbalance between Aboriginal people and big business.

Many saw a simple dichotomy: corporate wealth, political clout and legal talent on the one side; morality and a rising tide of support from a dedicated coalition of land rights activists, environmentalists, non-government organisations, academics and churches on the other side.

Any stereotype that clearly distinguishes the good people from the bad has a seductive attraction. (Let me stress that in business you can find a countervailing stereotype that clearly labels opponents of economic development as luddites or social parasites.) Such stereotypes are dangerous because they close our minds to inconvenient facts.

So I explained to my audience that, while we were talking, geologists employed by the world's largest diversified resources group were exploring for minerals in the heart of East Arnhem Land in the Northern Territory on land that was subject to a native title claim. Arguably, the people of Arnhem Land retain more aspects of their traditional culture than other Aboriginal communities. What was important was that the exploration team was there with the full support of the local community, because Rio Tinto Exploration had concluded an historic agreement, which would benefit the local Aborigines, irrespective of whether the exploration proved successful.

As it happened, our exploration team did not find a viable ore body on this occasion, but the contacts and goodwill generated have led to other agreements and a continuing relationship with Arnhem Land people.

I reported that Rio Tinto was the only major resource company to have a formal memorandum of understanding with Australia's peak indigenous representative body, the Aboriginal and Torres Strait Islander Commission (ATSIC). ATSIC commissioners are democratically elected and come from every state and territory in Australia. They speak for the inhabitants of the inner city and country towns whose challenges are different, but no less real, than the others that they represent—the Aboriginal Australians who still identify closely with their ancestral land and live in isolated communities.

I explained how my company had set up a philanthropic foundation dedicated to helping indigenous Australians improve their lives culturally and socially. The efforts of the Rio Tinto Aboriginal Foundation complement the economic benefits of direct and contract employment as well as business development programs that are supported by specific Rio Tinto operations.

Some idea of the gap between perception and reality can be gained from the words of Dr Lowitja O' Donoghue AC, an Aboriginal trustee of the foundation. She is better known to most Australians as the founding chair of the Aboriginal and Torres Strait Islander Commission. Speaking at a launch of a New Directions-Aboriginal Australia and Business Exhibition in Canberra in November 1998, Dr O' Donoghue said: 'Rio Tinto is a good corporate citizen and is committed to working with Aboriginal people to achieve their goals. Aboriginal people have come to understand that it is possible to accept grants from a mining company, not to buy their favours but to be able to make changes which will have long-term effects on their lives and their communities.'

While the stereotype that miners and indigenous communities are inevitably at loggerheads is wrong, it is not true to say that relationships between Rio Tinto operations and local communities have always been satisfactory. Nor does Rio Tinto profess to have a perfect understanding of—and solutions to—the aspirations and problems of Aboriginal communities today. At best we would claim to be a part way along a steep learning curve and, hopefully, somewhat ahead of our competitors. What I can say is that the company now has a much clearer vision of how it wants to be regarded by Australia's indigenous people and has put in place both policy and processes to realise that vision.

To understand why the impression of conflict between miners and Aboriginal Australians is so prevalent it is necessary to understand that, for most Australians, Aborigines were invisible until relatively late in the twentieth century. Despite the iconic image of the bushman, twentieth century Australians have, for the most part, been city and town dwellers. For most of this century Aborigines were estimated to be about one percent of the population, many of them living in places well off the beaten track. Aborigines in the towns and the cities often assimilated or did not broadcast their ethnicity to their predominantly Anglo-Celtic neighbours.

The history books connived at this invisibility. Australian school children learned that, while some violence occurred, the European colonisation of their sparsely inhabited continent was essentially peaceful. That Aborigines apparently disappeared from large tracts of land leaving little trace other than some distinctive place names was largely put down to a lack of immunity to Western diseases. The emphasis was very much on the achievements of the European pioneers, little was to be gained from dwelling on the fate of the original inhabitants, other than to record the efforts of valiant missionaries who sought to teach the remnants of 'a dying race' Christian resignation.

Today we know this to be a censored version of Australia's history. It was a bloodier and more tragic affair than we were taught when I went to school. Disease certainly decimated the native peoples but we are now ready to acknowledge that the dispossession was indeed violent. We now are beginning to grasp that many of those who survived the bullets and the epidemics died of what sounds like sheer despair.

Thanks to the research of historians, we are beginning to grasp what colonisation felt like to those who were colonised. In more recent years, the science of anthropology has enabled non-indigenous Australians to acquire a degree of empathy with indigenous culture and institutions that seemed impenetrable or non-existent to the early settlers. Moreover, a postwar world is more alert to the dangers of racism and the consequences of ethnocentricity. As the scale of the historical loss and suffering experienced by Aboriginal society was appreciated it has become evident that many of the contemporary legal, economic and political institutions and practices of Australian society unwittingly perpetuated the problems of modern Aboriginal society.

It was in the 1960s and 1970s that Australians began to systematically explore the situation of Aboriginal Australians. Many did not like what they found. Statistical evidence mounted that one of the world's most prosperous nations included an impoverished minority that lived a comparatively short life. With little voice in parliament or any other deliberative body, this minority was excluded from economic advancement and social improvement by lack of education and paternalistic regulations that were ultimately at odds with the values of postwar Australian society. The problems of Aboriginal Australians were compounded by a considerable degree of prejudice on the part of some Australians who could not distinguish cause from effect when they witnessed the social problems afflicting some Aboriginal communities.

Change was inevitable, but it was equally inevitable that whatever changes occurred would be politically contentious. Australia's federal structure of government is appropriate in many ways to the practical realities of administering a land mass roughly the same size as that of the continental United States, but with around six percent of the US population. One result of the federal structure is that responsibility for the majority of Australia's Aboriginal population rests with state governments. These six governments have given economic development a high priority, and any changes that have threatened to curb economic development have been viewed with suspicion by state legislatures.

The year 1967 saw nine out of ten Australians support a referendum that gave the Commonwealth government overriding power in Aboriginal matters. It was also the decade when agitation for land rights gained a head of steam and found support among non-Aboriginal Australians. When Gurindji stockmen on a Northern Territory cattle station walked off the job in 1966 with a demand for higher wages and a land claim, they were championed by a well-known Australian author and won a good deal of public sympathy. Nine years later, the then prime minister of Australia, Mr Gough Whitlam, made a visit to the Northern Territory to hand over the leasehold title to 1250 square miles of the Wave Hill pastoral lease to its traditional owners. In the seventies a conservative Australian government, under prime minister Malcolm Fraser, passed legislation that would eventually transfer control of about half the land in the Northern Territory to Aboriginal people. However, of all the states, only South Australia, under the Dunstan Labor government, passed land rights legislation that effectively granted freehold title to significant portions of that state.

Many attempts to establish Aboriginal land tenure were unsuccessful during the 1970s and 1980s and the chief reason was that Australian common law did not accept the idea of communal native title. In this, Australia differed from other countries with a history of British colonisation. The perception was that Australia was *terra nullius*—an unoccupied land—at the time of this colonisation.

Because war had never been officially declared between the colonists and the original inhabitants, there were no peace treaties, and no official acknowledgement that Australia had been settled by conquest. In 1971, Mr Justice Blackburn, hearing a case brought by Arnhem Land Aborigines, concluded that a doctrine of communal native title did not form, and never had formed, part of the law of any part of Australia. It was his opinion that Australia came into the category of a settled or occupied territory. *Terra nullius* was reinforced.

As scholars delved deeper into the realities of settlement they accumulated facts unknown to or, tactfully ignored by, their predecessors. The hypothesis that Australia had been peacefully settled became very difficult to sustain. The sense of unfairness among Aboriginal people was heightened when comparisons were drawn with what was happening to their counterparts in Canada, the United States and New Zealand. A new generation of educated, articulate and forceful Aboriginal leaders worked hard to mobilise both domestic and international support for their cause. They wanted many things; better housing, education, health, compensation and political representation. But, above all, they wanted ownership of land because land was the keystone to their cultural identity. Without control of land to which Aborigines had an historical and spiritual connection, it was argued that many well-intentioned social and economic initiatives would fail.

For farmers, pastoralists and miners the seventies and eighties were decades of promise and frustration. In particular, international demand for Australia's minerals and energy was growing as our country became engaged in the phenomena of Asian economic development. Yet, paradoxically, as the economic importance of resource development to Australia became more pronounced, the minerals and energy producers became aware that public sanction for their activities was wavering. In part, this was because mineral exploration, once seen as a vital and heroic endeavour to build a strong nation, was tarnished when it was presented as an infringement on Aboriginal territory and an affront to Aboriginal cultural beliefs.

That the Australian mining industry did not support radical changes to Australia's property laws was seen by many land rights supporters to be a simple expression of corporate greed. More thoughtful people recognised the capital intensity, long planning horizons and inherent uncertainties of developing a major economic ore body and did not confuse concerns about land access with opposition to the aspirations of Aboriginal Australians.

Actual mining operations affect only a very small part of the Australian land mass and, given the nature of the industry, that will always be the case. Mineral exploration is another matter. Because economic ore bodies are extremely rare, their discovery is typically a long and expensive process, which depends on access to large areas. Nevertheless, modern technology means that much useful information can be gained from satellites or from aerial surveys, so that the actual physical presence by exploration camps and drill rigs can be confined to a few promising areas. Compared to the vast acres under pastoral leases, mineral exploration was hardly a major threat to Aboriginal communities.

That, however, was not the perception. In the long struggle for formal recognition of the importance of land to Aboriginal people it was normal to suggest that resource development was a growing threat to the cultural integrity and social cohesiveness of Aboriginal communities. On the other side of the divide, the representatives of primary industry and tourism, as well as shire councils and state authorities, were concerned that the recognition of native title would threaten existing titles to property and limit future development. They saw a future of open-ended land claims that would devalue current property rights.

In Rio Tinto in the eighties there was a two-pronged approach. On the one side, we scrutinised the various land rights proposals to determine possible legal and financial consequences. We wanted to know the extent that these measures would affect the viability of our current and our future operations. At the same time, the company set out to gain a deeper understanding of the issues. This latter search brought senior Rio Tinto management into contact with prominent Aborigines, politicians, social scientists, government officials, church leaders and others.

Efforts to build stronger bonds between our operations and their Aboriginal neighbours were partially successful. However, greater progress could not be made so long as Australian Aborigines felt that the Australian legal system failed to embody recognition of some form of native title of a kind that Mr Justice Blackburn had said did not exist. Without that legal recognition there would always be the perception that negotiations between a mining company and Aborigines would be an uneven contest. In the absence of native title, the most powerful negotiating tactic available to Aborigines was to use the often complex administrative process to delay the onset of exploration, while drumming up support in the court of public opinion. Such an approach has been described as the 'politics of embarrassment' and it was an effective approach in some instances.

There was a paradigm shift in the early nineties. It came after a decade of legal argument in what became known as the Mabo case. In one of a series of historic judgements, the High Court of Australia acknowledged that, for the inhabitants of an island in the Torres Strait, which runs between Queensland and Papua New Guinea, native title did exist and could be protected by legal action. Subsequent decisions handed down by the High Court have strengthened the negotiating base of Aboriginal land claimants.

The Mabo decision served to both clarify and confuse. While the principles underpinning native title are relatively clear, the devil is in the detail. Determining those details could take a very long time and, according to cynics, make many lawyers very rich. You do not have to be opposed to land rights to recognise how uncertainty can destroy investor confidence. There have been many gloomy forecasts about what native title will mean for the Australian economy. A series of legislative responses has eventuated but there is little doubt that courts will still be used to test the laws.

In Rio Tinto, we understand these concerns but we are not as pessimistic as some others in business. Our experience suggests that it is a mistake to believe that legal agreements will guarantee a harmonious future for a resource development. In the last decade especially, we have come to appreciate that legal agreements and contracts are important but that to guarantee good relations with the neighbouring communities (and in the Australian context that can include groups living a hundred kilometres away) you have to build and sustain a relationship of trust. Building such a relationship takes time, resources, determination and specialised skills.

In Rio Tinto, we are increasingly emphasising that the traditional competencies that were the hallmark of our successful resource operations are no longer sufficient. Superior engineering, metallurgy, financial marketing and other business skills are still essential. Today we must match them with equivalent standards of social and environmental expertise so that our operations can comprehend and accommodate the concerns of the people they most directly affect.

In terms of our relations with our Aboriginal neighbours, no written agreement or reliance on legal rights can guarantee an arrangement built on trust. Only actions can do that. That is why the company has persisted with a relationship-building program in the face of legal challenges to some of its titles. We have frankly acknowledged the common law position of Aboriginal people and have not used native title claims as an excuse to criticise the recognition of native title. After some years of this approach, we are starting to see the benefits.

One example of this approach is in the Pilbara region of Western Australia. There, Hamersley Iron has recently completed the construction of the Yandicoogina iron ore mine and its associated rail corridor. The previous mine development, Marandoo, was characterised by Aboriginal opposition and was delayed for two years by the confrontation. The new mine could have been similarly delayed if a purely legalistic approach had been adopted by either the company or those Aboriginal people with links to the land. The company established an Aboriginal Liaison Unit in 1992 and in subsequent years, the trust that I speak of was established. Consequently, when the Yandicoogina development was mooted in 1996, negotiations were conducted in a much more enlightened environment and an agreement was reached in 1998. The Yandicoogina Agreement eventuated, not just because of the efforts of the negotiating team, but because Hamersley Iron had worked hard to establish a sustainable and equitable relationship with the Aboriginal population of the Pilbara.

The goodwill and trust enjoyed by Hamersley is the ultimate product of a corporate philosophy that recognises that indigenous people were in the area long before mining commenced and will be there long after it finishes. It leads us to support activities that will persist after Rio Tinto has left the area. People who have cultural roots that extend back thousands of years prefer that approach.

Similar processes have been applied to produce agreements in central Queensland for the Hail Creek coalmine and in exploration agreements in the Northern Territory and Western Australia. Work towards agreements is also proceeding at two sites in Western Australia and two sites in Queensland.

I cannot speak for the mining industry as a whole, but Rio Tinto's experience is that most Aboriginal communities do not oppose exploration and mining development in principle. Increasingly they see involvement in these efforts as a potential route away from welfare dependency. Thus, we are finding that, as Aboriginal people gain greater control over their own destinies, they are more willing to work with us if there is benefit in doing so. The Memorandum of Understanding (MOU) with ATSIC mentioned earlier is a manifestation of the desire to go further in the area of Aboriginal business development. Inclusion of government bodies as partners in this work can increase the chances of formation and sustainability. We have followed with a second MOU with the Federal Department of Education and Youth Affairs and a contract with the Department of Employment, Workplace Relations and Small Business. Both of these arrangements are aimed at increasing education and employment in the regions where we operate.

Rio Tinto is committed to continuing its work in improving its relationships with Aboriginal people. We wish to co-operate with them in arriving at arrangements that are mutually beneficial.

I wish to acknowledge Rio Tinto for the position that allows me to write this article and thank Michael Bell and Janina Gawler for assistance in its preparation.

What's the Alternative?
Rick Farley

The core of the reconciliation debate is the future of race relations in Australia. How we all manage that debate will shape Australian society and our standing with the rest of the world. It goes to the heart of our national psyche and our national identity. It is the debate we have to have, if for no other reason than that the issues won't go away. They will continue to fester and reduce our vitality as a nation until we deal with them.

There is a range of events now that will keep indigenous issues high on the public agenda—the Sydney 2000 Olympics, when 20,000 international media will be turned loose on Australia; the centenary of federation in 2001; the report of the Council for Aboriginal Reconciliation to the Commonwealth parliament at the end of 2000; the United Nations 'please explain' about native title legislation; court decisions on native title; and proposed amendments to cultural heritage protection arrangements between the Commonwealth and states. The issues certainly are not going away. In that context, the critical questions become how we manage them, how long it takes and how much collateral damage we incur along the way.

I have been involved in the reconciliation debate for about ten years now and came to it from a very pragmatic perspective as the executive director of the National Farmers' Federation. I have learned many things over the decade and have come to the simple view that there is no alternative to reconciliation; at least no alternative acceptable to me and, I hope, to most Australians.

Without reconciliation, we will be a divided nation with racial tension and racial strife because indigenous people will not give up their struggle. They have survived until now, against all the odds, and will continue to fight for their human and legal rights. They see it ultimately as a question of the survival of their culture, a war against cultural genocide. There can be no retreat in such a war, even though some battles may be lost. So, in very stark terms, Australia can either be an inclusive, harmonious nation or one split by race issues. I reject the latter and therefore must embrace the quest for harmony.

Facing up to facts
Eventually, Australians will have to come to grips with the facts about our treatment of indigenous people. Even if we don't want to do it, the rest of the world will increasingly hold a mirror up to us and we will not be able to avoid it forever.

That mirror will show many things. The history most Australians were taught is wrong. Australia was not a land belonging to no one—*terra nullius*. It was owned and occupied by hundreds of Aboriginal and Torres Strait Islander nations. They resisted invasion by European convicts and settlers and more people were killed than the number of Australians killed in Vietnam. Yet most history books don't record that these wars occurred.

By any standard, indigenous peoples have been treated disgracefully. They have been slaughtered in massacres, their women abused, their children taken away and their human rights ignored. They still die younger, have greater health problems, lower education and employment rates and more of them are in jail than any other sector of the Australian community. The rate of youth suicide in Australia is amongst the highest in the world and the rate of indigenous youth suicide is higher still.

The mirror will show that indigenous Australian culture has survived, despite the many attempts to kill it off (whether intentional or non-intended, malevolent or well-meaning). In fact, it is the oldest living culture on earth; something the rest of the world believes should be protected and celebrated, even if we don't.

The mirror will also show that indigenous peoples have legal and human rights which cannot be ignored. There is a growing body of domestic and international law where those rights can be pursued. The High Court has rejected the myth of *terra nullius* and ruled that some residual indigenous property rights continue to exist in the form of native title. The Commonwealth's efforts to wind back those rights are being questioned by the United Nations. The UN is also reporting on whether the Australian government is in breach of its responsibilities to indigenous people under treaties and conventions it has signed. Domestic legislation in relation to racial discrimination, cultural heritage protection and the environment also provides fertile ground for the indigenous rights agenda.

The bottom lines as I see them are: indigenous peoples have legitimate grievances which are significant issues of natural justice; there are many avenues for them to pursue their rights; they won't give up because ultimately their culture and identity are at risk. This is a recipe for huge social and political dissension unless it is managed carefully and sensitively.

Lessons I have learned

Having established, I hope, the case for reconciliation as a priority in national debate, I do not want to pretend that resolution of the issues is easy. There are profound problems along the way. Reconciliation is the interface between many cultures and different laws.

In the first instance, there are huge challenges to public administration policy. The system of government in Australia is highly centralised. Peak industry and community groups deal directly with the Commonwealth on public policy—the ACTU, National Farmers' Federation, Minerals Council of Australia, Australian Council of Social Services and so on. Yet under indigenous law, no one can talk for someone else's country. There were over 300 separate indigenous nations in Australia. Clan and family groups have responsibility for caring for particular land and waters. The concept of a peak body, able to speak for all of the country, is alien to indigenous law and culture. This creates a fundamental tension—our system of public administration is centralised, but the only way to deal effectively with indigenous issues is at the local and regional level.

Second, traditional boundaries and areas of responsibility for country have become blurred. Indigenous peoples have been moved and shifted around extensively. Their history is a history of dispossession. Different peoples were pushed back from the coast by settlement, jumbled together on missions and reserves, and had to leave large inland grazing properties as the result of the equal wages decision in the 1960s. It therefore can be very difficult to identify the right people to speak for country and exercise traditional responsibilities for it. The exercise requires time and resources and finally can be resolved only by indigenous people themselves. There is no whitefella who can tell indigenous people their responsibilities for country under their traditional law. This, once again, creates problems for policy makers. How can policy be developed, or timely approvals granted for industrial development, when government and industry are not sure with whom they should be dealing, and when many indigenous groups are in dispute about the matter? This situation is not the fault of indigenous peoples, but it is the reality we have all inherited.

Third, indigenous peoples don't want to be totally absorbed into an homogeneous Australian community. They have their own culture, which has survived for over 60,000 years, and they want to protect and enhance it. They have rights to do this under the common law. They also have special rights as the first peoples of Australia under international law—rights that are not available to the rest of the community.

The challenge for non-indigenous Australians is to accept and respect this wish for a distinct identity by indigenous people, while they still remain within the overall Australian community. The challenge becomes even greater when another cultural difference is added to the equation.

In European society, there is an expectation that information will be available freely. There are libraries, extensive media coverage of events, the Internet, the 'information superhighway'. But in indigenous society, some information is not available. Some information is never released generally and only handed on when people are judged ready to deal with it.

This was put into sharp focus for me by Galarrwuy Yunupingu during the native title debate in 1993. My proposition to him at the time was: 'Galarrwuy, you're a senior law man. It would help debate if you were able to talk about your relationship with country. If there was more knowledge by whitefellas, there would be greater understanding and that might help to generate some solutions.' I thought this was a pretty reasonable position—make more information available, which will assist understanding, and out of better understanding will come a better debate.

Galarrwuy just looked at me for a moment and replied, 'Why do you whitefellas have to know everything?'

That about sums it up. The enormous jump in mindset that non-indigenous Australians have to make is to respect, and accept as different, a culture and laws they can never fully understand.

The ingredients

In order to develop an agenda for reconciliation, it is first necessary to understand what we're talking about. Many indigenous people and many other Australians have a problem with the concept of reconciliation. They ask, 'What is there to reconcile? There never was an initial coming together of indigenous and non-indigenous Australians, so how can we come together again?'

Personally, I don't think the word matters. To me, the question is how to generate better relationships between the first peoples of Australia and those who came after. What do we have to do to reduce racial tension and strife and move towards a more harmonious community?

I believe there are three key ingredients—acknowledgement of the true history of Australia; education; and a legislative process for dealing with 'unfinished business'.

Acknowledging history is fundamental. Until the community has a common understanding of what has occurred in the past, there is no firm foundation for moving ahead together. From an indigenous perspective, it involves acceptance by the wider community that they are the traditional owners of Australia, that they were invaded, that they resisted, that atrocities were committed, and that they still suffer unacceptable levels of disadvantage. Those are the facts of the situation. It is the reality of Australia's history. That being so, I can see no problem in acknowledging it. In any case, if we do not, the rest of the world will do it for us—we will not be able to stick our heads in the sand forever.

Acknowledgement does not imply guilt. It is simply telling the truth about our shared past. Saying 'sorry' does not imply guilt either. I can be sorry about an event over which I have no control—I am sorry that our land and rivers are ravaged by salt; I am sorry that many Australians are unemployed and homeless; I am sorry for the victims of natural disasters; I am even sorry that South Sydney has been kicked out of the national rugby league competition. But that does not mean I bear any guilt for those events. All it means is that I recognise the pain arising from what has happened and want to communicate some human warmth to those who need it.

Saying 'sorry' to indigenous Australians is evidence only of the generosity of our spirit. Hundreds of thousands of Australians have done it through the Sea of Hands project and Sorry Books. So have most state and territory parliaments. So has the senate. The resistance of the prime minister to the 's' word can only feed the view that his government does not approach the reconciliation process with the warmth and generosity necessary to heal the wounds of the past and move forward together.

The second key ingredient to the process of reconciliation is education. There are three important roles education can play. It can help counter ignorance and racism by presenting the facts about Australian history and giving non-indigenous people an insight into Aboriginal and Torres Strait Islander culture. In many ways, better understanding is the first step towards mutual respect, which is a cornerstone of reconciliation. The goal of indigenous people has always been to have Aboriginal studies as a mandatory component of school and university curricula. Schooling, of course, is a decision for the states and there has been varied progress. New South Wales premier, Bob Carr, made the point at the State Reconciliation Conference in 1999 that today's generation of students is in a unique position—they are the first to grow up with the truth about Australia's treatment of its first peoples. They therefore have an enormous opportunity to improve relationships.

The education system is also a tool for achieving more equitable social outcomes for indigenous people, many of whom are trapped in a cycle of poverty. The cycle goes like this— if you don't have a good education, it is harder to get a job; if you don't have a job, you can't afford good housing; if you don't have a functional house, health suffers; if you don't have good health, your ability to participate in the education system is reduced...and so on.

There are other dimensions to the issue. Without education and a job, you are more likely to end up in the criminal justice system. The proof of that is plain to see as indigenous people are grossly over-represented in the justice system now.

The benefits of education and employment also disseminate quickly in indigenous communities because they apply not only to the immediate family, but to the extended family as well.

Education of the wider community is the third task. Many Australians have grown up in ignorance of indigenous culture and issues. Many have had little or no contact with Aboriginal and Torres Strait Islander people. In that climate, reconciliation obviously is more difficult.

The Council for Aboriginal Reconciliation has started to address this issue. Local reconciliation groups and community study circles have been formed, assisted by the churches and the union movement. But much more needs to be done.

One of my personal hobby horses always has been the need for a coordinated national public information campaign about native title. Neither the Keating nor the Howard governments ever undertook such a campaign. The issue consequently has been characterised by uninformed debate, some of it generated for base political reasons, and unjustified fears. It is incomprehensible to me that government is prepared to spend millions of dollars on public information about the GST, health issues, drink driving and a raft of other issues, but has never been prepared to devote resources to informing the nation about one of the most significant legal and social developments in our history.

The last essential ingredient to encouraging reconciliation is a defined process to address the issues and focus public debate. That was recognised by the Commonwealth parliament when it unanimously passed legislation to establish the Council for Aboriginal Reconciliation in 1990. Under the legislation, the council is required to report to the parliament by the end of 2000 on whether a document or documents would advance reconciliation. The council was also asked to advise the minister on the form and content of such a document(s), and whether it would benefit the community as a whole.

The council has been through an extensive process of consultation with the indigenous and wider community. It has decided that there is value in a document of reconciliation and plans to release it in two stages. The first will be an inspirational statement about reconciliation and will be presented to the nation at Corroboree 2000 in Sydney in May. The second stage is the council's report to the parliament, which will be presented in December. It will recommend four action strategies that it wants to be given effect by a legislative framework. The four strategies—dealing with disadvantage, economic independence, rights and sustaining the process—will be foreshadowed in May.

The council's legislation expires in December, so it plans to establish a new body, Reconciliation Australia, as a foundation independent of government, to carry on the work towards reconciliation.

The prime minister has said reconciliation cannot be achieved by the end of 2000. That is self-evident. The real issue is the speed at which the Commonwealth parliament responds to the council's document and its formal recommendations. The longer it delays, the greater the capacity for public disquiet and frustration, and the more indigenous people will be forced to pursue their agenda in the courts and international forums.

The politics

The Howard government has never been comfortable with the reconciliation process or the indigenous agenda. Indeed, it is uncomfortable with social issues in general and different in that respect to previous Liberal governments.

But it also must be recognised that reconciliation and the associated indigenous agenda are a very complex set of issues and difficult for any government to deal with. The Hawke government reneged on national land rights and the Keating government never proceeded with the social justice package that was the third element of the Mabo negotiations. That is why indigenous peoples have increasingly pursued their agenda in the courts and internationally. No political party has consistently given them confidence that the political process will deal with their issues effectively.

But therein lie the problems for Australia and the shape of our society. The reality is that indigenous people will never give up. They are fighting for the survival of their culture and have human and legal rights that can be pursued by many means. If they have to stay in the courts for centuries, they will. If they have to embarrass Australia before the rest of the world, they will.

Their immovable position now is that there must be a legislative framework to deal with 'unfinished business'—the broad areas for action identified by the council. They don't trust the politicians to deal with the issues unless they are required to do so by statute.

The prospect facing our community is for an increasingly bitter and divisive debate until there is a clear process for dealing with the indigenous agenda—a process which has their confidence. The more indigenous people are forced to press their case, particularly in the courts and internationally, the more fuel will be added to the fires. Ultimately, there will have to be some resolution, some reconciliation. The critical political questions are how long it takes and how much hurt there will be along the way. The People's Movement for Reconciliation and Reconciliation

Australia will be important factors in this equation. The extent to which they can focus and mobilise public opinion will have a big bearing on the speed of the politicians' responses.

In these circumstances, perhaps the penultimate question is how much pain we can save ourselves as a society. That's where leadership comes into play. Leadership can focus and guide the debate, and reduce the pain of an extended struggle. Leadership must come from all those interests that are integral to the debate, but the first steps must come from the government and indigenous people. And the first movement should come from the prime minister as the leader of our nation, in the interests of Australia's national identity and standing in the world.

This is My Life
Mary Darkie

I'm Mary Darkie, I'm 23-years-old and live with my husband and two children. We live in a remote community in the Great Sandy Desert in the Kimberley Region of Western Australia. I moved here in 1992 to be with my husband in his country. I work in the community school as an administrative assistant.

I want to talk to you about growing up in the desert and the impact of Kartiya (non-indigenous people) on me and my family. My attitude has gone from friendship to mistrust, to accepting people as individuals.

I grew up on a cattle station about 200 kilometres from here. The station was on my grandfather's land and it had passed on to his children. Aboriginal people owned the station and employed managers to look after the cattle business.

When I was a child I played in the bush and went hunting with my family. All the adults used to go out a long way hunting and us kids used to wait at the station gate for our parents to come back. We would swing on the station gate and tell stories till they returned. When the parents returned we would count how many goannas they had and the children would go on home with their parents. Most of the time I would be the last one sitting on the gate and sometimes it was already dark. When my parents returned they would have caught up to 40 goannas. They would share these with my uncle and other family members.

At that time the manager and his family lived on the station with us. They had two sons and we always played together. Once I nearly drowned in a dam and one of the manager's sons saved me. There was another little girl with them with whom I became friends and we played together at my house. She would invite me to her house too and we would play in the fishpond there. She shared all her dolls and toys with me and we took her out bush with us.

When I was six-years-old my parents decided to send me to a nearby community where there was a school. I had to stay in the dormitory during the week and could go home on the weekend. I stayed in the dormitory with other station girls and a Saint John of God sister looked after us. She was kind to us and we had a playroom with lots of toys that I loved with all my heart. I was happy in the dormitory but we were not allowed to see our extended family during the week and that was really hard.

Back on the station there was a new manager. He ran the office, store and cattle business. He was good to everyone. At Christmas he would put on a big party and get a truck in from town with lots of toys and presents. Everyone liked him very much and trusted him with everything. We did not know that he was good on the outside but bad on the inside. He was taking money out of the company and destroying the station.

After he left, there was no more money to continue the station business. Other non-indigenous people knew what had happened but my family still did not know why the station had failed. When we tried to get more funding to keep the station going we got the blame for not looking after it. We had no choice but to leave the station because we had no money to run generators for our electricity or get supplies for our store. We felt sad to leave, and leaving our country hurt a lot. We expected that we would always stay there.

After all this had happened I lost trust in non-indigenous people. I carried a lot of hurt and anger and blamed all non-indigenous people for what had happened. I thought all non-indigenous people were the same; that they were bad people and wanted to steal what we had. Some of my family didn't understand what happened but others, like me, felt angry.

When I got older I married and moved to another community. I started working in the community school as an administrative assistant. While I was working I started a course in community administration. I did this study because I wanted to know more about book-keeping so I could understand what was happening to my family's and community's finances. I did not want what had happened to my family to happen again.

In the school where I worked I started to see non-indigenous people in a new light. The people I worked with were not bossy and pushy and they tried to understand indigenous people. It's sometimes hard for them to understand our ways but they still try. They were willing to accept our culture and share in what was happening in our lives. With us they would celebrate our joys and mourn our losses. They encouraged me and other indigenous staff to take up studies and helped us to complete them. They cared about us and wanted us to achieve good things. They encouraged us to become qualified for jobs in community administration, teaching and health. They taught us to be strong and proud and stand up for ourselves and our community. When I felt down and worthless, someone would encourage me and push me along. Sometimes I would say, 'I'm not like you. I can't do this,' but my tutor would say, 'You're just as good as anyone else.' When I was told these things I would feel good and strong inside and I could go on.

I was starting to see non-indigenous people as individuals and not all the same. I got to know individuals personally and developed friendships with them. It was during this time that I started trusting non-indigenous people again.

All this helped me to believe in myself. I was working in a position where non-indigenous people listened to me and respected me. At home my family was proud of me and I was able to help them with their finances and their dealings with non-indigenous organisations. I also felt proud of my Aboriginal culture.

Reconciliation is about getting to know each person individually. It means letting go of old ideas that all white-skinned people are the same or all black-skinned people are the same. All people are different; they may have the same colour skin but inside, each person is unique. It's what's inside each person that's important. I sometimes think we live in a crazy world that we always have to divide people into separate groups.

Reconciliation also means letting go of anger, hurt and blaming. I had to let go of these things in order to get to know people as they really are. We cannot forget the past but letting go of anger and hurt allows us to move forward.

Breaking the Cycle
Boori Monty Pryor

For 40,000 years or more Aboriginal people have lived, finding ways to be in rhythm with the world around us. In doing so, we have become the oldest, continuous, living culture in the world today with the oldest songs, stories, dances, paintings, and a very special understanding of respect and family through powerful oral traditions.

Then for 200 years we were inhumanly separated from our families, our land, our songs and dances, our stories, our lore. We found ourselves in darkness, facing the horrendous truth that we were slowly being separated from ourselves, our spirits and souls left to float out there somewhere, forever.

Then in that darkness came some light, for in 1967 there was a national referendum that overwhelmingly said 'Yes' to giving Aboriginal people the right to vote and in doing so, be allowed to be citizens in our own country. How weird does that sound? Citizens in our own country.

I grew up during that time and my heart goes out to all my elders who fought hard, some dying in the battle, to give me the power to write these words. I include my white elders in my love and thanks for there were many, many white people who fought side by side with my old people to get us all to where we are today.

It is now the year 2000, 33 years since that vote was cast. That's 33 years to, as some people say, 'get over it.' It's hard to imagine that any race of people could 'get over it' in that short period of time, considering the horror 'it' was, much of which is only being spoken about in the last few years.

In the last 30 years, Aboriginal people have suddenly been allowed to be part of the race, the human race, again. We have been allowed to love and treat ourselves like humans when in the years before that, we had been told we were animals.

That in itself is a huge task, finding ways to love yourself through your own culture when you have seen that culture so decimated and fractured almost to the point of destruction. That's why I feel so blessed with the power of the wisdom that my old people have passed on to me. I'm humbled to be part of such great families and see my mum and dad, uncles and aunties, leading the way with such grace and poise and dignity. I can't do anything else but follow their lead. I see the way they deal with the many suicides that happen in our families, the alcohol and the drugs, all the things they had happen to them and are now seeing those same things happening to their children and grandchildren, yet they stand tall, tell stories of sadness with great humour, have love in their hearts and always have that shimmering ray of hope shining cheekily through their eyes. From my heart to theirs, I thank them once again.

During the past 200 years there have been many laws put in place to dispossess us from our mother earth. These laws are inhumane, unjust and have left many deep scars in the souls and hearts of my people. There's a story my mother tells of when she was going to marry my dad. She had to have documented proof that either she or her intended husband had at least 50 percent white blood running through their veins. A full-blood could not marry a full-blood. Children were separated from their mothers at birth; their souls lost, their bodies abused, making their journey through life a sad and painful one. I have sat, talked and listened to many people on this journey. I have looked into their eyes. There is no way to describe what I see, it's just too painful. And for the children with white blood running through their veins, the question is always there. How did this white blood get there in the first place? Was it through the raping of black women, or was it through love and consent?

Then there are the Trust Funds where money was taken from Aboriginal workers and put into Trust accounts. None of the money held in these accounts ever reached my father or many thousands of other Aboriginal people who worked so hard developing the land for white people.

To heal this situation, the first steps have to be taken from within all of us. To do that we must all admit we have a problem and listen to the voices from the past that have never been heard. It may not be all good news, but at least it's there for all to see. Life is a great teacher. If you listen with your eyes, your ears, and your heart you will become strong and powerful. Try to do this without your heart and you will become lost in anger and misunderstanding. Being selective about history only deepens the wounds of ignorance. This leads to the passing on of pain from one generation to another.

Through my work as a teacher, performer and storyteller in front of many hundreds of children each week across five states in this country, I see in the eyes of these children the chance to diminish the pain that has crippled the country. For our young kids are the ones, given the right medicine or information, that can take this country to a new level where everything can be sorted out by honest discussion.

I've had to work a lot of things out in my life, both family and personal, that have been very traumatic. One step in the wrong direction could have been death, so I've had to make the right choices. I've done this by leaving myself open to all sorts of tests—physical, mental, spiritual—any of which I could have died from and many times I nearly did. But what I found emerging from the other side was a better and stronger me. This is what we all must do for ourselves—find ways to fight the demons within us. Don't sit on the fence or on your backside and expect everyone else to do the dirty work, then blame everyone else because nothing has been done. Start your own journey, then you have a chance not to pass all the garbage and mistakes of the past onto your children and they in turn do not pass it on to their children and so on. We all have the chance within us to break the cycle.

I never preach when I speak in front of people; God knows, if anybody can talk about being preached to, it's Aboriginal people. Through leaving myself open I have learnt how to teach through sharing because we all have something to give. We all have the chance to be presented with the right material to change ourselves. Sometimes I have people who sit in front of me and expect to be changed just by being there. Well, it doesn't work like that. People have to find the courage to alter their own way of thinking. In this way, I never try to change people. They have to change themselves. I just relate to them through stories, personal ones about my journey through life to where I am at present. They can be sad, happy, beautiful, soulful, uplifting stories—all of these things and more. The stories are given when needed to explain the plight of my people. I suppose I tell it best when I do it through these stories.

Just recently, one of my nephews committed suicide. He was on his motor bike. He came off at high speed and lost his life. The demons within his soul had done their work. I remember being at my mum and dad's place when we heard the news. We all went over to pay our respects to my cousin and his mob. There were many tears, but lots of laughter and lots of great stories told; again, another way of using stories for survival. This time dramatic, funny stories of fishing, crocodiles and Hairymen.

I had to head back to Melbourne the next day so I was going to miss the funeral. My mother rang me and told me this sad story: As the church service finished and my nephew's coffin was raised high on everyone's shoulders to be carried out, a few feet behind stood his son who was about five or six years-old at the time, tears streaming from his eyes, his arms raised to the heavens and his little voice piercing the air saying, 'Daddy, please come back. Don't leave. Please come back.' His voice echoed through the church and eventually those sad words found their way back into his little heart.

My niece, who has great spirit and energy, sometimes gets lost. In her efforts to make her way successfully through her teenage years she gets herself into lots of trouble; so much so that she ended up in the Juvenile Justice Centre for young girls in Brisbane. It just so happened that at the time I was booked to do a day at the centre to talk to the kids about finding ways that could work for them to help them survive. I had a great day telling yarns about life that made them laugh till they cried and some stories that had them looking for answers within themselves. I learned so much by being in their presence.

We were all sitting down to lunch and I was listening to some of their stories. One of these young girls was excitedly telling a story about the cell she was in and how she was checking all the writing on the walls when she noticed a message of love from a young girl to her boyfriend. That message was written by her mother to her father.

As I left the detention centre on that day, I got into a taxi headed for the airport. The driver had a dry sense of humour, a sharp wit and was a great storyteller so I listened closely and was rewarded with a gift.

Early one Friday night this cabbie picked up a fare. It was a young Aboriginal boy. The young boy sat very quietly in the passenger seat. The cabbie repeatedly asked his fare where he wanted to go. Still nothing from the boy. The cabbie tried again, when the boy suddenly produced a knife. 'Give us ya money.' With this the cabbie grabbed the knife from the boy's hand and whooped him about the head. After a while he sat and spoke to him.

The cabbie was very honest in his concern for the boy's welfare. He called around on his phone to a few places that might be able to help the situation that had been dumped into his lap, but with no success. He didn't want to take him to the police station because he thought the boy would be lost within the system. The cabbie took up to three or four hours in an effort to try to find an alternative to sending this young boy to jail—all this on a Friday night where serious money was to be made. What a heart-warming gesture.

At one stage he managed to squeeze out of the boy his home address but when he took him there he was greeted by the boy's father—drunk, angry and yelling abuse, telling him to take his kid because he didn't want him. Finally, the cabbie tracked down one of his friends and went round to his place. The boy waited in the taxi while the cabbie spoke to the man. The friend had a lawn-mowing business and wanted to know what the boy was like as a worker. 'I dunno,' the cab driver replied, 'but he'll never make it as a hold-up artist.' They both laughed, then got the boy to come in to meet the family and have a cup of tea.

Then there was silence from the cabbie as we stopped at a red traffic light. He looked across at me and smiled, then said, 'That was five years ago. I ring him from time to time. He's doin' fine.' The smile stayed on his face and as the lights changed he went onto his next story.

These stories have a great deal to do with us all. My nephew's little boy had the baton of pain passed on to him as he cried for his father in that church. As he grows he will have to fight hard to break that cycle. The young girl reading her mother's writing on her cell wall also has to find ways to break the cycle. Luckily the young boy took the right cab that Friday night in Brisbane and has a great chance of making things right for himself and his children.

Many of my people die of broken hearts; some don't wait for this to happen, they take their own lives and at every funeral someone stands up and says, 'They have gone to a better place.' Why should we have to die a terrible death to find a better place? Why can't the place we're leaving be better than the one we're going to?

We're all walking around in pain. Aboriginal people because they're living with the truth and white people because they find it hard to deal with the truth. As an Aboriginal man, I find I have to justify my existence on this earth every day and I get tired and angry, very angry. I've worked very hard to deal with the anger inside me and in doing so have become better not bitter. I have been rewarded greatly for searching for the light in my own spirit first. I call them gifts for my soul. They are glimmering lights springing up all over the country.

One such light is an 11-year-old girl from Basket Range Primary School situated in the hills near Adelaide. This young girl sat and wrote me the most beautiful letter. As I read her words, my heart felt safe and I cried, shedding many tears, but the tears that I shed were safe and flowed freely with love and joy because as a boy I was told, 'If you don't laugh, you cry; if you cry you die.' We spoke to each other, learning as we listened. She also included a six-page summary of her thoughts on *Maybe Tomorrow*, the book about my family and my work in schools. I have read her letter many times and was grateful for the opportunity to eventually meet this shining light and attend her school. It was a great day, one I will keep in my heart forever; and when I'm standing in front of people justifying my existence and the pain gets too much, I will call on the light of that day for its healing.

That healing light is there for us all. There are many of them appearing across our country everywhere because lots of people have started on their journey. I hope you read this and decide to face the demons within and begin your own journey creating a light for someone else to see. Just like someone else did for you.

A New Confidence
Robert Milliken

Lloyd McDermott handed me his card as we sat down to talk in his Sydney office. 'Mullenjaiwakka', it said. 'Barrister at law.' For 57 years, McDermott had played the game of white Australia. He went under a European name, had a job that brought him status, a home in Sydney's rich eastern suburbs and enough money to send his daughter to a private school. Hardly the image middle Australia sees, or sometimes wants to see, of Aborigines. McDermott is Australia's first Aboriginal barrister, and still one of only two indigenous barristers practising in New South Wales. Four years ago he decided it was time to reclaim his origins and to take back his tribal name from his childhood in central outback Queensland where he grew up in a tent.

Mullenjaiwakka is one of a growing number of indigenous Australians who have defied the odds. They are what middle Australia would call success stories. They have 'made it' into the world of influential, rewarding jobs, six-figure incomes and homes in the 'better' suburbs. They are the reverse side of the sad, bad stories the media harps on about Aboriginal Australia.

For the most part they belong to a recent phenomenon, people who have emerged since the explosion of Aboriginal politics in the early 1970s that brought new opportunities for young blacks, particularly in education. Sport, the arts, small business, education and the tourist world's discovery of Australia's rich Aboriginal heritage have helped to turn many of these figures into household names: Ernie Dingo, the actor; Charles Perkins, the political activist; his daughter Rachel Perkins, the actress and filmmaker; and Gary Ella, the rugby star—to name a few.

Others are less well-known, but are making their marks with equal impact: Linda Burney, deputy director of the NSW Department of Aboriginal Affairs; John Moriarty, a millionaire designer and businessman; and Paul Ah-Chee, an outback entrepreneur. All represent a giant leap forward for indigenous Australians. Although these achievers are still a small minority, they are a positive sign of things to come. And it is largely through these, the ranks of Australia's first generation of educated, self-reliant Aborigines, that the movement towards reconciliation has been led.

I first met some of these people when I was researching an article in 1999 for *The Eye* magazine on the subject of a new Aboriginal middle class. The idea was meant to suggest the arrival of a new generation of independent, self-reliant Aborigines. But it was highly contentious, and few of those who fell into this category willingly subscribed to being identified as middle class. First of all, how can you talk about a middle class among a race of people whose deplorable standard of health and welfare mocks the very notion? Then there's the fact that middle class itself is a white term whose meaning in black eyes stands for everything that almost wiped the Aboriginal nation off the map: push, expansion, individualism. How can this term have any meaning, people ask, to a race where sharing and obligations to one's community take precedence over the trappings of individual achievement?

Aboriginal achievers who consciously join the middle class risk being pilloried by their own people as 'uptown niggers', 'flash blacks' or 'coconuts', a derogatory term meaning black on the outside, white on the inside. Yet advances are being made that would have been unthinkable 20 years ago, certainly a century ago. And some manage to turn this conflict on its head with a dash of dry humour. Ernie Dingo told me how he deals with it. When he is not travelling to exotic places like the Canadian Rockies, filming episodes for television travel programs, Dingo and his wife live in a comfortable house in Brisbane, surrounded by magazines on homes, gardens and how to make your money work. 'A few mates and I call ourselves Bluppies—black yuppies. I feel no discomfort because it's been happening slowly for more than 100 years.'

Now, in March 2000, I was back with Mullenjaiwakka at a crucial point in that long journey. Australia was preparing to mark later in the year reconciliation with its indigenous people, a process launched formally in 1991, and supported by both sides of politics, with a target date of 2001, the centenary of federation. Now came one of the most breathtaking reversals of a political promise in memory. John Howard, the prime minister who had pledged on his re-election in 1998 'genuinely' to commit himself to reconciliation by 2001, had just ditched this commitment—not in the upfront manner of his original promise but in a backdoor interview in a daily newspaper. Howard, the short-term political survivor, had decided to play to the disenchanted heartland of rural Australia, where opinion polls indicated indifference towards reconciliation prevailed. For this he was prepared to sacrifice a great moment of Australian history. And in doing so he had let down the Aboriginal leaders and achievers who had put much faith in the process. But, as I discovered, their faith in the longer run has not been broken.

This is largely because their own stories have called for much bigger tests of faith to get them where they are today. Mullenjaiwakka did not go to school until he was nine. His mother taught him correspondence lessons in the tents where he spent much of his north Queensland childhood. Through the Anglican Church, he won scholarships to high school and university. 'I believe education for Aboriginal people is equally important as land rights.' At his Anglican school in Queensland, he suffered racist taunts. 'They called me Jacky. But I was a good athlete, a good rugby union player and I could use my fists. That was something the white kids revered.' In his youth, Mullenjaiwakka was one of the first Aborigines to become an international rugby star. Later it irked him that, up to the mid-1980s, only five Aborigines had ever played international rugby for Australia. So in 1995 he helped to set up the Lloyd McDermott Rugby Development Team, a non-profit organisation aimed at helping talented young Aborigines make the most of their rugby and netball skills through training camps and overseas playing tours. In 1999 this venture also found jobs for 18 young Aborigines. Fundraising dinners for the team are held at NSW Parliament House; Mullenjaiwakka's friends in the legal and rugby fraternities have supported them.

A good example of reconciliation. But, at 60, Mullenjaiwakka finds reconciliation 'difficult' and 'confusing'. 'It's a good middle-class concept,' he says. 'For proper reconciliation you have to have an equal bargaining position. But the Aboriginal people aren't coming from a position of strength to the people they're reconciling with.' His preference is for something more radical: a treaty saying indigenous Australians had never ceded sovereignty to the 'invaders' and that they should remain an Aboriginal nation within a nation. This would never be accepted by most Australians, and certainly not by John Howard, and Mullenjaiwakka knows it.

'I realise reconciliation is the only game in town. The knockers would say I want to divide Australia. But we were the ones who were divided. In America they call their indigenous people nations—the Sioux and the Navajo who run their own affairs today—and in Canada they call their aborigines the first nations.' In the absence of a treaty, Mullenjaiwakka believes the minimum Australia should do is acknowledge Aborigines' past custodianship of the land and apologise for past injustices. 'I will never say reconciliation has occurred until the disadvantages in housing, health and over-representation of blacks in prisons has been rectified. And until the numbers of Aborigines in important jobs—teachers, doctors, judges, politicians—reflect our proportion of two percent in the population as a whole. Until these things happen, reconciliation is an impossible dream.'

It seemed a sad reflection. But Canada indeed has shown a way of how it can work. After a Royal Commission inquiry, the Canadian government in January 1998 made a 'Statement of Reconciliation'. It talked of the 'diverse, vibrant Aboriginal nations' and their 'responsibilities as custodians of the lands, waters and resources of their homelands' before Canada was founded. Instead of the word 'sorry', the Canadian government offered 'profound regret for past actions of the federal government which have contributed to these difficult pages in the history of our relationship together'. But it went further in making verbal amends for the residential schools, a system that separated aboriginal children from families and obliterated their traditional languages and cultures, not unlike the assimilationist policies Australia adopted up to the mid-twentieth century by taking Aboriginal children from families and dumping them in missions. The Canadian statement acknowledged the physical and sexual abuse suffered by children in the residential schools: '...we wish to emphasise that what you experienced was not your fault and should never have happened. To those of you who suffered this tragedy at residential schools, we are deeply sorry.'

Linda Burney wishes Australia could take a leaf from Canada, say sorry without fear, and move on. 'And the sun still comes up in Canada each morning,' she says. Burney is a member of the Wiradjuri nation from the NSW Riverina district, where she grew up in the 1960s. She did not meet her father until she was 28. Her non-indigenous great aunt and uncle on her mother's side helped to raise her. Education was Burney's passport out of her deprived background and she has made education, for Aborigines and non-Aborigines alike, a focus of her life. This broadening of mental horizons is the core of reconciliation for her: 'I'm passionate about it.'

In 1979, Burney was the first Aborigine to gain a diploma of teaching at what is now Charles Sturt University in Bathurst, NSW. She did not teach for long. Two years later she started working on education policy with the NSW Department of Education, a process that saw the state introduce an Aboriginal perspective to the school curriculum, the first of its kind in Australia. This was the first of a series of influential policy-related jobs for Burney, leading to her latest role as deputy director of the NSW Department of Aboriginal Affairs. Along the way she has been on the board of SBS, the public broadcasting network, and has spoken at United Nations conferences in Geneva on indigenous populations. Burney is involved in two big historic issues that are meant to pull

Australia together in 2000: she chairs the NSW State Reconciliation Committee and is a member of the Centenary of Federation Council.

It is a formidable commitment, but it is easy to see why Burney is in demand. She is a small, attractive woman with an articulate grasp of issues. If Burney is middle class, she seems to have been propelled there by her commitment to advance Aboriginal causes rather than Linda Burney's cause. Recently I spent a day with her, starting in the early morning at her comfortable home in a gentrified part of inner-Sydney, where she lives with her daughter and partner, Rick Farley, a prominent lobbyist, former executive director of the National Farmers' Federation, and now a consultant on native title claims. At a series of talks during the day, her audiences were typically all white: a meeting of the staff of the Centenary of Federation Council, then a lunch attended by well-heeled business men and women hosted by the *Readers Digest* at Ampersand, one of the trendiest restaurants in Sydney. Most at the Ampersand tables had never seen an Aborigine before, let alone heard their stories. Burney made the most of this: she held the room with her presence.

When she was a child there were no such Aboriginal figures bridging the divide, no indigenous achievers to capture public attention, no Aboriginal stories in schools. In the short span since then, the pace of change has been remarkable. What Burney has seen makes her convinced the reconciliation process is bigger than John Howard, and that it will outlive his government. She points to Moree, the northern NSW town that most people remember for its racism, the town that infamously banned black kids from its swimming pool, where Charles Perkins and the 1960s 'freedom riders' got into a dust-up with whites when they tried to desegregate it. Now Moree has erected signs proclaiming itself a centre of reconciliation.

'You're humbled by this sort of thing for a town that was so racist,' says Burney. 'The real success of reconciliation is happening at local government level, where people have to live together. What the government in Canberra is missing is the emotional energy, where so many people have made journeys from being redneck to supporting reconciliation absolutely. The business community has moved a long way, and so have many ordinary Australians.'

Burney believes two big reforms are needed before proper reconciliation can happen. First, the inequalities in health, housing and prison incarceration for blacks must be overcome. Second, Australians must accept our history before 1788 as much as since then: there must be constitutional recognition of Aborigines as the first nations. 'This should be accepted as a non-threatening aspect of how Australia sees itself. We're still a long way from this.'

But edging closer. As a symbolic healing of old and painful wounds, reconciliation always had the capacity to become a people's movement, even if political leaders run away from it. Burney says: 'We now have the first generation of Australians who have grown up with the truth: the massacres, the diseases, the stolen children, the stolen land. We grew up not knowing the truth. That's going to have a profound effect. It has increased the resolve of ordinary Australians to keep on with this process. That can't be lost because there's one man in Canberra who can't sign up to this stuff. The resolve is that if the prime minister can't be part of it, other people can.'

Of the Aboriginal achievers I met, one whose personal story touched me deeply was John Moriarty. People had told me he was the richest indigenous Australian, a millionaire several times. He may well be. Moriarty owns an Aboriginal design business, Balarinji, which he runs with his non-indigenous wife, Ros. The company's designs have been painted across two Qantas 747s, and its furnishings, clothes and corporate designs have been sold in America, Japan, Europe, the Middle East and the Caribbean. The business has prospered largely on the strength of this overseas recognition, with recognition following in Australia only later. An example of cultural cringe? Moriarty says: 'Aboriginal design is seen overseas as something absolutely special. A handful of Australians see it like that. But not many. The attitude in Australia is to see it as special only when it's been appreciated overseas.'

Moriarty started the business in Adelaide in 1983 and moved to Sydney 13 years later as it expanded. His studio is now in one of Australia's most historic buildings, the old Customs House at Circular Quay. Outside a plaque marks the spot where Captain Arthur Phillip raised the Union Jack on 26 January 1788. Here was historic resonance: returning in a position of power and strength to the spot where Moriarty's people's oppression began 212 years ago. Just how far Moriarty has travelled is revealed in poignant black-and-white pictures on the studio wall, showing him frolicking as a baby in a dugout canoe with his laughing mother in the Gulf of Carpentaria, where he was born into the Yanyuwa tribe in the 1940s.

Moriarty is a stolen child. When he was four, he was taken from his mother. He was put into an Anglican Church home in Mulgoa, west of Sydney. His mother was not told. She had no idea what had happened to him. They were reunited when he was 15. After his schooling Moriarty became an apprentice fitter and turner. It brought him into contact with 'New Australians', the postwar wave of European immigrants, who taught him to play soccer. Like Mullenjaiwakka, his sporting talents brought him recognition. He was selected for the Australian soccer team. Later he travelled through Europe in pursuit of his soccer career. 'I was able to start thinking I was not a second-class citizen forever, as many Aborigines are conditioned to thinking.'

How does someone with his background, who was needlessly deprived of his mother's love and attention for ten years of his childhood, approach reconciliation? He is not bitter. As a first step, Moriarty believes Australia must learn more of its past if indigenous and non-indigenous Australians are to understand each other. 'We're the oldest living civilisation on earth, yet our system doesn't bring out our tribal and spiritual base. My mother and grandparents died without passing on their knowledge. A lot more people will die with these secrets of what this country is all about. The measure of a good society is to be able to acknowledge the individuals who make up that society.'

A watershed for indigenous Australia was the 1967 referendum, when Australians voted overwhelmingly to end constitutional discrimination against Aborigines and to give the Commonwealth government power to legislate on their affairs. The achievements of Moriarty and others are a sign of how far Australia has come in the relatively short time since then. But behind their stories are sobering statistics that remind Australia of how far it still has to go. Indigenous babies are more than twice as likely to die at birth than non-indigenous babies. More than half the deaths among Aboriginal men happen before the age of 50. Aboriginal people are more likely than others to have reduced mental and emotional wellbeing due to violence, removal from families, poverty and racism, according to the Australian Bureau of Statistics in its 1999 report, *The Health and Welfare of Australia's Aboriginal and Torres Strait Islander Peoples*.

There is still only a handful of indigenous doctors, lawyers and health workers, far too few for a race desperately needing these skills. But advances are happening nevertheless. More than 8,000 Aborigines attend university today, compared with 1,600 in 1990. There are 4,800 Aborigines in apprenticeships, six times the number in 1995. The proportion who stay on at school until the final year, 33 percent, has almost quadrupled since the mid-1970s.

And one who sees hope in these positive signs is Gary Ella, youngest of the three famous Ella rugby brothers. Born in 1960, about a decade before indigenous affairs sprang to the forefront of Australian politics, Ella grew up in an extended family of 12 children in La Perouse, on Botany Bay. Their house had no hot water, one power point and Gary and six other boys shared one bedroom. 'It was fun, but not an easy upbringing.' The sporting prowess the Ella brothers showed at school helped to transform their lives. Gary became manager for Aboriginal and Torres Strait Islander Relations at the Sydney Organising Committee for the Olympic Games. When I talked to him at an inner-Sydney cafe near the Olympics headquarters, he was every image the cool, corporate man.

He reflected how the last 40 years had broadened the opportunities for young Aborigines in sport, how talented athletes had more choice than ever to move from the country to the city. There are now large numbers of Aborigines playing in major city competitions. 'Those players are becoming extremely wealthy and are living very tidy lifestyles.'

Ella said: 'Growing up, I always felt Australia was racist not because people made conscious decisions but it was just instinct. Taxi drivers always asked me where I was from: I couldn't be an Aboriginal person because I sounded educated.

'In the bush these negative images persist. But the reconciliation process has helped to change things by putting more indigenous stories into schools. I spoke on reconciliation at Barker College [a well-to-do private school on Sydney's North Shore] and the kids asked all sorts of questions. It's made kids hungry for knowledge. There's a slow shift from the stereotype image of Aboriginal people being lazy to one of Aborigines achieving things and maintaining links with their culture.

'We have a new confidence in Aboriginal and Torres Strait Islander communities—more confidence about going out and achieving your ambitions and running your businesses successfully. We have a lot more people in that class than we've ever had. That's been a phenomenon of the past 10–15 years. It came about by beating down doors that were closed for a long time, but are now starting to open. Australia as a society has become more open-minded about giving indigenous people a fair go.'

Linda Burney too believes reconciliation will come, despite the inadequacies of the country's political leadership on this. 'Healing in Australia is a profound, long-term and incremental thing,' she says. 'It's about people. It's a tough road, but it's been only ten years out of 212 years. I think we'll get there. It won't be in the next 12 months, it may not be in the next five or six years. But inevitably we'll come to an accommodation, where we're recognised constitutionally and morally as the first people of Australia. This is what reconciliation is about.'

The Stolen Generations
Robert Manne

We encounter, in contemporary politics, two quite different situations both of which rather misleadingly go by a single name—reconciliation.

The first takes place, characteristically, at the end of a bitter and protracted civil war, like that between Protestants and Catholics in Northern Ireland. In such situations both sides have once regarded their cause as pure, their enemy's cause as foul. In the course of their struggle both parties have lied about their own side and the enemy. Both have committed and been the victims of vicious crimes. Eventually both sides have come to accept the futility of further conflict. Both are required to recognise now that justice has not belonged exclusively to their own side. Both must show some contrition. Both must show some capacity to forgive. Both must, in short, accept that the creation of true peace requires more than the laying down of arms. This acceptance draws both sides, after the exhaustion of battle, along the difficult path towards reconciliation.

There is, however, a second kind of process also called reconciliation. It is most purely seen in the contemporary quest for reconciliation between Aboriginal and non-Aboriginal Australia. Here the acts of injustice have come exclusively or almost exclusively from one side alone, as the expression of a radical inequality of military, political, legal, economic and cultural power. Because of this inequality the group with power has dispossessed the powerless of their land. It has destroyed resistance, where necessary by military means. After the dispossession it has surrounded the dispossessed remnant in a system of supposedly protective but in fact astonishingly oppressive law and treated the people whose mode of life it has destroyed with patronising condescension at best and with withering contempt at worst.

During the period of dispossession and its aftermath some members of the powerful group may recognise the injustice of the situation in which they are implicated. With time their numbers grow. Eventually very many members of the group of the powerful may come to feel, in regard to the historical process of dispossession, intense shame. In response to their sense of shame they may begin to seek a reconciliation with the descendants of the dispossessed. This search for reconciliation will differ from the process at the end of a civil war.

Reconciliation between former enemies requires a recognition, on both sides, that acts of injustice have been done. Reconciliation between the powerful and the powerless requires the powerful to acknowledge, without equivocation, that grave injustices have been committed. It requires, however, from the powerless only that they accept the sincerity of the apology, the appropriateness of the acts of reparation, and that they can find it in their hearts to forgive.

Historical understanding and imagination lie at the heart of both kinds of reconciliation. In the reconciliation between former enemies both sides are obliged to revise their national histories, to deconstruct their national myths, to untell their national lies. In the reconciliation between the powerful and the powerless it is the responsibility of the powerful to write into their national histories an understanding of the injustices they have done, or, to put it another way, to incorporate into their own histories the self-understanding of those they have wronged. So long as the political leaders of former enemies after a war resist unpleasant historical truths about their own side reconciliation will not arrive. Similarly while the political leaders of the powerful resist attempts to revise their nation's story in the light of the knowledge of the harm their forebears have done, the prospects for reconciliation with those who have been wronged are dim.

It was only in the early 1990s that the process of reconciliation in Australia gained real momentum. In 1997, as part of this movement, the Human Rights and Equal Opportunity Commission published its report, *Bringing Them Home*, on the question of Aboriginal child removal. In recent times no episode has stirred Australian conscience more deeply than the story of the systematic and frequently forcible removal from their mothers, families and communities of thousands upon thousands of babies and children of mixed Aboriginal-European descent. Among other things, *Bringing Them Home* recommended that the Australian government offer a formal apology to the stolen generation and their families. The Howard government famously refused.

From this moment the political process of reconciliation and the historical question of Aboriginal child removal became intertwined.

What follows is my attempt to outline the history, as accurately as I am able in a limited space, of the policy and practice of Aboriginal child removal in the one area where the Commonwealth government had responsibility, the Northern Territory. It is my conviction that an understanding of the terrible and tragic history of Aboriginal child removal and the general recognition in Australia of what this episode signifies is now one vital element in any quest for reconciliation between Aboriginal and non-Aboriginal Australia. It is towards such an understanding and such a recognition that this essay is aimed.

II

In 1911 the Commonwealth government took over from South Australia the administration of the Northern Territory. It was almost precisely at this moment that the rounding up of 'half-castes'—most usually of children born of Aboriginal mothers and European fathers—began. The policy appears to have been the brain-child of the first Commonwealth chief protector of Aborigines, Dr Herbert Basedow.

His scheme, for the institutionalisation of the Territory's 'half-caste' children at Darwin received strong support from the acting administrator, Samuel James Mitchell. 'In my opinion,' Mitchell wrote to his minister in Canberra, 'one of the first works to be undertaken is to gather in all the 'half-caste' children who are living with Aborigines. The police could do most of this work. No doubt the mothers would object and there would probably be an outcry from well-meaning people about depriving the mother of her child but the future of the children should I think outweigh all other considerations.' The policy course was set.

At its origins some of the most basic ingredients of official thinking over the removal of 'half-caste' children could already be seen. Only the foolish humanitarian could think the grief of an Aboriginal mother at the loss of her child could weigh seriously in the moral scales against the benefit to society and to the child of rescuing it from the prospect of a worthless and degraded life among the blacks. At its origins and over the next 50 years the policy and practice of child removal was grounded in an astonishing indifference to two of the most fundamental of all human needs—the bond of the child to its mother and the rootedness of individual identity in a culture.

Where were these rescued 'half-castes' to go? In the north of the Territory the police protectors, who gathered them in, brought the children to Darwin, at first to the general Aboriginal reserve, the Kahlin Compound; later, from 1924, in order better to segregate the 'half-caste' from the 'full-blood', they were taken to a nearby three-bedroom house.

In what conditions did the 'half-caste' children live? In 1927 the superintendent of Kahlin Compound reported on the new life in the 'half-caste' home. 'The building is not only too small, but it is very much out of repair...the floor is rotten...the shower is out of order...In the kitchen the stove is unfit for use and the sink, together with the table, collapsed, causing all slops to fall on the floor.' Worst of all was the overcrowding. It is difficult to believe but none the less true that by the late 1920s, 76 babies, children and young adults were living in a cottage suitable for a single family. The inmates were locked in for 12 hours or more. Several children slept on the floor. There was no artificial light or entertainment, not even enough knives and forks to go around. An inspector who visited the Darwin Half-Caste Home in 1936, genuinely shocked by what he found, thought the food unfit for human consumption.

In the southern half of the Territory—in the corrugated iron shed known as the Bungalow, erected first in the centre of Alice Springs and then re-erected at Jay's Creek, conditions were even worse. In 1924 a journalist, M.H. Ellis, visited the Bungalow. He described the place as 'a horror' where the souls of 50 human beings were being destroyed. In 1929 the Reverend Davies visited the Bungalow at Jay's Creek. 'The accommodation provided,' he wrote, 'exhausts my power to paint adequately...a very rough framework of wood was put up and some dilapidated sheets of corrugated iron roughly thrown over it...The children...lie on the floor...The ration scale has been deplorable...The whole place makes me boil that such a thing can be tolerated in a Christian country.' It was in this very year that the Commonwealth embraced as its child removal rationale the ambition to elevate the 'half-caste' to the 'standard of the white'.

So seriously was this ambition taken, so concerned were the authorities that the 'half-castes' might revert to their Aboriginal ways, that they strictly forbade all contact between their charges and Aborigines of the 'full-blood.' The superintendent of the Bungalow even attempted to prevent 'half-castes' and 'full-bloods' worshipping together. On behalf of their travelling missionary the Aborigines' Friends' Association protested to the minister:

> We would ask also that the privilege hitherto granted to the representative of the association in visiting the Half-Caste Children's Home at Alice Springs be continued under the new arrangements. By keeping in touch with these native children our representative has been able in his long camel tour to give their mothers some welcome information about them and act as an intermediary between them. Mothers are mothers the world over, and the native women come long distances if they know Mr. Kramer is passing with his camels, to get some information about their children at the home, and it comforts them to have an assurance that they are well looked after by the government.

The child-removal experiment in the Northern Territory caught the attention of no less a figure than the prime minister, Stanley Bruce. In 1927 a letter on his behalf was sent to the premier of South Australia.

> There are at the home at Alice Springs a number of quadroons and octoroons under five years of age who could hardly be distinguished from ordinary white children. My colleague [the minister for home and territories] is assured that, if these babies were removed, at their present early age...to homes in South Australia, they would not know in later life that they had Aboriginal blood and would probably be absorbed into the white population and become useful citizens.

The premier was unconvinced. 'To give effect to this suggestion,' he replied, 'would be greatly to the disadvantage of South Australia...These persons with Aboriginal blood almost invariably mate with the lowest class of whites and, in many cases, the girls become prostitutes.'

In this exchange between the prime minister and the premier, about the future of a handful of stolen children in the Half-Caste Home at Alice Springs—about whether or not the stain of Aboriginal blood could be erased—the alternative versions of Australian racism in the 1920s were rather neatly outlined.

No one endowed the sorry business of child removal with a grander social and geopolitical purpose than the architect of Aboriginal policy in the Northern Territory between 1927 and 1939, the chief protector, the progressivist intellectual, Dr Cecil Cook. During his protectorship no more than 3,000 Europeans were settled in the Territory. They were vastly outnumbered by Aborigines—18,000 'full-bloods' and 800 'half-castes'. Cook was particularly obsessed by the menace posed to White Australia by the 'half-castes'. Anxious brooding on rates of birth convinced him that in one or two generations the Territory's 'half-castes' might outnumber whites. He was also deeply concerned about the fact that some of these 'half-castes' were the result of sexual encounters between Aborigines and those of 'alien' coloured blood. His nightmare vision was of the emergence of a sinister new hybrid race in the north brought about by the intermixing of Aborigines, Asiatics, Pacific Islanders and low-grade Europeans—'multi-colour humanity', he once called it—which would in 50 years overwhelm white civilisation in the Northern Territory.

How was such a nightmare to be averted? Dr Cook's plans were clear. All 'half-caste' children in the Territory's Aboriginal camps would continue to be collected by police and institutionalised in the state-run homes of Darwin and Alice Springs. In these institutions the 'half-castes' were to be segregated from the 'full-bloods'. The girls were to be given a rudimentary education, trained in the domestic arts and released, at age 14 or so, into service in respectable white homes. The boys were to be prepared for work as station hands although, as he sought to achieve with his 'half-caste apprentice regulation', on wage levels equivalent to those of whites, not blacks.

Dr Cook was, however, concerned not only with the social but also the biological future of the 'half-castes' under his control. As chief protector under the Northern Territory ordinance, Cook wielded immense power over the lives of Aborigines, including the right to approve or disapprove marriage. During his protectorship, marriages between 'half-castes' and 'full-bloods' were, in practice, forbidden. More unusually—and for this he became notorious in the Territory and beyond—a vital dimension of Cook's policy was to arrange for the marriage of 'half-caste' girls to European males. In part such marriages would help ease one of the great social problems of the north—the scarcity of available white females. In part it might reduce the incidence of miscegenation in the north—the tendency of young men to seek their sexual pleasures with what was then termed in the Territory 'black velvet'. Most deeply of all, however, Dr Cook's scheme to broker marriages between 'half-caste' females and white males represented in his mind the most promising long-term solution to the 'problem' posed to White Australia by the 'half-caste'.

Dr Cook's thinking here was shaped by the fashionable pseudo-science of eugenics, which taught the virtues of state-engineered human breeding programs. Cook believed that if the state encouraged marriages between 'half-caste' females and white males, eventually, over four or five generations, the stain of Aboriginal blood could be bred out altogether. For Cook and for those who thought as he did, such as the Western Australian protector of Aborigines, A.O. Neville, the prospects of the progressive 'breeding out of colour' were bright. They believed that the Aborigines did not belong to the negroid race but were the remote ancestors of the racial stock of Europe, the Caucasians. Because of this, a systematic interbreeding program of the kind Cook favoured would contain within it no danger of what was called at the time 'atavism' or 'biological throwback'.

Although the public servants in Canberra were somewhat sceptical of the prospect for success of Dr Cook's marriage scheme, whenever necessary the government gave Dr Cook their support. On 25 May 1933 it was officially recorded by the first secretary of the Department of the Interior, J. A. Carrodus, that it was 'the policy of the government...to encourage the marriage of half-castes with whites or half-castes, the object being to "breed out" the colour as far as possible.' In Western Australia Neville was also an enthusiast. On 8 June 1933 the following remarks were given to the press:

> The decision made by the Commonwealth government to adopt as definite policy the encouragement of marriages of white men and half-caste women with a view to raising the standard of

> mixed blood to that of the whites, is nothing new in this state. I have foreseen it for years, and sponsored it as the only outcome of the position. The blacks will have to go white.

At the first ever national conference of Aboriginal administrators, held in Canberra in April 1937, which Dr Cook attended, the most important motion advocated a nation-wide policy for the absorption or biological assimilation of the 'half-caste'. Without such a commitment it would not be merely European settlement in the Northern Territory, as Dr Cook suggested, but the very future of White Australia that would be in doubt. 'Are we,' A.O. Neville inquired of the conference, 'to have a population of 1,000,000 blacks in the Commonwealth or are we going to merge them into our white community and eventually forget that there were any Aborigines in Australia?'

In the world-view of A.O. Neville and Dr Cook, the first move in the policy chain that could achieve the breeding out of colour and thereby the solution to Australia's Aboriginal problem was, precisely, the segregation of the 'half-castes' from the 'full-bloods' by means of the systematic removal of 'half-caste' babies and children from the Aboriginal settlements and camps. Their eugenic solution to 'the problem' of the 'half-caste'—breeding out the colour—represents one of the most shameful moments in the history of the Australian state.

In 1939 the policy and practice of child removal in the Northern Territory changed gear. Dr Cook had always been a fierce opponent of the Christian missions. His successor, the former colonial administrator from Papua New Guinea, E.W.P. Chinnery, was not. In 1940 Chinnery decided to close the government's 'half-caste' homes in Darwin and Alice Springs and to transfer their inmates to a new Roman Catholic home on Melville Island and a new Methodist home on Croker Island.

As it turned out, these plans were interrupted. After the Japanese bombing of Darwin in January 1942, virtually all the 'half-caste' children in the Territory were evacuated south, chiefly to South Australia (where one group was housed in horse stables at Balaklava) and to New South Wales. At the end of the war most of these children returned to the Territory and the practice of child removal resumed. The Christian island homes reopened. In addition, two new 'half-caste' missions were created—the fundamentalist Baptist Retta Dixon Home in Darwin and the Anglican St Mary's Hostel in Alice Springs.

In the Territory's policy and practice of child removal there were, after the end of the Second World War, important elements of both continuity and change. Although the removal of 'half-caste', or what were now being called 'part-Aboriginal', children from Aboriginal settlements or camps continued to be more or less universally practised, one begins to see, in the correspondence of the officials administering the policy, the first signs of troubled conscience and of a dim awareness that the removal of babies or children from their mothers, families and communities might involve considerations of a serious ethical kind.

In mid-1949 the administrator of the Northern Territory, A.R. Driver, was asked to respond to an inquiry of the United Nations Association on the welfare of Aborigines. He conceded that 'certain restrictions' were indeed placed on Aborigines 'even though they are at variance with the complete ideals of the Universal Declaration of Human Rights'. The first such restriction he mentioned (and justified) was 'the removal of part-Aboriginal children'.

Six months later, a senior Territory patrol officer, Ted Evans, was given the job of airlifting five 'half-caste' children from Wave Hill station. 'The removal of the children,' he reported on his return to Darwin 'was accompanied by distressing scenes the like of which I wish never to experience again.' Evans's report appears to have become well-known in Darwin, Canberra and beyond. When an old friend of the Aborigines, Dr Charles Duguid, delivered a speech in Adelaide in October 1951, he described the removal of 'half-caste' babies as 'the most hated task of every patrol officer'.

Duguid's speech sparked considerable public interest. As a consequence, the Menzies government's minister for territories, Paul Hasluck, asked Darwin for more information about child removal. The acting administrator began his reply thus:

> Aboriginals are human beings with the same basic affections that we have and the Aboriginal mother has a real love for her children, especially those of a tender age. We cannot expect the normal Aboriginal mother to appreciate the reason why her part-Aboriginal child should be taken from her.

None of this, of course, caused either Darwin or Canberra to consider that what they were doing was wrong. The new sensibility might have been different from the age of Cook, but the racial condescension still ran very deep.

Hasluck's intervention led to the clearest statement of the Commonwealth's policy regarding Aboriginal child removal in the Northern Territory since the time of Dr Cook. It became official policy that 'partly coloured Aboriginal children' could be removed from settlements or camps so long as the written permission of the director of native affairs was obtained and so long as he considered the removal to be in the best interests of the child. The administrator at Darwin, F.J. Wise, had recommended that no child under the age of four, except where the question of danger arose, should be removed. Hasluck disagreed. 'No age limit need be stated. The younger the child is at the time of the removal the better for the child.'

It was only in 1952 that the question of maternal consent became a matter of official interest. According to the new guidelines, the director of native affairs did not need maternal consent. What he did need was to be convinced that 'a painstaking attempt has been made to explain to the mother the advantages to be gained by the removal of her child'.

This proved an unstable policy base. After 1953 parental consent, frequently a maternal thumbprint, became a requirement before removal. Yet it was at this time a spurious form of consent. In March 1959 the welfare officers of the Territory assembled for a week's conference. The memorandum that followed their meeting spoke, frankly, of the 'strong pressures being brought to bear on the parent to release the child'. It also acknowledged that some of the children who entered the 'half-caste' institutions from the Aboriginal settlements or camps were strictly forbidden from ever returning home, and that, as a consequence, such children lived always with a powerful sense of 'forceful separation from their mothers and families'.

At the end of the 1950s, then, the officers of the Territory, who administered the policy of child removal, admitted in their private deliberations that parental consent was obtained by pressure and that the children experienced their separation as an act of force. They also admitted, in 1957, that the policy pursued in the Territory for almost 50 years had failed. Although the policy of Aboriginal child removal had been, an official in Darwin now argued, 'well-conceived and well executed', it had finally been discovered that as soon as the children left their institutions 'the burdens of their mixed blood heritage' had proved too great. 'Rapid deterioration has flowed—especially in the case of girls'. What, then, was to be done? In its wisdom the government now decided that the 'mixed blood' children (the terminology had changed) should be removed not only from their parents but from the Territory in which they had been born. The children, it was now argued, 'should be given a chance to develop quite normally in southern states where they will pass unnoticed in a community which is conscious of no colour problem.' Perhaps, if they were fortunate, they might be mistaken for an Italian or a Greek. A new chapter in the tragedy of Aboriginal child removal had begun.

III

What, at the end of this story, can we conclude? The following seems to me clear.

For 50 years Aboriginal children of mixed descent were removed from their mothers, families and communities, as a matter of course, often by a process of force. It was only during the 1950s, and then with considerable ambiguity, that the issues of maternal consent or of the evaluation of the life prospects of individual children were even raised.

Throughout this period, in the Northern Territory, the decisions about child removal—which would determine the fate of hundreds of human beings in the Territory, many thousands in Australia as a whole—rested exclusively in the hands of politicians, public servants, policemen and patrol officers. Before the 1950s in the Territory, no legal process was involved.

Throughout this period, the decisions of those who administered the policy did not rest on the need to find or prove negligence or that the children were in danger of harm. It was not from harm that the mixed-descent children were rescued but from their Aboriginality. Or perhaps, to put it differently, it was the fact of their Aboriginality that represented, to the policymakers and implementers, the source of harm.

Throughout this half-century, no doubt, the child removalists sincerely believed that they were acting in the best interests of the child. This did not, however, prevent them from sending children to institutions of utmost squalor in the early period or from turning a blind eye later to the many instances of abuse—of physical beatings, sexual interference, moral humiliation. Even more deeply, the belief that the separation of Aboriginal children from their family and culture was in their best interests was the expression of a racial arrogance that seemed so natural and that went so deep as to be altogether invisible to those whose thoughts and feelings, whose policy and practices, it shaped.

Those who took Aboriginal children from their mothers and communities simply could not see how terrible was an Aboriginal mother's grief at the loss of her child. They simply could not see how terrible was the pain and bewilderment of Aboriginal children at the loss of mother, family and world. It was in this inability to grasp the depth of Aboriginal suffering that the racism of child removal was most clearly expressed.

The Howard government has never made it clear that it accepts, without equivocation, that the policy and practice of Aboriginal child removal was wrong. It is not only that the prime minister has consistently refused the recommendation of the Human Rights and Equal Opportunity Commission to apologise. In 1999 hearings began in earnest in Darwin in a civil action for damages brought against the Commonwealth government by two members of the Territory's stolen children, Lorna Cubillo and Peter Gunner. In his opening address counsel representing the Commonwealth, Douglas Meagher QC, made it clear that his client regarded the motives of those who administered the child removal policy as not merely well-intentioned but also as noble and wise. Shortly after, the minister for Aboriginal affairs, senator Herron, gave the after-dinner address at a conference on Aboriginal politics hosted by *Quadrant* magazine. By so doing he associated himself with a small group which was at the time involved in a campaign to characterise the Aboriginal babies and children taken from their mothers as 'rescued' not 'stolen'. By so doing he associated himself with an editor, P.P. McGuinness, who argued that those Aborigines who now claimed to have been unjustly separated from their mothers and communities by agents of the Commonwealth government or the states were suffering from a kind of collective hysteria, which he diagnosed as 'false memory syndrome'. By so doing the Australian minister for Aboriginal affairs associated himself with a campaign whose purpose was to characterise one of the most terrible instances of human rights abuse in twentieth century Australia as a hoax. When, on 1 April this year, it was revealed that the minister had made a submission to the senate quibbling with the use of the term 'stolen generation' and asserting that a *mere* 10 percent of Aboriginal children had been separated from their families between 1910–1970, it came as no surprise.

The meaning of all this seems clear. In public the Howard government will not apologise to the stolen generations. In court it is willing to defend the policy of Aboriginal child removal as benign. In private many members of the Howard government believe that this indeed is true. The Howard government has shown itself blind to the different kind of racism which animated the policy of child removal both in its earlier eugenic and its later assimilation phase. While a government like this holds power in Australia the prospect of reconciliation—a process which is premised on the general understanding by non-Aboriginal society of the terrible wrongs that have been done to the Aborigines—remains bleak.

Forgive us our Trespasses
Aban Contractor

Reconciliation between black and white Australians is perhaps our greatest challenge. It is not about allocating blame. It is about dealing with our past, warts and all.

And it is made more difficult because Australians know so little about that past, and the bits we do know we do not like. In our hearts we know that the government-sanctioned policy of forcibly removing Aboriginal children of mixed Aboriginal–white parentage from their families to bring them up as white Australians was wrong. We know that it is almost impossible to find an indigenous family not scarred by that policy. We know that if a white child had stood in a black child's shoes, we would, at least in retrospect, have been appalled.

Yet, that policy was law and well-intentioned people helped implement it. Many of those people have been hurt by the stories of the stolen children. The reputations of some, long-since dead, are passionately protected by their children. Sons and daughters, whose parents had lived in poverty while doing God's work in church missions scattered across the outback, cling to old diaries and photos that might provide a clue to a stolen child's past for fear loved ones will be blamed. Now, the gate-keepers of those documents and of the other side of the story are being encouraged to speak. It is a slow process and they are only just coming out of the woodwork.

Ask church leaders how easy it is to convince those people of the need for reconciliation and they freely admit it is a difficult task. A member of the Records Task Force, set up to implement the recommendations made in the Human Rights and Equal Opportunity Commission's *Bringing Them Home* report, says those people feel defensive and intimidated. When church leaders apologised they apologised, at least in part, for the actions of missionaries and other mission workers who had betrayed their duty of care and for participating in what has been shown to be an unjust and destructive practice.

But for members of the stolen generation confident enough to speak publicly about their childhoods, reconciliation is not about them forsaking the church and all they have been taught, nor is it about finding villains. It is about reclaiming their identities as Aborigines and having that respected.

Reverend Dr John Brown of the Uniting Church believes reconciliation begins by acknowledging how others have experienced history: 'In the case of Aboriginal Australians, by imagining how you would feel had those things been done to you.' As part of that process, he says, it is important for those within the church to admit that they did get caught up in a government agenda which preached assimilation. The fact that it was also the ethos of the time and that many in the church agreed with that agenda only made matters worse.

Brown says the push for making one homogenous people was clearly documented. In 1937 Aboriginal 'protectors', the men responsible for Aboriginal policy and its implementation in each of the states, met in Canberra. The Aboriginal protector for Western Australia, Mr A.O. Neville, spelt out how the Aboriginal problem should be dealt with. He believed in the theories of the time, that full-blood Aborigines had weak genes; left to themselves they would die out. The half-castes would not. Aboriginal traditions would therefore survive and the problem be perpetuated for all time. The solution? Take the children from their families and bring them up in a white environment.

Despite the clear implications of that policy, Brown says many in the church believed they were providing opportunities for Aboriginal children; that the way forward was to give them the same opportunities given to other children. 'What happened though was at least a partial blindness to the injustice of removing children by force,' he says. 'In some cases the missionaries didn't know it was happening, but it wasn't all unknowing. The churches failed to perceive the injustice of assimilation and the racism that is implied in that.

'Most missionaries were good people; kind, compassionate and had a sense of justice, but some didn't. And, quite clearly some at least, abused children.'

Many missions helped implement a policy that disparaged Aboriginal culture as inferior and as something that needed to be replaced by all that was Western, modern and Christian.

The auxiliary Catholic bishop of Canberra and Goulburn, Pat Power, agrees. He believes that an important part of reconciliation is admitting to past mistakes, no matter how well-intentioned at the time. To that end, church records need to be handed over so that Aboriginal people can discover their origins and meet their extended families. But, he concedes, the records are not in good shape. *A Piece of the Story*, launched in November 1999, lists 140 different Catholic institutions, many of them no longer in operation. And that was why, Power says, individuals who had kept old journals, appeal letters and maps could be harbouring a valuable source of information and denying someone the possibility of a direct link to his or her past. The ACT Churches Council, working with the Australian Institute of Aboriginal and Torres Strait Islander Studies, is already mapping out how best to access records held by churches and mission organisations; the states are expected to follow suit.

Power knows that former missionaries are in an invidious position. He compares them to Vietnam War veterans, who have also paid the price for implementing in good faith government policies that became intensely unpopular.

Much of the good work done by those missionaries has gone unrecognised, Power says. 'We need to recognise the very real love those people often showed to those youngsters in their care; many genuinely feared they would not survive in the bush.'

There were church members who actively campaigned to improve conditions for local Aborigines. For example, the bishop of North Western Australia, John Frewer, worked tirelessly to raise funds for Aboriginal missions in a diocese that covered an area of 1.5 million square kilometres, despite confronting apathy and opposition among many of the squatters who 'didn't like the church taking an interest in the damned blacks'. And church synods often drew ministers' attention to the 'inadequacy of the monies voted by the government for the welfare of Aborigines'.

According to its 1930 year book, the diocese of Bunbury appealed to the Aborigines Department to increase the number of reserves for Aborigines and to provide them with water, bathing and washing facilities, and proper conveniences. The diocese also protested against the injustice of 'clean and properly clothed Aborigines and half-caste children' being refused entrance to state schools. In the face of public indifference, individual campaigners like the Reverend F. Boxall, were instrumental in forming the Australian Association for the Amelioration of Aborigines. *The Church News* regretfully observed in August 1932 that Boxall—also chief campaigner for Aboriginal aid in the Bunbury diocese—had not been able to arouse enough public opinion to support his cause.

The co-chair of the National Sorry Day Committee, Audrey Kinnear, knows that the path to reconciliation is a difficult one to walk. Taken at the age of four from the Maralinga Lands, she was placed in a mission home some 300 km away. She was 30 when she made contact with her mother, a member of the Yankuntjatjara people. She never knew her white father. The missionaries, she says, treated her well. 'I don't remember any abuse. I know the church thinks we've forsaken them, but we're just reclaiming our identity, trying to find the missing parts in our lives.'

And no matter how kind her carers were, they were not family and she does not believe she was better off.

'We were removed to turn us into whites. We ended up being outcasts in our own land. Displaced, sometimes for life. We can catch up with our families but can't make up for the losses. It takes a lifetime to recover. We were just a bloody nuisance, that was what the Aboriginal people were.'

Musician Helen Moran was taken in 1960 from Condobolin in central New South Wales. She spent her second birthday in an orphanage. Six of her grandparents' 11 grandchildren were taken that year. She and her twin brother were fortunate; they were kept together. Looking back, Moran believes her family needed help and that government intervention was necessary. But she was denied access to her family and her Aboriginality.

When Moran turned 18 she and her foster mother began searching for her biological family. 'I found out I was Aboriginal when a dark-skinned aunty opened the door and told me I was,' she says.

'The court records show we were removed because of neglect...but my parents were living in those conditions, in a little place outside town, to stop us being taken by welfare. We were living in a two-room shack. It was a very vicious circle.'

Moran counts herself among the lucky few. Her foster mother supported her search—travelling with her, paying for things like birth certificates, scouring through cemeteries and church records together. Her foster mother was told Moran's biological father had abandoned her mother, leaving her with six children.

'It was an absolute lie,' Moran says. 'We were taken away by the courts. My foster parents weren't told we were Aboriginal. When the act [governing] information for adoptees was changed in 1990 I got the information...My manila folder just had scrawled on the inside "mother Caucasian, father Aboriginal". That's our only recording of our Aboriginality.'

Again, Moran was lucky; the revelation did not drive a wedge between her and her adopted family. Instead, they were saddened by the deception and grieved for her maternal mother's loss.

Like many Australians, Moran has mixed feelings about the reconciliation process, saying it operates on different levels for different people. She has been touring Australia with Aboriginal singer-songwriter Johnny Huckle, performing at music festivals and indigenous concerts. She is pleased that the church has come out so strongly in favour of the cause. And she, too, has no illusions. It will be a long hard road for all sides.

'The grassroots movement of people is genuine and honest,' she says. 'The healing process has begun. But non-indigenous people and people come from very different places...Aboriginal people are still learning about the stolen generation and learning about their history. There are a lot of mixed blood, half-caste [Aborigines] who still find it difficult to come to terms with rejection from their own people. Who's a real Aborigine and who's not? Urban Aborigines, rural and traditional—they all have their own cultures. But everybody is affected, Aboriginal or not. Everybody has to come to terms with what their forefathers did. Aborigines have to come to terms with their loss and embrace the children that were taken and learn how to be Aborigine in the contemporary world. It's difficult for everybody.'

Like many in the church, Moran and Kinnear are adamant: what happened is not something you just get over; Aborigines cannot simply cut their losses and move on. Only when Australians have a taste of what it was like to be taken can they understand, and only then will the healing process begin.

For Kinnear, who became a nurse and the inaugural chairwoman of the Aboriginal Health Council in South Australia, talking is as good a place to start as any. She says people are almost immune to the stark pictures that appear on their television screens of indigenous Australians living in third-world conditions, and they turn the page when they see yet another stolen children story in the newspapers. But when you talk it makes a difference.

For people like John Bond and Ricki Dargavel, who helped organise Sorry Day on 26 May 1998 and the Journey of Healing in 1999, reconciliation is like coming together after you have had a fight. It is about talking, it is about having the courage to think in new ways, and sometimes it is about the symbolic—memorials to the lost generations, signs that say, 'You are now entering Ngun(n)awal land'. Dargavel tries not to think about what the federal government has and has not done because it only muddies the waters. Bond believes leadership at all levels of government is vital, otherwise, he says, you find yourself marooned in the courts, wasting millions of taxpayer dollars.

'Reconciliation is measurable and achievable,' Bond says. 'If we get it right Aboriginal Australians need not die 20 years younger than white Australians. New Zealand and Canada have made huge progress in the last decade and we could do the same.'

To those who label reconciliation a movement for middle-class, white Australians, Dargavel and Bond say 'take another look'. One million men, women and children have signed their names in Sorry Books across the country, thousands more put their names to a Sea of Hands outside Parliament House in Canberra. Bond says there has been a change in the

Australian mindset, including a recognition that society only truly works when there is a generosity of spirit.

Reverend Brown believes the expressions of sorrow have been genuine and important. 'A whole generation of people, despite what the government has refused to do, have acknowledged that it [the forced removal of Aboriginal children from their families] should not have happened and that there is a continuing aftermath that must be dealt with compassionately and fairly,' he says. 'We didn't know ten years ago about the stolen generation, we didn't know in our guts what had been done to those people. Now we do.'

Reflections on Race and Reconciliation
Lillian Holt

My story is inextricably linked with race and all its ramifications within this magnificent country of ours. Call it what you want—racism, white supremacy—the realities of race in this country have moulded, wounded and informed me. And make no mistake, they have done the same to non-indigenous people. For what has diminished me, as an Aboriginal woman, has also diminished white people. For our journeys are the same; our stories are the same; our histories are the same. And race politics and practices for the past 200-plus years have informed our views of each other. If we can understand that connectedness we are well on the way to healing and reconciliation.

Racial ideas, concepts, practices and policies have disempowered indigenous peoples worldwide, and it is only relatively recently that we are in a position to question its cunning and cruel power play; its insidious effects on us as indigenous people.

Some of these historical legacies are not pretty. Indeed, they are painful. But to deny them is to further deny our integrity and to scar our soul. As Viragina Woolf said: 'You cannot tell the truth about others, until you can tell the truth about yourself.'

John Pilger speaks of 'the secret country'. Secrets keep us sick. We need to open up and share. I believe that only by talking about such issues, strained and strange though they may seem, will we ever set foot on the path to the Wise country, as opposed to merely just the Clever Country.

• • •

I was born on Cherbourg Aboriginal Settlement, Queensland, 55 years ago. I was born there because my paternal grandfather was sent there, in either 1919 or 1922 (the records vary) from a cattle station in central western Queensland. Cherbourg, originally called Barambah, was set up in 1908 for so-called 'disadvantaged or difficult Aborigines'. I'm sure my grandfather was in the latter category, for, as the story goes, he objected to the treatment meted out to my father—a young stockboy—by the local station owner.

My mother was taken to Cherbourg as a very young child from north Queensland. She died in 1987, and to this day, nothing is known of her age nor her relations. There is no written record of her existence on Cherbourg and yet she lived as a young girl and grew up there as a young woman, before getting her exemption certificate. Exemption certificates for Aboriginal people were the rule of the day and both my mother and father received them. In essence, they deemed that one was now 'civilised' enough to live in mainstream society and, in some cases, it was actually stated on the certificate that one was 'no longer an Aborigine'.

Born in 1945, I was a teenager in the sixties. The world was my oyster and I had a whale of a time. There were a few firsts and I was feted; for example, I was the first Aboriginal person to work at the ABC in Queensland. I started there as a fresh-faced 17-year-old in 1962. I worked there for four years, and then began studying. And so began what was for me a life of either studying or working full-time.

The sixties were heady times. Of major significance was the referendum of 1967, a milestone in Aboriginal affairs. I now existed in Australia's eyes.

Yet despite finally being counted as part of the population, it was in the sixties that the realisation of 'difference' began to creep in. Through the actions and attitudes of others—who began to point out my 'otherness', my 'race', my 'difference'—I was gratuitously given the subtle and not so subtle messages of an assuredly white supremacist society. I felt like a stranger in my own land, a curiosity, an exception.

I was completely excluded from the surfie scene, which dominated the era. Surfie girls were, most often, blonde, blue-eyed and white-skinned with slight European noses. Broad noses and brown—let alone black—skin were not encouraged. The surfie look was considered the epitome of beauty. Both boys and girls were bronzed but not too brown and certainly not black! Whitefellas were able to control how tanned they got! Whitefellas, it seemed, were always in control when it came to skin colour—theirs and others.

I was relieved to find that the black struggle in America in the sixties had also identified colour as a major factor in struggle and existence. For as they proclaimed, 'If you're white, that's alright; if you're brown, stick around; if you're black, stay back'. Ever since then I have been acutely aware of a hierarchy of skin colours whereby some colours are more marketable and acceptable than others. Including my own.

Such factors enabled me to survive into the seventies when the Commonwealth government took action. After the referendum of 1967, the 1971 census counted Aboriginal people for the first time. In 1972, the Department of Aboriginal Affairs officially came into existence. Money, policies, platitudes and jobs abounded. The panacea for the 'Aboriginal problem' was pursued, at full pace.

If the sixties were heady days, then the seventies were giddy ones. Institutes for research were founded and experts materialised. People such as myself benefited as I became the first Aboriginal executive officer for the National Aboriginal Education Committee (the education advisory body to the federal government) and then gained an overseas study award to do postgraduate work in the US. I returned in 1980 and became involved in Aboriginal adult and community education, in which I worked for the next 16 years. Once again, the world was seemingly my oyster. Ultimately I progressed to principal where I adapted, advanced, assimilated, aspired—and even, on occasion, was admired.

But something did not quite fit. By the mid to late eighties I was extremely disturbed by the use of deficit language in the endless writings and research about Aboriginal people. Aboriginal people were often portrayed as disadvantaged, handicapped, deprived, etc. A whole 'industry' it seems, was built around deficit terminology which can best be described by the joke about the old, indigenous bloke, sitting on a slag heap, reflecting on life. He says: 'First of all, they said I was primitive, then I was a savage, then a pagan, then a heathen, then uncivilised, then handicapped, then deprived, then culturally deficit, then marginalised, then a victim, then dysfunctional, blah, blah, blah, *ad infinitum.* My position in life hasn't changed but I sure have one hell of a vocabulary.'

By the nineties, it was left to Aborigines to explain to curious, well-meaning, ignorant mainstream Aussies what it was all about. The past had caught up to the present. The governments of the day had failed to offer an explanation of why money was needed in the first place; and that given the historical legacies, there was a need for unequal distribution for equal outcomes. Media releases at the time proudly proclaimed what the government was doing and the huge amount it was costing. But never a hint of why it was needed and why the cost; never a remote allusion to Artistotle's insight: 'The equal treatment of unequals is the most unequal treatment of all.'

Inevitably, a climate of resentment developed, specifically in relation to 'black money'. It started out as a sarcastic trickle and then turned into a torrent. Just when I thought I had played the white man's games, got his accreditation and successfully negotiated his systems, it started. By *it*, I mean the interrogation; the suspicion. Hence, I was frequently asked when I went to a conference: 'Was the government paying for it'? I was asked, sometimes menacingly, whether the college car was a government car; whether I was buying my house, or was it a government house? I was sure that they would not ask a white principal the same questions.

But questions did not have to be asked. The looks, the stares, the glares, the attitudes, were enough. In vain, I searched for that plentiful pot of gold that blackfellas were supposed to be getting. Indeed, I stood up at a conference recently—after listening to whitefellas complain about how much money Aboriginal people are getting—and said that if any whitefella in the audience knew where my share was, I would use it for two purposes: either to go and live overseas to get away from Aboriginal specific racism; or to get a nose job, like Michael Jackson and have my skin whitened, so that I would no longer be 'cosmetically apparent' and would just 'fit in'.

Today, I work in a remote community. It's called a university and the ignorance is alive and well and festering. Platitudes and policies abound about cultural diversity; about migrants and international students and their contribution to this country. Multiculturalism is applauded. (Not that I am opposed to the latter.) But in all the discussion, I have not heard one word about the contribution of Aboriginal people to this country; for example, the pastoral industry being built on the backs of Aboriginal stockmen such as my father and grandfather who worked long hours for which they were paid in rations of bully beef, flour, tea and sugar. Instead, since being there, I have been asked why Aboriginal people should get special privilege: Why do we need a separate centre? Why are there not more Aboriginal doctors and lawyers? Why do not more attend university? Why do they drop out? Why, why, why?

And yes, it is my job to answer questions. Yet the stupidity and rapidity of it all is fatiguing. The amazing array of questions asked with monotonous regularity indicates to me that mainstream Australia does not know its own history. Most non-indigenous Australians do not know about exemption certificates; they do not know that it was official policy for people such as my mother to be educated only to fourth grade as they were considered not capable of anything beyond; they do not know of the apartheid system in missions, settlements and reserves with lights out by ten at night and written permission by the white superintendent to visit the local white town.

This 'not knowing' by whitefellas of what has happened in their own backyards, for yonks, both fascinates and infuriates me. Fascinates me, because such institutional hierarchies are supposed to represent all that is worth knowing. And infuriates me, because often more is known about South Africa and New Zealand and their racial issues than about our own country.

This not knowing has diminished whitefellas. Generational ignorance has left them bereft, regardless of whether it is recognised or not. And I say that in all sadness and kindness. It is this not knowing that creates the ignorance and stereotypes, which we as indigenous people deal with regularly—even daily.

This not knowing seems to be a luxury of white supremacy, which allows people to refrain from the pain of pondering. It allows for filtering, denying and discarding that which is uncomfortable; and there is no doubt that Aboriginal existence in this country has been and continues to be too uncomfortable for most to contemplate. As Sister Veronica Brady says, Aboriginal people are the shadow side of white Australia, which is afraid to look because of guilt, shame, blame, anger, defence. Yet, in looking, in interrogation lies liberation, as my closest white friends have attested. And with liberation can come reconciliation.

Thus, if we are to have a true reconciliation, I believe there is mammoth work to be done. Not so much on the outside but on the inside. For too long only the structural has been addressed and now it needs to be accompanied by the spiritual.

The time has come, I believe, for 'physician, heal thyself'. But in order to heal oneself, one first has to *know* oneself. One has to know one's history —warts and all. There is an old Russian proverb which says: 'Dwell in the past and you lose one eye, forget the past and you lose both'. I am saddened that the past has been conveniently and consciously or unconsciously forgotten, of late, in recent debate. For I believe that the past informs the present and the present informs the future. The past can be used as a revered elder or tutor to the young present.

After 25 years of official government policies and structure of one sort or another, there is currently a strange impasse—crisis, even—in race relations in this country. In the past decade I have felt the mean spirit of attitudes in this country in a way I have never felt it before. And I believe, rightly or wrongly, that it has to do with the virulent ignorance and arrogance of white supremacy. If you do not believe that white supremacy exists, there is an easy way to test it: go and mix with Aboriginal people. Not for just a day or a week or a month. The longer, the better and the more obviously Aboriginal-looking they are, the better. Hang out with them, walk with them in the streets and accompany them into shops, pubs, and public places. Then wait for the reactions of other whitefellas to yourself and to the Aborigines you are with. Try it. I urge you. For you will learn something not only about yourself but about your own mob, who will most often see you as a 'race traitor'.

Most of my best white friends tell me that the only way they learned about white supremacy in this country was through mixing with Aborigines. A kind of 'learning by proximity' or absorption. They tell me that their encounter was a healthy and liberating one as they were able to 'interrogate their own oppression' as whitefellas. For I believe that unless we go beyond the mask and dig deep, it will remain a superficial encounter. Kissing and making up doesn't really matter unless you deal with what you came to fisticuffs over in the first place. And as for 'sorry', if it's not heartfelt, then it means nothing, as far as I am concerned. All sorts of people say sorry and, at worst, not mean it, or, at best, continue the behaviour. I'd rather have a whitefella say to me, 'I have awoken to myself, my own spirit, my own dispossession. I am prepared to look at myself and not just you.'

I think that the time has come for Australia as a nation, to do just this. Maturity can be part of the new millennium. We in Australia are superbly situated to embark on such a journey. For it is a young country of European occupation coupled with an ancient ancestry of Aboriginality and is blessed with an abundant and accommodating landscape.

There are no innocent bystanders in our mutual history. On the other hand, neither should there be any terrified ones. We can all make a stain on the silence. It was Adrienne Rich, the American writer, who said: 'You can lie with words, but you can also lie with silence.'

An Opening to New Seasons
Tim Costello

I grew up in Blackburn in the eastern suburbs of Melbourne. Though I cannot identify any particular person who uttered the precise words, I remember it being said that Aborigines were 'stupid, dirty and lazy'. More disturbing is the recollection that those sentiments seemed to be widely shared by many of the adults I knew and respected.

Nevertheless there was considerable concern in churches including my own for Aboriginal people. The work of the Aboriginal Inland Mission (AIM) and the United Aboriginal Mission (UAM) with these 'ancient primitive people', as we then described them, was very familiar to us. We prayed for the missionaries and for conversion of the Aboriginal recipients of the gospel. We had missionary deputations to our church who showed us slides of indigenous peoples, said to have come from a tribal state where they had been captured by fear of evil spirits and 'witch doctors', but who had subsequently 'yielded their lives to Christ'.

Most exciting was when one of our church families adopted a 'full-blood' Aboriginal girl. We were encouraged to admire the care and compassion of the adoptive parents who had taken on this responsibility, and would provide an education and Christian training.

Indeed Joy's arrival was a landmark event for our church at Blackburn. There were no other ethnic groups represented there and the term 'multiculturalism' had not even been coined; indeed, the only foreign-sounding name I knew when growing up was 'Barassi'. But sadly, Joy, who seemed to 'enjoy' family life for a short time, 'ran amok'.

In prudent tones it was explained to us that she had gone 'walkabout', a manifestation of a restlessness which was understood to course through her very veins. We were never told what happened to Joy except that something foreboding had occurred.

It certainly never occurred to me or to those growing up in our church that we had occupied and finally appropriated Aboriginal land. The sense of wrong flowed in one direction: Aborigines were sometimes hostile and unwilling to appreciate the enormous benefits offered to them by the missionary schools, health services and churches. How could they be so ungrateful?

As I write this piece I am glad at least to be able to celebrate that some small steps toward reconciliation have been taken since those myopic days. My own children and their friends are not growing up with those particular attitudes. Happily in the last 30 years there has been an extraordinary shift in what we say to our children about Aboriginal peoples. Our kids now learn to respect the way our indigenes knew how to survive on one of the harshest continents on earth. Their ecological harmony with this awesome continent is a thing of wonder and it attracts our admiration. Also my children have grown up knowing that, thanks to the Mabo decision of 1992, Aboriginal land and title has been found in a court to have survived the European settlement which began in 1788.

But despite the distance between these two snapshots of family attitudes there is still a long way to go on our journey of reconciliation. A more recent step has been an improvement in our readiness to hear the cry of the Aboriginal people whom we have so systematically oppressed. Some of it has been clearly articulated in the *Bringing Them Home* report which describes the removal of Aboriginal children from their homes as recently as the 1950s. The tears shed by some federal politicians eloquently touched a nerve for many of us and we went on to weep in private after reading that remarkable report.

One of the earliest recorded stories in the Hebrew scriptures is that of God hearing and responding to the cry of slaves in ancient Egypt. Liberation begins with hearing aright, and we can be glad that, as we have been taught in the Exodus story, we have begun as a nation to hear the cry of our indigenous peoples and to honour their anguish. With Norman Habel in his book called *Reconciliation: Searching for Australia's Soul*, we have all come to understand that no serious reconciliation is possible until the suppressed stories are told in public, especially by the oppressed party, and the underlying source of the alienation is exposed.

But after this 'truth principle', Habel speaks of the 'justice principle' which is also inherent in any reconciliation process. In his book *Exclusion and Embrace*, published in 1996, Miroslav Volf examines the problems of justice-seeking in admirable detail. He points to the mistakes of Christians who have judged 'between cultures with [what they claimed was] divine infallibility'. He draws attention to the fact that Christian groups in Europe have continued to fight 'one another bitterly over the beliefs they claimed were directly revealed by God'. Volf also examines the Kantian view that universal justice can be based on pure reason and the view of Rawls that it can be discovered through a consensus of all reasonable people. He finds that both these approaches always situate 'justice within a particular vision of the good life', and hence they cannot indicate the route to true justice any more than can a divinely-inspired text.

Volf finds unsatisfactory even the postmodern view that an acceptance of 'radical difference' is the only route to justice. He argues that this leaves us unable to discriminate the 'weeds' of justice-seeking from the 'flowers', and it takes away our motivation to struggle against injustice. He agrees with Alasdaire McIntyre's claim that all views of justice need to be seen in the context of their 'traditions' because they mitigate against the sterile exchange of assertions and counter assertions, and because they can provide resources for settling disputes about where true justice lies. But even in this view Volf sees danger because any tradition will tend to want to prove itself more rational than the next.

I have quoted Volf's deliberations in some detail because I like his conclusions which focus on the use of the word 'embrace'. He points out that the Christian tradition is never pure, but that it embraces a number of views of justice, and 'represents a merging of streams coming from the Scriptures and from given cultures that a particular church inhabits'. Even the early Christians 'lived and thrived without the secure closure of a system; [so] there is no reason why we cannot do the same'. We should be open to 'discordant worlds that all project multiple voices into the same space'. Volf suggests that we can enlarge our thinking by letting the voices of others 'resonate within ourselves' so that at least competing justices have a chance to become 'converging justices'.

So that there are good theological grounds for endorsing the 'double vision' that may result from such an 'enlarged way of thinking', Volf reminds us of the story of Jesus (a Jew) and his encounter with the Syrophoenician woman which begins with his refusal to heal her daughter because she was a Gentile. She then successfully challenges him to extend his mercy beyond 'the lost sheep of the house of Israel', and immediately after this event, Jesus begins to express His own double vision by healing and feeding the Gentile crowds. Volf remembers how Dietrich Bonnhoeffer has told us that faith enables us to 'take into ourselves the polyphony of life, instead of pressing life to "a single dimension."'

But this 'double vision' is not easy to achieve, and this is where the concept of the 'embrace' comes in. We need to do justice and that is more important than any mere reflection on justice; so, as we struggle to do justice, what we need is to see it 'through the eyes of the other—even the manifestly unjust other—and be willing to readjust our understanding of justice and repent of acts of injustice': certainly we must always sustain an 'initial suspicion against the perspective of the powerful', but both sides must be willing to 'embrace the other' if we are to practise the 'double vision' required of true justice-seeking.

In order 'to agree on justice you need to make space in yourself for the perspective of the other, and in order to make space, you need to want to embrace the other'. 'I am not', Volf continues, 'talking about soft mercy tampering harsh justice, but about love shaping the very content of justice'. God treats us as family. In the Hebrew scriptures we hear about his relationship with the people of Israel, and in the gospels we hear about the father who quite unjustly throws a party for the return of his prodigal son. This is the embrace at work.

Using the work of Carol Gilligan, Volf points out that, 'If our identities are shaped in interaction with others, and if we are called ultimately to belong together, then we need to shift the concept of justice away from an exclusive stress on making detached judgements and toward sustaining relationships, away from blind impartiality and toward sensibility for differences.' Volf settles for a justice which, alongside the grand prophetic vision of it 'rolling down like a river', we take 'small steps' toward learning to live together, embracing the other whilst keeping true to ourselves.

And so, we might ask, where do we go, and what sort of small practical steps can we take? One impressive attempt to achieve Volf's 'double vision' in my own city of Melbourne has been the development of a walking trail. A number of well-known sites in Melbourne are described in a booklet for the trail. Called *Another View*, it is written by the Aboriginal research/writer, Robert Mate Mate. He tells how for hundreds of generations the Kulin people lived as hunters and gatherers on the banks of the Yarra Yarra River, moving to the Dandenong Ranges in the winter, and how the 'site selected by the first settlers for the village of Melbourne was precisely the place most favoured by the Kulin for interclan gatherings.'

It is certainly a shock to see in our mind's eye the corner of Collins and Spencer Streets in Melbourne as the booklet describes it, 'once covered with she-oak trees and...traditionally the borderline between the Woiworung and the Bunerong tribes of the Kulin nation'. The tribespeople wore possum skin cloaks, each comprising about eighteen skins. 'The inner side of the pelt would be scraped clean with a mussel shell and when dry incised with lines to make it more flexible'. And at Kings Domain near the Botanic Gardens, we learn that there are the skeletal remains of 38 Aboriginal people under a large granite rock marked by the National Aboriginal Flag. Until 1988, these remains had been locked in a vault in the State Museum of Victoria. The artwork which accompanies the trail has a 'cluster of five painted ghostlike Eucalypt poles, adorned with the spirit people, the Rainbow Serpent and the red ribbons' in honour of the Aboriginal people of Unungan (Victoria).

I was delighted to discover the existence of this trail and intend to arrange for my congregation to further embrace their double vision by seeing these sites through Aboriginal eyes. We can so easily think that this new vision is merely quaint, but as we let it 'resonate' within us, we begin to welcome the unexpected insights it brings. For instance a recent paper printed in Museum Victoria's internal newsletter, *The Horse's Mouth*, was brought to my attention after a colleague heard Gary Presland speak at the East Melbourne Historical Society. It points out that our insistence on four seasons—summer, autumn, winter and spring—derives from European ancestral landscapes, and perpetuates an inappropriate myth in Australia. Not surprisingly, in Kakadu National Park, Aboriginal knowledge of nature's cues and cycles has been substituted and used as a landscape management tool.

By working closely with the Wurundjeri Aboriginal community at Healesville, a group of landscape architecture students and staff, particularly David Jones (the author of the *Horse's Mouth* article) have developed a model of five seasons with two variations to accommodate the flood and fire cycles in the Upper Yarra Valley. These seasons are marked by such things as the presence of active female butterflies, or the croaking of Growling Grass frogs. This kind of seasonal sensitivity could bring us much closer to our true climatic cycles than can any European four-season model. The latter only leaves us to be reliably disappointed each year with our failure to experience the dramatic turn of seasons which is deeply embedded in our psyche from our reading of English literature. If we want to embrace this land, we urgently need to achieve some double vision by allowing the Aboriginal seasons, which are responsive to what really happens around us, to resonate within.

But when all's said and done, how difficult is reconciliation really going to be? It can sound difficult when we speak of Volf's 'double vision', but taking another perspective, we are all members of the same species, and recent analyses of genetic findings suggest that we are much more alike than we are different. As Kelly Owens and Mary-Claire King point out in their article in *Science*, October, 1999, 'The possibility that human history has been characterised by genetically relatively homogeneous groups ('races'), distinguished by major biological differences, is not consistent with genetic evidence.' They tell us that skin and hair colour and facial traits are 'quite literally superficial, in that they affect exposed surfaces of the body', and that they involve 'limited numbers of genes with very specific physiological effects'. More than 80 percent of genetic variation is between individuals of the same population, and only ten percent of human genetic diversity occurs between populations from different continents. They conclude that the notion that there are major genetic differences across 'races' is nothing but a myth which has caused incalculable suffering.

When we extrapolate from such genetic findings, we realise that the enormous gap we non-indigenous Australians expect to find when relating to an Aboriginal person is simply not there. This is because only a very small amount of human variation is described by the superficial differences of appearance, the ones which we use to 'recognise' an Aboriginal person. As described in my recent book, *Tips from a Travelling Soul-Searcher* I have found, even sitting in a circle on the earth under a strong sun in central Australia, that it was easy to find common ground with Aboriginal colleagues who have chosen to remain living psychologically and geographically far from the busy towns of the eastern seabord.

I was recently asked to suggest a symbol for the new millennium. I chose Uluru, as my family had only recently journeyed together to see it for the first time. But since then I have read of Norm Habel's choice of it as a symbol of reconciliation as well. I can do no better than to quote him as he says, 'The rock—the symbol of the centre, the place of sacred power but also the place of historical shame—an indigenous golgotha. The stolen children—the symbol of human suffering, indigenous pathos and deep healing, the symbol with whom many non-indigenous Australians now identify—an indigenous suffering servant. The land—…an indigenous holy land.'

The single vision with which my church saw Joy can never return. I live in hope that my own children will learn to practise Volf's 'double vision' as they work and live with all people but especially those who identify as Aboriginal. I pray that they may eventually experience the true embrace of a reconciled Australia.

A Bitter Wind
Drusilla Modjeska

In the winter of 1997 I was asked to give the formal after-dinner speech at the NSW Premier's Literary Awards. It was to be a celebratory occasion with guests gathered in praise of good writing and I did not want to dampen the evening by taking up a sombre issue. Yet it seemed to me that I could not speak publicly on the subject of writers and writing without reference to the painful events that were unfolding in the wake of the report of the national inquiry into the separation from their families of the generations that we have come to know as stolen.

All that winter I had been living quietly, writing each day and following public events on the radio and in the press. As I say in the speech, I felt that when historians come to look back on that year, the writing that would be best remembered would not be the literary works we were there to celebrate, but the testimony of the separated children. I was particularly aware of the perspective of history as I was myself writing about the past, and much of that winter had been immersed in the First World War. Or rather, in the lives of artists—then young women—who lived through the bitter divide of that war. Political events can and do affect even the most private and domestic aspects of our lives; I could see it in their past and feel it in my present. The question that presented itself and to which I turned my attention that night was how, as writers, we might make sense of a shared and painful history, for which we were not responsible but in which we are nevertheless implicated, without losing sight of the value of what we do.

March, 2000

• • •

The European winter of 1914 was famously bad. As the troops dug in for a war that the hopeful were still hoping would be over by Christmas, Virginia Woolf wrote to Violet Dickinson that, 'There is a bitter wind directly one gets out beyond the trees.' And in her diary she wrote during yet another *great downpour*: 'I am sure however many years I keep this diary, I shall never find a winter to beat this. It seems to have lost all self-control.'

It is at one's peril that one draws too close a parallel between a meteorological and a political climate, but I was thinking of that bitter European winter as sleety rain rattled the windows and thunder rumbled and roared around the edges of our city earlier this winter, great clouds hanging over the ocean. As it happens I had been writing about the Great War, about the way it pushed and shoved at writers and artists. Virginia Woolf, who's always good for a quote, said that after it was over nothing could be written about in the same way; not even a strawberry on a plate could appear as it had appeared before that savage war.

Now we're not at war, and I'm not suggesting that we are, but it seemed to me during this unusually bad winter, when it was indeed bitter once one got beyond the trees, that this too is a time of upheaval and conflict in which ways of thinking, and perhaps even of writing, are being challenged and changed in the most painful ways. I am sure I am not the only one to have had the sensation of waking up to find myself in an Australia I barely recognise. Or rather, more to the point, an Australia I would rather not recognise. In a rhetorical climate in which we are daily encouraged into the most selfish and defensive forms of individualism, when sentiment parades as feeling, and productivity matters more than morality, I find myself fierce in defence of old-fashioned and slightly embarrassing words like *community* and *responsibility*, and also confronted by what, beyond the rhetorical flourish, might be meant by them.

In this climate, it seems to me that the most important book—if not the best—that has been published this cold and chilly winter has been *Bringing Them Home*, the report of the national inquiry into the separation of Aboriginal children from their families. If I were a betting man, as my father used to say, I'd bet that this is the book that will be remembered by the historians of the future when it comes to writing the narrative of this divided moment in our culture; for the story of those children, and the struggle for land that surrounds it, is like an open wound through our history. It is a story that demands absolutely that we attend to words like community, and responsibility. And morality. And shame. And apology. So powerful is their story that if I were given to poetry, which I am not, I might think the skies were weeping and the thunder rumbling as this great land of ours rolled and heaved to shake us into remembering that there are forces at work here much greater than our small and greedy selves.

Talking of poetry, there is a wonderful poem by the American poet Edna St Vincent Millay which I discovered for the first time this winter:

> To what purpose, April, do you return again?
> Beauty is not enough.
> You can no longer quiet me with the redness
> Of little leaves opening stickily.
> I know what I know.
> The sun is hot on my neck as I observe
> The spikes of the crocus.
> The smell of the earth is good.
> It is apparent that there is no death.
> But what does that signify?
> Not only under ground are the brains of men
> Eaten by maggots.
> Life in itself
> Is nothing,
> An empty cup, a flight of uncarpeted stairs.
> It is not enough that yearly, down this hill,
> April
> Comes like an idiot, babbling and strewing flowers.

She wrote this poem, as it happens, at the end of the Great War, and published it in 1921, seven years after Virginia Woolf's great downpour of a winter. She had reason to know what she knew. I am reading it to you now because it says in a few elegant lines what I am struggling to say in several pages. And I read it to you because it brings us back to the realm of feeling and image and language, which is after all our stock in trade.

So if we are to speak of language, let us consider two tricky words that have been getting a good deal of use lately: *guilt* and *shame*. There's been a lot of slippage from one to the other, a lot of dodging and frank dishonesty. And a chronic lack of discrimination.

The prime minister has been at pains to point out that we ourselves personally are not responsible for stealing the children; it was enacted by previous generations. Leaving aside exactly when this practice stopped, and leaving aside the quite astounding statistic that as recently as 1993, two percent of our Aboriginal children were 'in care' compared to 0.2 percent of our non-indigenous children, let us think for a moment about this question of guilt. It is probably true that most of us in this room tonight, in our bookishness, have relatively comfortable consciences when it comes to active, knowing acts of racism. Probably. By the same token I doubt that I am the only one to feel a complex and disturbing set of emotions, not least of which is shame.

Guilt is not the same as shame, and trying to get out of one doesn't let us out of the other. Guilt, an emotion drummed into many of us by a Eurocentric god, operates in the realm of personal breach. We are guilty of those things we have done that we ought not to have done. Some of those guilts are imposed on us; others keep us awake at night.

Shame, on the other hand, operates in the realm of honour and dishonour, responsibility and our common humanity. A nation can be shamed, or a tribe, or a family, or a child. Shame can be imposed on others, and can be brought on oneself. And while guilt is often limiting in that it focuses on individual acts of wrong-doing, shame can be a spur back into a common humanity, if not community, by the recognition of forces much greater than our small guilty selves. I think it was Robert Manne who said that the prime minister's refusal to apologise was a lost opportunity in the spiritual development of the nation. For recognition of the shadowy side of life, of our capacity for cruelty and our own ugly impulses, our flawed past, can make way for integration as well as reconciliation. Generosity is a good antidote to shame, and until we find it in ourselves to step forward as white Australians and face that shame, none of us can sleep easily on this continent, or claim the riches that are also in our past.

As Edna St Vincent Millay helps us realise, spring is *more* potent, not less, for allowing into it the knowledge of maggots and death, of rot and decay. If we cannot understand this, we are left like idiots, babbling and strewing flowers, as if there were no death, as if there were no dark side to our history. As if it weren't up to us how the cup is filled, or that flight of stairs carpeted. As if we had no choice.

In July this year, on a day when the sun had put in one of its rare appearances this winter, a meeting was held here in Sydney for women to join together under the banner of *Women for Wik*. Three women spoke at that meeting of their own experience: Lowitja O'Donoghue, Jean Carter and Marlene Wilson.

They spoke with the kind of articulate simplicity writers would die for, about their experience as young children suddenly taken from their mothers. They told stories similar to those we read in *Bringing Them Home*, of mothers running behind welfare cars, weeping outside police lockups, of being turned away from the institutions that housed their children. In Jean Carter's story, the car was outside the house when the children came home from school and they weren't even allowed inside to say goodbye.

A great deal moved me, as it did every other woman in that room, about the stories and the way in which they were told. Over and above everything else I was deeply struck by the strength and open-heartedness of the women telling their stories. They were fierce, in that they understood absolutely the travesty of all that had happened to them, but they were not bitter, or hostile, or sentimental. And they were certainly not defeated. In their different ways they are all formidable women. And in that strength they left open, wide open, the possibility of reconciliation. Where is our strength to meet theirs? When can someone like me, speaking on an occasion like this, use the word community to mean all of us without having to dodge through the thicket of pronouns—us, them; you, me—thereby perpetuating the divide one wishes to speak against. When can we, any of us, say *us* to mean all of us without falling into a chasm of uncertainty. Who speaks in whose name?

When we left the meeting, the friend I was with, who had grown up here in the fifties, said that she was thinking of all those Germans who kept saying they didn't know anything. She says she remembers, a wispy sort of child memory, that she did know, and when she inquired she was told, 'oh well, they're orphans', or 'they're neglected', or 'they're getting an education'. In other words, there was a gloss; the stories a white Australian child was told were of buds stickily opening. Why is it so hard for us to tell ourselves, and our children, the truth?

I didn't grow up here, but that doesn't absolve me of anything, and having grown up in the south of England in a family that had a good splattering of uncles in the Indian Civil Service of the Raj, I'm hardly in a position to say anything about anything. But the moment at which I felt an acute sense of personal shame, or perhaps I should say the moment at which I felt the stir of history, as if a dark bird had flown over me and I'd been cast in its shadow, was when Jean Carter spoke of being born on the salt pan at George's River. I felt it as a shock: the enormous disjuncture between her Sydney and mine. And I felt it most uncomfortably when she and Marlene Wilson both talked about being taken to Bidura Children's Home in Glebe, where they were dipped in lye and had their clothes removed with tongs; and when they talked of walking along Glebe Point Road, calling out to the boys in their crocodile on the opposite pavement for news of their brothers.

I lived in Glebe when I first came to Sydney, 25 years ago now; I was a student on the then generous Commonwealth Scholarship, with no need to work anywhere other than in the library. You could still rent a room for ten dollars, food was cheap, it was the seventies, we all had heaps of love affairs and nobody locked their back doors. Glebe was heaven. To me. And almost certainly to the Eora people who lived on Blackwattle Bay in 1787. But not to the children in Bidura which was there when I was a student; we walked past it, smooching along with books under our arms. And it certainly wasn't heaven for Jean Carter and Marlene Wilson who were there not so many years before, for no other reason than the colour of their skin, separated from family, mother, culture, land.

It is a shameful story, and we will all feel it in different ways. I felt it that day as if another map had been laid over streets I'd mapped for myself in the most egocentric and naive of ways.

I felt it also last year when in celebration of turning 50 I went with a friend similarly afflicted to the Kimberley. It was the first time I had been into red Australia and it was the first time I had visited an Aboriginal community. That this is possible for someone like me after so many years in this country is a comment in itself. I won't berate myself for that. But I will say that we stood at Long Arm Point on the southern head of King Sound with the silent houses behind us and the roar of the tide in front of us, looking across to islands of rock-bleached white in the Sound, as inhospitable as a Gulag. The awesomeness we felt was not just for the grandeur of the land, but the weight of history pressing. As we drove inland into the red Kimberley, through a landscape we saw as Fred Williams and the descendants of its original inhabitants see as peopled with fabulous mythological beasts and animals, we traced the history of massacres, of pens that were built under the scarp to collect the tribespeople who were taken in chains to Derby and Broome. And we slept on Ngarinyin land with the stars as companions and the bush, bright in moonlight, casting shadows as troubling as ghosts across our swags.

When I accepted this invitation to speak tonight, I thought about how to speak at an event that is after all in celebration of the best of this year's writing, and the question that posed itself was how to celebrate at this moment of shame, when there is division all around us, and so much is unresolved. It was Edna St Vincent Millay who showed me the way through. Rather than pretend there is no shadow, we need—or at any rate I need—to attend to it and allow it into the celebration, to feel it weighty in our hands, and in our hearts.

When I look at the shortlist for tonight's awards, I see that there is a lot to celebrate. There are the familiar names that have already done so much to carpet the stairs: Thea Astley, Rob Drewe, Les Murray, Peter Porter. And I see Peter Read's name and think he should be speaking and not me because he is one of the few who've tackled the questions direct. And I see the roll call of historians with their thoughtful perspectives on ideas, and the past; and Barbara Blackman and Mark Raphael Baker, with their vastly different stories, who share in common the desire to integrate personal memory and public history. And with particular pleasure I see the names of Alison Clark and Robert Dessaix, whose strong voices come from knowing the chill wind that blows out there past the trees. And the new names of Sallie Muirden and young Emma Lew who, if I were that betting man, I'd say will both one day be familiar, though I hope neither of them stop being surprising. All of them, all of you, all of us, are mapping and remapping our streets, our country, our past. It's what writers, at their best, have always done. And that too should be celebrated.

I think of Katharine Susannah Pritchard with *Coonardoo* that won a prestigious prize in 1929 and then couldn't be serialised in the *Bulletin* as the story of a white man's love for a black woman, and the tragic consequences of her disinheritance, was considered too shocking for the Australian reading public. I think of Christina Stead in whose name a prize is to be awarded tonight, and the years she spent in poverty and personal despair struggling to find publishers and an audience during the Cold War when everything she stood for was reviled. And I think of Patrick White up at Dogwoods, coming into town to the fancy parties with oranges in his string bag. I think of Oodgeroo Noonuccal who was given the name Kath Walker and deprived of her language. I think of Faith Bandler, queenly at the reconciliation conference a few months ago, berating the government as *wicked, wicked, wicked*, as the stolen generation report was published and the prime minister was insisting on the emptiness of symbolic gestures. And I think of Dorothy Green, in whose name there is no prize, and the lesson she taught those of us who knew her and read her and were taught by her, that if there is any hope for any of us, thinking and feeling must be brought back into relationship with each other, so that thought is fully felt, and feeling given the rigour of thought. We must feel, not deny, our history, and give our feelings a just and tangible, well-thought shape. No soft options either way. No babbling idiots strewing flowers.

And maybe that historian of the future who will remember this year by the stolen generation report will be up here winning a prize when we are all dead and gone, and if she is, maybe she will glance our way, and say that this was a good year for writing, 1997, and a good decade. She might even remember Virginia Woolf and her strawberry on a plate, and say there are moments, and maybe this is one of them, when change comes like a blast of chilly air, and maybe for her it will be easier to honour everyone, black and white, old and young, man and woman, who is out there past the tree line. Maybe for her *us* will be just another pronoun. I am being optimistic. But then, it is, after all, an occasion of celebration, and just imagine, if you can bear to, what the alternative would be.

Aboriginal Disadvantage
Noel Pearson

Lest I be promptly if discreetly arrested by comrades from the left and condemned to some remote Gulag, let me first tell you my starting point. My first concern lies with the situation and prospects of the marginal and dispossessed in this country. My anxiety stems from the primal belief that we all have a right to a fair share of the common wealth of this country. It also stems from an obligation which those who come from outsider communities cannot easily escape—a sense of responsibility for the future of my mob.

Like my elders and colleagues in Cape York, I am worried for my mob. Our situation is not good and our future not bright. I am anxious about the rising inequality that threatens the future of my people, as I am about the growing numbers who are joining my people in the formation of an Australian underclass. Not only must we strive to arrest this rising inequality, we must ensure that our people eventually get our fair share.

However, there are so few new ideas about how this noble, grand and long-held objective might actually be achieved. We seem to just hold on to our ideals as a matter of philosophy and intellectual debate in the academies whilst the real society and economy unravels in front of our eyes, driven by the public policy ascendancy of those who accept that the growth of an underclass is an unfortunate but inevitable result of larger economic forces about which nothing can be done.

We need to focus on locations. We need to work on locations. We need to devise strategies for places. We need to encourage, stimulate and organise around places. We need to apply ourselves to the predicaments and opportunities of locations.

Let me be parochial. We need to encourage fidelity to and reinvestment in our home locations. On this last point, let me speak to people who come from the other side of the tracks. The abandonment of our mob by the meritocratic left as we rise up in the world is a shameful tendency. How are dismal places going to develop if their success stories not only pack up and move uptown but tragically never look back? We have to, at the least, worry for home and maintain a life-long interest and contribution to its wellbeing.

Mark Latham[1] has pointed out all too clearly the fact that advantage and disadvantage invariably centre on place and that locational disparities in Australia are on the increase. The location and people I worry about are the indigenous community of Cape York Peninsula, being the former missions and fringe communities north of Cairns.

Our parlous economic and social situation is notorious; you have all heard the statistics that are so outrageous that they are routinely greeted with numb acceptance.

Imagine if the average life expectancy of the town of Gatton was only 50 years and sliding. Imagine if the population of Cairns was in prison to the same proportion as the people of Hopevale or Arrakun or Lockhart River. Imagine if over 38 percent of the 15 to 45-year-olds in the town of Atherton had a sexually transmitted disease. Imagine if kidney or liver failures or heart disease were proportionally the same for Gympie as it is for Cape York. Would we be as numb and complacent about the statistics as we are when faced with the reality of the social disaster of Aboriginal society on Cape York Peninsula? No. There would be nothing less than a state of emergency. The government initiatives that had prevailed and failed hitherto would be fundamentally questioned and radically revisited. Government would allocate political energy and resources as a matter of disaster relief priority.

That the social situation of Cape York has displayed these steadily worsening statistics for more than two decades now makes even more horrific our failure to have any policy clue or to have developed any even vaguely urgent initiative that discloses some understanding that there is a social crisis. The problems are so overwhelming that even the Aboriginal society comes to accept its own state of dysfunction.

The creation of the welfare state is one of the great civilising achievements of our democracy. It gave expression to our social responsibility towards others in society—the aged, the vulnerable and those temporarily

---

1 Mark Latham, *Civilising Global Capital*, Allen & Unwin, 1998.

disengaged from work in the real economy. It gave expression to our democratic commitment that government belonged to all of us. It was at least the one thing in which we all had a shareholding. And it was legitimately charged with the responsibility of redistributing resources in society so that opportunity could be enjoyed by all.

This commitment was politically bipartisan and it produced the largely egalitarian society Australians so fondly recall—egalitarian that is putting aside the indigenes.

As we know, the welfare state was developed in an industrial economy when work was abundant. It goes without saying that structural unemployment has challenged one of the central assumptions of the welfare system that was devised in the old economy. Rather than unemployment being a temporary condition, where the state guaranteed income maintenance for people moving between jobs, it became a permanent condition for increasing numbers of Australian bread winners and their families.

Today we routinely see third and fourth generations dependent upon income assistance through the social security system. These people are trapped in the welfare safety net. Welfare dependency for these people is not a temporary halfway house. It has become a permanent address.

Our people in Cape York first took our place in the welfare safety net around 1970. The coming of equal wages in the pastoral industry in the late 1960s particularly contributed to the removal of Aboriginal people from the miserable bottom end of the real economy into welfare. Families moved from the cattle stations where they received rations for work, or at the most unequal pay, to settlements and to the fringes of country towns where the primary source of income was the social security system.

In retrospect, the removal of Aboriginal people from the pastoral industry was a monumental policy failure. The dilemma facing policy makers at the time the equal wages case was being debated was this: on the one hand, Aboriginal stock workers were being discriminated against in relation to their wages and conditions and this could not continue, but on the other hand, it was clear to everyone that the institution of equal wages would result in the whole-scale removal of Aboriginal people from cattle station work to social security on the settlements—and the latter path was chosen.

Of course, with hindsight this choice has had tragic consequences.

First, the cultural impact of the removal of Aboriginal families from their traditional lands in pastoral properties was obviously massive and today inestimable.

Second, there are the social results of the removal of Aboriginal workers from work on the stations to no work on the settlements.

Third, we would not have had the difficulties in relation to the Wik case and the issue of coexistence of native title on pastoral leases had Aboriginal groups remained on these properties.

Was there a third option available to the policy makers? My own regret is that the resources that were made available by the federal government, through the social security system when people were removed to the settlements, were not instead used to subsidise wages for continued work in the cattle industry. Rather than the federal government committing to the provision of resources through the social welfare system on the settlements, those same resources could have been applied to the improvement of Aboriginal wages and living conditions on the stations. I believe the social results would have been much better.

There are no doubt lessons to be learned from this policy experience. Let us turn to the settlements and discuss the effect of the removal of Aboriginal people from discrimination in the outside real economy to the internal economy of the settlements that increasingly constituted social security payments.

For those of us who take seriously our social responsibilities and who passionately understand and support the important achievement of the welfare state, the Aboriginal experience of welfare in Cape York raises troubling issues for us. It has become patently obvious that the passivity and disempowerment of our welfare condition is, together with racism and the legacy of our colonial dispossession, the fundamental causes of dysfunction in our society.

The problem with the welfare economy is that it is not a real economy. It is a completely artificial means of living. Our traditional economy was and is a real economy. Central to the traditional economy was the imperative for able-bodied people to work. If you did not hunt and gather, you starved. Life in a traditional economy was extremely hard and involved struggle and work. And the bottom line—namely nature—came bearing down on people, demanding work. This is the same with all kinds of subsistence economies.

The whitefella market economy is also a real economy. Central to the market economy is the imperative for able-bodied people to work. If you do not work you starve. The bottom line, namely the market, comes bearing down on people demanding work.

Common to the real economy of traditional society and the real economy of the market is the demand for economic and social reciprocity. This reciprocity is expressed through work, initiative, struggle, enterprise, contribution, effort.

The key problem with welfare is that it inherently does not demand reciprocity. I call it a gammon economy. The fact is that the absence of reciprocity from welfare income support to able-bodied people makes the resource counter-productive. It is counter-productive for individuals and it is corrosive of society.

The gammon economy of welfare has had tragic social consequences for people on Cape York. Steadily but surely over the past 30 years it has torn our society apart. It has made proud and decent people helpless. It has corrupted a truly wondrous social system, based on reciprocity and care, into social dysfunction. In its daily battles against our traditional values, our culture and our kinship relationships, it routinely overpowers love.

It was and is our failure to properly distinguish between welfare and the real economy that has seen us pursue, advocate, design and deliver policies which have more usually exacerbated problems or placed band-aids over weeping sores because they were conceived within that paradigm.

At this point we need to distinguish between positive and negative welfare. I am attacking negative welfare—that is, the provision of income support to able-bodied, working-aged people without reciprocity. It is this that is poisonous and socially corruptive.

In order to understand the social dysfunction of Aboriginal society in Cape York, it is my view that its primary cause is negative welfare. I believe that the provision of income support to able-bodied working-aged adults without reciprocity is the source of our social problems and the starting place for any solutions.

In identifying negative welfare programs as a source of social problems, we must immediately recognise that these programs represent extremely valuable and important resources. These resources have the potential to be extremely beneficial and will be critical to the process of social recovery that we are seeking. But in order for these resources to be beneficial rather than destructive, we must fundamentally transform them. We need to insert the principle of reciprocity into the welfare resources. If we do this, we will leech out the destructive element. We will turn negative welfare into positive welfare.

By instituting reciprocity into the resources, we will transform programs that currently induce passivity and dependency into programs that enliven and empower people and which demand responsibility from individuals.

I will soon turn to the central question of how the state needs to work with the Cape York community to transform negative welfare into positive welfare. Before doing so, let me share with you three observations about negative welfare.

Negative welfare involves an economic relationship and an economic transaction between the state and the able-bodied individual. The state gives resources to the individual much as a gift, as a matter of entitlement under the current rules of our welfare state. The economic transaction and relationship is gammon. It does not involve reciprocity.

Secondly, negative welfare is also a method of government. It is a method that proceeds from the nature of the economic relationship; that is, the method involves a powerful party, being the state, having resources and power, delivering resources and services to powerless people. The relationship sets up a situation of activity, responsibility, power, decision-making and initiative on the part of the superior party;

and passivity, reliance and dependency on the part of the inferior party. The negative welfare method of government permeates our current system of government insofar as it deals with social policies.

Whenever the state deals with individuals and communities too often it does so on the premise that the state will be able to save and serve people on the ground. The state is reluctant to transfer responsibility to people on the ground. Because the state holds the resources, it is the powerful party, and whilst the state desires to solve social problems, its inherent methods are frequently the source of the problem.

Thirdly, negative welfare is a mentality, a mindset. It is a mentality that accepts that welfare resources to able-bodied people should not involve reciprocity. It should be provided as a matter of social right. It is a mentality that accepts that the capable, responsible and powerful state should serve programs to incapable, irresponsible and powerless people on the ground. This mentality is not only held by those dependent upon negative welfare but it is also held by the state.

Recognition of these aspects of negative welfare I believe is a key to conceiving its reform. It is obvious that the process of transforming negative welfare into a positive resource involves a transformation in the role of the state from a disabler to an enabler.

Before turning to how the state needs to be transformed, let me first identify another problem of our system of government, which also concerns Mark Latham: the fact that it does not provide holistic strategies to addressing social problems and needs.

In my view it is these two problems with our current system of government that we must reform. We must ensure that government does not continue to deliver negative welfare and operate in the modes and mentalities of negative welfare, and we must ensure that government programs on the ground become holistic.

Mark Latham has pointed out all too clearly the problem of what I call the hydra of government. And the ideas for reform for Cape York Peninsula that I will soon outline were largely inspired by his insights and ideas. I believe that the traditional bureaucratic methods for overcoming the problems caused and the opportunities lost as a result of uncoordinated government departments and programs—namely, establishing interdepartmental committees and working groups, talking about intergovernmental and interagency approaches, developing bilateral and trilateral agreements and so on—have not worked and will not work.

We need a more fundamental change to the way we approach government input into the management of places. In Cape York we need to establish a new interface between the outside structures of government, the Queensland government, the Commonwealth government and the Aboriginal and Torres Strait Islander Commission and the Cape York community.

It is at this interface that we need to meet our two basic policy challenges—turning negative welfare into a positive and making all inputs into the region holistic. The interface needs to become the meeting place between the state and the Cape York community and its leaders. All government programs and inputs into Cape York need to be negotiated through this interface. The state would negotiate with Aboriginal community representatives at this interface, design programs and develop co-operative agreements on how these programs will be delivered on the ground.

It is at this interface that the 15 health programs and the 200 education programs and the dozen economic development programs that various agencies are presently administering in a disparate, conflicting, overlapping way, are brought together into a better coordinated and holistic effort.

The joining together of the resources of the various governmental silos can only happen at an appropriate locational management level. It can only happen through a partnership with the community, through its agencies and its representatives.

As I conceive it, the interface would be legislatively charged with the responsibility and duty to make government inputs into Cape York holistic and, furthermore, to transform negative welfare into positive resources. When we talk about leeching out the poison from welfare and de-welfarising our approach to the development of our communities, it means that we have to decide honestly and carefully where the negative welfare mentality is. This means that we, the Aboriginal people of Cape York, have to think hard about the way in which resources are provided to our communities, and then within our communities, work out whether they are being provided for nothing in return from individuals and therefore inherently damaging our society; whether they are promoting independence or dependency; whether they are promoting responsibility or irresponsibility; whether they are doing any good or bad, and whether they can do better.

We then need to develop the policies and make the decisions about changing the way in which things are done in our communities, and the way in which economic resources are distributed throughout our society. Then we need to negotiate with the state how we can, in a new partnership, ensure that all of our welfare provision into Cape York is in the form of positive resources that enable our people rather than disable them.

As I have explained, there are valuable resources that are currently embedded in negative welfare programs. These programs can be transformed by instituting reciprocity. It is my view that reciprocity needs to be demanded and implemented at the community level. I have great doubts about the institution of reciprocity by the state alone because the state simply lacks, in the Aboriginal community at least, the moral authority to do this effectively.

Furthermore, it is the community that is best placed to define the reciprocity that its able-bodied community members should be bound to. Given the opportunity, the community can devise imaginative and enterprising ideas that give expression to the reciprocity principle. It is the community and its leaders who need to develop strategies for the development of their community. It is the community that needs to develop ideas that address the educational, health and recreational needs of their people, so that individuals are empowered and engaged in the solution of their own problems and those of their families and communities.

When we think about reciprocity at its most simple level, the community needs to ensure that if there is an income support program that has been provided for a specific purpose—say for the wellbeing of children—then it should be the children that benefit from these resources. Ensuring that welfare resources are used for the purposes for which they are provided is the least reciprocity that needs to be implemented. And there will be endless ideas if we approach the challenge of turning negative welfare into positive resource, if we approach it with imagination and a preparedness to innovate.

For example, we need to engage Aboriginal parents in the education system. At the present time, it is as if the schools in the communities are colonial outposts of the state; the same with the health clinics and the hospitals. There is very little relationship and engagement on the part of the community with these service structures. The education of children is left almost entirely to the state and the terrible outcomes speak for themselves.

Parental and wider family involvement in the education system in the communities is an area that is ripe for new ideas and new approaches. Making the school a focal point for the community, through the involvement of community members and the development of adult education programs, would underscore the primary importance of education for the future of the community. It would boost children and attach value to education, both for children and their parents.

Similarly in relation to health services, it is now patently clear that the resolution of our health problems will not be achieved through a passive system of state delivery. What is required is an active engagement on the part of the community in overcoming our health problems.

Communities in Cape York need to be given the responsibility to implement reciprocity and responsibility amongst its members. What this all means is that the state must see itself as a partner and, at the most, a junior one. The state must cease to see itself as the sole service provider, particularly when it comes to social policy. The objectives of the state, to resolve social problems, will not be achieved without effective community engagement. If it is to enable communities and individuals, it must understand that good policy ideas and initiatives can be generated within the community. Not all good policy ideas come from the state.

The Aboriginal affairs policies that the state has historically developed have almost invariably been moribund and have created the very problems we are seeking to resolve. There is simply not enough innovation, risk, enterprise and imagination within the policy mentality of the state, and until it develops these capacities, we must recognise that the community can be the source of creative ideas and solutions—if only it is unleashed.

Unleashing the creativity and initiative of the community involves some structural change. That is why the establishment of a governmental interface is important. The state must come to the interface with resources and the preparedness to devolve responsibility, to amend its programs, to overhaul its priorities, to make efficient decisions, and to be amenable to the community, taking the role of senior partner in devising and implementing strategies.

The Aboriginal community must come to the interface with the preparedness to take responsibility, to put negative welfare behind us, and to be involved in the solution of our own problems. The state's role will be one of ultimate but minimal regulation and the provider of the resources. It will continue to be involved in the delivery of services and its expertise and resources will be accessible to the people of Cape York but its role will be negotiated with the community.

Where the state should retreat in favour of the community taking responsibility for something, then it must do so. Of course, we must recognise that the problems with the methodology of negative welfare— that is, the problem of capable people attempting to serve and to save passive and supposedly incapable people—is not just present in the relationship of the state structure to individuals but it can be present in the relationship of community structures and individuals, and indeed within the family structure.

So the establishment of a regional interface will not be sufficient in itself. The regional interface will need to devolve responsibility to the communities of the peninsula and the community structures in turn will need to devolve responsibility to families and to individuals. Rather than entrenching hierarchial bureaucracies of governance, we need instead to encourage and facilitate freedom of initiative at the ground level. Indeed, not only encourage freedom of initiative, but our system of governance should mandate this through the institution of a complete economic and social reciprocity.

I believe that we can in Cape York Peninsula overcome our incredible problems. I have never before believed this. Knowing the scale of the problems on the ground and its steady deterioration, I too came to numbly accept the statistics. And make no mistake, our challenge is huge. How do we lift the life expectation of a society by at least 20 years?

As anyone familiar with the history of Aboriginal affairs in Queensland well knows, the state has in the past pursued policies and played a role that has been deliberately malign. These policies have produced many problems. But the two problems—that of the state's propensity to deliver negative welfare and the bureaucratic hydra of government—are problems that even sympathetic governments have produced as well.

Without desiring to unravel the fabric of Aboriginal society through negative welfare, this is what the state has done nevertheless through its historic policies and methodologies.

We will not be able to meet our challenge unless the state is prepared to transform its relationship with our community from being disabling to enabling. This means our community will need to seize responsibility. Premier Peter Beattie has committed the Queensland state to partnering us in a new relationship and in the development of a new method of governance for indigenous Cape York. The federal minister for Aboriginal affairs, senator John Herron, has similarly committed himself to partnering us in this quest to develop a new relationship with the state in right of the Commonwealth.

These are fundamental ingredients to the achievement of a new direction—commitment by the state and the Commonwealth to the common cause of enabling the people of Cape York to take charge of their own communities and their own problems. I think there is a bipartisan preparedness in this country to addressing the problems we are talking about and this represents an important opportunity for us.

The private sector will need to be the third party in this enterprise. Only by incorporating Aboriginal people in the real economy will we achieve our goal of taking our share of the country. Of course, the critical ingredient will be the provision of resources by the state. When we say that negative welfare is destructive, we mean that it needs to be changed, not that the resources should be denied or diminished.

In fact, the process of social and economic recovery will require significant increases in access to resources by indigenous communities. By inserting real economy principles into the resources that flow into our community, we will not only arrest and eventually reverse the social disintegration that it is presently causing. We will develop the necessary initiative, capability, responsibility and esteem that will orient individuals to re-engage in the real economy—and that must be the objective of our strategies, to use the resources provided by the state to develop our people, through the promotion of education, through tackling grog, through positive engagement in our own health and of those around us, through the development of an economic base, so that we can eventually take our fair share of the country.

In the future in Cape York there is no reason why our people cannot live within and move successfully between two real economies and societies. We can maintain our traditional society and economy and we can engage in the outside market economy and society and our children can move with great facility between the two, provided that we ensure that the resources that the state provides us, and indeed the resources we generate ourselves, and which we distribute within our own communities, are no longer in the form of negative welfare.

Leaders in disadvantaged locations like Cape York have to develop a conscious and long-term strategy for their home regions and communities. They must be involved, in the front line, of working with the state to reform welfare resources that come to their people into sources of personal empowerment. They must understand the central importance of education and the encouragement of enterprise, achievement and success amongst our people. They must understand the fact that our social responsibility is not just individual, it is collective.

If the state is prepared to adopt an enabling approach to its role, and the community leaders of the Cape York are prepared to take responsibility, I believe that we can recover our society from our egregious social and economic predicament and eventually take our fair share and our fair place in the country.

Unfinished Business
Kim Beazley

I learnt at a young age about some of the tragedies imposed on Aboriginal families by totally misguided white bureaucrats. My parents were interested in Aboriginal issues, and we were privileged to count among our family friends Aboriginal people, including Margaret Tucker, who had been taken from her mother at 13 and brought up to be a domestic servant. The shocking story was told with great dignity and forbearance. I wish more Australians could have heard this story first hand. Margaret's autobiography, *If Everybody Cared*, should be required reading for young Australians.

My father, Kim Snr, spoke often on the need for Aboriginal land rights at Labor Party conferences in the 1940s and 50s, long before many Australians studied these issues. My father always wanted a better education system for Aborigines, a matter that is still a major priority today. My father believed white Australians needed to find out more about their indigenous neighbours. In a sense, he was one of the first senior people in the party to advocate a reconciliation process.

Because I was lucky enough to know Aboriginal people, and to have learned their history from people I trust, I am always surprised to find Australians who doubt the terrible wrongs they suffered. As historian Henry Reynolds has proved, it only takes a little research, a little willingness to ask questions and pursue answers, to uncover the truth. It is not hard to find Aborigines willing to share their stories. They are a remarkably generous people when you consider their history.

That's why I am so offended when I hear people talking about the 'black armband' approach to Australia's history, as if attempts to uncover the truth are somehow unpatriotic, that the only history to be tolerated is one of triumphalism. We have a lot to be proud of when looking back at the last 200 or so years of European settlement. The human race being what it is, however, there are shameful and barbaric episodes. Unless we confront these, and try to make amends, we will be a lesser nation. That's what reconciliation means to me.

I'd like to see schoolchildren learn about the massacres of Aborigines by early settlers, and the spirited resistance of the Aboriginal people. In Queensland alone it is estimated 10,000 indigenous people and at least 1,000 Europeans died as a result of frontier fighting. There were many good people in the judiciary and among settlers who saw crimes against Aborigines and tried to stop them. Aborigines too showed their preparedness for reconciliation. The black cricketer, T.W. Wills whose family had been killed in a massacre at Cullinlaringo, Queensland in 1861, nevertheless agreed to take part in the Aboriginal cricket team's tour of England seven years later.

Our children need to learn about how Aborigines fought for their land and were then dispossessed. They need to study the harrrowing stories of the stolen generation, and how some like Lowitja O'Donoghue and Margaret Tucker still went on to become leaders among their people. They need to ponder the injustices of mandatory sentencing, the burden of which falls unfairly on indigenous people. It's part of understanding what it is to be an Australian, of who we are and how we came to be here.

It is easy to celebrate the positives about the Aboriginal communities in our country, and we are always quick to do so. We are proud of their spellbinding artworks, the great sporting prowess of many Aboriginal people, the gripping stories illustrating the spiritual links between the peoples and their land. Scholars from around the world come to our country to study Aboriginal culture. Aboriginal paintings can be seen in the most avant-garde arthouses from New York to Paris. We all marvel at the spectacular skills of AFL's Michael Long and Maurice Rioli, rugby league's Anthony Mundine, rugby union's Andrew Walker, and of course, Cathy Freeman.

To understand these people properly—and to claim them as fellow Australians as we do—we need to know their history. We need to reconcile ourselves to the part we played in their past—for good and evil. Only then, can we ask them to be part of a real reconciliation between our communities—one that is meaningful for all of us, and one that allows us to move forward as a really unified nation.

When Nicky Winmar, Australian rules football star, pulled up his football jumper to show a rowdy crowd taunting him with racial slurs that he was proud of his black skin, we knew we had a long way to go. That moment, seen by thousands on national TV, was a revelation to many young Australians. It was a sign that racism was alive and well in Australia, and that the suffering of earlier generations of Aboriginal and Torres Strait Islander people hasn't ended.

It was a sign that reconciliation is unfinished business.

Australians appear to have contradictory views on this issue—they want to look to the future, but are unclear about the past. This is not surprising. The republican debates of 1999 showed us that we Australians are not experts when it comes to our own history, and politicians are no different from the rest of the population. Each political generation seems to have had to rediscover Aboriginal Australia, and the way has been littered with false starts.

In the 1960s many more Australians knew and approved of Martin Luther King's stance against racism in the USA than knew of the struggles of Australia's blacks to win citizenship and equality.

And yet there have been some high points where the system has worked, where we can be proud of our institutions and traditions.

The 1967 national referendum, after which the federal government was able to take over responsibility for many Aboriginal issues from the states, was one of the high points. It led to true citizenship and voting rights for many of our indigenous people. Another great landmark was the passage of the Whitlam government's Racial Discrimination Act in 1975, and later, the Land Rights (Northern Territory) Act, devised in the Whitlam years and passed into law under Malcolm Fraser's prime ministership.

In all these cases, changing social and political attitudes in Australia coincided with the emergence of indigenous leaders with the capacity and the will to confront injustice and to campaign publicly for change. They worked with and on behalf of people who had been abused and ignored for too long, and were prepared to struggle for change. From the Pilbara to Wave Hill to Redfern to Fitzroy and in due course to the lawns in front of the federal parliament, they carried forward a courageous campaign.

Another more recent high point was the High Court's decision in the Mabo case in 1992, when the highest court in the land came to grips with Aboriginal prior occupation of this country, after two centuries of the legal system's virtual silence on their origins.

The Mabo decision was central to the unfolding of the reconciliation process. The pride and reassurance that flowed to indigenous Australians from this recognition of their prior rights has been real and measurable. It truly affirmed their cause, and gave many of them confidence that our system of justice can recognise and empower them.

In reaching this decision in the case of Murray Island's Eddie Mabo, who unfortunately died only four months before the result of his long-fought case, the High Court brought Australia into line with other countries. We finally joined New Zealand, the US and Canada in recognising that our indigenous people were the prior owners and custodians of this continent long before European settlement.

In truth, the judgement was remarkable to the rest of the world only in the time it took to arrive. The court found that so-called native title was derived from and resided in the customs, beliefs and traditions of the indigenous Australians. Furthermore, this title was now embraced within the common law of the nation.

Of greater significance, the court found that—although this title was vulnerable to extinguishment by executive and legislative acts since European settlement—it could survive, and indeed had survived in some places.

There has been a kind of saw-toothed progression in the case for Aboriginal rights in Australia, and this case was no different.

The Mabo exhilaration was closely followed by a deliberate fear campaign, promoted by many Coalition leaders, to spread misinformation and panic in rural and regional Australia.

The Keating government, in the context of the Coalition campaign, framed a legislative response to Mabo in 1993. It did so in the face of total non-cooperation from the federal Coalition parties. The conservatives did not seek to deal with the newly discovered rights of our indigenous people, they sought to deny and suppress them, and in some cases to attack the High Court judges who had made the native title findings.

In government the conservative Coalition tried to wind back the rights of Aborigines found in both the Mabo and the later Wik cases.

The Wik decision by the High Court found that where an incidence of native title was not inconsistent with a later grant of interest in land, the two titles could coexist. While affirming the primacy of property rights granted since European settlement, it recognised the rights of Aborigines on land that had been appropriated for other uses. Many pastoralists had already recognised the rights of Aborigines to have some access to their lands for ceremonial and hunting purposes.

The Wik decision could have been a major instrument of reconciliation, recognising that the needs of both parties could be accommodated. The Howard government did not see it that way.

The Howard government on gaining office in 1996 set out to gut the Native Title Act and to reverse the Wik decision. Its Native Title Act 1998 soon attracted the attention of the UN committee overseeing the Convention for the Elimination of Racial Discrimination, to Australia's lasting shame. The committee has found that the act is inconsistent with our obligations as signatories to the UN convention.

Reconciliation has certainly not been plain sailing in the Howard years: John Howard just does not seem to understand what is important to Aboriginal and Torres Strait Islander people. He did a cruel thing when he held out hopes on the night of his second election victory in October 1998 when, totally unprompted, he named Aboriginal reconciliation as one of the important areas for his new term of government. 'We have our own way, but our commitment and our sincerity in areas like this is just as deep and just as great as that of the Australian Labor party,' John Howard said.

Yet, less than 18 months later he let slip in a newspaper interview that he was no longer committed to getting the reconciliation document completed before the centenary of federation in 2001.

In light of the leadership vacuum on Aboriginal policy in the Howard years, it is not surprising that opinion polling carried out for the Council for Aboriginal Reconciliation shows that white Australians are still confused about the plight of indigenous people.

It was disheartening to see that 52 percent of respondents to a Newspoll survey, published in early 2000 did not see Aborigines as disadvantaged. This comes at a time when on any scale you can think of—life expectancy, children's health, educational attainment, poverty levels, unemployment—Aborigines are a third-world nation within a rich Western one.

Statistically, their disadvantage is stark. It's a worrying trend that white Australians seem to blame them for this—they see the symptoms but not the causes. The research showed that there was a firm view (61 to 31 percent) that Aborigines get too much government assistance, and also a strong idea that funds for Aborigines have not achieved much (78 to 15 percent).

Yet, Australians do seem to be keen on reconciliation. A remarkable 62 percent believe the nation should formally acknowledge Aboriginal people as the original owners of the land, and 64 percent want to see recognition of their dispossession. On reconciliation specifically, 57 percent supported a document of principle, while 37 percent did not. A very heartening 81 percent believed a process of reconciliation is quite or very important.

When people read the draft document prepared by the Council for Aboriginal Reconciliation there was more support than opposition to it.

In the past, Aboriginal affairs were left in the hands of a few interested politicians. Now the Aboriginal people speak for themselves. Over the last 30 years, there has been a great increase in numbers of Aboriginal leaders who are willing and able to articulate the views of their people, and the Council for Reconciliation has been a good example of this.

The contradictions in the polling show that political leadership will be crucial in assisting Australians to build bridges with their indigenous neighbours. The Australian Labor Party has high ideals on this matter. It has earned us all sorts of insults from the conservative side of politics, not least the charge that in government we tried to impose a blanket of 'political correctness' over the debate to stifle dissenters.

That was never our aim. We have had dissenters within our own party on this subject. That is well known.

But in government, Labor leaders from Gough Whitlam, through Bob Hawke and Paul Keating, have shown consistent leadership on this fundamental question of human rights and equality.

We remember Gough handing over the lease to Wave Hill station in the Northern Territory to Vincent Lingiari, in 1975, nearly ten years after Vincent had led an Aboriginal stockmen's strike over appalling conditions, and lack of pay, on what had once been the Gurindji people's traditional lands.

We remember Bob Hawke unveiling the Barunga petition from Aboriginal elders in what was literally his last act as prime minister in Parliament House. Bob called for reconciliation to proceed, preferably in an agreed document, 'The important thing is what's in our minds and in our hearts,' he told them.

We remember Paul Keating's Redfern speech in 1992 when he said: 'We took the children from their mothers. We practised discrimination and exclusion. It was our ignorance and our prejudice. And our failure to imagine these things being done to us.'

On some issues, it is important to show the way, to give expression to our better natures. It might be thought to be clever politics to sit silently and allow ignorance and prejudice to prevail, but it is not good leadership.

Mr Howard's stubborn refusal to countenance an apology to Australian indigenous people for the wrongs of the past appears to be the major sticking point to getting agreement on the formal reconciliation document, put together so painstakingly by the Council for Aboriginal Reconciliation since it began in 1991. It is true that a majority of Australians according to the polls are not in favour of such an apology.

Nevertheless, if an apology is what the indigenous people of Australia overwhelmingly want in a reconciliation document, it is up to a national leader—someone who claims to govern 'for all Australians'—to deliver.

Reconciliation will mean nothing if it is offered as a watered-down document to pander to the prime minister's sensitivities, instead of something that can be embraced whole-heartedly by Aboriginal and Torres Strait Islanders.

The wonder of it, and the shame of it, is that the Aboriginal and Torres Strait Islander people are hanging in there, offering us a way forward, as they have been for so many years. The challenge for the prime minister, on behalf of all of us, is to swallow his pride, and accept that offer in a spirit of national unity.

We know from the experience of other countries that the achievement of reconciliation will be a long journey. No one suggests that the signing of a national document will complete the process. Indeed, not all Australians will agree with it. Nevertheless, it would be a significant first step. It's time to take that step.

A Humbug-free Zone
Peter Garrett

The music and words of Aboriginal artists have a greater force and eloquence, and elicit deeper insights into the whole business of reconciliation, than any essay can attempt to provide. Listening to the music, as well as reading about it, is highly recommended.

Pretty much devoid of rhetoric and infused with the experiences of growing up black in white Australia, the output of Aboriginal contemporary musicians might best be described as timely songs of pain and hope. As a consequence of their recent holocaust there is little to match indigenous music in terms of depth of meaning in the contemporary arena. The chart-hunting posture of most white bands, whose work is often copycat, with success usually measured by volume of sales and overseas acceptance, is pale and limp by comparison.

To the observer, it appears that the work of indigenous artists is grounded in the fact that young Aboriginal people have grown up in a disconnected world, where their identity has been engulfed by the events of history and where Aboriginal communities face huge challenges of survival. In this situation, and in the face of various official expressions of concern which in their eyes have contributed little, it is plain speaking—the opposite of humbug—which is preferred.

Much of the music—the expert and the instinctive, the great, the good and the ordinary—is deep like the ocean. A palpable sense of loss seems to infect most songwriters. Song titles such as 'Eulogy for a Black

Person', 'Island of Greed', 'Treaty', 'We Shall Cry', 'Black Fella White Fella', 'Took The Children Away' give some sense of what the music is about. Often there are cutting observations on the nature of black-white relations; witness singer Kev Carmody's stinging rebuke of theft of land as state-sanctioned behaviour in 'Thou shalt not steal'. (1990)

> In 1788 down Sydney Cove the first boat people land, and they say sorry boys our gain's your loss we're gonna steal your land. If you break under our British law then sure you're gonna hang. Work your life like a convict with a chain on your neck and hands, and they taught us, woah black woman thou shalt not steal, hey black man thou shalt not steal. The land's our heritage and spirit yeah, the rightful culture's black, we're sittin' here just wonderin' when we gonna get that land back, they taught us, woah black woman thou shalt not steal, said hey black man though shalt not steal.

At the same time these mourning and acerbic elements coexist with residual expressions of hope that some good can come of the current situation. Always there is the proclamation that there is much to be proud of in Aboriginal culture. Younger artists like Christine Anu and Nokturnl draw more from their own street experiences, with music that has less folk or rock elements and more dance. Underneath though, the simple fact that Aboriginal culture is in the midst of a tough struggle is a constant theme.

Indigenous artists are burdened by twin conflicting expectations, from both Aboriginal and mainstream society. In Aboriginal society, the expectation of the musician's extended family and community for a continuing relationship with family members and the obligations to family and home, must somehow be reconciled with the demands of touring schedules and extensive absences that are a necessary part of the life of a professional musician. For artists who hail from outside the main city centres in particular, this conundrum has stymied a number of careers. It is a tension, one suspects, that can never be completely eased.

The second set of conflicting expectations arises from the fact that any degree of prominence of an Aboriginal artist creates the expectation on the part of black and white society that he or she will be a spokesperson for their people. Often glossed over by mainstream media are the complexities of indigenous culture, as journalists simplify or aim for a cover-all statement which may misrepresent the views of the artist. Add to this the tendency to lionise successful artists, and the possibility of burnout is always present.

Despite these tentacles, most performers manage to keep their voice true to their people without suffering too much misreading, but they are seldom long in the mainstream. Without a healthy and accommodating indigenous media, and the ABC's commitment to indigenous programs, most writers would despair of ever being able to genuinely explain the meanings and events that have shaped their music.

At the same time as colonial secretary Earl Grey instructed governor Phillip to 'effect a settlement with the natives' and the House of Commons Select Committee on Aborigines (1837) advised that relations with the inhabitants of New Holland be 'fair and just', Aboriginal people were still a majority who had been in possession of the continent, and had been singing songs of life and meaning about their home since the beginning of memory. But they were a people under siege.

Recent historical writings of Reynolds and others make clear that the indigenous experience on the ground, once the British arrived, was one of constant erosion of their territory and subsequent devastating impact on health and clan. That all this was suffered without any ensuing settlement or meaningful compensation for stolen land and heartache, provides the backdrop for today's movement towards reconciliation and, not surprisingly, the substance of much of the modern music created by Aboriginal artists.

The dispossession was quick and almost complete. The assimilation settlements like Papunya in central Australia and Hopevale in far north Queensland were already overflowing and fracturing by the early sixties, when touring country and western singers, like Slim Dusty and Buddy Williams who often made the trek to towns outside Melbourne and Sydney, finally arrived in remote parts and introduced the first sounds of Western music to Aboriginal people. Most were unable to attend these early concerts which were well beyond people's means and mixed audiences were discouraged, but local communities discovered Western music via tapes and albums that followed in the wake of these early tours.

It is now understood that music and dance for ceremonial purposes which include all aspects of Aboriginal society is central to the lives of Aboriginal people. The form and content of ceremony music is a far cry from the country laments and renditions of boogie-woogie which made up the typical fare of visiting performers. Even though there are reports of young Aborigines playing with makeshift amplified instruments as early as 1973, so great were the distances and the costs of moving people and gear around the hinterland, that until the establishment of the Centre for Aboriginal Studies in Music (CASM) at the University of South Australia in 1980 and later that decade the formation of the Central Australian Aboriginal Media Association (CAAMA) in Alice Springs, which provided a springboard for emerging performers, these early bands remained nameless. Beyond the confines of the dusty camps, their music was never heard.

It is remarkable how quickly fully-fledged performers emerged, first from South Australia, the Northern Territory and the Kimberley, and later from towns and cities all over the land, once there were vehicles for identifying and developing talent. In part one suspects that this rapid emergence of Aboriginal bands was inspired by the walk-off from Vestey's Wave Hill station in 1966, led by Vincent Lingiari, which was an early beacon for musicians, many of whom directly or indirectly drew succour from the event and made reference to the walkout in song. Added to the reflections on the conditions faced by their people, and it seems likely that this event, along with other recorded examples of resistance to poor treatment, fuelled a creative explosion which belied the small Aboriginal population from which the artists were drawn. But the establishment of CAAMA and institutional support from arts councils which encouraged indigenous music in the ensuing decade, meant that nascent Aboriginal talent had some means of being heard and appreciated.

From South Australia and CASM came the pioneer band No Fixed Address led by drummer Bart Willoughby who featured in the ground breaking documentary *Wrong Side of the Road* (1982) which detailed the progress of two aspiring black bands facing police harassment, bureaucratic indifference and chronic poverty attempting to make it in the big smoke. Then followed songwriters of high calibre including Buna Laurie who fronted Coloured Stone and the enigmatic Jimmy Chi from the Kimberley who went on to write the successful musical *Bran Nue Day*.

In the space of about ten years numerous bands and performers emerged, assisted in part by these bodies and newly established indigenous radio networks supported by governments of the day. In the 1980s, politicians saw nothing sinister in providing the means for young indigenous musicians to survive and have their music heard. A live circuit in the Northern Territory in particular had evolved, following the footsteps of the country and western pioneers, who by the late seventies and early eighties had begun to venture outside of whites-only venues in the towns and visit settlements where the audience was predominantly black.

The emergence of the Warumpi Band, from Papunya in the Northern Territory, with Victorian guitarist and songwriter Neil Murray joining singer George Rurrambu and the Butcher brothers, Sammy and Gordon on bass and drums showed with the release of *Big Name No Blankets* (1985) how quickly and competently Aboriginal musicians had mastered the modern rock idiom. The Warumpis, with gravel-voiced charismatic singer Rurrambu, showed great promise, conjuring up visions of an Aboriginal Rolling Stones. However lame such a comparison may seem, their raw sound and direct lyrics, enhanced by Murray's arranging and composing skills, created a huge buzz in the east. Plagued by personnel changes and the contrary demands of family and professional life, the early impetus was not sustained, but of late a reformed Warumpi are again making powerful music.

Notable amongst bands and performers who spread out across Australia were Coloured Stone, originally from Adelaide via the Great Australian Bight; Scrap Metal featuring the Pigram brothers from

Broome; Kev Carmody, a Dylanesque troubadour from Queensland; Archie Roach based in Melbourne; and Yothu Yindi from North East Arnhem Land—all played regularly on the rock circuit. The latter group led by Mandawuy Yunupingu, brother of Aboriginal leader Galarrwuy Yunupingu, achieved a significant degree of national and international success on the back of the hit single 'Treaty' from the album *Tribal Voice* (1992).

'Treaty' was a particularly well-developed song combining a confident and fresh sound with lyrics directly aimed at the question of reaching satisfactory agreement between Aboriginal people and white Australia, a notion that had been variously described as a 'compact', or 'settlement'. It also included a middle bridge sung in the Gumatj language of the region, which exposed more people to the sound of indigenous language than any other source of Aboriginal culture. As with much Aboriginal music of the time, the sentiment was plain.

> Well I heard it on the radio, and I saw it in the television
> Back in 1988, all those talking politicians
> Words are easy words are cheap
> Much cheaper than our priceless land
> But promises can disappear, just like writing in the sand
> Treaty yeah, treaty now.
>
> This land was never given up
> this land was never bought and sold
> The planting of the union jack, never changed our law at all
> Now two rivers run their course, separated for so long
> I'm dreaming of a brighter day, when the waters will be one.

Yothu Yindi, more than most indigenous acts, skilfully managed to combine the distinctive facets of clan and region, belief and custom, with the modern vehicle of a pop music outfit. As traditional owners of the land, they brought authority and credibility to the process of music making and judiciously enlisted support from various non-Aboriginal people who were excited about the impact a successful Aboriginal act would have in communicating Aboriginal culture to the mainstream. A number of white artists including Paul Kelly and Midnight Oil provided song writing and touring support. Management, recording and producing chores were shared with whites, who acted in part as filters, in part as skilled specialists, to give the music as much accessibility as possible in order to reach a wider audience.

One of the themes consistently highlighted in contemporary Aboriginal music is the notion of land; the loss of land, the relationship to land, the spirit in the land, the treatment of land by modern Australian society. Professor W.E.H. Stanner, the distinguished anthropologist, said of this much-used word, 'No English words are good enough to give a sense of the links between an Aboriginal group and its home land. Our word *home*, warm and suggestive though it be, does not match the Aboriginal word that may mean *camp, hearth, country, everlasting home, totem place, life source, spirit centre* and much else in one. Our word *land* is too meagre and spare.'

The prophetic call by Warumpi Band from 'Too Much Humbug' is heard again and again:

> I believe the time will come when everyone will join us
> And understand our way of life
> And how we care for this land. And we shall cry for our land

In 'Eulogy for a Black Person', (1991) Kev Carmody writes:

> Lay me down in the sacred ground
> Keep me from the cold
> Wrap me in the deep warm Earth
> Where the stars can see my soul
> Take me where them trees stand tall
> By the waters in the river bend
> Let me face the rising sun
> Commend my spirit to the wind

This recurring them is again picked up when Christine Anu, whose people hail from Thursday Island, writes of water which brings with it 'Life for me and you' (*Stylin' Up*, 1995). The response of poets and artists as the debate about Mabo and Wik plays out, and the reluctance of certain sections of the community to accommodate this attachment, notwithstanding that the courts have validated its existence, adds 'bucketloads' of poignancy to the music.

But it isn't only black musicians who have addressed these issues. There have been a number of folk and country musicians, including Slim Dusty, Ted Egan, John Williamson, and rockers Paul Kelly, Shane Howard, Midnight Oil, Neil Murray as a solo artist and others, who have tried to find expression in their music for the situation faced by their colleagues on the wrong side of the track. Neil Murray, after years of living in the bush and touring with Warumpi Band has made a number of eloquent albums including *These Hands* and *The Wondering Kind* which detail the see-saw existence of living as a white Australian in an Aboriginal world.

The seminal 'From Little Things Big Things Grow', a duet performed with Kev Carmody, is one of many fine Paul Kelly songs which have chronicled the Aboriginal condition. As well as writing songs like 'Maralinga' and 'Special Treatment', Kelly has written songs and produced albums with a number of indigenous artists, notably Victorian Archie Roach. His intensely personal first album, *Charcoal Lane* was suffused with the experience of living rough on the streets weighed down by the body blows suffered by Aboriginal people whose identity was all but dismembered. Archie Roach with his wife Ruby Hunter, a writer and performer in her own right, have found great critical acceptance and an expanding audience for their intense and melancholy work. They, along with a growing number of other black artists including country singer Troy Cassar-Daley and the Pigram Bothers, now make their living as professional musicians, a rare feat in the highly competitive music entertainment field.

In 1986, Midnight Oil along with Warumpi Band travelled through central and northern Australia in the Black Fella-White Fella tour, including many remote desert communities in the itinerary. This was a first-time occasion for many of the audience as well as for the members of the band and the spectacle of wrecked cars, ragged, poor settlements in dry and fierce landscapes overlaid with ever-present, red desert dust remains a vivid memory.

Even though the tour included the tropical north, mining towns, remote coastal settlements and aimed to play to mixed audiences wherever possible, the overwhelming sense that remains is of a timeless, still strong culture, ruptured by violent displacement, struggling to come to terms with a mammoth loss. Yet in the midst of this diasporic setting numerous bands and singers had amazingly sprung up, seemingly out of nowhere, and started composing and performing—Sunrize Band, Areyonga Desert Tigers, North Tanami Band, Blekbala Mujik, and a host of others were producing creditable material that documented their experiences and expressed their dreams for the future. This dramatic spawning of music groups was repeated across the Commonwealth.

In the midst of great poverty and uncertainty, Aboriginal people, partly through the songs of this generation of musicians, are managing to survive. The culture has proved resilient, its creative capacity to make music is astounding and continues to this day. But the way too high levels of infant illness, early death, incarceration and youth suicide—indeed of most indices of human wellbeing that dog many Aboriginal communities—still ought to trouble any fair-minded Australian.

It is apparent that these statistics have come to mean different things to different people. There are some who have greater access to the airwaves than Aboriginal musicians, who contend that Aboriginal people are actually privileged. For these people and for the politicians who give them implicit support, the Aboriginal population has already been given too much. The 'special treatment' they speak of contrasts with Paul Kelly's song of the same name.

> Grandfather walked this land in chains
> A land he called his own
> He was given another name
> And taken into town

> My father worked a twelve hour day
> As a stockman on the station
> The very same work but not the same pay
> As his white companions
>
> I never spoke my mother's tongue
> I never knew my name
> I never learned the songs she sung
> I was raised in chains
>
> I got special treatment
> Special treatment
> We got special treatment
> Special treatment
> Very special treatment

The humbug that Aboriginal artists write about is evidenced by the angry denunciations of the 'Aboriginal industry'. One searches in vain for this juggernaut—made up no doubt of numerous Aboriginal judges, media magnates, CEOs, black politicians—which needs to be restrained. The complaints about a 'black armband view of history', whereby a fresh generation of researchers and survivors fill in a large gap in Australian history, ring hollow to the sons and daughters of the dispossessed, brought up through a school system where accurate knowledge of the past is meant to better inform the future.

Some believe the discontent about Aboriginal people asserting their legal rights or demanding a response to the Black Deaths in Custody Royal Commission or the stolen children report of the Human Rights Commission, stems from the psychic trauma associated with confronting massive end-of-century change. But it is also a reminder that our recent past is racist—an uncomfortable concept for most people—to the extent that race was an issue in immigration, that racial discrimination was part of the policies of the major parties and a reflection of our colonial state of mind as part of an empire.

My view is that what is most challenging in the drive for reconciliation, echoed in the pleas of Aboriginal songwriters, is that Australians are being asked to reconsider what constitutes our national make-up as informed by our collective history. Is it more than a series of explorer figures, colonial tales and victorious adaptation by Europeans to a hostile and different environment? Ands if it is more than a potted, blameless record from a 1950s primer, then what does this newly discovered history tell us about ourselves?

Alongside numerous successful indigenous athletes and painters, so many Aboriginal musicians are making a substantial contribution to the life of Australia. They reflect the creative vitality of indigenous communities; the strength of their compositions belies the events of the recent past. Their music exists not only to entertain but to inform and provoke the Australian community to whom the pleas to settle with the past are made, and upon whom the responsibility to act, now squarely rests.

The final word belongs to Warumpi Band:

> Black fella, white fella
> It doesn't matter what your colour
> As long as you a true fella
> As long as you a real fella
> All the people of different races
> Of different lives in different places
> It doesn't matter what your name is
> We got to have lots of changes
> We need more brothers if we're to make it
> We need more sisters if we're to save it
> Stand up, stand up and be counted...stand up

Negotiating Co-existence
Djon Mundine

Most non-Aboriginal people, both Australian and from other nations, have their first (and possibly only) contact with Aboriginal people and Torres Strait Islanders through viewing Aboriginal art or attending a cultural performance or event. In the last two decades of the last century, acclaim for Australian indigenous visual art, dance, theatre, moving image, writing, and to a lesser extent music has reached unheard of heights both critically and financially. Yearly returns for indigenous visual art of all types now totals $180–$200 million and—like minister Ruddock's government figures to the UN of money spent on indigenous Australians—paint a rosy picture. But similarly, all is not what it seems.

Indigenous practitioners, dealers and other art workers in fact receive only an estimated 30 percent of this figure. A combination of bad middlemen, so-called friends, bad advice, imitators, forgers and just plain thieves, accidentally and consciously conspire to deprive indigenous artists of their just rewards. In practically all instances, non-indigenous players still miss the concept of this art as intellectual capital or property.

White Australia has been slow to see any substance in indigenous cultural values since European arrival here in 1788. Like most of western Europe, white Australians did not define indigenous cultural expression as 'art' for the first 150 years of the colony, even after artists such as Picasso had appropriated other so-called 'primitive art' imagery from Africa into their compositions. Nearly all indigenous art was personal, event, and site orientated. Made of materials that were destroyed by the participants as part of the performance or by natural degradation, the art was for a time and for specific people to consume. This art that existed largely as a mental concept was the exact opposite of art as Western material object to be stored away under lock and key. There were art forms of a more durable nature—images incised in rock surfaces or living tree trunks, or paintings of great ingenuity on rock gallery walls. These have dated to at least 25,000 years before the present.

As the market and intellectual value of indigenous art has risen astronomically, history seems to be repeating itself. Not seeing the art as a gesture of reconciliation or an attempt to communicate, white Australia has merely discovered it as another resource to exploit, pollute and desecrate to death—a continuation of the colonial frontier. There is seemingly no philosophical meeting place where there could be an incorporation of indigenous beliefs and social customs. In places such as Alice Springs or Darwin, which are major indigenous art centres, 'dreaming' tracks and sacred sites within the town boundaries are often well known. Given the tourist industry, one would have thought it would be in the towns' interest to incorporate this indigenous view of the land into town planning and design.

This trade in art has not been a one-way street exchange. Indigenous artists actively took advantage of the initial interest of specialist art collectors (mainly from the USA) and the ever-increasing demand for their art in two ways. Firstly to subsidise their meagre incomes from selling their art and, secondly, to convert the wider Australian communities to indigenous values. In 1963, in one of the most widely known instances, the people of Yirrkala created the Yirrkala Bark Petition and presented it to federal parliament to state their ownership of their lands. This powerful use of art to effect political change is most probably unique in the nation's history. It now sits in Parliament House alongside the letter from Queen Victoria; 'in her own hand', when she gave permission for federation to happen from her Balmoral Castle in England. Many other indigenous land claims have used art—either song, dance, or visual art—as direct evidence or to reinforce other evidence in their cases. They illustrate forms of spiritual and intimate relationships between people and to the land itself For white people to create an industry of forgeries of these carte blanche is a gross crime.

White Australia has 'used' indigenous art in three major ways over the last century. Firstly, after almost totally denying its status as art for the first hundred years, the Australian art world included the art of the first Australians in several significant exhibitions to extend the length of Australian art history. Indigenous visual art as painting on, or engravings in, rock surfaces have been dated to around 25,000 years before the present as against the short history of 200 years for non-indigenous art. References to indigenous art allow Australian art to have a history as long as that in western Europe.

The second use has become more prevalent since World War Two as Aboriginal art became more widely known and popular outside Australia. Governments began to showcase this art as proof of white Australian sophistication (in their recognition of it) and as proof that all those terrible stories of genocide, deprivation, and racism that outsiders had heard about were wrong. Here were happy, smiling blacks.

Aboriginal performers and artists are paraded before the world but rarely with any self-representation. There is a curators' joke that the only good artist is a dead artist—they can then never contradict what you say about them nor get in the way of your limelight. In many, if not most, of the above instances, these art appearances were without living artists or at best a token inclusion as living exhibits. This practice still continues. I have been to international functions where the indigenous parties spoke for something like five minutes after listening to hours of delivery by non-indigenous experts telling our international audiences the real indigenous history, what Aboriginal people really felt.

The third use is a definitional one. By defining what was 'authentic' indigenous art, white Australia defined who in effect was indigenous. Thus the art of the people of the south-east would be seen as something less than indigenous. The only 'authentic' indigenous art was defined as being created in the remote, largely northern communities; the others were somehow less pure and even contaminated. This same criteria was, of course, never applied to Western art; Picasso was not contaminated when he was influenced by African art imagery but Albert Namatjira was producing a pale imitation of Western art when he completed his water colour landscapes. This view, not entirely extinct, changed significantly around the 1960s and a new generation of practitioners, refusing to be so-defined, are thriving. It is still trotted out every so often 'in the spirit of reconciliation' [sic]. As a reply argument to my criticisms of the Elizabeth Durack–Eddie Burrup affair, it is suggested that I am not really an Aboriginal so my points don't count.

Up to the 1950s a group of white Australian artists and intellectuals, in what they thought of as a positive step, attempted to incorporate indigenous art into their own art and to promote this idea. This was fine in the 1950s but today indigenous artists are successfully speaking through their own art and curators. Which makes the case of certain artists appropriating imagery and identity itself in some cases, ridiculous in the extreme, and simply playing out a form of neo-colonialism. Having taken or destroyed most of the physical resources, white Australia is now moving on to the intellectual property. In an amazing intellectual standing-on-your-head position, these people see this as a reconciliation. This can only be a shallow reading and appreciation of indigenous art, as cliched as wearing a beret to pretend to be an artist.

To appreciate and admire Aboriginal cultural life doesn't mean that you walk around naked, painted in ochre. You can admire and incorporate into your personal and social life indigenous practices in deeper forms. A relationship and respect with the environment is one; acknowledgement of the traditional land owners at public events is another; indigenous smoking ceremonies to open events and buildings is another.

A statement often made by white Australians is that, as part of reconciliation, indigenous people have to contribute instead of taking all the time. When the Mabo and Wik rulings were made, it destroyed the notion of *terra nullius*, the uninhabited land. These rulings were made using Australian law by the highest courts in the land. After losing 7,500,000 square kilometres of land—a piece of real estate 30 times the size of the UK—to white Australia, one would have thought that this was a sizeable contribution. The paltry few hundred million per year paid as social welfare payments since World War Two are really insignificant if one measures the billions and billions of dollars extracted from the continent each year. This could hardly be seen as an adequate rent or payment for the resources of the continent according to white Australian market values.

Indigenous Australians have realistically never wanted it all back nor wanted to force common people out of their homes; however this is never seen as a gesture of reconciliation. A significant number of the ruling classes and the Liberal–National Party Coalition government have never accepted the Mabo and Wik decisions and tried to live with them or try to negotiate a position.

The dictionary meaning of reconciliation is listed as: to make friendly after estrangement, to purify after a desecration, to heal, to harmonise, to make compatible, but also to make acquiescent or contentedly submissive. Although like the rest of Australia, indigenous people would like to reach a form of healing, this can only be meaningful with action; it must be pragmatic and economic as well as symbolic and spiritual. A number of concurrent strategies need to be pursued—remedial, economic, educational.

The Council for Aboriginal Reconciliation defines reconciliation as: to achieve recognition and respect for the unique position of Aboriginal people and Torres Strait Islander peoples as the indigenous peoples (the first peoples) of Australia through a national document of reconciliation and by acknowledgment within the Constitution of this country. Reconciliation certainly does not mean, as a recent *Canberra Times* headline suggested, 'Aborigines fought and lost; they should get over it'. It isn't an Aboriginal problem, it is a white problem. The reality is less about reconciliation that it is about negotiating co-existence.

The reconciliation process needs leadership. There is already a platform of leaders in the community, however at the top—the government and the prime minister—there is failure; a failure of vision, generosity and leadership. Real reconciliation means a collaboration on real terms not paper gestures.

Doubtful Island
Hannah McGlade

Doubtful Island is one of two small islands on the south west coast of Western Australia. It is located in the traditional country of my grandmother, Ethel Woyung and her people from the Wheelman, Bremer bay and Quaalup tribes; and, it is my country in spirit too. The land is wild but beautiful. It is bounded by the Fitzgerald River National Park, with its unique and diverse wildlife and is recognised internationally for its world heritage value.

According to my grandfather, Roddy McGlade, Doubtful Island was named as such after a ship passing in the night failed to negotiate its way through the two islands. The ship's captain wondered if he could make it through to the other side; he thought it doubtful but tried anyway. He didn't succeed—the ship became lodged and stranded. So that is Doubtful Island, a place my grandfather speaks of with great wistfulness and affection.

The island and surrounding country was divided up by the colonial government shortly after the arrival of the Europeans to the Swan River colony in 1830. The land was swiftly procured by the Hassell family, who for over a century established themselves as the most substantial pastoralists in the south west of the state. How did they manage such a feat? Certainly it was facilitated by the colonial legislature or legal system of the time which established, by way of the various native protection acts, the 'assignment system'—and the enslavement of thousands of Aboriginal men, women and children.

My grandmother, Ethel Woyung, was born in Jerramungup around 1875 and lived to a great old age, perhaps a hundred years. She was given her European name 'Ethel' by Ethel Hassell, the matriarch of the Hassell family. Grandmother Ethel Woyung spoke well of Ethel Hassell, who in turn said of the local people:

> ...all the years I was with the natives, though my husband frequently told me they were the greatest blackguards under the sun, I never heard a native woman say, or saw her do anything that could offend the most delicate or sensitive woman.

By 1910, Ethel Hassell lamented the fact that there were so few of her 'dusky friends' left. She spoke despairingly of them as 'a fast disappearing race'. These descriptions reflect the government policies and laws of the time, policies and laws which are now frequently described as 'genocidal', and recognised as being aimed at the destruction of races and cultures. I know from first-hand experience as a child growing up with my beautiful grandmother how successful these policies were. They left scars, imprints on the minds and spirits of the survivors.

An Irishman, Jim McGlade, took Ethel Woyung for his wife when she was a young girl. They lived together all their lives as man and wife and had six children. Jim McGlade was a commendable man, as it was the case that 'not many white men were prepared...to live with a dark girl and accept fully the responsibilities of his handsome family'. Nonetheless, Ethel and Jim McGlade lived in breach of the law, the Native Welfare Act 1905, which prohibited relations between Aboriginal women and non-Aboriginal men. They managed to avoid prosecution, which would have entailed the break-up of the family, by living in isolation in the bush—Jerramungup, Quaalup, Doubtful Island—a lonely existence away from their respective families and communities.

They had some close calls. One day a Sergeant McCallum called; he was inquiring whether my grandmother was in fact a native. He declared that she was not a native but a 'Chinese' woman—she was fathered by a indentured labourer or 'coolie' from China, one of the many brought to Australia by the Hassell family. Perhaps he also felt some loyalty to Jim McGlade, a policeman's son.

Ethel did not ever believe that times could change, and so she always lived in the 'old days'. Consequently, my life as a child with my grandmother was marked by indescribable sadness. I would pester Granny, when feeling bold and with a sense of mischief, to tell me Nyungar stories or even some of those Nyungar words. But she would shoo me away with some annoyance, and tell me not to ask her wrong things like that. Before she passed on though, she gave me her Nyungar name, Woyung, and that is something special. I don't know the meaning of my name though; Granny Ethel spoke a dialect that has now been lost. Although my grandmother grew up with her traditional people whose stories were fortunately recorded by her namesake, she did not pass them down to me.

However, I read them recently in a book by Ethel Hassell who, being fascinated by the culture and traditions of my grandmother's people, recorded many of these stories in her account, *My Dusky Friends*. This manuscript is invaluable as it is the only written account of the people and the traditions of this period. I recently read the book and was somewhat taken aback. I knew that these were indeed my Nyungar ancestors she was describing in her observations about '…their unfailing humour and child-like ways, and merry laughs at such trivial things'; or the way that 'a native is observant, it is part of their life to watch and to notice'; and how, 'a native, like a child, has a keen sense of justice, if they think they are not justly treated, they quietly early one morning walk off'. Ethel Hassell also wrote of 'women's booliah' or wizard stones: if you hold them in your hand and wish hard for a nop cullum or baby boy, you might just get your wish. And, I remember that my baby son came to me only after I brought home the pretty stones from the Quaalup river. My son is also from my grandmother's country, as the pelicans or butalungs who live there came to him very early on. So the genocide was not as complete as it may have seemed. I do not think anyone can kill the Nyungar spirit; it is timeless, like this country.

I wonder what my grandmother would have thought about the Racial Discrimination Act introduced in 1975. She lived with her radio at her side and always listened for the ABC news broadcast. Its passage in parliament signified the full circle in Australian racial relations, from the overt racial discrimination of the segregation and protectionist eras to its legislative prohibition. But I do not think that Ethel Woyung believed in it.

As a child I learnt the shamefulness that the dominant white Australian culture placed on Aboriginality. It was very bad and degrading to be an Aborigine. The schoolyard of the 1970s defined this for me—I was one of them, an 'Abo', 'boong', 'nigger'. My family was a real minority; the only Aboriginal kids in the whole school populated by Australians of Anglo-Celtic origin and recent English immigrants. There was no refuge. If I want to, I can still hear the kids running past me with their catchcry, 'eenie, meenie, miney mo, catch a nigger by the toe'. My head would swing around; did they mean me? No, not that time, they were just playing. Sometimes they meant me, I was 'burnt toast' in polite language. Most times on the netball court though I was the 'fairest and best'; that was my payback I suppose. Sometimes, girls from other teams would comment on what a 'nice tan' I had, and when feeling brave I'd respond, 'I'm an Aboriginal' and watch them recoil in horror, as if they would catch something nasty from me.

And what did the schoolbooks teach us about being Aboriginal? They were not as obviously nasty as the taunts but probably more insidious, presenting a negative and shameful image. Pictures of naked Aborigines, standing one legged and clutching at spears—was this me, I could only wonder? We were a pest and hindrance to the great civilisers, settlers and discoverers, Captain Cook and the like. I can still remember kindly Mrs Miscavich who proudly showed the class a newspaper photo of myself taken on a visit to the Aboriginal Advancement Centre, holding a coolomon and adorned in the traditional beads. I cannot recall any other positive memories. I immersed myself in a make-believe world of mystery books whilst my sister and brother found themselves in fist fights on their way home from school.

And so it was, more than 20 years later, with a law degree and university teaching position, I read an article, in the state's only daily newspaper the *West Australian*, about a state Liberal politician, Ross Lightfoot who had claimed publicly that:

> Aboriginal people in their native state are the most primitive people on earth.

And then he went even further, stating:

> If you want to pick up some aspects of the Aboriginal culture which are valid in the twenty-first century that aren't abhorrent, that don't have some of the terrible sexual and killing practices in them, I would be happy to listen to those.

I was in a state of shock! Could times really have changed so little?

It wasn't that I hadn't experienced racism after my schooldays; university was no easy feat, especially as I was a minority of one and a world away from the young white students from the predominantly upper-middle classes. I remember an incident which occurred while I was attending a postgraduate training course required for our admission to the legal practice. A group of students, dressed in their expensive suits, recounted (with apparently great fun) an alleged episode involving a law firm which had persuaded some native title claimants to withdraw their claim for 'a carton of Jack Daniel's'. But, they said, it would be to no avail as their 'so-called ancestors would only claim it later on'. I went cold to the bone. So we were no longer just drunken alcoholics; post-Mabo we had become liars and imposters! My natural instinct was one of denial or disbelief. I could not speak and was a little girl again, silenced.

Although I immediately brought the incident to the attention of the course supervisor it was 'vehemently denied' by those involved—who were apparently offended by the complaint—and it was subsequently found by the administration that I, 'being who I am', had 'misheard' the incident. It was also thought that law students in this day and age, could not possibly hold such ignorant and racist views.

Senator Lightfoot's position, by contrast, was upfront and highly publicised. I found it unbelievable that someone as prominent as a member of parliament could publicly promote such racist, bigoted views. And for what reason? Because he was 'vehemently opposed' to the teaching of Aboriginal studies—for the first time ever—in West Australian schools. I decided to make a complaint to the Human Rights and Equal Opportunity Commission (or HREOC) under the recently enacted provisions prohibiting racial vilification, which was defined as a public act 'reasonably likely, in all the circumstances, to offend, insult, humiliate or intimidate another person or a group of people'.

Shortly after the article appeared in the *Western Australian*, and, after the lodgement of my complaint, Ross Lightfoot went on to gain a seat in the federal senate. In his maiden speech to federal parliament—made during National Reconciliation Week—he again repeated his earlier statements. I subsequently learnt that he had in fact been making such statements since 1993, with no chastisement from the Liberal Party, which he represented. This time though, he was rebuked and apparently threatened with expulsion by the prime minister, John Howard, and less than an hour after the maiden speech returned to the senate and made the following statement:

> I wish to unreservedly apologise to any Australians who may have been given offence by the remarks I made. I respect the Aboriginal people of today and strongly support practical measures to address their disadvantage.

Senator Herron, minister for Aboriginal affairs, claimed that Australia was a democracy and senator Lightfoot had a right to his personal opinions. In latter correspondence to HREOC the senator claimed that the statements were 'a legitimate opinion based on research and observation'. Lightfoot went on shortly thereafter to join the federal Aboriginal affairs committee, the decisions of which are fed directly to the powerful cabinet.

I, on the other hand, began my descent into the murky world of anti-discrimination law. It wasn't as if I had no knowledge of this area of the law; only up until this point it had all been theoretical. I had decided in 1997 to commence a masters degree, focusing on the effectiveness of anti-discrimination mechanisms for indigenous peoples. I wanted to know if these laws, which appeared to offer justice to a people who are discriminated against, really work as they should.

Although I applied to state and federal race discrimination commissioners to access cases and undertake voluntarily any research they may have required, the doors were shut to me. I was confined to a study of case decisions, the majority of which had concluded that no race discrimination had in fact taken place. Often this conclusion was reached in stark contrast to the evidence.

In this same year HREOC itself, as part of the twentieth anniversary of the Race Discrimination Act 1975, initiated a review of the act. With respect to Aboriginal people, my analysis of the review highlighted the following:

> Racial discrimination is very difficult to prove, and harder to establish than sex discrimination;
>
> Very low damages are awarded for successful complaints of racial discrimination;
>
> The only clear act of racism against Aboriginal people identified by the commission is the refusal of service in hotels.

Nonetheless, armed with a law degree and an awareness of these issues, my initial attitude was still relatively optimistic.

Almost at the near end of my time with HREOC, I can no longer claim this to be true. I started a law degree with a belief that law could empower Aboriginal people—we could seek justice from this apparently fixed and neutral system that all had to obey. But my experiences have been disturbing, to say the least. What a journey I have travelled through—comparable to some kind of very racialised Alice in Wonderland tea party.

My case with HREOC was assigned to conciliation officer after conciliation officer, none of whom were ever Aboriginal persons. There was no conciliation; the senator refused outright to participate and rejected the jurisdiction of the commission. After two years in the 'conciliatory' phase, the complaint was referred to the Commission Hearing level for determination. The case of Hannah McGlade v senator Ross Lightfoot was determined by commissioner Peter Johnstone on 21 January 1999. I had some knowledge prior to the hearing that things may not go too smoothly. I felt pressured by the commission, on more than one occasion, to produce all sorts of particulars, witnesses, and other evidentiary matters. And yet the procedure was designed to be an informal one, to allow access by the disempowered. I had a legal qualification yet could barely keep my head above the water.

My case was not actually ever determined by the commission. It was dismissed under a section of the act, section 25x, which allows the commission to dismiss complaints it considers 'frivolous, vexatious, misconceived or lacking in substance'. Great fuss was made by the commissioner over the issue of parliamentary privilege, despite the fact that the complaint was always with respect to comments made outside parliament. Somehow, issue of parliamentary democracy and the senator's 'apology' in parliament became crucial to the determination—or more correctly, lack of it.

> Given that the respondent's remarks were made in a political context and were the subject of a later apology in the Commonwealth parliament, representing a rejection of opinions of the kind that had given offence in this case, and balancing that in the situation where such matters are accessible to public debate and repudiation by right thinking persons, it seems to me

inappropriate and an exercise in futility to proceed to a determination of this complaint.

The atmosphere at the hearing was charged and I was amazed at the acrobatics that were taking place before my very eyes. From the transcript of proceedings, though, it appears that I gave as good as I was getting, even when the going got personal, and my 'quite possible future in the law' was referred to by the hearing commissioner.

I have experienced repercussions arising from my action in making a complaint to HREOC and utilising a legal system against a powerful figure such as a member of parliament. But like most indigenous lawyers, my objective in pursuing a law degree was never to become part of the 'esteemed' legal profession; I was driven by other motives. I believe that 'effective' measures and remedies for racial discrimination are required of the law—as is stipulated by the International Convention on the Elimination of all Forms of Racial Discrimination—a binding international human rights treaty. But even more importantly, I believe that reconciliation requires an honest acknowledgement of wrongs committed and a proper redress and reparation for racial discrimination perpetrated, whether individual or systemic. But I do not know if this is possible. What I do know, however, is that the opportunity is denied by the hypocrisy of a legal system, which prohibits racial discrimination with one hand, and yet allows it with the other.

Reconciliation, Law and the Constitution
Melissa Castan

Not long ago this nation underwent an attempted overthrow of its constitutionally entrenched monarch, just as so many other nations experienced in the closing decades of the twentieth century. Like many such attempts, the coup failed, but unlike most others, this one was accompanied by no rioting, bloodshed, demonstrations or even military or political retaliation. The supporters of the two (or three?) sides congratulated or commiserated with each other, a few harsh words were expressed, and everyone went on with their usual business. Twenty-four years prior another overthrow had occurred: that time the parliamentary leader was ousted. Similarly, no bloodshed or military intervention ensued, a new leader was duly elected and the normal processes of government, law and order continued uninterrupted.

The key to such peaceful transition processes is often attributed to the stability and flexibility of the legal and political order in Australia, an order that has evolved out of the English constitutional model of parliamentary sovereignty and the rule of law, combined with a doctrine of separation of powers, and a federal arrangement that shares power between the central government and the states.

Despite the admiration we might have for a legal and constitutional order that is capable of accommodating fundamental threats to stability of leadership, we should not lose sight of the inherent defects that underpin our system. The historical basis of Australia's Constitution and law was grounded in certain economic imperatives, but also some important social and cultural factors. The expulsion of indigenous Australians from their lands and their exclusion from the political system, along with a legal order that tolerated (if not encouraged) brutality and cruelty to the disenfranchised, is a fact of Australian history that is fundamental to assessments of the validity of the legal order today and hereafter. Australia's constitutional and legal order may be one of the most dependable, adaptable, popularly supported, and indeed successful systems evident. However until our legal system redresses the fundamental defects that underpin and undermine its application and acceptance for indigenous Australians, reconciliation of our past history with our present aspirations for justice will remain unattainable.

Since time immemorial the Aboriginal people settled, governed, owned and had custody of the continent of Australia. For the first peoples of Australia the land was and remains the essence of their culture, society and identity; intrinsic to their legal system, organisation and nationhood. The denial of indigenous sovereignty and ownership of Australia amounted to a denial of indigenous existence; the assertion and promulgation of the *terra nullius* doctrine in the laws of the new colony prepared the foundation for much of the wrongs that were perpetrated upon indigenous peoples during the time of European settlement and beyond.

Australia's modern legal system was founded on assumptions about the identity, polity and (non)existence of indigenous peoples; these assumptions were usually incorrect, arising out of mistake, ethnocentric perspectives or racist bias. Nevertheless such assumptions laid the foundation for the following two centuries of legislative control, 'protection', disempowerment and dispossession. If sovereignty is now understood as being derived from the authority of 'the people', then it is clear that indigenous Australians never ceded sovereignty, although the Australian legal system has never fully accepted this.

Indigenous rights should be recognised in law, not only on the basis of their first possession of the lands, but also on the basis of substantive equality, an essential part of justice and Western law from ancient times to the modern era. Further, we must legally recognise that indigenous peoples, although entitled to equal rights as are all Australians, have distinct cultural identities, and as such they must be free to assert, preserve and develop their cultural identity. The right to self-identification and expression, particularly for minority cultures faced with being subsumed by a different, majority culture, is an important aspect of Western liberal legal culture, and inherent in international standards.

Laws and legal systems can be slow to change, and unresponsive to new challenges (although they don't have to be). This was particularly so regarding the enlarged doctrine of *terra nullius* which underpinned the denial of indigenous sovereignty, legal systems and proprietary rights in the colonial and post-colonial period. That expanded doctrine, based upon the writings of Locke and de Vattel, justified imperialist expansion into territories inhabited by 'uncivilised savages', and formed the basis for English and international law regarding colonial acquisition. Such law treated 'desert uninhabited' lands as amenable to all of the laws of England (or other relevant colonial power) as applied by the settlers, whereas 'occupied' lands, whether conquered by force or ceded under treaty or surrender, retained their legal system, at least until altered by the colonial parliament or royal prerogative. Justice Brennan explained in Mabo v Queensland (No. 2): 'The theory that the indigenous inhabitants of a 'settled' colony had no proprietary interest in the land thus depended on a discriminatory denigration of indigenous inhabitants, their social organisation and customs.'

The English and Australian legal systems thus developed on the perpetuation of the false basis that the territory was 'practically unoccupied' and peacefully annexed (see Cooper v Stuart, 1889). That foundation principle appeared unassailable until the Mabo No. 2 case challenged the legal orthodoxy, and the High Court confirmed that indigenous ownership of land was reality, and the legal fiction of *terra nullius* was discarded, redefining the parameters of Australia's legal landscape.

If we can look past the frailty of the title guaranteed by the court in Mabo No. 2, the case represents the turning point in the reconciliation of Australia's law with its history, acknowledges the past's 'unutterable shame', and recognises the wide-reaching effects that the inaccurate assumptions underlying the legal system could have upon a group of people.

The absence of any meaningful or positive statements concerning the position of Australia's indigenous people as part of the constitutional and legal landscape represents more than mere oversight or historical anomaly. The 'great Australian silence' that Stanner referred to in his 1968 Boyer lectures is no longer a feature of the anthropological, historical or cultural outlook, but the Australian Constitution, the foundation document of the federation, remains strangely silent on the subject of this country's first peoples.

The Australian Constitution had little if any input from indigenous people. Where it did reflect their existence within the legal and political landscape, the Constitution was negative and exclusionary: section 51(xxvi) empowered the federal parliament to make laws with respect to 'the people of any race, other than the aboriginal race in any state, for whom it is deemed necessary to make special laws.' Section 127 commanded that 'aboriginal natives shall not be counted' in the calculation of the census.

These sections were included in the Constitution to ensure that the states could continue to regulate the so-called 'people of coloured or inferior race', and to undercut their rights and freedoms, underpinned by the assumption that the aboriginal people were a 'dying race' whose populations were too unreliable to count. These views of course reflected the racially prejudiced attitudes that were prevalent at the time of the drafting of the Constitution, but those views, and the relevant Constitutional sections, continued unaltered for a considerable time during the last century. Such an obvious denial of basic human rights are no longer accepted by the Australian community, and indeed the wider international community. International treaties and declarations have for some time prohibited violation of people's civil and political rights, particularly on the basis of racial discrimination.

The 1967 referendum, which deleted section 127, and amended section 51(xxvi), reflected the rejection of such a fundamentally discriminatory constitutional model. Although it is often perceived that the passing of the national referendum was the moment when indigenous Australians 'got the vote' or became 'citizens', it is well recognised that the public perception of the significance of the referendum was probably in excess of the reality of what was achieved, or indeed achievable. The modification of section 51(xxvi) simply allowed the Commonwealth to legislate regarding all races, whereas previously only the states had legislative power over the 'aboriginal race'. Similarly the deletion of section 127 gave no 'rights' to Aboriginal Australians; it merely allowed them to be counted as people for the purposes of 'reckoning' the number of people in the Commonwealth for the allocation of seats in the House of Representatives. The changes to the census count, and the expansion of the federal parliament's powers represented an important symbolic shift in the wider electorate's recognition of the multiple breaches of the human rights of indigenous people, however there was little practical change to the laws or the administration of the law as an immediate result of this symbolic change.

There still remains some considerable debate on the scope of the Commonwealth's power over Aboriginal people, given the amendment in 1967. Does the discriminatory origins of the 'races power' permit the Commonwealth to pass laws that are 'for' Aboriginal people, but which are detrimental or regressive with respect to their civil, political, economic, social or other rights? It is argued that as the purpose of the 1967 alteration to the Constitution was to remove discrimination against Aboriginal Australians, 51(xxvi) cannot be understood as authorising detrimental laws targeted at these people on the basis of their 'race' (even if we accept this problematic designation as having some meaning). Justice Kirby said in the Kartinyeri (Hindmarsh Island) Case that if the Commonwealth's power under 51(xxvi) was construed as authorising detrimental and discriminatory laws, that interpretation 'would be a complete denial of the clear and unanimous object of the parliament in proposing the amendment', and so he decided that the Commonwealth could not use the 'races power' to make laws that have an adverse effect upon Aboriginal Australians.

However, the High Court judges did not all agree on the scope of section 51(xxvi) in that case, and there is substantial support for the interpretation that allows the Commonwealth to use that power to make laws about Aboriginal persons, irrespective of those law's beneficial or detrimental effects. This means that the Constitution still includes power that could permit the Commonwealth to pass laws that are racially discriminatory and detrimental, and also to derogate from its own anti-discrimination standards in the Racial Discrimination Act 1975. This analysis would mean our Constitution contravenes a number of international treaties and covenants to which Australia is a party, such as the Convention on the Elimination of all forms of Racial Discrimination and the International Covenant on Civil and Political Rights.

At a fundamental level, the Constitution represents the primary law of the nation. It establishes our system of government and assumes participatory democracy as its elementary principle. The Constitution should reflect the reality of prior indigenous ownership and first discovery of Australia, as well as the imperatives of equality and difference, both in order to come to terms with our past, and to shape the future. But further than that symbolic or aspirational objective, the Constitution needs essential amendments that enshrine and protect the basic human rights standards that contemporary Australians (wrongly) assume are recognised, protected and enforced.

There are strong arguments for alteration of the preamble to the Constitution to include acknowledgement of the first occupancy and 'custodianship' (or even sovereignty) of Australia by Aboriginal and Torres Strait Islander peoples, and even the recognition of ongoing rights arising out of that status as Australia's first peoples. Such alteration, by process of national referendum, would represent a widespread recognition of the fundamental omissions that are apparent in the Australian Constitution, and thus manifest the progressive development of 'reconciliation' across Australia. There are however some questions about the influence that a preamble has on the interpretation of the wider Constitution, and it has been suggested that there would be no scope for using such an alteration as a springboard for recognition of further rights or freedoms. If this were the case then expressions of goodwill and symbols of recognition would do little at the legal level for protection of indigenous rights and prevention of breaches of human rights. However the nature of the referendum process itself may have wider effects on Australian society at large, much as the 1967 referendum result represented a nation-wide shift in attitudes.

Substantive laws that would protect rights fall into two broad categories; laws that entrench rights within the Constitution or a statutory bill of rights which would enliven enforceable rights, and laws which commit a declaration such as a reconciliation treaty, the document of reconciliation or other type of declaratory statement into legislative form, articulating aspirational yet unenforceable principles.

The Australian Constitution guarantees few fundamental rights and freedoms. These were not considered necessary by the drafters of the Constitution because they believed that the parliament was best equipped to balance the competing needs of governments and individuals. We are now the only common law country that has shunned a bill of rights that protects and promotes human rights for all Australians, including indigenous peoples. Australian parliaments and executive governments have been loathe to entrench a bill of rights, for fear of putting fundamental freedoms beyond their reach, and into the hands of the independent judiciary.

Canada and New Zealand have enacted mechanisms for recognising and enforcing indigenous rights. The experience in those nations has been to develop sophisticated (and even practical) laws and policies that reflect the underlying rationales for indigenous rights, and reconciliation of these with competing national interests. In Canada the Charter of Rights and Freedoms and the Constitution Act 1982 protect 'existing aboriginal and treaty rights' and these rights can prevail over inconsistent legislation. In New Zealand the principles of the Treaty of Waitangi have to be accommodated by the government, and general rights are protected under the Bill of Rights Act 1990. Although neither instrument is entrenched in the sense of a constitutional document, the Bill of Rights is safeguarded; if proposed laws are to derogate from people's rights and freedoms, this must be explicitly expressed in the parliament at the time the law is passed.

Many indigenous and non-indigenous Australians feel that frustration and divisiveness characterise the reconciliation and native title debates in this country. The negotiations, hearings and even litigation that have evolved out of protective legislation may be complex and take time, but the issues themselves are complicated and deserve properly constructed legal and political solutions. Nevertheless the experience of other nations has not necessarily been dominated by intractable legal impasses and divisive judicial outcomes. The preservation of indigenous rights through constitutional or statutory means appears to have led to a greater prominence for the objective of reconciliation in Canada and New Zealand. Their courts have endeavoured to develop mechanisms that balance competing indigenous and non-indigenous rights and values, and to construct a legal framework that reflects and enhances reconciliation, rather than friction.

The protection and entrenchment of indigenous rights has not only affected the judicial enforcement of rights. Governments in both Canada and New Zealand have moved progressively in the articulation and protection of indigenous rights. In Canada for example, limited self-governing agreements have been made with the Inuit peoples of the northwest territories, and provincial powers have been accorded to the Nunavut territory. In New Zealand, Maori fishing rights have been accommodated in a fisheries arrangement that acknowledged the need for a just settlement of Maori claims, the public interest in the sale of public assets, and the demands of commercial enterprise. Not everyone agrees with the details and implementation of these accords, but they certainly are concrete acts of reconciliation.

These political agreements reflect an authentic level of reconciliation; law, politics and rights have coalesced around an acknowledgement of competing needs and interests, and the legal and constitutional processes are in place to negotiate largely satisfactory outcomes. Does such a coalition arise because indigenous rights are legally protected, or were those rights protected in the first place because of a certain level of respect and acceptance of their fundamental nature by the wider population? This 'chicken and egg' dilemma may be unanswerable, but until Australian governments show leadership to develop a culture of respect for rights our legal, constitutional and political system remains incomplete and deficient. Whether this is accomplished through an alteration to the Constitution or an ordinary statute is not of such importance. It will be the fact of enactment that conveys the essential message of reconciliation.

Even without a bill of rights, there are still opportunities for Australia to demonstrate respect for indigenous rights and status. This could be through adoption of a document such as a domestic 'treaty', a reconciliation declaration or the Council for Reconciliation's proposed draft document for reconciliation. This document is envisaged as an aspirational expression of community responsibility, understanding and goodwill towards indigenous Australians. As a symbolic commitment to further strategies generating real outcomes for communities, and setting standards for work environments and public institutions, no doubt it will be a worthwhile sign of enduring change in the collective attitudes of Australian society in general.

But as with an alteration of the preamble, symbolic statements are of limited value unless they manifest an underlying development or shift in awareness and protection of indigenous rights. Real acknowledgement of our legal history, and the abuses of indigenous rights can and should be redressed by the law, and that must mean by the Australian parliaments. Thus such a document, after community consultation, should be enshrined in federal and state statutes, so that reconciliation objectives become a legal reality, and further protection, development and even enforcement of reconciliation strategies is guaranteed.

Leaving aside these examples of future laws that would further the reconciliation process, there is currently the opportunity and an obligation for the Commonwealth government to make a stand for basic protection of human rights and human dignity. When state and territory governments fail to honour their obligations and responsibilities to all members of the community, then it becomes incumbent upon the federal government to act. For example, mandatory sentencing laws deny the courts adequate discretion in the administration of justice. While they are said to be non-discriminatory, in fact they apply disproportionately against indigenous offenders, often for seemingly trivial offences. The Commonwealth should not be swayed by arguments of 'states' rights' when fundamental human rights are so blatantly undermined by these types of laws, which not only contravene international standards, but offend Australian concepts of justice and fairness.

Further matters of substantive economic and social inequality, such as standards of health, education, housing and employment must of course be addressed, and programs to meet these needs are essential. However reconciliation is a wider concept that cannot only be about prospective socio-economic strategies. Reconciliation (whatever that term may mean) must include the resolution and recognition of the role that law and the Anglo-Australian legal system have played in the devastation of the Aboriginal and Torres Straits Islander peoples, as well as protection from continuing oppression. Statutory implementation of concrete acts of reconciliation and justice cannot be delayed indefinitely.

Whether it is the protection laws associated with policies of dispossession, assimilation and child removals, or the administration of criminal justice under laws that superficially appear unbiased yet are applied in a manner that reflects entrenched racism, or the laws that denied basic civil and political rights, such as voting, political participation, citizenship and freedom of movement and association, the legal system of Australia has characteristically reflected the denial of indigenous identity, presence, laws, and rights. Indigenous people have been subjected to all manner of abuses, such as kidnappings, false imprisonments, thefts, murders; in fact any number of recognised criminal acts, under the authority of 'the law'.

Now the legal system and the parliaments must redress those crimes, and contribute to the reconciliation process in a substantive and fundamental manner. Constitutional and other legislative amendments must now be presented to the Australian community, so we can take our legal and constitutional system forward with proper acknowledgement of the past, and confidence for the future.

I would like to thank Sarah Joseph and Julie Debeljak of the Monash law faculty, and the participants of the Indigenous Human Rights Conference (February 2000, Southern Cross University), who stimulated and informed my thinking for this piece.

Does Australia Have a Human Rights Diplomacy?
Pera Wells

Question:
How was it possible for Australia's foreign minister to make a definitive statement in December 1999 on Australia's past and future, without any acknowledgement of the process of reconciliation, while devoting considerable time to Australia's support for the act of self-determination in East Timor?

Answers:
(a) The foreign minister considered that reconciliation is not relevant to Australian foreign policy—that it is essentially a 'domestic matter'.
(b) The process of reconciliation is the kind of issue that can get in the way of productive relations with other countries and so the minister chose to ignore it.

Which answer would you choose? Maybe both are correct, but neither is right.

• • •

The minister for foreign affairs, Alexander Downer, gave a speech at the National Press Club Canberra, 1 December 1999 entitled 'Australia at Year's End—Retrospect and Prospect.'

An online search of the minister's speech picks up no references to the words: reconciliation, Aboriginal or indigenous. Two hits were found for 'human rights'.

The first reference was to the Universal Declaration of Human Rights, 'which reflects many of our values'. Downer went on to say that, 'Our values strengthen Australian foreign policy, helping to maintain our traditional ties with North America and Europe, and to build and strengthen links within other regions, including Asia.'

The foreign minister's approach to human rights diplomacy is based on a two-pronged strategy of maintaining traditional ties with Western allies (we share the same 'universal' values) and building links within other regions, including Asia (where we exert influence on the strength of our values).

There has been a strong tendency in Australian human rights diplomacy to assume a Western sense of superiority over our Asian and Pacific partners. For many years, Australian diplomatic representatives have asserted that Australia can and should play a leading role in promoting respect for human rights, particularly in the Asia-Pacific region.

Not surprisingly, the only other reference Downer made to human rights was in the context of East Timor:

> One point I've often made is that East Timor stood in the way of establishing a genuine long-term and productive relationship between Australia and Indonesia. Proof of the damage the issue had caused to our relations with Indonesia can be found in the widespread view in Australia that we could only promote Indonesian ties at the expense of dropping East Timorese issues—that we had to ignore East Timor despite continuing human rights concerns, Australia's historical ties with the island, and its close geographic proximity.

Downer believed it was necessary to get East Timor out of the way, so that Australia could develop a genuine long-term and productive relationship with Indonesia. Is this a reasonable analysis of how relationships develop between nation states—or is it more likely that genuine relationships develop through open and compassionate dialogue about sensitive issues, including human rights?

Let us imagine that people in Indonesia feel so strongly about the human rights situation of Aborigines that the Indonesian government decides that it cannot develop 'a genuine long-term and productive relationship with Australia'. How would we feel? What would we want our foreign minister to do—keep quiet or demonstrate a readiness to listen to Indonesians' concerns about Aborigines and enter into dialogue with a view to finding a way forward for genuine reconciliation?

This essay is an attempt to explore why dialogue on the process of reconciliation—actively supported within Australia—has not become integral to Australia's foreign policy, particularly our human rights diplomacy.

The Howard government seems to regard the process of reconciliation as something which will not impact on the balance of power within our society and therefore be of no consequence for Australia's international relations or standing in the Asia-Pacific region.

It is worth recalling that the 1991 commitment to a ten-year 'process of reconciliation' resulted from the inability of the Hawke government to achieve bipartisan support for formal acknowledgement of the right of indigenous people to self-determination or for a treaty or Makaratta with Aboriginal people.

The issue of the right of Aborigines to self-determination became significant when prime minister Whitlam declared in 1972 that his government's policy would 'restore to the Aboriginal people of Australia their lost power of self-determination in economic, social and political affairs'. The Aboriginal tent embassy was first set up in Canberra at this time and other symbols of 'sovereignty', such as the Aboriginal and Torres Strait Islander flags have gained ambiguous status.

With respect to the Aboriginal flag, Hugh Collins wrote:

> Is it a distinctive identity within the Australian nation? Or is it an incipient nationhood of an Aboriginal people? That ambiguity reflects a tension within Aboriginal politics, but the effectiveness of the symbol derives largely from its capacity to represent either notion and thus to unite both.

The Howard government is dismissive of such ambiguities and has firmly rejected the idea that Aborigines have a right to self-determination. The government has extended this position into its human rights diplomacy. In August 1998 Downer stated that Australia did not support inclusion of the concept of self-determination in the draft UN Declaration on the Rights of Indigenous Peoples which is being negotiated in the UN Working Group on Indigenous Populations:

> We don't want to see a separate country created for indigenous Australians. We will...be arguing...that it might be better to use the term self-management rather than leaving an impression that we are prepared to have a separate indigenous state.

Australia has participated in every session of the UN Working Group on Indigenous Populations since it was set up in 1982. There have been many debates about inclusion of the right of self-determination in the draft declaration and over the years Australian government and indigenous representatives have registered support for self-determination, not as a static concept, but an evolving right. For example, former ATSIC chairperson, Lowitja O'Donoghue stated in 1993 that:

> The call for self-determination in the Declaration on the Rights of Indigenous Peoples is not a new or different right that applies to us as indigenous peoples....Self-determination for the members of

the United Nations has taken many forms. The same will happen, I believe, in the evolution of self-determination for indigenous peoples. There is not a single future to which we must conform, there are multiple futures. And multiple futures within the same environment.

Downer's suggestion that the right of self-determination equates to a right of succession has no basis in international law, but it does have relevance to East Timor. Interestingly, the Howard government has worked with the concept of self-determination in its diplomacy towards Indonesia. And it has done so by making a direct link between the process of reconciliation and an act of self-determination.

The prime minister, Mr Howard, wrote to president Habibie on 23 December 1998 setting out the government's views on the future of East Timor. The letter stated that in the government's view, the long-term prospects for reconciliation would be best served by the holding of an act of self-determination at some future time, following a substantial period of autonomy.

This quote is from the government response, dated June 1999, to the recommendations of the report of the Joint Standing Committee on Foreign Affairs, Defence and Trade. The report was called *Improving but... Australia's regional dialogue on human rights.*

The government response includes one other reference to reconciliation: 'In its contacts both with the East Timorese and the Indonesian government, the government has also emphasised the importance of a process of reconciliation between various East Timorese factions.'

There is no reference in the government response to the Australian process of reconciliation, no mention of issues relating to Aborigines or indigenous people. How, it must be asked, can Australia have a meaningful regional dialogue on human rights without engaging in substantive discussion on these issues?

Where one would at least expect to see evidence that Australian human rights diplomacy is engaged with the process of reconciliation is in the newsletter of the Department of Foreign Affairs and Trade on human rights and indigenous issues—the January 2000 edition is a disappointment.

Within federal government circles, it has long been understood that it is necessary to uphold Australia's credentials on issues of racism to protect Australia's international standing as a middle power. In the early 1960s, when the United Nations began work on a draft Convention on Racial Discrimination, the Menzies Liberal-Coalition government set up an interdepartmental committee to 'confer regarding Commonwealth acts that contain certain provisions discriminating against the employment of persons of Aboriginal descent...and to report on the desirability of removing discrimination.'

The committee reported that there was growing international and domestic pressure against racial discrimination:

> Any 'white' country having an underdeveloped 'non-white' population was liable to close international scrutiny...Up to the present, Australia has largely escaped strong international criticisms for its handling of Aborigines.

The committee however concluded that there was an 'urgent need to remove, as far as practicable, instances of racial discrimination in Australia in order to ensure that Australia's international reputation and influence are not to be seriously endangered'.

The report of the committee formed the basis of the brief to the Australian delegation to the United Nations General Assembly in 1964. It explained why Australia, in company with other Western states, had abstained in 1963 on the draft resolution on the racial discrimination convention. The principal difficulties with respect to Australian acceptance of the substantive articles of the draft convention were:

> (a) some legislation in Australian external territories (such as PNG) could be seen as discriminatory;
> (b) the Commonwealth imposed restrictions on the right of Aborigines to leave Australia;
> (c) Aborigines do not everywhere have the same political rights as 'other' Australians;
> (d) in the pastoral industries there were no standards of equal pay for equal work.

How limited in scope this list now seems today, particularly against the background of the High Court decision on Mabo (1992), the Native Title Act (1993) and *Bringing Them Home*, the report of the national inquiry into the stolen generation (1997). But precisely because of these developments, the relevance of this convention to the situation of Australia's Aborigines is now of pressing international concern.

It has taken over 20 years for CERD, the United Nations committee set up to overview implementation of the convention, to raise urgent questions about Australia's record on racial discrimination. In August 1998, CERD made Australia the subject of an early warning/urgent action, the first and only time a Western developed country has come under such scrutiny.

Decision 1 (53) of 14 August 1998, requested the government of Australia to provide information on 'the changes recently projected or introduced to the 1993 Native Title Act, on any changes of policy... as to Aboriginal land rights, and of the functions of the Aboriginal and Torres Strait Islander social justice commissioner.'

The Australian government provided a detailed submission to CERD in March 1999. In response CERD found that the amended 1993 Native Title Act 'appears to create legal certainty for governments and third parties at the expense of indigenous title' and expressed concern about the 'continuing political, economic and social marginalisation of indigenous Australians.'

Calling on the government to address these concerns with the utmost urgency, the committee urged Canberra to reopen discussions with indigenous representatives with a view to finding solutions acceptable to indigenous peoples that comply with Australia's obligations under the convention. The Howard government rejected the CERD decision as 'insulting' and 'unbalanced'.

A year later, in March 2000, the government was called upon to make a further presentation to CERD. By this time another issue was on the agenda—whether mandatory jail sentencing laws in the Northern Territory and Western Australia were in breach of Australia's obligations under international human rights instruments. The CERD report, issued on Friday 24 March, concluded that mandatory sentencing laws did discriminate against indigenous Australians and breached UN conventions on human rights to which Australia was a party. The committee made a number of recommendations, including that the federal government override Northern Territory and Western Australian laws if necessary, and review its amendments to native title laws.

Once again, the government rejected the CERD report as 'unbalanced' for not taking due account of the government's submission. The presence and presentations of Aboriginal leaders at CERD meetings have clearly begun to carry greater weight in the eyes of committee members than the efforts of government representatives. Over the years, and particularly since the early 1980s when the UN Working Group of Indigenous Populations was set up, Aborigines and those working in sympathy for their causes, have become increasingly adept at leveraging the growing international interest in indigenous issues to exert pressure on Australian governments.

This time the government over-reacted. A chorus of federal ministers issued statements, including the attorney general, who asserted that international human rights instruments were irrelevant to the domestic issue of mandatory sentencing and that the federal government would not use its powers to override state or territory legislation. He said that the government had made 'some complaints to the UN hierarchy' about the CERD report, implicitly confirming media reports that the foreign minister had put pressure on the UN to sanitise its earlier report on mandatory sentencing.

The Howard government's sense of incredulity that the United Nations could find any fault with Australia's record shows how superficial Australia's human rights diplomacy has become, and how it has moved to an increasingly defensive posture on Aboriginal issues. By the end of March, the foreign minister issued a statement advising that 'Cabinet had determined that it would now be appropriate to review how Australia participates in the UN treaty committee system.' In effect the government proposed to attack the United Nations' human rights regime, rather than cooperate with CERD (and other agencies) with the intent of better protecting the human rights of Australia's indigenous people.

This government's basic position is that indigenous issues, including the process of reconciliation, are domestic matters and therefore not a proper subject for foreign influence or intervention. This position is untenable. The tensions that have emerged in the CERD context signal that the process of reconciliation is not working domestically and that there is growing international concern about the situation of Aborigines. Eminent Australians, notably Gustav Nossal, have made it clear that government attempts to suppress international interest in indigenous issues in the context of the Sydney 2000 Olympics will be counterproductive.

What is needed in Australia's human rights diplomacy is an appreciation that Aboriginal people, custodians of one of the world's most ancient cultures and value systems, offer a distinct and valid perspective to the global understanding of human rights. The Australian government has the responsibility to work openly for this understanding, in close consultation with indigenous people. No longer should major statements by the foreign minister focus only on trends in trade and investment, defence and security issues; high priority should be given to how relationships between people living on this continent are evolving, what this means for the process of reconciliation and for Australia's capacities to contribute to the international community including the work of the UN in promoting and protecting human rights.

Justice for All as Long as You're White
Petro Georgiou

We are a nation that celebrates its commitment to justice, equality, freedom and tolerance. Yet we are also a nation in which a child can be imprisoned for stealing a toy, for breaking a window or riding as a passenger in a stolen vehicle.

In 1997, the Northern Territory government introduced a mandatory sentencing regime for most property offences. That regime removes judicial discretion in the sentencing of juveniles. It demands, for example, that a child aged 15 or 16 convicted of theft for a second time must be incarcerated for 28 days—regardless of the value of the item stolen. A 17-year-old must be incarcerated for two weeks for a first offence, three months for the second, and a year for the third. There can be no appeal against the sentence.

Confronted with national concern over this legal regime, politicians in the Northern Territory have admonished the rest of Australia for criticising their legislation. Derided as southern do-gooders from leafy suburban electorates, critics of mandatory sentencing are told they do not understand the law-and-order crisis in the Territory, which necessitates locking up children.

In 1997, the Northern Territory introduced mandatory sentencing following considerable hype over rising property crime. But the statistical data casts doubt on the very basis of those concerns. Figures from the Australian Bureau of Statistics and the Australian Institute of Criminology show that between 1995 and 1997 crime rates for many property offences in the Territory were in fact declining. Unlawful entry into dwellings fell by some 17 percent, whilst motor vehicle theft and unarmed robbery dropped by 19 and 20 percent respectively.

On a comparative basis, property offences in the Northern Territory were broadly comparable with national averages. In some categories—such as robbery and motor vehicle theft—Northern Territory offence rates were below those in many other jurisdictions.

The initial rationale for introducing severe laws to combat property crime was questionable. Today, the arguments supporting their retention are similarly flawed. We are told that mandatory sentencing reduces crime. Yet since its introduction property crime and imprisonment rates have increased. The 1998–99 annual report of the Northern Territory Police Fire and Emergency Services points to an increase in motor vehicle theft, unlawful entry to buildings and general theft since the introduction of mandatory sentencing.

In Alice Springs unlawful entry and criminal property damage has risen by 20 percent since mandatory sentencing commenced. The Australian Bureau of Statistics points to an increase in the Northern Territory prisoner population of 42 percent since the introduction of mandatory sentencing.

We are told by representatives of the Northern Territory government that mandatory sentencing is not just designed to deter—it also aims to punish, and punish harshly. But what type of society have we become when we respond to minor juvenile crime with a policy based primarily on revenge?

We are told that the Northern Territory laws punish only a small group of hardened offenders who are beyond assistance or rehabilitation. Yet the findings of the Human Rights and Equal Opportunity Commission paint a very different and disturbing picture.

The commission identifies cases of young Australians in the Northern Territory sentenced to jail for minor offences. It tells, for example, of two 17-year-old girls with no prior convictions sent to jail for two weeks for stealing clothes from roommates. It tells of a 15-year-old boy who broke a window after hearing of the suicide of a close friend. Mandatorily sentenced to 28 days, he himself tried to commit suicide.

These are not the stories of children beyond rehabilitation or assistance. Rather, these are stories of children struggling with difficulties which many adolescent Australians experience. As John Tippett, president of the NT Law Society explains: 'The sort of behaviour that once upon a time was regarded as pretty much part of the human process, the sorts of mistakes that people would once take into account as a momentary failure, the sorts of things that you might not give a great deal of consideration to in the ordinary living of life, in the Northern Territory can put you in prison.'

We are told that in the Northern Territory the mandatory sentencing regime applies equally to everyone. It does not. Although it looks neutral, in practice the Territory regime results in 'indirect' discrimination against indigenous Australians.

The vast majority of those who find themselves incarcerated for minor property offences are indigenous. A range of socio-economic circumstances and difficulties ensure that mandatory sentencing has a disproportionate impact on indigenous Australians. Remarkably, property offences in the Northern Territory, like fraud and white-collar crime, which have high levels of non-indigenous offenders, are exempt from mandatory sentencing.

In many remote indigenous communities an absence of education campaigns about mandatory sentencing laws combined with difficulties with English have left the population uninformed about the severe consequences of committing minor property offences. A lack of interpreter services means many children from these communities will understand neither the sentencing process nor the reason for their incarceration. Often interned a considerable distance away from families, the dislocation of indigenous children from their communities can have tragic consequences.

We are told that the mandatory sentencing legislation was necessary because the courts in the Northern Territory were excessively lenient. But I find it hard to believe that allowing a court to take into account the personal circumstances of a child who has stolen an apple amounts to going soft on crime.

The Northern Territory mandatory sentencing laws are cruel and inappropriate in a nation where our justice system is largely predicated on the ability of the courts to hand down a punishment that fits both the crime and the criminal.

Gordon Renouf, director of the North Australian Aboriginal Aid Service, explains that young indigenous Australians in the Territory are finding themselves in jail for the most minor of infractions such as the theft of a bottle of spring water. 'Not all the offences affected by mandatory sentencing are trivial,' says Renouf, but 'the non-trivial offences would in many cases have received a jail term anyway. The effect of mandatory sentencing is to make the offenders involved in trivial offences go to jail.'

In 1997, I refused to support legislation to override the Northern Territory's voluntary euthanasia law. I have no axe to grind against the Northern Territory. But it is unacceptable that any Australian child should be automatically incarcerated for minor property crime. The fate of such children, harshly and arbitrarily punished under an Australian judicial system, undermines our commitment to a society built on the principles of equity and justice.

Ed. note: In April 2000, Georgiou and two other backbenchers threatened to cross the floor, prompting Howard to meet the Northern Territory chief minister and broker a deal to keep juveniles who commit minor offences out of the NT mandatory sentencing system.

Embracing New Voices: Reconciliation in Canada
Peter Jull

Australians interested in reform of indigenous policy often look at the Canadian experience. The two countries are so much alike in size, history, economy, and federal structure—even their extreme differences may be 'alike'. Much of Australia endures +40 degree Celsius days in January while much of Canada has -40 degrees, equally extreme for migrants from temperate Europe.

Unfortunately Canada's indigenous policy is often dismissed in Australia as too exotic in its legal assumptions or history to be relevant here. However, a few details should not obscure some very large truths and trends which apply equally in both countries. The real shift away from the 'two solitudes' of indigenous and non-indigenous realities, a term often used for Canada's English and French language zones, came after 1945 in response to world conditions. After the Depression, the Second World War, and the defeat of aggressive racism embodied by Hitler, ideals bloomed with the postwar economic boom and fledgling United Nations. Affluence and ideals meant little, however, if the original peoples of national territory were isolated by skin colour, social disadvantage, and legal discrimination.

In 2000 there is commemoration of the 1000-year anniversary of the first known European landings in Canada by Leif Eriksen and his Norwegian crew sailing from the Norse Greenland colony. Inuit and Indians easily repelled attempts to settle, but Europe probably had more contact during fishing and whaling voyages than we know before Cabot claimed Newfoundland for King Henry VII in 1497. Cabot named the 'Red Indians' Newfoundland's Beothucks, but when Queen Elizabeth visited in 1997 to celebrate his voyage, Indians from across Canada stood by in mourning while the premier called for a minute's silence for that 'disappeared' (ie. extinct) people.

Several European peoples had seasonal fishing stations ashore but successful permanent settlement by the French began in the early 1600s. Those and earlier settlement attempts endured terrible sufferings, the whites often surviving winter only with indigenous help and medicine. Once established, the little English and French colonies and the colonists were pawns in the long-running struggle for world control between France and England, punctuated by treaties and trade-offs, ending with the Seven Years War and peace in 1763. King George III then decreed that the Crown must respect the 'Indian nations' and that only the Crown could deal with their land rights. This policy has shaped both Canadian and American policy to this day.

Initially, of course, the leadership of generals, including George Washington, was especially desirable so that such cool heads could prevent foolish settlers from enraging the Indians by grabbing their lands or women. The costs of fighting wars against the guerrilla tribes of North America, and frequent shame of defeat, made eighteenth and nineteenth century Britons turn pale. (The best survey of Canada's indigenous–white history, J.R. Miller's *Skyscrapers Hide the Heavens* has been newly revised and reprinted.)

Once the era of wars was over, and Canada repeatedly saved from the Americans thanks to inspired Indian leaders and their countless unnamed fighters, the civil authorities took over. Farming, forestry, resource extraction, harnessing rivers, and all the growth of modern Canada meant dispossessing indigenous peoples—a process that continues to this day.

Better-educated indigenous people, both in terms of schooling and awareness of Canada's official ideals of justice and equity, found some sympathy in the better-educated postwar Canadian public. But most Canadians remained amazingly ignorant. 'I thought they were all dead!' said astonished children of educated parents c. 1970 when told that the nice lady playing with them was an Indian. She was one of a group of friends from the national capital Ottawa sharing Christmas in a snow-bound forest chalet. Canadians knew that Brant and Tecumseh had saved Canada long ago, but today...? Weren't Indians merely quiet remnants withdrawn into the northern forests, away from 'modern' noise and industry, perhaps appearing as cooks or helpers in logging, survey, or fishing camps, content to stay out of sight and out of mind?

'The Indians'—ie. first nations from the Nuu-chah-nulth (Captain Cook's Nootka) and Haida on the Pacific coast to Innu (Naskapi or Montagnais in older writings) Mi'kmaq and Newfoundland's extinct

Beothuck on the Atlantic—had seen their reserved lands, once a minimum guarantee, become their sole allowed territory. Even the Cree and Dene peoples ranging across the mid-north to the tree-line were under constant threat from outside to turn land to 'productive', that is, non-indigenous, use.

The postwar 'discovery' of the Inuit, or so-called Eskimos north of the tree-line, ie. one-third of Canada's land territory, is full of irony. Living far beyond the end of roads, they were little known, so Canadians could see in them many happy qualities to accompany their novel artworks now reaching the south. Their smiles for the camera and iconic designs—for example, the snow-house—helped shore up Canadian identity vis-à-vis their all-too-absorbing American neighbour. Overlooked by all but a few officials, traders, and others ministering to their health needs, Inuit seemed cheery and a national tonic, unlike the grumpy Indians. When pressed, of course, Canadians admitted that Indians had good cause to be grumpy about 'the white man.'[1]

More recently Inuit have been seen, correctly, as determined protectors of the Arctic lands, seas, and ecosystems, and people determined to maintain their unique language and culture. Fighting the odds through development hearings, land and sea claims, international environment action, and national and regional constitutional forums, their struggle has often seemed one for the soul of the country against the excesses of Big Business, Big Oil, Big Mining, and Big Government.

While urbanised Canadians may not comfortably contemplate fundamental change to their own economic patterns, they have recognised that parts of the country not yet despoiled by industrial society may be worth protecting. Despite conferences, glossy booklets in both official languages, sanctimonious official gestures, swarms of PhD'ed experts, and endless exhortation, it has not been our Western rationality which has been saving the hinterland but socially deprived, discriminated against, ill- or un-educated hunter-gatherers who know precisely what is at risk and who are prepared to put everything on the line to protect it.

First nations and Métis have been no less active in this process, although Inuit have had a more reassuring domestic and international profile, the latter in part due to the Inuit Circumpolar Conference, an Inuit 'commonwealth of nations' uniting Siberian, Alaskan, Greenlandic, and Canadian Inuit as usefully as the British Commonwealth and Francophonie enrich Canada's other cultural traditions. Inuit have drawn Canadians into their great emptiness and redefined national existence. That is, the 'empty

---

1 'The white man' is not a gender insensitive term but rather the term used by indigenous and colonised or formerly colonised peoples all over the world for European intrusion or domination in their homelands. Virtually the only women involved in the early stages, of course, were missionary nuns engaged in teaching or medical work in places like frontier Canada.

north', far from awaiting the transforming hand of purposeful whites, as long fantasised in Britain and southern Canada, is now recognised as part of a circumpolar Arctic region of many indigenous peoples and ancient cultures with particular needs and imperatives. It has given Canada a new dimension and a new field for action. Instead of imposing white political models on other cultures painfully or even disastrously in the circumpolar past, the last decades have seen new awareness in governments and new accommodations or reconciliation with hinterland peoples.

Canada, Denmark (with Greenland and the Faroes), Norway, Sweden, and Finland in the Sami (Lapp) lands, Russia in fits and starts, and USA in Alaska are all practising and exploring new modes of public administration. Historically, politically, and morally, post-1788 Australia belongs to this far northern world in all but climate and location, not only as one among continent-scale nations like Russia, USA, and Canada, but as a country established by the explosive European expansion into new regions from c. 1500 onward.

Like Australia, Canada's vast hinterland is inhospitable to conventional European lifestyles but important for the national economy and identity. This hinterland (in both countries) might be better called an 'indigenous hinterland' because despite the presence of isolated resource and supply towns, and extensive activities like Australian grazing and Canadian forestry, indigenous peoples continue to live in their traditional territories and maintain significant elements of language, culture, lifestyle, economy, and social tradition. While non-indigenous workers come and go, indigenous people are at home. Even long-term non-indigenous town residents usually retire to the faraway south. One of the strange features of hinterland life is the boastfulness of those who have spent 15 or 20 years in Darwin or Yellowknife, vis-à-vis those who are newcomers, while real long-term residents—Yolngu or Dene or Inuit—are implicitly left out.

The recent furore about hinterland Australian laws which target and jail Aborigines, in practice, has highlighted dispossession and desperation of indigenous peoples on frontiers of settlement. In postwar Canada, the federal government moved strongly to avoid such outcomes in the Arctic and Sub-Arctic; that is, to avoid repeating the nineteenth century frontier which left indigenous peoples aside, sick, poor, and powerless. With 'northern territories' making up 40 percent of Canada's land area—that is, territories in which the national government could initiate or enforce important policies— there was scope for considerable action.

Various good intentions have been tried since the war, and many have failed, or had unforeseen results. When it became clear that the white newcomers intended not only to dominate local society, but control the political system and tear up the ground or drill through the sea ice in search of riches, indigenous peoples mobilised. They began to offer their own political solutions, coded as 'aboriginal rights' or 'land rights'; terms as full of self-determination as 'provincehood' to northern whites (or 'statehood' in Darwin). When northern white leaders shouted about equality, 'We're all northerners!', the indigenous reply was derision. After all, the whites had the good jobs, good housing, access to southern goods, long life-spans, and made all the decisions.

In this situation, as in northern Australia today, matters became complex. Northern whites draped themselves in good old-fashioned liberal values: the indigenous groups were being racist, they said, or separatist (a pregnant term in a Canada haunted by Quebec's secessionist movement), while the whites were merely trying to bring full Canadian citizenship and institutions into a backward area. Ottawa, for its part, was eager for northern resource development which northern whites enthusiastically supported, while indigenous peoples wanted environment and land rights questions answered first. Nevertheless, with indigenous political activism rising all across the country, and Canadians all too aware of injustices and evils of the past, the notion of handing large areas of the country over to some get-rich-quick whites in a few northern outposts never had much appeal. The debate raged for years, and despite their isolation and small numbers, indigenous peoples slowly won key elements of Canadian public opinion. Ottawa's modern 'northern policy' implicitly but firmly developed three main aspects.

Firstly, native title would be transformed through negotiation with indigenous peoples into legally enforceable agreements and packages of benefits, or 'regional agreements' as Australians call these Canadian outcomes; secondly, no large-scale transfer of land and resources ownership or jurisdiction from Ottawa (which held both) to northern territory governments would occur until indigenous land claims were settled; and finally, further constitutional development in northern territories must only proceed when both territory governments and the principal indigenous organisations agreed (or where Ottawa continued to reserve and protect the indigenous interest if such agreement was not possible on minor issues).

The result of this policy has been the easing of racial tensions (which became bitter in the 1970s), the sort of indigenous-newcomer cooperation in social and economic areas of which postwar idealists dreamed, and a confident multi-racial society. A new mixed political economy has emerged, one in which old dogmas of left and right, socialism and capitalism, hardly remain. Governments have always had to play a large role in the hinterland, and private initiative has always been a condition of survival whether one was there serving God, the Queen, one's igloo-dwelling family, or the Hudson's Bay Company. Environmental protection is built into the system through strong decision-making co-management bodies made up of indigenous and other environmental experts. Far from opposing all developments—which have proven more at the command of world commodity prices than government, developer, or indigenous will—indigenous groups have been happy to seek or support clean projects with job and revenue benefits. Political institutions at local, region, or territory level are all indigenous-friendly or indigenous-designed. In 1999, for instance, the large Eastern Arctic region of the northwest territories became a new territory, Nunavut, meaning 'our land' in the Inuit language, with a premier and cabinet drawn from among the large Inuit majority in that region which is somewhat larger than Queensland. (For more detail see my 'Negotiating Indigenous Reconciliation: Territorial Rights and Governance in Nunavut', *Arena Journal*, No. 13, 1999, pp 17-23.)

Nunavut's new premier, Paul Okalik, visited Australia to talk about Inuit land rights and Nunavut, so we may hope he returns to share insight on indigenous governance. In early 2000, meanwhile, the northwest territories chose former Dene land rights leader Steve Kakfwi as its new premier, he being the seventh indigenous activist leader to become NWT premier in the past couple of decades. These premiers have inherited an administration which was largely created to serve indigenous needs so although it now seems outwardly like any provincial government, the content of its policies and programs is indigenised.

Recent Canadian experience in the hinterland gives the lie to fears and racial prejudice which many whites in Australia or Canada direct at racial reconciliation. The Canadian experience has been so successful that the 1996 report of the Royal Commission on Aboriginal Peoples proposed such 'regional agreements' or 'treaties' for the whole of Canada. These would not impinge on existing land ownership or use, or on the public institutions of the settled southern Canadian public. They would, rather, attempt to re-organise indigenous communities on a more viable basis and address constraints on their development and wellbeing. Nevertheless, a scare campaign run by a few vested interests, eg. fisheries, and slowness of federal and provincial governments to respond with information and public leadership on the issue, has endangered the Nisga'a Treaty in the northwest of British Columbia (BC) province. British Columbia is a region often compared with Queensland in its lamentable history of race relations. However, BC polls in recent years have shown broad public support for indigenous rights settlements, something unimaginable when I was cabinet secretary there in the mid-1970s. The Nisga'a have been trying for a hundred years to settle their claims and their moral win in Canada's highest court in 1973, the Calder or Nishga decision, was Mabo-like in its import.

Calder was a national psychological breakthrough, like Mabo, and many areas of indigenous reform gathered momentum despite successive changes of government. Before long discussion and fractious meetings, attempts at negotiation, talk of practical outcomes, and the ultimate icon of Canadian political importance—constitutional amendments entrenched in 1982 and televised constitutional conferences from 1983 between prime minister, premiers, and indigenous leaders—showed that a new age had dawned. Retreat was useless. After a national constitutional conference in March 1987 failed to agree on indigenous self-government clauses, a weary federal prime minister hoped to tiptoe away from indigenous reform. That ended with the explosion of a 290-year-old land rights issue at Oka in 1990, a quiet Mohawk reserve at the mouth of the Ottawa River, provoking sympathy actions across the country. Canada now had the unenviable experience of its tanks lined up against a tiny village where Indian women, children, and men tried to go on with their lives, sharing the TV news with Saddam Hussein's tanks threatening Kuwaitis and their neighbours. Pent-up indigenous anger across Canada should have surprised nobody. It forced governments to return to the clear evolution of postwar policy through recognition and devolution of powers and funds to indigenous local and regional communities.

Canadians and their governments know there are limits to indigenous patience. They know that governments cannot blithely ignore or legislate to override rights recognised belatedly by the courts; that they cannot withdraw constitutional commitments promised by their leaders; that they cannot ignore pain and suffering such as removal of children or residential school abuse; and that they must offer continuing dialogue and reforms and maintain plausible hope for a better indigenous future. Perhaps most of all they know now that indigenous leaders are practical men and women. They have shown as clear vision, skill, and articulateness as the best non-indigenous politicians and can sway the Canadian public no less effectively than premiers and prime ministers. With so much past injustice and continuing disadvantage behind their words, they have an emotional and intellectual authority which the daily 'mainstream' political flim-flam rarely equals. Meanwhile, in a country where 'native' is a word in general use for 'indigenous', the irony of the national anthem's opening words, 'O Canada, our home and native land!', is lost on few people today.

Canadians did not set out with a road-map to reconciliation. Instead, they found it through trial and error, through articulate voices debating or shouting, through court cases, media coverage, a change of generation in politics and high officialdom. The history and shape and entire understanding of what the settlement of Canada and its development had meant, was being replayed and relived across the huge northern areas of seven provinces (and is still going on there) and across the northern territories from the 1960s onwards, confronting Canadians with the shabbiness or crassness of their own myths. The social costs for ancient cultures and their children today, and environmental costs to a supposedly vast and unspoiled land which was now being spoiled at a great rate, became front page news for the first time in history. Angry schooled indigenous youth in cities and in indigenous organisations funded by Ottawa in multi-year formula financing—perhaps Canada's best and bravest innovation—kept a wealth of issues before governments and public. Better this, Canadian leaders recognised, than random or long-running Ulster-style violence.

For over a generation and a half, indigenous and non-indigenous Canadians have negotiated or re-negotiated the fundamental assumptions of national political culture. It was bracing and has produced a larger, richer, more complex, more interesting, and more satisfying country. Narrow late Victorianism and British Empire triumphalism was a strait-jacket. Canada became a new country.

If Canada has been changed, the exploding populations of indigenous communities face new practical problems, too. Just as a generation of gifted spokespersons and idealists were savouring some ease in middle age, an angry new generation—better educated, with more mainstream experience, and full demanding citizens both of indigenous 'nations' and of a diverse federal multicultural Canada—has arisen demanding more immediate socio-economic improvements. The framework has been established by one generation and now another must make it work. Indigenous scholars like Taiaiake Alfred offer tough critiques of indigenous society and the leadership and cultural confidence needed for rebuilding.

Building the framework for renewing indigenous-white relations was not so hard as many imagined. Indigenous Canada is no longer tidily out of sight, but has joined the Canadian community. Its many problems are now shared with a wider public surprised by their extent. Reconciliation is not a new forgetting of old peoples. Rather, it is a welcoming of new voices, new energies, and new ideas long hidden or ignored to an enlarged country more aware of itself and more mature.

Not Much Progress
Geoff Clark

Early in 2000, Indonesian president Abdurrhaman Wahid embraced East Timorese leader Xanana Gusmao on the tarmac at Dili airport. The Australian government welcomed this potent, symbolic act of reconciliation and president Wahid's apology for 24 years of oppression saying, 'It's important to have a good political relationship'.[1]

Only one day earlier, Australian prime minister John Howard signalled that he would scale back his commitment to advancing the cause of reconciliation in Australia during 2000. Mr Howard does not believe in apologies or symbolic gestures.

We can only wonder what it will take to make a significant advance in the reconciliation process in this country. We don't have a history of civil war or terrorism. (However, we shouldn't lose sight of the fact that one of the last state-sanctioned attacks on Aboriginal people resulted in the massacre at Forrest River in WA in 1926—an event within living memory.)

Perhaps the elected representatives of the Australian government feel relaxed and comfortable and unchallenged about race relations. Perhaps they feel they should follow opinion polls that suggest a majority of the population is not very committed to reconciliation.

---

1 Foreign minister Alexander Downer, ABC Radio news report, 29 February 2000.

Yet political leadership isn't about following opinion polls. A majority of the population remains opposed to the introduction of a Goods and Services Tax but the political leadership in this country has committed itself to that course.

Reconciliation, as it is generally understood, has mainly been the white man's concern. While reconciliation meetings in local town halls have filled to overflowing with sympathetic non-indigenous people, the process has only briefly offered any relevance to Aboriginal and Torres Strait Islander people.

A troubled process

The only test of reconciliation is to ask: 'What will change as a result?'

Recent events, including prime minister John Howard's withdrawal, confirm that the answer, at this time, remains: 'Nothing much'.

There seems to be widespread acceptance that there are issues dividing Aboriginal and Torres Strait Islander people from the rest of the community. From the prime minister down, most parliamentarians and other leaders seem to understand that this country's indigenous population misses out on opportunities for full and equal participation in the community. They seem to recognise the need for some sort of fundamental change to the relationship between the broader community and the first peoples of this land. But they have trouble understanding the nature of that need.

Endless debate about what change is needed has become the substitute for action—an evasion of the real issues and an obstacle to progress. Much of what passes for public comment on reconciliation is propaganda designed to whittle away the argument for change.

So, too, is the talk about achieving reconciliation by improved standards in health, housing, education and employment opportunities. It's demeaning to reduce the core issues about why we are a divided society to simple, basic citizenship entitlements. That's just another form of handout. It's both assimilationist and an evasion to offer services that are due to us as of right. Poverty, ill-health and lack of opportunity do not distinguish Aboriginal and Torres Strait Islander people and do not define indigenous identity. White people also suffer poverty, illness and unemployment.

Indigenous people are seeking the ability to exercise choice in our lives. So much of the history that has shaped this country has denied us any choice. It's the legacy of the historical relationship that has created the need for reconciliation.

Nowadays, to talk about reconciliation is to refer to a football game without goal posts or accepted referees. Instead of booting around ideas about what should be done to or for indigenous communities in the name of reconciliation, non-indigenous Australians need to commit themselves to a bipartisan process for listening to what we have to say.

Let's be honest about this—if reconciliation was working, the debate on native title would not develop the way it has, driven by propaganda and hypocrisy. Prime ministers and independent senators would not conduct negotiations on policy decisions while Aboriginal and Torres Strait Islander people stand outside the parliament.

And governments must stop insisting that we now abandon our separate identities as Aboriginal people and Torres Strait Islanders. It's a perverse, if not hostile, position for politicians now to argue that the path to reconciliation should traverse assimilation. They spent two centuries reinforcing the idea that Aboriginal and Torres Strait Islander people are different to the Australian nation and may not have a place in it. Now they want us to surrender our distinct cultures and identities.

As far as reconciliation goes, Australia may need a role model to get itself back on track. It needs to look at the process in South Africa where social change preceded the process of community healing. The community embraced a process known as Truth and Reconciliation that placed a premium on facing up to the issues of the past before moving on.

In this country, we have yet to make a similar quantum leap. We do not yet have a commitment from politicians to an ethical and transparent process for debate on how to heal division. Undeserved attacks upon ATSIC, for example, reinforce division and play to the suspicion and resentment towards indigenous people that clearly exists in the community. What we need is national leadership that will bridge the gap between attitudes and action.

And it's probably time to stop being coy or evasive about what action is required to achieve reconciliation. Personally, I doubt I will be satisfied with anything less than a treaty. I believe the majority of indigenous people share that preference. We need a treaty, and we need it sooner rather than later.

Where it began

The concept of reconciliation grew out of the calls for a treaty or a makarrata made by Aboriginal activists in the 1970s.

In the 1980s, prime minister Bob Hawke came up with the idea of a 'compact' between indigenous and non-indigenous Australia. This developed later into 'reconciliation' as people tried to evade the implications of a treaty.

'Reconciliation' was seen as less confronting, especially as the Burke government in WA had just sunk the push for national land rights.

I remember that Robert Tickner, as minister for Aboriginal and Torres Strait Islander affairs, was keen to set up a process that would run for some time and gradually warm up the community to the idea. He was also keen that the process shouldn't be the captive of a particular political leadership. So reconciliation became the government response to a political movement.

There was a lot of debate among indigenous people about what reconciliation should attempt to achieve. Some of us saw it as a precursor, that it would be a smokescreen behind which we could gather overwhelming support for a treaty.

But a problem emerged immediately with the government's step in appointing the members of the Council for Aboriginal Reconciliation. Aboriginal and Torres Strait Islander people saw this as the government hijacking the process.

We did hold some hope while Patrick Dodson was on the council. Patrick was our hero, our champion, dating from the days of the Federation of Land Councils. We saw him as someone with a strong view on our rights and ambitions.

But with the loss of Patrick Dodson from the council we could only be suspicious of the government's motives. Again, the government made new appointments to the council without taking account of the views of indigenous people.

So the process has become an empty one in recent years. 'Reconciliation' now means preaching to the converted. There's no effort to engage the whole community or challenge the status quo. The word itself has now been soured and anything attached to it will fail to hold the interest of most Aboriginal and Torres Strait Islander people. They will just walk away from it.

The priority now is to generate a new agenda, perhaps find another word for what we are trying to achieve. We also need to find people who haven't used up their credibility and goodwill to carry forward that agenda.

What people want

Many Aboriginal and Torres Strait Islander people hold the opinion that reconciliation has never had a chance. At the moment, we are part of the community but we sit outside it.

I said earlier that we seek the opportunity to exercise choice. Indigenous people have always been told where to go, what to do, where we can socialise and with whom. We have been directed as to who we can marry and when and where we can practise our cultures and beliefs. We were told it was for our own good.

We want to see a difference where it matters—on the ground, in day-to-day life. We want to see a change in the relationships at neighbourhood level—within the local shire, with police, business, and the state government.

In some areas, local reference groups offer promise. They include local government, Aboriginal or Torres Strait Islander people, police, the mayor, the local doctor. They're just groups of people from all walks of life looking at the common good and wellbeing of their community. It may be that reconciliation can build from there—allowing people the space to actually sit down and openly and honestly discuss issues that affect all of us. But that won't be enough.

Many non-indigenous people seem to think that reconciliation is coming to terms with the past or the atrocities of the past. The average person might think Aboriginal and Torres Strait Islander people deserve compassion, and wants to see that compassion formalised along with some form of recognition. Some Australians believe they need to make their peace with indigenous people so they can be proud of a shared heritage and history. But this is not enough, either.

Restoring faith

From the time Bob Hawke advocated a treaty there was no turning back. Once the word was mentioned, there could never be a satisfactory fall-back position. It's out of the box and it won't go back in.

We need legislative certainty to resolve outstanding issues such as a tribunal for the stolen generation, recognition for customary law, a process for implementing national land rights and proper political representation.

There may well need to be reconciliation among Aboriginal and Torres Strait Islander people as part of the process. Communities have different experiences of settlement and face differing circumstances today. One continuing problem is that our communities compete for limited resources to support programs and initiatives. There is a residue of suspicion and resentment between communities that succeed with their bids and those that don't. So we need to do some work among ourselves to gain agreement on what we want from any treaty or reconciliation process. And we need to move ourselves on from our traditional role of supplicants seeking assistance—a role in which we have far too much experience.

This is where an elected chair and deputy chair of ATSIC have key roles. It shouldn't matter who the individuals are—if the community can trust and believe in an elected leadership, as people who genuinely represent their interests, then we can foster internal discussion and reconciliation amongst our own communities.

The ATSIC structure gives people in Aboriginal and Torres Strait Islander communities a system for representing their interests at national, state and local levels. Governments need to respect and respond to this form of representation.

The way forward

The question for all parties is: where would we rather be as a nation? If we don't get a result from the reconciliation process, will we be happy with ourselves?

To restore the process it's time to restore the goal posts and anchor them immovably. Improvements in citizenship entitlements—health, housing, education, employment—serve to mark progress towards a level playing field but the ultimate goal must be commitment to respect the specific rights of indigenous peoples.

We look for pathfinding leadership that is, ideally, bipartisan and free of political opportunism. And it must involve discussion and negotiation with the elected representatives of Aboriginal and Torres Strait Islander people.

The history of our dealings with governments, even in recent years, leaves us suspicious. Decisions and agreements reached during one term are too easily revoked during the next. We need an explicit commitment about our place in the community that will endure changes in political fortunes.

A document of reconciliation should capture several elements. It should be a formal document between representatives of the Aboriginal and Torres Strait Islander peoples and federal and state governments as representatives of the wider community.

It should address the structural relationship between the Aboriginal and Torres Strait Islander peoples and the Australian state. It would commit Australian governments to a policy of self-determination as an internationally recognised right of the first peoples of this land.

It must refer to a process for resolving land issues.

It must address the concerns of the stolen generations—specifically with a formal apology from the Australian government acceptable to them and a process for compensation.

It must include protection from racial discrimination, possibly through a bill of rights.

It should make reference to indigenous customary law.

In addition, it must provide an independent economic base for Aboriginal and Torres Strait Islander existence that removes the reliance on annual appropriations from parliaments. There are a number of options for achieving this.

Whatever title we choose to give it, it's obvious that a document of this type would be a treaty. As an agreement between two groups of peoples it must be an effective legal document.

Some people try to tell us that Australia can't sign a treaty document with own people but this is nonsense. Countries with similar legal systems (New Zealand, Canada and the United States) have signed treaties with their own people. Treaties don't turn back the clock. They define the place of indigenous peoples in the context of a changed social and political reality but with reference to our pre-existing rights.

A treaty between Australians and the indigenous peoples of this land could actually lead to devolution in the reconciliation process. With a document that outlines a set of national principles, we can encourage regional bodies (local government, ATSIC regional councils, etc) to negotiate over local interests.

This is the ideal way to bring reconciliation home in ways meaningful to every person, rather than leaving it to think-tanks or universities or other elite bodies. It would encourage governments to start practising the politics of inclusion, rather than exclusion. Indigenous people would no longer be the unrecognised presence in local and national affairs.

Once we agree to move towards a treaty, the process need not be protracted. If we can engage in a process with bipartisan leadership and a commitment to ethical behaviour, it's possible to conclude negotiations within two or three years, rather than another decade.

ATSIC, as the voice of the indigenous population at a national level, is the appropriate body to negotiate the treaty document with the federal government. However, we would need to allow time for adequate consultation with our constituents at every stage.

At this time, it's easy to forecast the decay of the reconciliation process as disillusionment rises all round. The public mood seems uncertain—there's some willingness to respond to the issues, but that willingness lacks direction. It needs something to focus that interest and goodwill.

That goodwill is largely due to the efforts of the Council for Aboriginal Reconciliation over the last decade. The council has nurtured interest through its state and local networks. Bodies such as the Australian Local Government Association, the churches, trade unions and other community organisations have played an important role. ATSIC commissioners have also contributed to raising awareness of issues and finding local resolutions.

But national leadership is required for the reconciliation movement to continue to hold prominence in the national psyche. The behaviour of the prime minister of the day is as important in this matter as in issues such as tax reform or constitutional change.

If the prime minister fails to provide reassurance and commitment, Aboriginal and Torres Strait Islander people are likely to continue to lose interest. If the prime minister cannot reach out and include indigenous people in decision-making processes, I believe the nation would see a return to more strident levels of activism from indigenous people.

It must register with all Australians that activism was the only means that has led to significant gains for our people—the 1967 referendum, Eddie Mabo's High Court actions, the tent embassy, deaths in custody, protests at the Commonwealth Games in Brisbane and at Commonwealth Heads of Government Meetings, the 1988 Invasion Day actions. If activism is to be our only recourse in future, then so be it.

But I hope that the Australian government will come to value the importance of 'a good political relationship' with the indigenous peoples of this country, just as it values the same between the Indonesian government and the people of East Timor.

If it meant gaining a treaty for our people, I'd even be willing to embrace an Australian prime minister.

Reconciliation is a Two-way Street
P.P. McGuinness

Reconciliation will not come this year. Nor will it come, if some of the advocates of reconciliation between the Aboriginal population and the rest of the community have their way, ever. It is convenient for them to blame this on the prime minister but like the Greens and certain other groups, they are not interested in compromise or settlement. The Greens, as former WA senator Peter Walsh has pointed out on a number of occasions, are not interested in compromise nor in reconciliation between their demands and the desires of the rest of the community. Nor will they keep promises, stick to the terms of agreements, or ever honestly adhere to a deal once made. Every advance is ground won, to be used in a ruthless campaign to conquer still more ground, regardless of the truth of their claims. The same goes for some of the advocates of reconciliation.

The extraordinary gap between the opinions of the minority of self-styled progressive middle-class people who see themselves as the opinion formers and leaders of the Australian community and the vast majority of that community, who increasingly are rejecting holus bolus the 'enlightened' leadership being offered them has never been greater. The results of the qualitative survey, using focus groups, commissioned by the Council for Aboriginal Reconciliation indicate that the prime minister was absolutely right in saying that the end of year deadline for a statement was unachievable. The Newspoll results published shortly after the leaking of the council document show equally clearly, though perhaps not quite so overwhelmingly, that the people will not be sold a bill of goods in the name of reconciliation.

This marked separation of community opinion from that of the *soi-disant* progressives also ensured that the republican referendum was defeated. It now seems that those who claim to have the right opinions, and the right to influence policy, are as far removed from general electoral opinion as was the aristocracy in pre-revolutionary France. They are out of touch, they hold those they govern in contempt, and they see any disagreement with their own views as a sign of ignorance, prejudice or bloody-mindedness. In some cases the progressives see it as incumbent upon themselves to conduct a campaign of education and persuasion to convince others of the rightness of their own views; in other cases they see their appropriate course of action as using every device of law and political lobbying to impose their own views upon an unwilling community. The term education when it is used clearly to mean indoctrination is always evidence of an intolerant agenda, one which assumes that there is a single truth which others have to be browbeaten or bullied into accepting.

Many of the progressives in exasperation resort, publicly and privately, to denigration and abuse of the wider community. Racist and redneck are the favoured epithets, along with reactionary, rightwing, mean-minded, mean-spirited, lacking in vision, profiteering, and so on—it is a range often deployed in the reporting as well as opinion columns of newspapers and the other media. The ABC is a frequent offender, with few of its mouthpieces apparently capable of distinguishing between their own callow opinions and revealed truth. Lawyers are especially prone to losing faith in democracy when the community refuses to follow their fashionable lead; they seek to use international conventions to overrule domestic law, especially when those conventions have been negotiated and entered into without any real discussion in the Australian community. A favourite technique in this process can be best if somewhat crudely described in the words of the classic reassurance, 'I'll only put it in a little way, and if it hurts I'll take it out again.' Conventions are negotiated by cabals of lawyers and bureaucrats meeting in remote capitals who assiduously reassure their masters at home that there is no real force in the commitments into which they are entering, and they are simply entering into the consensus of high ideals of the leading democracies of the world.

Thus it is difficult to find anything strongly objectionable in the Convention on the Rights of the Child, and anyway it would require legislation to incorporate it into domestic law. As we found in the Teoh case (the convicted drug dealer who was saved from deportation on the false grounds that the fate of his children had not been adequately or explicitly considered in the light of the convention even though their welfare had been taken into account) its words can be twisted to mean much more in legal practice than they apparently mean, and they can be imported into domestic law by courts whose contempt for democracy is becoming more and more apparent. The ridiculous doctrine of 'legitimate expectations' on the behalf of people who have never heard of a convention is invoked. Equally with the International Convention on Civil and Political Rights which was grossly and abusively reinterpreted in order to introduce a concept of privacy alien to its original drafters, at the same time ignoring the provisions with respect to public morality and decency which are scattered throughout the fundamental international treaties and conventions on human rights. The offence of the Tasmanian parliament in maintaining a law which infringed on the private consciences of homosexuals was much less than the offence of a federal parliament which used dishonest means to exceed its constitutional powers.

The belief that somehow the Northern Territory and Western Australia can be bludgeoned into changing their popular mandatory sentencing laws is the most recent example of this contempt for democracy. These laws, which are certainly full of defects, are misrepresented as being used against innocent or trivial offenders when this is simply not true. Repeated breaking and entering, no matter what is found in possession of the criminal after he or she has cut and run and had time to dispose of much of the evidence, is not trivial. But the now habitual misreporting, indeed willfully dishonest reporting, to be found in much of the media, especially the Canberra press gallery, is at the heart of much of this. Yet another example is the affair of the kerosene baths, where the use of a tiny amount in dilution of kerosene in the bathing of elderly patients of nursing homes suffering from scabies was continually presented as if the poor old people had been placed into pure kerosene. A kerosene emulsion for treatment of scabies is an accepted if not modern treatment, and much cheaper than proprietary medicines. This kind of legislation by dishonest reporting and intellectually dishonest lawyers is becoming almost the norm. It is particularly egregious in the Northern Territory where the majority of the legal profession, while asserting belief in the separation of powers, a concept few of them understand, have appointed themselves, including many members of the bench, as an unofficial opposition. The legal system there is not financially corrupt, but it is certainly arguable that it has become intellectually corrupt.

To attempt to invoke the Convention on the Rights of the Child to overrule the WA government is objectionable in the extreme and ought to be resisted on constitutional grounds, whatever the faults of their sentencing law. The constitutional status of the NT is very different; it is not a state and the latest attempt to persuade even its own residents that it was ready to become one ended in decisive rejection. But to continue to overrule their laws, as the federal parliament did so unconscionably in the 'voluntary euthanasia' matter, must bring into question the whole future existence of the Northern Territory. Perhaps it would be better to agree that it is a failed experiment and return it to direct Commonwealth governance, or perhaps split it and turn Darwin and its hinterland into a separate free city within the Commonwealth. The worst thing that ever happened to Darwin was not Cyclone Tracy but the subsequent influx of southern carpetbaggers. Many of them came from Canberra, whose own experiment in self-government has been even worse than the Northern Territory's. The sooner federal territory is cut back to the minimum prescribed by the Constitution and the people of the Australian Capital Territory absorbed into the NSW local government system the better.

The move towards reconciliation between Aborigines and the wider community was certainly worthwhile. But it has been poisoned by exactly the same intolerance of popular feeling which has become the hallmark of the nagging progressives. Rather than attempting reasonable persuasion along with an effort to understand what the feelings of others actually are, and whether they have any justifiable basis, there is resort to hysteria. The qualitative research has shown that whatever the reasons most people have for refusing to accept the draft statement on reconciliation they are certainly not racists. In this respect it should be the progressives who cast out the beam in their own eye rather than continuing to look for the mote in their neighbour's. The reality is that those who dislike the statement do so because they have been subjected to a continual barrage of demands for concessions on land rights, admissions of guilt and monetary compensation without any proper accounting or evidence of real progress. There is genuine goodwill on both sides in the reconciliation process. Unfortunately, there are also extremists who are only interested in the unconditional surrender of their opponents. Sometimes the reconciliation argument is reminiscent of the peace process in Northern Ireland or in the Middle East, with the majority desperate to end the ongoing crisis and stop the killings while the extremists on both sides are determined to continue hostilities at any cost. Of course we are lucky enough to have an argument which is much less bitter, and in which violence, let alone killing, is rare or non-existent. Moreover there is only a tiny and irrelevant fraction in Australia who hold ill-will towards the Aborigines; and in reality only a very small proportion of Aborigines who hold any real ill-will towards the non-Aboriginal population.

It often seems, and it is undoubtedly true in some cases, that the earnest advocates of reconciliation in terms unacceptable to the greater part of the population are much more interested in continuing hostilities than in achieving reconciliation. They are exploiting the Aborigines as cynically and ruthlessly as any squatter ever did. Or they are allowing their sentimentality to blind them to the actual circumstances which need to be addressed. This is particularly the case with the great and the good, such as the various prelates or indeed Sir Gustav Nossal who is certainly a great scientist but no politician or political analyst. From the United Front movement through the various peace and anti-nuclear movements we have seen again and again the gullibility of well-meaning people who are used by activists with quite different agendas to those they purport to advance. We have also seen the infiltration of people with their own political agendas into key positions in the bureaucracy and other institutions where they should in principle be disinterested advisers and administrators. Any attempt to identify these immediately evokes cries of 'McCarthyism', and indeed when it is done by the politically unsophisticated (as so many ASIO and ASIS operatives were) it can be just that. But we can observe the presence of committed Greens in departments where they have an axe to grind in their advice to government, and the same is true of some advisers on matters relating to Aborigines. The German government prior to the fall of Communism was much abused for the *berufsverbot*, its attempt to keep clearly committed fanatics out of the bureaucracy; these days it is being similarly attacked by pernicious sects like Scientology for having the good sense to read their own documentation.

As the unlikely comparison with the peace processes between the IRA and the Unionists, or the Israelis and the Palestinians, serves to demonstrate, our reconciliation process is by no means a matter of urgent and desperate need. The only deaths at stake are those coming from the failures of policy of the last 25 years which have produced the dreadful hopelessness and mounting suicides in Aboriginal communities. These do not require a peace treaty or a formal statement of reconciliation. What is needed is some real effort at overcoming actual problems by practical means—a good example of a practical measure was the use of army engineers to assist remote Aboriginal communities in establishing basic infrastructure. English language literacy and numeracy are also essential if Aborigines are to be able to administer their own affairs. Reconciliation is best seen as a slow and gradual product of sensible policy, not a single easily defined objective to which a deadline can be attached.

It will require the gradual growth of goodwill and a myriad of small acts of goodwill. What has really been lacking is goodwill on the part of so many of its advocates. But essentially, it can only take place if some form of what is often now used as a dirty word, assimilation, takes place. This ought not and need not imply the destruction of what remains of Aboriginal culture and tradition. But it has to involve the acceptance that the majority of Aborigines certainly do not want to live in the manner which their ancestors did before the arrival of the Europeans. They want most of what ordinary Australians take as their own birthright—access to education which will equip them to participate in the wider society, access to health and welfare systems, participation in the polity as a matter of course, opportunity for their best intellects and talents to advancement, social stability and order. Reasonable standards of housing, health care and education are part of all this. At the same time, as do most Australians other than the privileged urban elites they accept that they must reciprocate: in the language of Charlie Perkins: 'We have to get off our black bums'. The popular support for Work for the Dole schemes is shared by most Aborigines; they see the justice of the notion that welfare payments should not merely be 'sit down money', which is corrupting both to its recipients and to those who dispense it, who too often begin to believe that they themselves are somehow the providers of the largesse. The greatest problem facing many Aboriginal communities is that they are faced with a culture of welfare and preservation which is more or less consciously held by their white patrons—they are told what is good for them, they are told what their culture is or should be, they are told that they must stand apart from the general community, and they are even told that English language literacy and numeracy is somehow inimical to their own culture. That is, they must stay in permanent tutelage, as far as their relationships with the rest of Australian society are concerned to those who have appointed themselves their protectors and insulators from the evil global or national culture which will destroy what is unique about them.

The reality is that of course the Aborigines have to adapt to co-existence with, and therefore sharing with, the rest of the Australian community. As former NT senator Bob Collins has pointed out in his report on the state of Aboriginal education there, it is absurd to expect the Aborigines to be able to deal with all the complex problems involved in land rights, royalties, a degree of self/local government, and so on without equipping them with the necessary skills. By definition these are incompatible with traditional Aboriginal culture. But instead of improving the educational standards of the NT the resultant of the last 30 years of effort has been the reduction of the generation of Aborigines under 30 to almost total illiteracy. It is clear that English language literacy must be the highest priority of education in the NT and in all other remote areas where there is an Aboriginal population; while literacy in the original mother languages is a nice idea, and use of such languages should never be discouraged, there is simply no point in giving the highest priority to a language in which there is no written literature and which gives no access to the levers of power in the general community. Fairly large increases in expenditures on Aboriginal education are obviously needed, but there is no point in this unless there is a sensible policy designed to combine the skills of conventionally trained, and intellectually adequate, graduate teachers (a minority of the university output) with Aboriginal interpreters themselves trained to act as teachers' aides, and, hopefully, as teachers in their own right.

But it is often forgotten that the majority of Aborigines do not live in remote areas but in the cities and provincial towns. Indeed, the majority of all those who claim Aboriginality in the census also live in mixed families, that is where one of the partners is a non-Aborigine. Too often the debate about reconciliation is dominated by the problems of remote area Aborigines, Northern Territory or other. In fact reconciliation is as much an urban as a country or provincial problem. In this context it is impossible to escape the fact that the Aboriginal and Torres Strait Islander Commission is an unrepresentative body in which only a minority of Aborigines take sufficient interest even to vote. So glaring is the problem that the Australian Electoral Commission has attempted to obfuscate the issue: it no longer publishes detailed figures of the voting for ATSIC which make it possible to compare the numbers eligible to vote with the numbers voting. But we do know that only about a quarter of Aborigines in the Sydney district bother to take any notice of ATSIC elections.

That is, the issues of reconciliation are far more complex than is conceived by those who think of it in terms of either apologies or statements which concede the maximalist demands of those who are not even true representatives of Aborigines. The ills of Aboriginal society and communities are acute, their condition often desperate. A bit of reconciliatory behaviour by the propagandists would be a good starting point for some genuine progress.

True Stories and What We Make of Them
Inga Clendinnen

Lecture 1: Incident on a beach
I begin with the story of an incident on a beach. The place is the southwest coast of what we now call Western Australia. The year is 1801. A French scientific expedition is coasting those shores, with the official blessing of their first consul, Napoleon Bonaparte. Their main job is to collect samples of flora and fauna which might be useful back home in France, but they are committed scientists, and they are curious about the human population too: indeed, one of the naturalists aboard has a special interest in the infant discipline of anthropology. But while they have seen the smoke of many fires they have not sighted a single native, until they surprise a solitary man, fishing in waist-deep water. The encounter is not encouraging: as the Frenchmen advance, waving glass necklaces at him, he shouts, who knows what, shakes his fish spear at them and disappears into the scrub.

Then they come upon a man and woman digging for shellfish. The man runs, but the woman, 'seized with fright', we are told, flings herself down and flattens her face and body into the sand, arms and legs bent 'like a frog on the edge of a pond'. The Frenchmen surround her. One lays presents beside her—a mirror, a little knife—while another quickly checks to see whether she still has her front teeth (Dampier had reported that the people he encountered had lost theirs.) He finds that she does.

Then, hoping she might stop crying, the men withdraw 20 feet or so. But she remains pressed into the sand, save that she once lifts her head and looks at them. So they come back and pick her up and hold her suspended so they can examine her. Then, 'as she still would not stand, they laid her on her back on the sand.'

The leader of the expedition continues the account:

> I saw then that she was pregnant—that is probably what prevented her from fleeing...this woman had a small round face with pronounced features...She was of small stature, but well-made...I judged from her breasts that she had had many children, although she appeared not to be more than 20 or 22 years old. Her only clothing was an old skin...a piece of the same skin forming a kind of pocket, which contained several small onions, similar to the roots of orchids...At last, as this woman showed no sign of life, we left her. We were hardly more than 30 paces from her when we saw her stealing away on hands and knees into the bushes, leaving behind our presents and her stick.

This is the story as Nicolas Baudin recorded it in his report to his superiors. The story was told honestly: Baudin was confident that he and his men had conducted themselves correctly, and that they had done no harm. Clearly they intended none. In one sense the woman was lucky: these strangers didn't rape her, they didn't abduct her, they didn't kill her. Three centuries earlier Spaniards might well have done any or all of those things. The Frenchmen had treated her gently. Of course they would not have treated a Frenchwoman met on a beach like that, but these heirs to the French Revolution certainly recognised her as a fellow human, black and near naked though she was—they gave her both time to stop crying, and her little gifts, and they molested her only in so far as their scientific purposes required. They were only doing their job—and they did her no harm.

Or so they thought. Now, consider the matter from her perspective. She had been surrounded; she had been paralysed with terror. One of the strangers had forced his fingers into her mouth. At that point she had been lying face down, so he must have turned her head to the side before he could thrust them in. Then they had lifted her and stared at her and tugged at her garment as she hung in their hands like a frozen frog. Then they laid her down and stared some more. And then they went away. So what had happened to her?

What is terrifying is that we do not know, even as we watch her press herself into the sand, as we watch her crawling away. We see her body, but we do not see her mind. What did she think was happening as she felt the hands of these very material apparitions? What did she think was happening to the child in her belly, the child she was desperately trying to protect from their sight and touch? And later, when she crept back to her people, how was she received? Was she received at all? Was she shunned? Was she killed? They would have been watching what happened. They would have seen her hanging in those strange bleached hands. What did they think had happened to the child in her belly? Did they decide to kill it, too? And the man who fled in terror, abandoning his pregnant woman to the strangers. Where would he find his manhood now?

We don't know the answers to any of these questions. All we do know is that no harm was intended, and that harm was almost certainly done. We also know the Frenchmen's story, a story told honestly from their perspective, despite all the things it leaves out, of what happened on the beach. We don't know the woman's story at all. We can only infer what it might have been by exercising our imaginations.

It is also worth thinking about the gifts the Europeans brought to bestow upon these as yet unknown locals: glass beads, knives, mirrors. This is the standard inventory of the smiling face of imperialism. Columbus took beads, knives and mirrors with him to America. Why knives? Because knives are seriously useful in any economy? Why beads? Because savages are vain? Because all men are vain? Why mirrors? A usefully portable fragment of white man's magic? A joke on the savage? The woman had just been subjected to the novel experience of the sustained European scientific gaze. Is she now being invited to scrutinise herself? She leaves the European things anyway—along with her digging stick, which is her essential equipment for life. What I most notice about this aborted transaction is that the Europeans bring no mirrors for themselves.

There is little point in apportioning blame close to 200 years after the event. What interest me are two things. First is the intellectual and imaginative exercise we have just been through in doing this little bit of history: retrieving just what happened, thinking about its possible consequences, deciding from their words and actions just what the Frenchmen were up to and the kind of men they were, and doing our best to imagine the thoughts and feelings of the silent players in the scene. Second, there is the separate matter of clarifying and examining our own responses to what happened.

What I feel, to my surprise, is anger. In part this is because she is a woman, young, pregnant and alone, she is being manhandled, and as a woman I resent that. But I have to admit to a deeper response which is an anachronistic absurdity. What I want to say is: 'Take your hands off her, you Frenchmen.' I see them as foreign intruders molesting my countrywoman, someone from my territory—a territory my forebears will not even enter for several decades, forebears who could well perform actions much worse than these earnest Frenchmen. Nonetheless, that is what I feel. And I do not feel in the least implicated in what was done to her: I am on her side. What, I wonder, do you feel?

As to why this small long-ago event should matter to any of us—well, I will make a large claim for it: I believe its examination is conducive to civic virtue, and therefore to the coherence of a democratic liberal state. The philosopher Martha Nussbaum identifies three qualities as necessary for responsible citizenship in a complex world: an ability to critically examine oneself and one's traditions; an ability to see beyond immediate group loyalties and to extend to strangers the moral concern we 'naturally' extend to friends and kin; the development of what she calls the 'narrative imagination': the ability to see unobvious connections between sequences of human actions, and to recognise their likely consequences, intended and unintended.

Nussbaum believes that these three things sustain the political health of a democratic nation, and so do I. I also believe that these things can be achieved, indeed are possibly best achieved, by the close analysis of past situations like the one we have just been looking at. Reflection on such situations liberates our imaginations to taste experiences other than our own—what it was like to be that woman on the beach, what it was like to be one of those rather embarrassed French scientists. That imagining expands our moral comprehension. We are also led to reflect on unobvious connections and the range of possible outcomes—what Nussbaum would call the narrative imagination at work.

Such analyses also help us to know ourselves more exactly, and more critically. For example, what is this territory I discover I feel so powerfully about? Why did I feel invaded, too? Some years back one of those books appeared which precipitate ideas lurking in the corners of the mind into clear view. Benedict Anderson asked what holds nations together. Think about it. What set of experiences signifies 'Australia' to you? What do you directly know of it? You know your family, your friends, the people at the school, your workmates if you still have a job, the lady in the corner shop if there is still a corner shop, the people at the fruit stall, a cloud of relations, your football team, some people on radio and television. You will have travelled over bits of it, some bits often if your social or economic work takes you there. But it is still a very patchy mental map. There will be suburbs even in your home city as unvisited as Marco Polo's China.

So where is 'Australia'? As Anderson makes clear in his *Imagined Communities*—it's in your mind. Nations are imaginary communities, and none the less real for that. And nations, especially democratic nations, especially democratic ethnically and religiously diverse nations like our own, cannot hold together unless they share a common vision as to how the world works, what constitutes the good life, what behaviour is worthy of respect, what behaviour is shameful. Present input clearly matters—the journalists of the ABC and SBS influence my image of Australia and the world every day—but our understanding of our nation is also profoundly shaped by our view of its past, of its history—however vague that view might be...

Lecture 6: What now?

It is only 32 years ago that Aborigines ceased to be 'protected persons', and were recognised as free citizens. Only 32 years ago did the belated drive towards political and social equality begin. The emphasis naturally fell on rights, especially the one which had become symbolic of Aboriginal exclusion. Some of those who fought hardest for that constitutional change have since admitted despair as they have watched the havoc wrought in too many Aboriginal communities by the unfettered right to drink.

Marcia Langton has written on the artful ways in which white Australians have concocted the stereotype of 'the drunken Aborigine', which identifies the Aboriginal drinker as debased by nature while leaving any number of addicted white Australians to drink themselves sodden with impunity. Langton also reminds us that whites deliberately used and continue to use alcohol, along with opium and other drugs, to seduce and control Aborigines, while simultaneously exposing them to contempt. That is true. However, it is also true that alcohol dependence has been shredding the social fabric of many Aboriginal communities, especially since the relaxation of that legal prohibition on drinking, with not much white encouragement beyond an eagerness to supply. There are probably more Aboriginal teetotallers per head of population than there are among whites—they know what drink can do. But alcohol has a killing grip on a lot of Aboriginal men, and on increasing numbers of women, too. Why has it proved so destructive for them?

I suspect there is a seriously useful historical anthropology waiting to be written on changing Aboriginal uses of alcohol, but today I want to focus on the dynamics of that recent process of social devastation by telling you the stories of just two communities, only a few hundred kilometres and two decades apart, and their very different relationships with alcohol.

I begin with a kind of success story about a group of Aboriginal mavericks, conscientious objectors to the claims of white authority, who lived, at least for a time, a resolutely independent life on the edge of a potentially hostile urban white community—the people of the camp at 'Wallaby Cross' (not its real name) on the fringe of Darwin. The time is the mid 1970s: that is, after only ten years' experience of that double-edged right to drink.

Normally outsiders, especially white outsiders, could not penetrate such a society, but a young Englishman called Basil Sansom managed it. A big Toyota truck and an easygoing disposition probably had something to do with it. Sansom also had the good anthropologist's ability to keep quiet, listen and look, and after a lot of listening and looking he was able to show us something of the life at the camp. He does this with the density of small and surprising detail which carries powerful persuasive force. What follows is no more than a thumbnail sketch drawn from his complex, affectionate, often admiring portrait.

The camp was one of several conjured into existence to provide safe drinking conditions for Aborigines visiting Darwin, coming in from pastoral or other seasonal work like buffalo shooting, or from reserves and missions. They came intent on following the great Australian frontier tradition of drinking their accumulated pay cheques to oblivion and back again. 'Safe' drinking meant drinking in congenial circumstances, free from the threat of violence or robbery and, above all, from any entanglement with whites, especially whites in authority—excepting, of course, the whites who supplied the alcohol.

The camp operated as an informal hotel for Aboriginal seasonal workers. It had another smaller but more regular source of income from the welfare cheques paid to its handful of old-age or disabled pensioners. Note that unemployment relief was not yet a prospect. The pensioners' money, distributed through a mind-bafflingly complex and fluid system of internal credit policed by the three full-time camp bosses, bought the pensioners company, respect and physical security, and protected drinking of their own small resources in their own small circle.

Perched lightly on illegal land, Wallaby Cross could provide such a haven because of the stunning political skill and discipline of its 'masterful men', as the three camp bosses were called. With minimal resources, always at risk of eruptions from within or invasion by white police or white hoodlums or a rival mob, the camp at Wallaby Cross was an example of modern Aboriginal culture in creative action, and it was a social and political tour-de-force: the maintenance of effective group autonomy in the face of deeply hostile circumstance.

It was also a purely contact-zone invention, so how 'Aboriginal' was it? Diane Barwick characterised contemporary Victorian Aborigines as living in closed communities of kin and friends, 'scattered through a world of whites' like a string of waterholes in a desert. That was not the way of things at Wallaby Cross. Its hotel role required it to take in people from different kin groups and regions, so while the first question asked of a stranger was still 'Which place do you come from?' and the second 'Which family?', these traditional bonds existed alongside other loyalties developed in work situations. Basil Sansom again: 'The reason why Big Maxie could get ol' Luke to use his expensive FWD Toyota to travel 200 miles down the track by offering a measly $20 as incentive was less a function of market forces, more a product of two intersecting biographies'—that is, it was a transaction based not on money, not on kinship, but on friendship.

This mixed group celebrated its shared cattleworking history in its 'Darwin style' of high pastoral-worker chic—big hat, big belt buckle, bright shirt, jeans, svelte boots. Even more important was the collective work done on the camp's own history. Disputes would be publicly aired and supporters publicly recruited until there was general agreement as to just what had happened, who was to blame, and what ought to be done about it. Sansom thought this public consensual history worked much as had the great traditional narratives, distilling an intelligible moral order and a set of workable daily rules out of potentially disorderly lives. What Wallaby Cross tells us is that even after generations lived deep inside the contact zone Aboriginal personhood remained a reflex of place and family tempered by individual biography, and that sharing and 'being level', not striving for individual advantage, remained a primary virtue. And it tells us something more remarkable. Traditional ceremonial remained deeply important even for this mixed group of very mobile persons. Camp authority had moved from oldfellas to youngfellas competent in dealing with both Aborigines and whites, which is about what you would expect in a society permanently in the war zone. But even these relatively young 'masterful men' had to be men of traditional knowledge, capable of organising the ceremonial life which was one of the camp's core attractions. Initiations were carried out in each of the two years of Sansom's stay, and a huge, expensive and successful corroboree staged out of collective camp savings.

In this modern moral economy, prestige came not from the accumulation of goods or even present power but from the efficient discharge of social roles—'Fighting Man', 'Law Man'—and even more from flair and grace in the performance of ceremonial roles—'Singing Man', 'Dancing Man', 'Bamboo Man', 'Dancing Girl'. The money-privileged drinkers drank, but their conduct was closely supervised, while around them an orderly, essentially traditional life went on, with the women sustaining their cooking hearths, caring for their families, feeding countrymen down on their luck. In a drinking camp in the Darwin of the late 1970s, we can still discern the enduring outline of what Stanner called 'The Abiding'. Wallaby Cross also demonstrates the depth of the habit of mutual support against outsiders—a habit of mind we see manifested in dozens of communities today. That is a real communitarian strength. White society cannot match it. But Wallaby Cross was a set of solutions appropriate to a particular time and place. Its people could celebrate the pleasures of alcohol without too much social damage because access to alcohol was restricted first by lack of cash, then by their lively commitment to other responsibilities, like family and ceremony.

My second story comes from this last decade, and points to a dangerous change. During the 1970s, there was a collapse in rural employment and unskilled labour everywhere, with Aborigines suffering first, and worst. There haven't been secure jobs for Aborigines right across the north since the old symbiosis between white pastoralists and black stockmen was broken. It has always been tough economic territory, a graveyard for white entrepreneurs' hopes for more than a century. It is a bitter paradox that the one industry which thrives is mining: mining which generates few jobs; which benefits some Aborigines financially but is acknowledged to be massively socially disruptive; mining which gobbles up and vomits the land which many Aborigines believe they have a sacred duty to cherish. Everywhere country towns are shrinking. Whatever jobs which do turn up will go to their white sons and daughters. In the cities, southern, central or northern, Aborigines suffer the employment fate which attends poor education, low social class, and prejudicial skin colour.

Chronic involuntary unemployment has forced whole generations into full dependence on government services and on welfare—citizens' rights from which Aborigines had been historically excluded, but citizens' rights which now exile whole communities, rural and urban, both from the real economy and from hope. Excessive drinking, with all its hideous consequences, has been one result.

This last decade has taught us all that purposeful, disciplined work is necessary for dignity and happiness, whether the work is hunting for bush tucker or working cattle or building houses or teaching or running an office. The same decade has seen heroin and other drugs consume our children and shred families, as kin steal from closest kin. The physical and the social isolation of Aboriginal communities exacerbates these toxic effects, but now an increasing number of white communities find themselves in precisely the same sinking boat, constructed out of chronic unemployment, welfare dependence, inescapable poverty, drink, drugs, demoralisation. After 200 years in parallel, our histories are at last beginning to converge.

It is this grim context which provides the setting for my second story, told by Alexis Wright in the book she calls *Grog War*, published only two years ago, in 1997. Her report on the struggle of the Warumungu people of Tennant Creek against alcohol makes shaking reading. Wright forces us to see, in wincing detail, the process of the destruction of individuals and of whole families by drink. She shows us a society drowning in violence and despair, with even the non-drinkers helplessly implicated in the general disaster.

Then the story changes as she shows us something else: how individuals and families can be retrieved by tough community intervention. In 1986, the Tennant Creek Night Patrol came into operation. Volunteers went out every night to pick up drunks, to stop fights, to risk their lives. A year later the Julalikari Aboriginal Council was set up, committed to loosening the grip of the grog on the people, and then an Aboriginal Rehabilitation Centre. And then, in 1994, the council began a relentless political and legal battle before the Liquor Commission of the Northern Territory for a reduction in the availability of alcohol to the whole community, white and black alike, by a restriction on trading hours, especially on pension days, and on the sale of the larger wine casks.

Two years after that, and after a ferocious battle with the licensees and a six-month-long controlled experiment conducted by the Liquor Commission, the council won. The prohibitions were made permanent, and the local police, the local hospital, the local municipal council and most Tennant Creek residents, regardless of colour, applauded the victory.

The council's position was simple, and revolutionary. They declared that the individual's right to drink was not absolute. The rights of the whole community, most particularly those of the children to nourishment, physical security and education, took priority. Now other communities are following the Tennant Creek model, or forging their own. Some are striving to remain 'dry', with no alcohol permitted and expulsion the penalty for possession. Others are choosing to fight on the issue of the involvement of the whole community in what for too long has been defined as an exclusively Aboriginal problem, and are seeking to limit the suppliers' 'right' to sell as much alcohol as they can, regardless of the social consequences.

Noel Pearson, always a man worth listening to, has recently made a courageous and clear-sighted analysis of the social malaise of the Aboriginal communities of Cape York. He argues that the imposition of welfare-dependence on able-bodied men and women living in communities isolated from any genuine employment opportunities is a poison as deadly as strychnine-laced flour, leading first to the deformation of traditional values, and then to their destruction. Individual pride and social purpose survived the injustices inflicted by white racism through several generations, but Pearson believes these handouts create a desolation which saps ambition, and leads men and women to acquiesce in their own victimhood.

So says Pearson. Only an insider of knowledge, courage and compassion would dare make such a diagnosis. Once made, even an outsider must recognise its justice. Pearson's solution is a return to a traditional emphasis on responsibilities as well as on rights—on reciprocity, on respect—and above all a return to meaningful work. For the young, that work will be the work of education. His ultimate hope is for the reintegration of the communities into the real economy, but his immediate concern is for their autonomous development towards self-sustaining subsistence, with full and equal educational resources available to the children.

Pearson has already effected one revolution: from now on there will be straight talking on these matters. There must be, because lives are at stake. He is also urging a second revolution: that the flow of power be turned upside down; that both decisions and the responsibility for them be taken by the communities themselves, with regional councils coordinating local programs and negotiating with government agencies for the necessary government resources. Nearly 30 years ago, W.E.H. Stanner said: 'it should now be simple wisdom to let Aboriginal people...run their lives their way, or our way, or somewhere in between, as long as they themselves run their lives, with whatever help they seek.' At last we are coming to agree. Aborigines could say we are very slow learners.

That second revolution—the local seizing of power—is already in process, as in the battle for Tennant Creek. Everywhere local leaders are deciding to rescue their own communities. The across-the-board figures on health, employment and education published by the Bureau of Statistics last August make a necessary political point, but they mask that changing on-the-ground actuality. To see that we need microstatistics. For example: out of Palm Island's population of approximately 3,000 there had been 20 suicides over a three year period. In 1997 alone there were eight. That is a lot of mourning in a small community. Last year, in 1998, there were two, early in the year. Since then there have been none. What changed? First, the islanders were given the hope of comprehensive change, with a sympathetic state government standing ready to help remedy the social and economic conditions which generate suicide. (Unemployment on Palm stands at 88 percent.) But what mattered immediately was that people from pre-existing local groups got together to identify individuals at risk, and then someone would stay close to them until the bad time was over. Call it responsibility. Call it neighbourliness. Call it organised love. It worked.

Aboriginal communities, whether remote or rural or urban, must handcraft their own solutions because the cures for their ills lie with the people themselves, not because they are to blame—I hope I have persuaded you that they are not—but because only they can do it. Only they can effect solutions to immediate and to long-term problems. Only they can devise ways to protect women, children and old people from violence. Only they can rescue the drinkers and the lost adolescents. Only they can decide to get children to school on time, and to make sure that the school is worth getting to in the first place. Issues of child welfare and juvenile justice absolutely require precise local knowledge as to relationships and personalities. The communities will not be alone: the stolen children report contains an archive of accumulated experience and practical models on all the major social issues, and now there are regional and national Aboriginal organisations committed to accumulating experience and expertise. Anyone nurturing a secret hope that such grassroots reforms will save money should be warned. Doling out welfare and leaving people to rot has always been the cheapest option.

The innovators will need good leaders at every level. I cannot get excited about the occasional excitements over minor corruptions inside Aboriginal organisations, especially in view of large-scale corruptions and opportunistic self-advancement by whites who seem to assume they are the natural leaders of the national community. We also have to remember that these so-called 'Aboriginal communities' are largely colonial residues, and that even where they are not, family and faction have tended to dominate. But leaders intent on the common good are already emerging, using skills learnt from white society in the service of their own people, from teaching in Aboriginal schools through working in Aboriginal health and legal organisations to invading local, state and now federal politics. Some of these leaders are people of remarkable presence and capacities. Looking at them I think, wistfully: 'Why don't we have leaders like that?'

They will need our heartfelt, unstinting support. Let any one of us who, in our comfortably upholstered circumstances, have tried to change one single element of our behaviour—giving up smoking, losing weight—remember how hard that was, so we can recognise and respect the discipline, the clarity of purpose, the moral tenacity necessary to effect the kind of bootstrap transformation I have been talking about. What is encouraging is that I have identified precisely those qualities in action at Tennant Creek and a dozen other places.

As for the great question of land: British-based laws of relationship, property and inheritance do not readily accommodate to the realities of Aboriginal historical experience. In darker moods I can sometimes see the native title movement as a giant red herring. In Victoria, Mabo and Wik together have as yet done nothing for the dis-located, re-located Yorta Yorta people, some of them descendants of the people from Coranderrk and Cumeragunja. Earlier this year their legally-provable 'attachment to the land' was found to have been 'washed away by the tides of history', or, to put it rather less metaphorically, obliterated by years of vigorous white intervention. The Yorta Yorta case is now on appeal before the full federal court. But for those who fail, and many will fail, the gulf between law and justice will gape wide, and that is a dangerous thing in a democracy. Land must also be found for those expropriated men and women living on the fringes of impoverished country towns or in corners of the cities; men and women who have been permitted no physical continuity with any land anywhere, and this not as a matter of law, but of justice. I am haunted by the image of that old woman described by protector Robinson, dancing the history of her country before a half-comprehending white man—country where soon there would be no place left for her to set her foot. Guaranteed access to traditional land is not a cure-all, but it is a necessity.

To return at the last to our beginning. Why concoct a single, simple, and therefore necessarily false tale and call it 'Australia's history'? Why not a cornucopia of true stories, which will tell us what really happened? Why deny the courage of those early settlers? Why deny their cruelty when sheep were taken or a shepherd speared? Why deny the horror when they took their guns and hunted down black men, women and children, helplessly running to nowhere? What most surely unites Aborigines now—what leads them to define themselves as Aborigines, whatever the percentages of blood—is their shared historical experience at the hands of whites, and that is a history that we, who are their fellow citizens, know too little about. It happened, but we were looking the other way. They know it in their bones, because it happened to their great-grandmother, their uncle, their brother—because it happened to them.

The settlers, despite their loneliness and fear, despite their cruelties, built a society where the centuries-old shackles of class were struck off in a generation. Egalitarianism was their achievement, not as an aspiration, but as a social fact: an egalitarianism initially exclusively designed for Anglo-Celts, excluding Chinese, excluding Afghans, excluding Kanaks, certainly excluding Aborigines. Over the last couple of generations that egalitarianism has expanded to include peoples from many different colours and cultures, so creating an authentically cosmopolitan civic culture of which I for one am very proud.

But there remains a scar on the face of the country, a birthstain of injustice and exclusion directed against that people who could so easily provide the core of our sense of ourselves as a nation, but who remain on the fringes of the land they once possessed. I don't much care what the United Nations says about us, although I know I should. But when I listen to the stories of what we incomers have done to the people we found here, generation by generation, in ignorance or malice or confusion—then I do care. That is why I have tugged you through all this history. We need history: not 'black armband' history and not triumphalist white-out history either, but good history, true stories of the making of this present land, none of them simple, some of them painful, all of them part of our own individual histories.

I am not suggesting that we shuffle backwards into the twenty-first century. I would recommend a crabwise approach, eyes swivelling sideways, backwards, forwards, with equal intensity, because while the past is past, it is not dead. Its hand is on our shoulder. As for what is to be done—I end with the words of the great British historian, E.P. Thompson: 'This is not a question we can ask of history. It is, this time, a question history asks of us.'

The Burden of the Past in the Present
Bain Attwood

A few years ago, in a course on Australian Aboriginal history I teach, I devoted a class to a debate on whether the Commonwealth government should apologise to the stolen generations. The students who argued for an apology were well prepared and their team presented their case in a compelling way but their opposition was nonplussed by the task I had allotted them and were unable to marshal a strong case, probably because they were unaware that there *were* thoughtful and well-reasoned arguments for opposing an apology though these were not ones that have been heard from the lips of its most vociferous opponents. And so I was pleased when in discussion time afterwards a sophisticated German exchange student expressed his opposition to an apology. 'For what reasons?' I queried him. 'It's too early,' he replied. What did he mean? 'Most Australians,' he told us, 'don't know enough about their history yet'.

I was reminded of his comment last year when at a symposium on 'the burden of the past' in Germany, South Africa and Australia at Monash University, Robert Manne also pointed out that whereas Germany had long recognised it has a burdensome past and that it had to deal with it, Australia has yet to even realise it has a difficult past which it must confront.

It is now 30 years ago that Charles Rowley emphasised the importance of 'History and Aboriginal Affairs' in the opening chapter of his landmark work, *The Destruction of Aboriginal Society*. He observed that 'the historical dimension of Aboriginal affairs [was] dimly seen' and claimed that this 'lack of a common fund of historical knowledge' hampered any attempts to address Aboriginal problems. During the last decade the Council for Aboriginal Reconciliation has similarly placed a stress on the importance of addressing the remarkable lack of public historical knowledge of Australia's colonial past, making 'sharing history' one of eight 'key issues' in reconciliation, and 'understanding and accepting the history of our shared experience' the first of five essential steps towards reconciliation. Most recently, the 1999 ABC Boyer lecturer Inga Clendinnen, following in the footsteps of W.E.H. Stanner's 1968 *After the Dreaming* and Bernard Smith's 1980 *The Spectre of Truganini*, has reminded us of the importance of sound historical narratives for any nation.

As Clendinnen noted, this need for 'real stories' or 'true stories' has been increasingly met since the late 1960s. Indeed, during the last three decades there has been a historical revolution in the way the past of this continent is represented in Australian history. Many Australians grew up learning a history that, in summary, began with Cook or some other European explorer discovering a land called Australia; told how brave and decent explorers and other men peacefully settled a land occupied by an inferior, primitive and passive people; and traced the disappearance of a dying race who had or would pass away into the past. By contrast, the new history begins with Aborigines and asserts their very long ownership on the continent; alters the foundational events and figures of the history by showing that the first discoverers, explorers and colonists of this land were Aborigines, not Europeans; describes the invasion of their land and documents the violent dispossession and the racial oppression subsequently inflicted upon generation after generation of Aboriginal people; and shows their resistance and survival. As a result, the old history has been exposed as a travesty; most importantly, it is now realised that Australia was not founded through discovery and settlement but by conquering another people—and so its legitimacy has been drawn into question.

This revolution has dismayed many conservatives, as their response to the High Court's Mabo and Wik judgements—both of which were the outcome of this radical change in historical understanding—testified. For example, one anguished conservative spokesman attacked the former in these terms: 'It is the disturbing feature of the case that...[the] judges have been prepared to change the foundations of the land law in Australia after that law had been settled for 200 years... The High Court was quite clearly changing what had been settled law'. The new history, he was revealing, was unsettling because it unsettles the old history of Australia, that settling history of a settled Australia which settled the minds of the 'settlers' and their descendants who claimed to have 'settled' it. This disturbance is hardly surprising: first, because history has long been important in giving people a sense of meaning, order and composure; and second because the old history rested and still rests upon the silencing of Aboriginal narratives. Aborigines' return to the history—something like a return of the repressed—has shattered the illusions of the old history and so torn away a familiar map of the past. As such it has provoked angry denials and denunciations from many of those raised on the old but false history. There have been many who have not *wanted* to know the old but suppressed historical truths that have been revealed again by the new history: Pauline Hanson complained that, 'This is not the history I was taught in school', John Howard sympathised 'with Australians who are insulted when they are told that we have a racist, bigoted past'. Subsequently, many have donned white blindfolds and rejected the new history that Howard has dismissed as 'black armband history'.

More commonly, perhaps, many have denied the relevance of the new Australian history. This history, they say, 'is the past and is past'; 'we can't change the past'; 'what is done is done, it cannot be undone'; 'we have to accept it for what it is'; 'there are challenges that lie ahead'. But what many fail to realise or accept is that history deals not so much with the past but the relationship between the past and the present. History, after all, always rests on their being a connection between past and present—on the past continuing to exist in the present in some form or other, either as memory or remembrance or all those 'remains of the day' that historians and others use to try and reconstruct the past, or as a legacy that shapes the present—and if the past doesn't exist in the present there can be and is no history. This apparent failure to understand the nature of history is common but it has particularly serious consequences in the context of reconciliation since Aboriginal affairs is a profoundly historical field.

Reconciliation, it is apparent, requires recognition of our history—an understanding of that relationship between past and present—in at least three ways. First of all, it depends upon an acknowledgement that the Aboriginal peoples *are* the original owners of this continent. Most non-Aboriginal Australians have considerable difficulty coming to terms with this history, since it entails at the very least recognition of Aborigines and Torres Strait Islanders' rights as indigenous peoples (rather than merely their rights as Australians), at most sovereignty. This is hardly surprising, given the nature of our history—the denial of Aboriginal land ownership at the beginning of European colonisation and so the absence of any negotiation of a treaty—and our histories—the stories which so determinedly tried to consign the moral issues of colonisation to the past, to make the stealing of the land and so forth '*past* wrongs'.

Reconciliation, however, depends on proper recognition of the status of Aboriginal people as aboriginal or indigenous, either in terms of a treaty, constitutional changes, a bill of rights that would enshrine indigenous rights, or restoration of much of the 1993 Native Title Act. Gestures such as the references to Aborigines and Torres Strait Islanders as 'the nation's first people', 'their deep kinship with their lands' and 'their rich and continuing cultures' in the new constitutional preamble which was defeated in November 1999 are empty unless rights are also bestowed upon Aborigines in accordance of this status; the preamble's representation of indigenous peoples as Australia's 'first people', it can also be noted, merely repeated the old history inasmuch as it serves to disguise (and so seeks to extinguish) the historical fact of Aboriginal sovereignty and nationhood prior to the conquering Australian nation. Australia needs a new beginning or foundation to its (hi)story, an instrument of reconciliation similar to that of New Zealand's Treaty of Waitangi which is now widely interpreted there as a charter for reconciliation since it recognises the legitimacy of both peoples' presence. So long as we lack such an agreement, non-Aboriginal Australians will be left with the nagging doubt that we are but 'a community of thieves'.

Reconciliation requires, secondly, recognition on the part of non-Aboriginal Australians of the shameful wrongs that our forebears have perpetrated upon Aborigines and Torres Strait Islanders. In the first instance, this entails an acknowledgement that these were not mere 'blemishes' like the prime minister has claimed; as Judy Brett has reminded us, 'blemishes are superficial imperfections, having little to do with underlying structures' and so it is hardly an appropriate term to describe 'a whole historical relationship between two races, one of which conquered and dispossessed the other'.

To recognise the historical facts of our treatment of Aborigines does not mean we have to or should indulge in simple-minded condemnation of our forebears; instead, it involves historical understanding of why they acted as they did so that we can reflect upon their actions as well as on our own attitudes and beliefs. In the case of the practice of separating Aboriginal children from their parents and kin, for example, this would mean a realisation that, while this policy was carried out for various reasons including humanitarian ones, it was underpinned by two widely held assumptions; a conviction that it was best that Aboriginal people disappear as a separate, identifiable group and a belief that it was 'for their own good'. The lesson to be learned? That evil lies in the presumption that we know what's best for Aborigines and that it's best that they become the same as 'us'. Reconciliation entails a recognition that such a presumption can only ever be morally wrong—in other words it's not a case of applying today's standards and values to the past, as the federal government claims, but a matter of adopting a measure for human conduct that is universal. Here, it is important to note that when Aboriginal people have called for an apology for the stolen generations they have not only sought an acknowledgement of the government policy and practice and its devastating impact but they have also wanted an explanation for *why* it happened; armed with historical knowledge, non-Aboriginal Australians can confess that our forebears sought to destroy Aboriginality, express our sorrow, ask that our ancestors be forgiven, and commit ourselves to ensuring that we do not repeat the mistakes of the past.

For the foreseeable future, the fate of reconciliation will also rest on recognition of the severe historical impact the various dimensions of colonisation have had upon Aborigines and Torres Strait Islanders—what can and should be called a holocaust given the scale of loss and the trauma that has been suffered; for example, Aboriginal people probably numbered between 750,000 and 1.25 million in 1788 but the European invasion brought decimation in its wake, destroying hundreds of communities and leaving only 75,000 by 1900.

To know and acknowledge such simple historical facts does not mean Australians should assume responsibility for a past to which they were not party; rather, it provides a point of departure for being able to imagine Australian history from an Aboriginal perspective, something too few non-Aboriginal Australians try to do. The crux of the matter, once more though, is not simply to know this past but to recognise the past in the present—to see that the horrible destruction of the past continues to burden the present of Aborigines and Torres Strait Islanders—and to take responsibility for helping to address this through *reparation*. (Isn't it odd that this term is seldom heard here yet is commonly used in the context of the German state and the Jewish Holocaust?)

Obviously our forebears cannot assume responsibility for that shameful past in the present since they are no longer here; but that duty, similar to that of honouring the Anzacs for example, can and should fall to us as their descendants and to our children and their children (and so we can apologise on behalf of our forebears who cannot). Nations necessarily rest on such historical consciousness—upon the sense of a chain of connection between them and us, between the past and the present and the present and the past. This is what it means to be a patriot. One can argue, as Noel Pearson has done, that if we can 'share and celebrate in the achievements of the past, indeed feel responsibility for and express pride in aspects of our past', surely we can 'feel responsibility for and express shame in relation to other aspects of the past'.

The recognition of the status of Aborigines and Torres Strait Islanders, the shameful wrongs perpetrated (often in the name of Australia), and the present consequences of colonisation, should, moreover, be ongoing in the same manner as we commemorate other aspects of our history. For example, just as we repeatedly mark Gallipoli on Anzac Day, year after year, and are proud to pay homage to our ancestors who fought for 'our' freedom and liberty, we should gather to pay our respect to the original owners of this land and remind ourselves of their dispossession and destruction. Non-Aboriginal Australians have, of course, been loath to recall the bad things our ancestors have done. For example, their killings of Aborigines on the frontiers have been forgotten even though the wars here were of much greater importance inasmuch as Australia was created through the invasion of the Aborigines' land (and so our indebtedness—our debt—to Aborigines should be all the greater); as Henry Reynolds and Ann Curthoys have noted, this forgetfulness is strange in a country that has been so good at memorialising its own sufferings and which reveres the fallen warrior and emblazons the phrase 'Lest We Forget' on monuments throughout the land.

National Sorry Day is one appropriate way of regularly commemorating the historical relationships between Aboriginal and non-Aboriginal people. It follows a tradition among many Aboriginal communities that reaches back to the 'Day of Mourning' held on Australia Day in 1938 and to Aboriginal rituals (known as 'sorry business' in some communities) for expressing collective grief that are probably tens of thousands of years old. Another forum is National Reconciliation Week, which begins and ends on two historically significant dates—27 May, which marks the passing of a national referendum in 1967 that is widely (mis)understood as the moment when Aborigines were recognised as Australian citizens; and 3 June, which marks the High Court's Mabo judgement that is seen as the moment when the native title rights of Aborigines and Torres Strait Islanders were recognised. By celebrating these events, remembrance can encompass not only the dispossession of Aboriginal landowners and the destruction of Aboriginal communities that followed but also the fact of non-Aboriginal recognition of Aboriginal rights. This is both right and necessary; Australia, like any national community, needs heroes and so our true stories about relations between Aborigines and non-Aborigines should also celebrate those who championed Aboriginal rights so that we have exemplars whom we can try to emulate.

In all this, reconciliation needs to be seen as a *process*, something which has a time scale of generations rather than years, not something that can be hurriedly concluded by statements of apology or draft documents. These are only appropriate if they are seen as part of ongoing historical understanding, recognition and reparation—points of beginning or landmarks on a long march, not the journey's end.

The Need for Scepticism
Christopher Pearson

First contact between blacks and whites in Australia was by no means invariably hostile. As Geoffrey Dutton pointed out in 1974, the contemporary paintings and sketches sometimes show sailors dancing hornpipes, to the considerable amusement of the natives, who've returned the compliment with a corroboree and a feast of fish. Sainson's *Sailors Fraternising at Jervis Bay* and Pellion's record of a similar encounter at Shark Bay, WA, are only two examples.

Dutton often used to say that, if only there had been a bit more courage and spirited engagement on both sides, how different the history of Australian settlement might have been. It's a very seductive line of argument; one which informs some of what's best about the ideal of reconciliation.

Whatever one's reservations about reconciliation, both in theory and practice, of which more presently, it's obvious that the process of settlement could have been better and more humanely managed.

History can be tyrannical and constraining. It's always possible to understand the past better and to think more creatively about the present in the light of what might have been had things been otherwise.

The problem in doing so is succumbing to retrospective Utopianism or its more dangerous present day versions. The most alarming is the attitude, almost universal among urban under-25 year-olds, that 'if it had been us rather than our forefathers there would have been no massacres'. Another extreme form of unexamined fantasy is that there might have been no alien presence; that the Aborigines might have miraculously been left in undisturbed possession of the continent *ad infinitum*.

It's a tribute to how incredibly badly history has mostly been taught in Australian schools and universities over the last quarter century that the territorial and economic imperatives of late eighteenth century English, French and Dutch imperial expansionism could be amnesed like this. It's also a salutory reminder of the ways in which all that false (or at best naive) instruction prompts young people to distance themselves from previous generations and to assert their own, effortless moral superiority.

Paul Keating pandered to it in his infamous Redfern speech: 'we committed the murders', when it's clear that 'we' refers to distant tribal forebears rather than to us at all. His rhetoric also tended to demean Aboriginal Australia by suggesting that it was deprived of any human agency in the historical process, almost without the capacity for retribution, let alone for unprovoked violence and massacre on the scale inflicted on the survivors of the shipwrecked *Maria* in South Australia, to name but one example.

By 1840, when the *Maria* came to grief on the Coorong, east of the mouth of the Murray, the river and its trading systems had already brought unparalleled disaster to the Aborigines living on its verges, in the form of introduced diseases to which they had no resistance. When this fact is noted it is too readily assumed that mentioning it is merely a way of blamelessly assuaging past wrongs, with some blithe Darwinian subtext about survival of the fittest. I mention it instead as a talisman against Utopian sentimentality.

There are often reckoned to have been two waves of highly communicable diseases, primarily smallpox and other viruses, which are thought—within little more than a generation—to have reduced some tribal populations by a third or more of their pre-contact numbers. Hunter-gatherer societies with complex kinship rules and relatively small groups of old men who were the only people fully apprised of their traditions are likely to have been in cultural crisis or collapse long before the formal settlement of South Australia. The absence of permissible categories of marriage partners—with all that that implies about existential crisis in relation to moiety and land—and dwindling numbers of people able to perform the ceremonies of initiation and increase may have been as devastating as superior fire power when it eventually arrived. Vast stretches of the Amazon basin were rapidly depopulated for similar reasons.

None of these considerations lessens the tragic dimension of the impact of European settlement or the present day responsibility for decent indigenous policy and bipartisan commitment to Aboriginal advancement. What they do serve to remind us is that the past is another country and that the politics of the warm, inner glow are to be distrusted, like the politics of present day moral triumphalism. The only approach intelligent enough to deal with obdurate problems of social policy is scepticism.

Yet scepticism is the attribute most crucially lacking in public debate on reconciliation. As the distinguished anthropologist, Kenneth Maddock recently observed in a review of The Australian Academy of Social Sciences' Colloquium, *Reconciliation*[1], the notion seems to have collectively immunised Australian intellectuals from even the most rudimentary caution:

> The authors create a stumbling block for themselves by taking the idea of reconciliation for granted as something which ought by its nature to be supported. That is to say they bear an unfortunate resemblance to cheerleaders, the girls that cavort and wave gaily coloured plumes when their football team runs onto the ground. They are part of the show. No one expects them to ask awkward questions.

My own main reservations about reconciliation as a vehicle are these: firstly it is a misnomer. It implies a once warm relationship that has somehow been ruptured when in fact the real problem is that there is virtually no connection except by television between Aboriginal people and middle-class suburban Australia.

Reconciliation also has resonances of a religious and specifically penitential kind, which will no doubt appeal strongly to the already penitent but which will tend to be counter-productive and deeply offputting to those of a more secular disposition who don't believe in inter-generational guilt.

From a sceptical perspective, it's tempting to see reconciliation predominantly as a way for parts of suburban white Australia to feel good about itself at minimal personal cost. While I'm sure it wasn't conceived as an invitation to moral narcissism at the expense of 'redneck' Australia, that is undoubtedly an element in the thinking of those holier-than-thou Sea of Hands mums from Hunters Hill and Camberwell, especially if they don't have any Aboriginal friends *as such*.

Meanwhile a lot of rural people, black and white, who have longstanding work, sporting or bar-room associations and friendships will be inclined to see the whole social engineering apparatus of reconciliation as an enormous cheek and humbug on the part of government bureaucrats.

Again, on the question of bureaucracies, from a sceptical position it's possible to read post-contact Australian history predominantly in terms of a series of failures of administrative engagement.

---

1 Published in the *Adelaide Review*, February 2000.

Hunter-gatherer societies with staggeringly high levels of inter-tribal violence don't develop the structures for formal representation when dealing with potential invaders. Endless pay-back systems, based on the belief that most deaths except in old age or battle are the result of sorcery rather than natural causes, militate against co-operation to confront a common enemy who is a greater threat.

In Herzegovina, as the very name announces, whatever the level of internal Balkan strife, it was 'Archduke John's land' and he spoke for his people. In Aboriginal Australia there was never—and still isn't—someone to speak and negotiate from a position of generally acknowledged authority on behalf of everyone. From a sceptical point of view ATSIC looks like a deeply unrepresentative clique, elected by a small percentage of those eligible to vote, simply because the Hawke–Keating government needed what it conceived of as a 'peak body' with which to deal.

The mixture of evangelical good intentions, expansionist practicality, bloodymindedness and the schizophrenic Letters Patent that bedevilled the white side of the administrative frontier are well known. To bewail the fact that nothing comparable to New Zealand's Treaty of Waitangi was achieved is idle. The organised resistance and political structures to force London to negotiate simply were not there.

Since the 1970s it has been fashionable to borrow from American rhetoric and talk of an 'Aboriginal nation' and the need for a treaty. Legally and numerically, it was always a nonsense to think of a deeply divided two percent of the population as a separate nation with whom a treaty could be devised. When this eventually dawned on the more sensible people in Bob Hawke's office, reconciliation by the year 2000 emerged to replace it.

John Howard's realisation that Aboriginal advancement and preserving a degree of consensus on the need for it is too delicate a process to be determined by a millennial timetable and contentious statements of intent, is not, as his political and journalistic detractors would have it, poll-driven. As several Aboriginal commentators have said, it is common sense. What the polls suggest is that working-class taxpayers want to see more achieved in the way of lasting progress in the Aboriginal affairs budget and less wasted on self-serving bureaucracies, both black and white.

Lingiari: Until the Chains are Broken
Patrick Dodson

There have been many sunsets since Gough Whitlam, the prime minister of Australia, trickled a handful of red soil into the hand of the old man whose name was Vincent Lingiari.

At that moment in 1975, the prime minister recognised the rights of Gurindji people in their land. It was also a recognition of other efforts, other times, and other people. It was recognition by the Australian government, of the kind of rights that the Pilbara pastoral strikers of 1946 had been seeking during their long, acrimonious battle with the Western Australian pastoral establishment. It was also recognition of the 90 percent of Australians who put up their hands in 1967 to begin the process of recognition for, and reconciliation with, indigenous Australians. It was a recognition by a prime minister that the work of healing the relationship between our peoples was under way.

I am sure that the two men in that simple ceremony knew the road ahead for their peoples was not an easy one. They both knew that there were many within the Australian community who felt, out of fear or prejudice, that any recognition of the rights of indigenous people threatened their own superior place in the Australian society.

The old man and his tall whitefella mate both knew that among their fellow Australians were those who believed that the yellow peril still sat on our northern doorstep, and that letting Aboriginal people off the reserve would lead to a breakdown in the moral fabric of our country towns and cities. They both knew more was to be done beyond the noble symbol of recognition represented by that simple ceremony. Rights and reconciliation had to be translated into justice, equality and a shared future.

• • •

For the past nine years or so, we as a nation, have been considering the reconciliation process. We have had many decent Australians work hard to help a national mind shift. There is still much to do.

In the middle of that, we have had the Human Rights and Equal Opportunity Commission inquiry into the practice of removing the children from their mothers, their peoples, their country, their culture, to the extent that the inquiry described this activity as genocide.

The nation has still not come to terms with this reality. There has not been an official apology from the parliament despite recent events. The federal parliament has expressed its Paddy McGuinness version of regret. It has not said sorry to the stolen generations or offered to deal with the issue of restitution in any other way than to suggest that the stolen generations try their luck in the courts where the same sincerely regretful government will continue to oppose them. Those individual Aboriginal people who were taken away now have to prove that the act of genocide was real, and that they were lucky to have survived.

Perhaps this inability to seize the moment highlights just how entrenched the assimilation mindset is when we are confronted with the realities of how the Aboriginal peoples were treated by governments. We are still chained to our thinking and continue to seek the station manager's nod of approval.

Reconciliation is a matter that takes place at different levels, if it takes place at all. The quality of our reconciliation will depend on our capacity to embrace all its aspects however difficult each may seem.

There is the personal level. This is the level of human encounter. If there is ignorance, hostility, discrimination or racism experienced then reconciliation will mean very little, but if there is concern, solidarity, inclusiveness and some respect, then reconciliation will have some positive responses. The importance of reconciliation will range up and down over how any of these encounters dominates in the lives of both peoples, Aboriginal and non-Aboriginal.

Then there is the reconciliation at the social level. These are the social policy matters that have to do with health, housing, education, employment, welfare and an economic base. Reconciliation here is about whether the particular government or the Aboriginal peoples themselves have done enough, or anything, to relieve the concerns that hit Aboriginal people so hard day after day. It is also about the shared responsibilities and obligations we have in the society.

Then there is the reconciliation of governance. This is about governments making laws that remove rights, or enhance them. Fundamentally it is about the content of the legislative enactments that effect or impact upon the Aboriginal peoples.

Finally, there is the reconciliation of recognition. The sovereign position that Aboriginal peoples assert has never been ceded. Recognition starts from the premise that *terra nullius* and its consequences were imposed upon the Aboriginal peoples, and certainly there was never any choice given to the Aboriginal peoples concerning the Constitution or the rule of law.

To have any substantial reconciliation we must encompass all these aspects, no matter how challenging that may seem. These foundations of reconciliation cannot be made of concrete that lacks the binding mortar of truth.

The Council for Aboriginal Reconciliation is in the final stages of its current existence. It will soon make recommendations to the parliament about the future of reconciliation, specifically whether a document or documents of reconciliation will advance the reconciliation process. How we could contemplate signing off on any document of reconciliation while our government stands accused of racial discrimination by the UN Committee on the Elimination of Racial Discrimination is absurd to me. My considered view is that a comprehensive framework agreement is needed, and that it should be legislated into existence.

It is needed for two additional reasons, what I will refer to as the 'unfinished business'. The first is to deal with the conditions of our existence as Aboriginal Australians within the Australian society, and the second is in order for us to survive as Aboriginal peoples in keeping with our own laws and customs within our own traditions and values. This is our Aboriginal unfinished business, questions concerning the survival of our being as a consequence of having been subjugated and disadvantaged through the necessities of defending our interests and meeting our needs since the arrival of governor Phillip; 'to be Gurundji' in the words of Vincent Lingiari. Such an agreement should define, and set out a path, to resolve all the matters of unfinished business between the parliament and the Aboriginal peoples.

It will also need to extend the period of time beyond the current Olympian and millennium sunset clauses and establish an independent body to facilitate and mediate the issues towards resolution.

Vincent Lingiari would not have taken such a cumbersome path. He and his people went on strike not only for the wages and conditions, but also for their right to be Gurindji; to have their land back under their responsibility and the capacity restored to enjoy the benefits flowing from the ancient law and custom of the Gurindji. The exploitative employment conditions, the sexual abuse, the inhuman living conditions, and the stripping of their dignity provided no other path than to stand up to the Cudeba, and to tell him that they would no longer be treated as dogs. It was time to stand for what was rightfully theirs. There was no further depravation and indignity to be experienced from the Cudeba. He did not stand alone, he had mates and bosses.

In 1966, the Gurindji leader had meetings with the Aboriginal organiser for the North Australian Workers Union, Dexter Daniels in Darwin, while he was there recovering from being kicked by a donkey. They had talked about how best to deal with the conditions on Wave Hill. Dexter talked about the delay in equal wages until December 1968. Here was a very sobering lesson for the Gurindji. No Aboriginal stockmen were called to give evidence in the union case beginning in 1965. This enabled the Conciliation and Arbitration Commission to scope their ruling in March 1966 to the government's policy of assimilation, and to accept the assertions of the pastoralist that the Aboriginal workers had no real appreciation of the meaning of work because of 'tribal and cultural reasons' and therefore should not be paid the same wage as the white stockmen.

Whether Dexter had ever heard of the great strike of the Pilbara Aboriginal people, or had told Vincent about the Aboriginal people at Newcastle Waters who had already gone on strike because of wages and conditions, we do not know. But he explained to Vincent that the strike was the proper way to make the Cudeba listen to his concerns. Vincent, when he returned to Wave Hill knew that there was some support from outside the compound on Wave Hill.

But in the context of what that old boss Vincent was trying to achieve, and what the Conciliation and Arbitration Commission and Lord Vestey's mob were compromising on, Vincent must have been under no illusions about just how hard the search for permanent justice would be. It would be very hard.

The rulers were saying, 'For our natives and their own good because we best understand what they need'. It had nothing to do with equal justice even though in the future Aboriginal stockmen would be included in the award. They said to us, 'You don't use your land like us, or how we want to, so we will make better use of it'. Then they drove us away from our lands and took away our responsibility under the law to protect and nurture the land.

They said to us, 'Your languages make no sense'. So they gave us a new one but would not give us schools in which to learn this new language.

They said to us, 'You have no work ethic so you shall work for nothing' and they indentured us and brought us back in chains when we ran away from their cruelty.

They said to us, 'You have no religion' and they offered us several versions of their own.

They said to us, 'Your mixed race children will not be safe and happy with you so we will take them and train them to be our servants,' and alienated several generations of us from our birthright.

All these things were imposed upon our people because the governments of the day believed that these things were 'for your own good'. Why they didn't think these things would be just as good for their children and themselves I'll never understand!

Vincent and the other Aboriginal people on the pastoral properties in the Northern Territory were asked to swallow this type of rhetoric for many years, and then live under its mystique for the rest of their existence. The young Aboriginal people of today should not be asked to have their rights treated in this way and their young white mates should not be burdened with this unutterable shame.

Millions of non-indigenous Australians have joined with us in the search for a better relationship based on equity and justice. Australians at every level of our society have put up their hands to be counted as supporters of a nation that holds as its core value a society based on mutual respect, tolerance and justice. This has been the approach many Aboriginal people have been prepared to adopt in seeking to achieve reconciliation between our peoples.

I have seen first-hand the benefits that the Australian community derives from the achievement of local acts of reconciliation within communities throughout Australia—how local governments can function more cohesively; how small rural communities can join together to obtain infrastructure resources; how the coordination of health services can be enhanced in a region by working together cooperatively within a spirit of reconciliation.

But more importantly, I have seen what can be achieved among our young Australians when they decide that the values of division and conflict promoted by previous generations are not the values that they seek to carry into the twenty-first century. I for one believe that the voters of 1967 and their children are prepared to defend the values of tolerance, acceptance and respect.

But rest assured that the spirit of the ten percent that rejected the basic decency of the 'Yes' vote in 1967 have not been swallowed up in the pit of their intolerance. They have taken new guises. They present themselves as moral champions whose only desire is to save indigenous Australians from the iniquity of welfarism and to provide young indigenous Australians with a future imbued with all the trappings of successful entrepreneurs. Then there will be no need for membership of a unique people whose values are considered outmoded and irrelevant in the modern world. All this for our own good.

The tools they use to promote their argument are not the coarse arguments of racial intolerance that sufficed in 1967. They present their arguments in the guise of academia and legal sophistry. They use the vehicles of institutions created to promote their particular views. The hard men of Vestey's still walk the corridors of power.

What can we learn from the Wave Hill strike and its entire context? The very first thing that an Aboriginal person learns is that there has to be something more than just trust in the government to look after our interest. There has never been a comprehensive challenge to the 'for their own good' approach. Every facet of government policy is premised on this same paternalistic approach.

When Vestey's boss, Tom Fisher, tried to win Vincent and the Gurindji back to Wave Hill, and to his regime of serfdom with fresh beef, Vincent and his people—even though they were hungry—told Fisher to take his beef back to the station. Vincent was not to be bought off. Neither should the young Aboriginal leaders, being feted as a new breed of pragmatist in tune with the global necessities of the modern world, be lured into vanities of illusionary power and influence.

If a boss in the law can decline two bullocks a week to defend his principles, then we who follow should consider with great care any deals that could diminish the principles of our senior holders of the law.

Neither should our non-indigenous supporters accuse us of an inability to compromise with new governments and its leader. If our bosses thought enough of the law and their responsibilities to the land to lead their families into exile and uncertainty, then the least we can do is honour their courage and integrity by defending the principles of our law, which run with the land.

It may be a harsh thing to say, but many actions of Australian governments have given Aboriginal people little faith in the promises governments make in relation to protecting and defending the rights of indigenous Australians. That is why we need a formal agreement that recognises and guarantees the rights of indigenous Australians within the Australian Constitution; an agreement that will allow the politically partisan games to be stopped and the real issues between us put on the table.

Such an agreement would help put the matters of unfinished business that underlie the causes of discord and division between us into a framework agreement. This framework agreement could be made formal by an act of the parliament and ultimately matters flowing from it enshrined in our Constitution. This is needed otherwise it will be no more than a gesture, a matter of government expediency.

If there is no agreement to be bound in this manner, then we can be sure that the hard-won gains of the past will be placed at serious risk, if not certain loss. The assimilation process will have won out. Aboriginal peoples can then stop considering themselves as unique to Australia. And for this we will be able to thank those amongst us who have become so acculturated that the distinctions are no longer meaningful.

It would have been like telling the Gurindji that they were just a class of stockman without any other rights than those that the Arbitration Commission was prepared to give to them. The Gurindji decided in the course of the strike that their relationship to Vestey's and the government must be founded upon their right to determine their own priorities, the directions of their lives and their own affairs.

As a nation we must be prepared to recognise that there is unfinished business between us and that the only way that this can be resolved is through a formalised agreement between our peoples. An agreement that decent Australians have to help to build in a fair, respectful and just manner. We can do it together if we are willing to have a serious try at achieving something worthwhile for our country. If we are not willing, or decide that it is all to hard, then to our children we will bequeath a nation without pride or dignity, unfulfilled and diminished.

The achievement of an agreement will call for courage and persistence. Because it is about principle and not short-term expediency, there is no room for fear or appeasement in this quest. It does not have to be achieved by 2001.

Too often we are told that constitutional change is very difficult and that the best we can hope for is two lines in a preamble, negotiated by a prime minister, a poet and a minor party in the parliament. Surely as Australians we deserve better. All Australians should reject any preamble to our national Constitution that denies the true status of indigenous Australians as the custodians and owners of the land, and suggests that we are nothing more than gardeners at the station homestead.

The rights of any group in the society—be they women, ethnic groups, returned service people, the terminally ill or young people—should never be treated with such disdain. Vincent Lingiari would rather go hungry than accept the enticements of free beef that were the price for his people giving up their struggle.

It is not about words, it is not about getting into step with the thinking of a new government. It is not about making sure that Australia has a piece of paper to show off at the Olympics. It is purely and simply about a recognition of Aboriginal people as a unique people within the nation of Australia with rights and responsibilities.

There is no right more fundamental to Aboriginal peoples than the right to self-determination, and the big man Vincent knew that if it was not exercised then it would be taken away by government.

Vincent Lingiari started us on the road to reconciliation. What is it that we Aboriginal peoples want at the end of this century that will provide the substantial reconciliation that will heal our country? To make clear what some of these matters might be on the reconciliation road let us consider the type of petition we would construct today in keeping with the spirit of Vincent Lingiari's petition to Lord Casey. It may read something like this:

> *Equality*: Aboriginal peoples have the right to all the common human rights and fundamental freedoms recognised in national

and international law, as well as to our distinct rights as indigenous peoples.

Distinct characteristics and identities: Aboriginal peoples have the right to maintain and develop our distinct characteristics and identities, whilst taking part in the life of the country as a whole. This includes the right to identify as indigenous. We shall not be subject to: actions which threaten our distinct cultures and identities; the removal of our children from our families and communities; taking of our lands and resources; or any other measures of assimilation.

Self-determination: Aboriginal peoples have the right to self-determination; a right to negotiate our political status and to pursue economic, social and cultural development.

Law: Aboriginal peoples have the right to our own law, customs and traditions, and equality before the national law.

Culture: Aboriginal peoples have the right to our unique cultural traditions and customs. This includes aspects of our cultures such as designs, ceremonies, performances and technologies. We have the right to own and control our cultural and intellectual property, including our sciences, medicines, knowledge of flora and fauna, arts and performances. Our cultural property taken without consent shall be returned to us.

Spiritual and religious traditions: Aboriginal peoples have the right to our spiritual and religious traditions. This includes the right to preserve and protect our sacred sites, ceremonial objects and the remains of our ancestors.

Language: Aboriginal peoples have the right to our languages, histories, stories, oral traditions and names for people and places. This includes the right to be heard and to receive information in our own languages. In courts, other proceedings and in the criminal justice system, we shall have the right to understand and be understood, through interpreters and other appropriate ways.

Participation and partnerships: Aboriginal peoples have the right to participate in law and policy-making and in decisions that affect us. This includes the right to choose our own representatives. Governments shall obtain our consent before adopting these laws and policies. Governments shall negotiate partnerships with Aboriginal peoples representative bodies at local, regional, state and national levels.

Economic and social development: Aboriginal peoples have the right to determine priorities and strategies for economic and social development. This includes the right to determine health, housing, and infrastructure, and other economic and social programs and, to the extent possible, to deliver these through our own organisations. There shall be recognition of the importance of empowerment for decision-making and development at regional and community levels. There shall be indigenous participation in all regional planning processes. Aboriginal peoples' shall have full access to, and equitable outcomes from participation in relevant mainstream programs.

Special measures: Aboriginal peoples have the right to special measures to improve our economic and social conditions. This includes the areas of employment, education and training, housing and infrastructure, and health.

Education and training: Aboriginal peoples have the right to all forms and levels of public education and training. We also have the right to our own schools and to provide education in our own languages. Aboriginal children living outside communities shall be able to learn their own cultures and languages.

Land and resources: Aboriginal peoples have the right to own and control the use of our land, waters and other resources. This includes the right to return of land and resources taken without our consent. Where this is not possible, we shall receive just compensation. Governments shall obtain our consent before giving approval to activities affecting our land and resources, including the development of mineral resources. We shall receive just compensation for any such activities.

Self-government: As a form of self-determination Aboriginal peoples have the right to self-government and autonomy in relation to our own affairs. This includes the right to determine the structure and membership of our self-governing institutions. Governments shall facilitate the negotiation of self-government and regional agreements.

Constitutional recognition: The federal parliament shall initiate processes leading to concrete constitutional change to recognise and protect the special place and rights of the Aboriginal peoples in the Australian polity.

Treaties and agreements: The federal parliament shall enact legislation establishing a framework for the negotiation of agreements with the Aboriginal peoples. Governments shall respect treaties and agreements entered into with Aboriginal peoples.

Ongoing processes: The federal parliament shall establish a discussion, research, information and negotiation forum to promote public awareness and to draft national legislation enacting principles of recognition, guidelines for public policy, and the framework for negotiation of agreements referred to above.

All of these matters have to do with the various levels of the way the reconciliation process is capable of operating and the complexity of the challenge of its totality. This has to do with the two broad dimensions that I outlined earlier—the Aboriginal Australian dimension and the Aboriginal dimension.

It recognises that governments are elected for periods of three years, which, more often than not ends up being less. It recognises the vagaries of human nature that cause politicians to focus on how they can get elected next time around. It recognises that politicians focus on the short, rather than the longer term. It recognises that the short term is not necessarily compatible with the long term. It recognises that ministers are often rotated among portfolios every few years and it is not possible for those people to become fully acquainted with the challenge of Aboriginal affairs within such a short timeframe, however desirable their motives or loyalty to our cause. We need now to develop long-term solutions for our future.

To paraphrase the governor-general, Sir William Deane: I am convinced that true reconciliation that is not based upon truth will leave us as a diminished nation. And I, like the governor-general am convinced that such reconciliation is possible.

Despite the words of his whitefella mate—'Vincent Lingiari, I solemnly hand to you these deeds as proof, in Australian law, that these lands belong to the Gurindji people and I put into your hands part of the earth itself as a sign that this land will be the possession of you, and your children forever'—Vincent and the Gurindji had to struggle for a further ten years against being put back into the chains of welfare, the threats of the pastoralist and the government's opportunism before his people were given freehold title [in 1986] under the Aboriginal Land Rights Act 1976. Maybe the security of this form of title itself is now at risk. Who will then stand with the Gurindji and Vincent Lingiari?

Soon it will be the in-gar-liwa (blue bone fish) time in Yawuru Country with the calming of the east winds that come from the deserts, the dry cool winds of winter. With the new moon, will come the offshore ocean winds that will bring the rains to the desert later in the year—a sharing of the gifts of the land and sea. This has been the way for millennia. The passing of the year 2000 and the Olympic Games in Sydney will not change the cycle of the seasons. Neither will there be a diminishment of our responsibilities to defend and secure our rights in the land and sea, our responsibilities to defend our law and culture.

Vincent Lingiari would have never compromised his responsibilities in the land, even to accommodate the political needs of his mate. He would never have relinquished his responsibilities in the law or his responsibilities in the leadership of his people for the sake of free meat from Lord Vestey.

Then neither should we be prepared to relinquish our responsibilities to defend and secure the legitimate rights of future generations of young indigenous Australians, by moving from one compromise to another because of the intransigence of a government that declines to recognise us as the first Australians with our own unique rights and responsibilities.

Finally, I would like to quote to you from the last paragraph of Frank Hardy's 1972 book *The Unlucky Australians*. I offer it to you as a challenge: should we be content to allow the house of recognition and reconciliation for which the Gurindji and others have laid the foundations, be left half-finished by builders not committed to the job?

> Will I, having written it, be free to turn to other books and obsessions, will you, having read it, be free to turn to the pursuit of happiness, will the lucky country remain free while the unlucky Australians are in chains?

Guilt, Shame and Collective Responsibility
Raimond Gaita

Mabo and *Bringing Them Home,* the report on the stolen children, are supported by historical evidence that is a cause of deep shame for many Australians. For some it has been a source of guilt. Such responses—shame especially—often express acknowledgement of a collective responsibility, sometimes directly *for* the wrongs done, but more often *to* those who were wronged by our political ancestors. It amounts to the acknowledgement that we are rightly called to communal responsiveness to those who are the victims of our wrongdoing or the wrongdoing of those who preceded us.

Others have responded differently. They have mocked an historically deep sense of shame, calling it a 'black armband' view of history. Often they say something like this. The practical—and therefore the *really* moral—thing to do is to stop brooding on the alleged wrongs committed against the Aborigines in the past and to get on with the task of providing them with land, health, education and other benefits. This (the thought continues) should not be done in response to the divisive idea that their history entitles them to it, but in response to their present needs assessed equitably alongside the needs of all their fellow citizens.

People who believe this are, I think, seriously mistaken because they treat the fact that the Aborigines are landless because they were dispossessed rather than because of a natural catastrophe as morally and politically irrelevant. More generally, they treat as irrelevant that their suffering is saturated by a justified sense that they have been terribly wronged. To ignore the fact that they have been wronged in any proposal for what is now to be done, to insist high-mindedly that *real* moral concern focuses on the present and the future rather than the past, is to compound their humiliation and our shame.

Justices Deane and Gaudron saw that quite clearly. When they said so in their judgement in Mabo, they were accused of using irresponsibly emotive language in the service of a transparent political intent and, therefore, of subverting the integrity of the court. Here is their language at its strongest:

> An early flash point with one clan of Aborigines illustrates the first stages of the conflagration of oppression and conflict which was, over the following century, to spread across the continent to dispossess, degrade and devastate the Aboriginal peoples and leave a national legacy of unutterable shame.

Later, when they justified their re-examination 'of the validity of fundamental propositions which have been endorsed by long established authority and which have been accepted as a basis of the real property law of the country for more than 150 years', they said:

> The acts and events by which that dispossession [of the Aboriginal peoples of most of their traditional lands] in legal theory was carried into practical effect constitutes the darkest aspect of the history of this nation. The nation as a whole must remain diminished unless and until there is an acknowledgement of and retreat from, those past injustices.

Anticipating criticism of their language, the justices explained why they spoke as they did:

> We have used language and expressed conclusions which some may think to be unusually emotive for a judgement in a court... The reason which has led us to describe, and express conclusions about, the dispossession of the Australian Aborigines in unrestrained language is that the full facts of the dispossession are of critical importance to the assessment of the legitimacy of the propositions that the continent was unoccupied for legal purposes and that the unqualified legal and beneficial ownership of all the lands of the continent were vested in the Crown.

It is important not to misunderstand them. When they acknowledged that their language was 'unrestrained', they did not mean that it was undisciplined and unsuited to a dispassionate appraisal of the facts and their relevance. A dispassionate judgement is not one uninformed by feeling, but one that is undistorted by it. This fact separates legitimate use of the words 'emotive', 'emotional' or 'rhetorical' as terms of criticism from illegitimate insistence that objective thought must always be separable from feeling.

Perhaps another, more dramatic example, will make the point more clearly. The descriptions of the Holocaust by Martin Gilbert and by Primo Levi are written with disciplined restraint. Those descriptions are dispassionate in the sense I claimed for the prose of Gaudron and Deane: though informed by feeling, they are not distorted by it. We know when we read them that they are written by men whose souls were lacerated by what they knew. It shows in their prose which we read, as Nora Levin put it, 'with bleeding eyes'. There is no other way to read them with understanding and no other way they can convey the reality of the evil they describe. This kind of truth and reality can only be understood by an informed heart. We see that immediately if we compare the reports of the murders with SS reports which are reports of the killing without any sense of its evil. Those SS reports are dispassionate in the sense of being uninformed by feeling. The effect is not to disclose reality objectively, but to obscure it.

Justices Deane and Gaudron claimed to speak as they did so that the 'full facts of the dispossession' and their significance to the legitimacy of previous judgements might be appreciated. By the 'full facts of the dispossession' they meant the full meaning of it, which can only be conveyed in prose that reveals its moral reality. It is not sober and truthful speech which they (implicitly) contrasted with their own, but speech in which a falsifying kind of restraint is mistaken for disciplined impartiality. One may reasonably dispute the accuracy of their descriptions. One may reasonably claim that, in its actual application, their language obscures rather than reveals the facts in their 'full significance'. But only specious assumptions about the distinctions between description and evaluation, fact and value, or emotion and reason can support the claim that the words of Deane and Gaudron are intrinsically unsuited to dispassionate appraisal of the facts and their significance.

Justices Gaudron and Deane were also accused of sacrificing the integrity of the law for the sake of (perhaps morally worthy) political purposes. As far as I am able to judge that is not merely false, but the very opposite of the truth.

It is clear that the justices desired a change in the law. It is also clear that they believed that those changes would benefit Aborigines. One should not conclude however that their primary intention was to change the law for the benefit of Aborigines. Their primary concern, as it shows in their judgement, was not with the effects of injustice on Aborigines, but with its effect on the law. In their judgement concern for the Aborigines is mediated and constrained in their judgement by that primary concern for the integrity of the law. Justices Gaudron and Deane made more explicit than the other justices the connection between that concern for the integrity of law and their belief that the 'nation as a whole must remain diminished unless and until there is an acknowledgement of and retreat from those past injustices'. That is why they were criticised so severely.

Concern for the integrity of law and a desire to redeem the nation's shame need not conflict. The law is, after all, the most important element in the definition of the political *persona* by virtue of which a person may have a national identity of which he or she may be proud or ashamed. By redeeming the law from the injustices in which it had become complicit the justices were, at the same time, redeeming (to some degree) the 'national legacy of unutterable shame'.

My reply, therefore, to those who say that Mabo and the persistent threat of (allegedly) irresponsible claims issuing from it are a threat to the national interest is as follows. On should not, as critics of Mabo tend to do, restrict the concept of national interest to economic interests and the interest of having an undivided body politic. If the dispossession of the Aboriginal peoples is one of the 'darkest chapter[s]' in Australian history, then justices Deane and Gaudron may justifiably have hoped that when their fellow citizens acknowledged this they would also accept its moral consequences—in this case, the material costs to the nation of the court's concern to purge the law of its complicity in the events of that dark chapter.

Even in politics we are, inescapably, moral beings. No adequate concept of our interests or of our wellbeing should ignore or diminish that fact. Justices Deane and Gaudron saw quite clearly that our communal and national interests include living justly and with a pride that we can honestly celebrate because we have acknowledged our shame. Shame is as necessary for the lucid acknowledgement by Australians of the wrongs the Aborigines suffered at the hands of their political ancestors, and to the wrongs they continue to suffer, as pain is to mourning. It is not an optional emotional addition to the recognition of the meaning of their dispossession. It is, I believe, the *form* of that recognition. The spirit in which their suffering is ameliorated must, therefore, be informed by the acknowledgement that those who suffered it were wronged—that to be wronged is a distinctive and irreducible form of harm. Pained acknowledgement of the wrongs we have committed or in which we are in other ways implicated is, according to the circumstances, either guilt or shame.

Mabo should, therefore, not be contrasted with the national interest. It should be seen as an expression of the kind of concern with law and justice which is essential to any conception of the national interest informed by an appreciation of the difference between patriotism and jingoism. Real-politik and other infatuations with 'political realism', depend on an unjustifiably narrow conception of what is in our interests as political beings. Applied nationally and internationally, they create unnecessary tension between the demands of justice and the national interest. And their disdain for moral concern in politics is inconsistent with most of the things in which people take national pride.

Who then should answer the call to acknowledge collective responsibility? And in what way? Clearly, those who are guilty by deed or omission and those sufficiently close to them in time to feel obliged to bring them to justice. Also those who are related to the guilty in such a way that they rightly feel ashamed. Finally, those who are related to the guilty in such a way that they should seek an appropriate figure—usually the head of an institution or of government—to apologise on their behalf and to acknowledge other responsibilities, generally, the responsibility to make reparation.

Obviously this last group will include many members of the first and second, but it may also have members who are not guilty and who are not ashamed because they do not have the kind of attachment to the country which would make shame appropriate. They might think of themselves merely as citizens of their nation, acknowledging certain rights and duties, but unable yet to speak in the first person plural in the way that is characteristic of those who are rooted in their country, who love it and who are nourished by its historically deep traditions. National shame requires an historically deeper and more intense attachment, perhaps a more *defining* attachment, to country than citizenship.

Discussions of these issues is sometimes muddied by the conflation of shame and guilt. Because remorse—which I take to be the pained acknowledgement of one's guilt—is taken as a paradigm of the acceptance of responsibility, people sometimes think responsibility must be restricted to what one has done or omitted to do. Moral guilt is indeed so restricted; the guilt of others can be the occasion for one's own guilt only if one failed to do something to prevent their deeds or at least to protest them. Perhaps that is why collective responsibility is so often taken to mean collective guilt rather than national shame. It is, after all, tempting to say that one's omissions must reasonably be judged to stand in some causal relation to the wrong deeds of others if one is justifiably to be held responsible together with their perpetrators—roughly, that one must reasonably judge that one could have played a part in stopping them.

That temptation should be resisted. If one soberly judges that one's actions could achieve nothing, one might nonetheless rightly feel obliged to protest, perhaps so it be known that, or merely so it be true that, at least someone cared that wrong was done to people. But in such cases, one must be in sufficient proximity to wrong done to them to give sense to the guilty thought that it was done and one did nothing to stop or to protest against it. That is not a thought that can justifiably occasion guilt in later generations, although they may rightly feel guilty for not responding, in ways appropriate to them, to the fact that their ancestors did wrong, because they have not offered reparation, for example.

Important though the distinction is between guilt and shame it is not always sharp. There are borderline cases as, of course, there are with any concept. More importantly, there is a condition which is neither guilt nor shame and which is not a state borderline between them. Ron Castan who played a prominent part in securing native title legislation, alerted me to it in discussion when he described the response of Adolf Eichmann's son to the fact that he was the child of one of the architects of the genocide of the Jews and gypsies. The oppressive and ineradicable gloom of that condition was neither shame nor guilt, but more like the condition the ancient Greeks described in their tragedies as 'pollution'. The fact that there is such a state which has aspects of shame and aspects of guilt and is not a borderline state, but a distinctive condition of its own, and the fact that it burdens people caught up in the evil deeds of others, may together explain why there has been such a confusion in public debate about the appropriate way to acknowledge the wrong done to our indigenous peoples.

Guilt and collective guilt appear simpler in their conceptual structure than national shame. That appearance should be trusted, on the whole, but there is an interesting complication to guilt, which may help us understand shame. It makes itself felt when one reflects on the response that many people have to Sophocles' play *Oedipus Rex*. Oedipus killed his father and married his mother. He did both unintentionally because of ignorance for which he was not culpable. Or, so I read Sophocles. When Oedipus realises what he has done, his horror is of the kind we would naturally call 'remorse'—its character is determined by his sense of the evil-doer he had unwittingly become:

> Now, shedder of father's blood, Husband of mother, is my name; Godless and child of shame, Begetter of brother-sons; What infamy remains That is not spoken of Oedipus.

The chorus does not doubt that Oedipus did evil: it shows in the quality of its pity for him:

> And now, where a more heart-rending story of affliction? Where a more awful swerve into the arms of torment? O Oedipus, that proud head! When the same bosom enfolded the son and the father, Could not the engendering clay have shouted aloud its indignation.

When reading Sophocles' play, and even more when watching it, few people would doubt that Oedipus and the chorus respond appropriately. Many question it on reflection, however, suspecting it is irrational, the expression of superstitions times long past, but psychologically understandable even now. In fact, as the philosopher Bernard Williams has pointed out in his book *Shame and Necessity*, urging that we must distinguish what we actually believe from what we think we believe, we are not so distant from such ways of thinking as we sometimes sincerely profess to be. He cites our law of torts as an example where responsibility is assigned and compensation demanded from those who played no causal role in the suffering of the litigants.

I do not, however, intend to argue for the rightness of Oedipus' response. To those who concede there is at least a case for it, I shall outline the more generous conception of responsibility that beckons even with something as severe as guilt. It shows in the response of the chorus. It doesn't blame Oedipus. That would indeed be irrational unless it judged his ignorance to be culpable, which it rightly does not. The stern pity of the chorus ensures that Oedipus does not evade his guilt by pleading, as he does in a later play, *Oedipus at Colonus*, that he was not culpable. Holding him in that way responsible, as properly responsive to the moral significance of his deeds, conditions what is morally possible for Oedipus and the chorus in the future. It is the exercise of a responsibility that Oedipus and the chorus have to the community which has been polluted by his deeds. Importantly, the chorus's pity is conditioned by a judgement which is severe but not 'judgemental'. It does not turn away from Oedipus in disdain, but towards him, expressing its sorrow for what he has (morally) become.

Such a non-moralistic desire severely to hold someone to their responsibility is, I think, what people express when they say that in calling for a national apology they do not thereby wish to lay blame. Sometimes they say they want merely to express their sorrow, even their grief. The trouble, however, is that the connections in our understanding between morality and blame are so close, that people then think such an expression of sorrow is not a moral response or, more precisely, that it is not a response which allows a moral description of what one sorrows over. It then seems irrelevant to the sorrow felt for the Aborigines that their suffering is largely a consequence of the fact, and is saturated by their awareness of the fact, that they were wronged rather than victims of a natural catastrophe, and that it was our political ancestors who wronged them.

Pollution is a good metaphor for the way an entire community can be affected by the guilt of its members including those who are not guilty. Some German poets and novelists were so deeply estranged from their country by the crimes of the Nazis that they could no longer write creatively in its language. Here it does seem as though the streams that nourish national identity, the love of country and its culture, have been poisoned, depriving them of the power fully to do so, at least for those with a certain kind of moral sensibility. Response to such pollution can of course be in various ways self-indulgent. The maudlin self-abasement that gives point to talk of black armband brigades is an example. But any distinction between authentic and inauthentic forms of such responses will depend on whether, and in what way, they are conditioned by a sense that one is answerable to the victims of the polluting crimes.

To talk of political ancestors is, of course, to rely on another metaphor, one whose task is to bring national shame within the conceptual ambit of familial shame. Sometimes the shame of parents for the deeds of their children depends on what they did or failed to do to or for their children, but it is not always so, and one would have desperately to be committed to the causal connotations of responsibility to believe that it is generally so when children are ashamed of what their parents have done. But reflection on familial and national shame brings into focus the deep and sometimes intense attachments to groups which form part of a person's sense of identity.

The role of the metaphor of ancestry in bringing national shame within the conceptual ambit of familial attachments is perhaps a function of what Bernard Williams has called the 'bonding interactive effects of shame'. In this respect shame is quite unlike moral guilt. Severe remorse is radically individualising. Remorseful suffering seems to be alone amongst the forms of human suffering in its need to resist the consolation which comes from the recognition that others suffer as we do. The commonplace fact that we may be consoled by the knowledge that we do not suffer alone informs Isak Dinizen's wonderful remark that 'all sorrows can be borne if you put them into a story, or tell a story about them'. Her point is not merely that stories characteristically are ways of making sense of the lives of their heroes. It is that they make the sense that they do—they are engaged in their distinctive sense-making project—against the background of compassionate responsiveness to the defining vulnerability of a common human condition.

Acknowledging that the guilty are, as I put it in *Good and Evil: An Absolute Conception*, radically singular does not mean that it is wrong to speak of national guilt, as people did of the Germans after World War Two. Such talk refers basically to the consequences for a sense of national identity of the fact that so many in the nation are guilty by deed or by omission. Although such people may have done their evil deeds under the inspiration of a corrupt nationalism, and although they were together complicit in the institutions which enabled the evil to be done and often disguised or denied, they cannot lucidly face the meaning of what they did in guilty fellowship with their compatriots. They can face it lucidly only as individual human beings.

Pride and shame, on the other hand, are fundamental to the kind of fellowship that makes community possible. It is a fellowship whose nature is determined by the way joys and sorrows change when they are shared. When that fellowship shows itself historically—as happens when people say, 'we of this nation'—then it is inseparable from the desire to celebrate achievements which shape an historically deep sense of communal identity. But if we are right to be proud, then sometimes we are obliged to be ashamed. The wish for national pride without the possibility of national shame is an expression of that corrupt attachment to a collective whose name is jingoism. Hugh Morgan, chairman of Western Mining Corporation, gave a good example of it when he responded to Mabo. 'Despite their high office, these people seem ashamed to be Australians. They seem to have no pride in their country and they strive mightily to melt it down and recast it, furtively, in a new self-deprecating and much diminished mould'.

Explaining to Frank Brennan why John Howard could not apologise in his capacity as prime minister though Howard had offered his personal apology, Peter Reith wrote: 'The government does not support an official national apology. Such an apology could imply that present generations are in some way responsible and accountable for the actions of earlier generations.' No explanation was offered of why the prime minister believed he needed to apologise personally.

How should we respond to what Peter Reith said in that letter and to the claim that, so long as one works to relieve the present misery of the Aborigines, there is no need to brood on past wrongs?

Imagine someone who says that he fully understands the wrong he had done in swindling a friend, and who also says that, while he is more than ready to make up his friend's losses, he feels no remorse and no need to apologise. Suppose he then indignantly denies that this compromises his claim to fully understand what he had done. He says that remorse is a useless and often destructive emotional addendum to the full understanding of what it means to be a wrongdoer. Such understanding, he goes on to say, entails only the desire to make good the damage to whatever degree one can. Now imagine the other extreme of this misunderstanding—someone who often and tearfully expresses remorse, but is never prepared to make reparation. Few people would deny that these characters have a desperately thin moral understanding. In the first the connection between remorse and the understanding the wrong he has done has come apart. In the second, the connection between remorse and reparation has come apart in the same way.

Is the same true of shame? Up to a point it is. The similarities are sufficient to yield a reply to those who say that protestations of shame unaccompanied by serious attempts to ameliorate the effects of the wrong done are self-indulgent and in the end harmful to the Aborigines. Would anyone deny it? Would anyone seriously say that shame is of itself an adequate response to the terrible plight suffered by most Aborigines, or that shame amounts to anything when it is separated from a serious concern with reparation? Relief of the material and psychological misery of many of the Aborigines will not count as *reparation*, however, unless the spirit in which that relief is given is informed by a recognition of the wrongs they have suffered. That is part of what we *mean* by 'reparation' and it is why we distinguish reparation from other actions which would bring the same material benefits to those who have been wronged. Acknowledgement of those wrongs as a source of torment distinct from and not reducible to their material or psychological consequences is, I believe, what the Aborigines desire when they ask for a national apology.

Thus far the analogy with remorse goes through. But is it right to say that those who declare that they know full well the terrible wrong their political ancestors did to the Aborigines, but feel no shame, have broken the connection between shame and understanding in the same way as the character in my example broke the connection between remorse and understanding?

It is, provided one adds the qualification that the persons involved must have the kind of attachment to Australia that could make shame appropriate for them. Clearly, people from other nations and citizens with no deep attachment to the country can acknowledge the wrong done to the Aborigines, and they can acknowledge also that the fact of those wrongs makes a moral claim on them. But their acknowledgement would not be shame (unless they were ashamed, as some people are, of being human). The attachment that makes national shame appropriate and sometimes called for is inseparable from the desire to celebrate achievements which shape an historically deep sense of communal identity. The pained, humbled acknowledgement of the wrongs committed by their ancestors, of those who are rooted and nourished by their country, who feel as do justices Deane and Gaudron, that those wrongs constitute a stain on their country, and whose joy in its achievements is thereby sometimes blighted—that acknowledgement I take to be one of the forms of shame. If it is not, then I do not know what to call it.

Peter Reith's claim that we cannot be held responsible for the crimes of our ancestors is true, therefore, only if one takes him to mean the kind of responsibility expressed in remorse, that is, in the pained acknowledgement of one's guilt. We can rationally feel remorse (feel guilty) only for what we have done or failed to do. But as well, or perhaps instead of, feeling guilty, we may feel ashamed, and that suggests a different notion of responsibility. Or, perhaps not a different notion so much as a different aspect of the same notion.

Martin Buber, a great Jewish religious philosopher, wrote: 'The idea of responsibility is to be brought back from the province of specialised ethics; of an "ought" that swings free in the air, into that of real life. Genuine responsibility exists only where there is real responding.' In remorse we respond to what it means to wrong another, which involves a new and terrible shock at their reality. Far from being intrinsically self-indulgent, lucid remorse makes one's victim vividly real. Corrupt forms of remorse, of which there are infinitely many, do the opposite. When our shame is the lucid expression of collective national responsibility for the wrongs done by our ancestors, we have risen in truthful response to the evil in our history—of the fact that it is *our* history. Because it is an acknowledgement of the fact that we must rise in truthful moral responsiveness to the meaning of what we have been caught up in, often through no fault of our own, it is rightly called an acceptance of responsibility.

In what way and to what degree the Aborigines may hold the non-Aboriginal community of Australia responsible for what happened in the past—some of it two centuries ago—is a matter for argument. But the fact that some of the crimes of our political ancestors were committed long ago does not mean that their victims should not require costly reparation of us. Nor does it mean that they should not call us to a sober acknowledgement of the responsibilities that determine our moral relations to them, and whose truthful acknowledgement is a precondition of our becoming, together, fully equal members of one political community. We may judge some of their claims to be excessive or foolish or even offensive. But such disagreements we must have with them—fully together with them—in the knowledge that we cannot unilaterally set the agenda, nor unilaterally proclaim what is reasonable and what is not. None of this means that non-indigenous Australians should descend into maudlin self-abasement. Nor does it mean that they cannot vigorously criticise indigenous proposals for reconciliation, or corruption in Aboriginal institutions and culture.

Long ago Yasir Arafat warned that the Palestinian problem was not merely a humanitarian problem, that its most serious dimensions could not be addressed by food and medicines sent to the refugee camps. The deepest needs of the Palestinians, he insisted, was for the political realisation of their identity as a distinct people. Australian Aborigines too are saying that theirs is not merely a humanitarian problem to be solved by better housing, schools and health services. They are saying that, as important as these matters may be, they must be dealt with in forums that acknowledge their need to find political identities which would be adequate to their history. Such claims were pressed before Mabo, but Mabo enhanced them and strengthened the demand for discussion of political structures that would best express the Aborigines' complicated relations to the Australian body politic—discussion of the kind found, for example, in books by Henry Reynolds (*Aboriginal Sovereignty*) and Nonie Sharp (*No Ordinary Judgement*).

Much of the exploration of those new structures is guided by the concept of self-determination. The vagueness of that concept has made it vulnerable to uncharitable attack. Its vagueness is not itself the expression of intractable confusion, however, even if there is plenty of confusion in its discussion. The vagueness of the concept is the expression of the fact that the Aborigines—together with the indigenous people in other parts of the world—are exploring forms of political identity and association which would adequately express the meaning of their dispossession. This exploration is radical and often novel to the classical traditions of Western political thought. Unavoidably, talk of self-determination does little more than gesture towards an outcome whose full conceptual character is unforeseeable. Such exploration of cultural and political identity is now necessary to the Aborigine's self-respect. Openness to it and to its unforeseeable outcome is a necessary condition of respect for them.

Simone Weil said that if one saw others as another perspective on the world, as one is oneself, one could not treat them unjustly. That means that we must be open to the distinctive voice of others, and that in turn means that we must encourage the conditions in which those voices can form and be heard. When people's souls have been lacerated by the wrongs done to them, individually or collectively, openness to their voices requires humbled attentiveness. When one's nation has committed those wrongs, shame is the form that humbled attentiveness takes. Without it there can be no justice.

There is little evidence of such attentiveness in the claim that historically we have little to be ashamed of and that, on balance, our history is a fine one. If we put together the thoughts that we have little to be ashamed of and that our history is 'on balance' a fine one, the relative weightlessness in these scales of the evil done to the Aborigines becomes apparent. The alternative need not be to conclude that on balance our history is a shameful one. It may be to resist such summing up. But if we insist on summing up, then we should not be surprised when Aborigines are insulted by the implication that the evil done to them should be treated as lightly as it is by those who sneer at 'black armbands'. Nor should anyone be surprised if they take such judgements as merely the further expression of the fact they have always been, and continue to be, only partially perceptible to the moral faculties of most Australians.

We must therefore not be sentimental about reconciliation. We should resist especially the kind of sentimentality expressed in Sorry Day, which good hearted though it may be, really hides from us the terrible evil the Aborigines have suffered and our responsibilities to them. More often than not, talk of reconciliation assumes that the road will be relatively smooth and the end welcome to all people of good will, if only indigenous and non-indigenous Australians will really listen to one another with an open heart. It might be so. But it might not. The assumption that it *must* be so, if minds and hearts are truly open, is inconsistent with anything that could seriously be called reconciliation. Anything really deserving of the name will be the result of an openness to the other which denies us the capacity to predict what will be consistent or inconsistent with an open heart and mind.

In 1997 Noel Pearson was moved to call some members of the Coalition 'racist scum'. This was at the time when the Queensland government together with the state's pastoralists steamrolled the federal government into treating a technical High Court judgement that native title could co-exist with pastoral leases (a judgement supported by a black-letter judge) as though it were a piece of gung-ho social engineering.

They thereby made a High Court judgement an extreme position in an acrimonious political debate. Seen against the action of the Queensland government (in its own way a naked and brutish display of political force), against the history of black/white relations which informed native title legislation, and against the fact that the court ruled that in case of conflict, pastoral rights prevail over native title, the response to Pearson appears prissy when it is not disingenuous. It shows, I think, that we are not yet ready to hear the full truth about the evil done to the Aborigines and to bear the pain of it. If we were, we would not have got so radically out of proportion our responses to Pearson and to the actions of the Queensland government and pastoralists.

An emasculated notion of conversation applied to politics, enables us to hide this from ourselves. Michael Oakeshott, the deepest conservative political philosopher of the postwar years, celebrated the idea of conversation as a way of understanding the life of the mind and of politics in his enchanting essay 'The Voice of Poetry in the Conversation of Mankind'. He insisted that strident, and even passionate, voices will destroy conversation. Even in academic life, however, that point has its limits. What is one to do with the many shrill voices in our intellectual history? How are they to speak to us? Must one first 'civilise' them? Civilise Plato, Augustine, Nietzsche, Schopenhauer and Kierkegaard?

The rhetorical force of those questions becomes more powerful when they are directed to our attempts to converse with those whom we or our political ancestors have brutally wronged. If we enter such conversations with a determinate idea of what counts as their civilised forms, then we are bound to shut our ears to what we do not wish to hear. It happens often in personal relations. More often than not the injunction, 'Try to be civilised' is a cruel reproach to those we have hurt, telling them not to make us uncomfortable by showing their pain. We then add humiliation to their pain.

Martin Buber was wiser about this. He said that the basic difference between monologue and 'fully valid conversation' was 'the otherness, or more concretely, the moment of surprise'. His point is not merely that we must be open to hearing surprising things. We must be open to being surprised at the many ways we may justly and humanly relate to one another in a spirit of truthful dialogue. It is in conversation, rather than in advance of it, that we discover, never alone but always together, what it means really to listen and what tone may properly be taken. In conversation we discover the many things conversation can be. No one can say what will happen when we fully acknowledge the evil done to the indigenous peoples of this land and when they see and accept that we have acknowledged it. More importantly, no one can say what should happen.

A Journey of Healing or a Road to Nowhere?
Lowitja O'Donoghue

There are moments in a lifetime when it seems timely to look back on where we've been, where we've arrived and where we're heading. This is one such moment.

We have just experienced all the fanfare of the dawn of a new millennium and the turn of a new century. It was a moment for collective soul searching and a great deal of sentiment and nostalgia. It was a moment for expressions of hope and optimism as we anticipated a new age. The world lit up with magical displays of fireworks—and none so wonderful and inspiring as the glittering *Eternity* sign on the Sydney Harbour Bridge.

And we all woke up the next day to realise that nothing much had changed—neither stock markets nor planes had crashed. Our microwaves, computers, ATMs and mobile phones still worked. Civilisation, as we have come to know it, had survived!

All this hype about a mere 2,000 years! It's ironic, and rather poignant really, when you think of my people and our 50,000 years of survival (against great odds) as the oldest living culture in the world.

As I write this essay, prime minister Howard has just bailed out of any commitment to a 31 December deadline for finalising documents of reconciliation, and has cast a shadow over the 27 May handover of the Reconciliation Council's documents.

This deadline was set nine years ago! Is it to languish in the 'too hard basket' forever? Given the government's record on native title, its slashing of ATSIC's funding and its refusal to offer an official apology for the stolen generations, it is hard to believe that the prime minister is genuinely committed to the cause of true reconciliation by the centenary of federation (as he claimed in his victory speech last election night). He's certainly not showing any leadership, vision or faith on the issue of reconciliation.

And as I reflect on where we've arrived, I cannot avoid thinking of the recent appalling and avoidable death of a 15-year-old Aboriginal boy in a Darwin juvenile detention centre. What a tragic waste of a human life—to die for the theft of some textas and pencils. This is surely not far removed from the petty crimes in Britain 200 years ago which led to the transportation of convicts and the invasion and colonisation of this country by British settlers. How little we have progressed in two centuries!

A decade ago the Royal Commission into Aboriginal Deaths in Custody recommended that 'imprisonment should be utilised only as a sanction of last resort'. This recommendation reflects provisions of the International Convention on the Rights of the Child, a treaty which we signed in 1990 and now dishonour.

Mandatory sentencing both disempowers and brutalises the magistrates required to enforce it and imposes on offenders senseless and cruel retribution for often trivial offences. And its consequences are racist. It is resulting in a generation of Aboriginal youth who see jail as an inevitability—their rite of passage to adulthood. A truly responsible federal government would demonstrate its leadership and commitment to reconciliation by intervening to overturn these state and territory laws.

So I feel a certain sense of despair when I look back on the events of the past few months. It makes me wonder whether my own personal journey has been a journey of healing, or has it been a road to nowhere?

I was recently asked to tell my own life story to some overseas visitors on holiday here from England. They wanted to know what were the formative influences which had shaped the direction of my life. What were the critical incidents which had led to a lifetime's work devoted to the cause of reconciliation?

It was interesting to think back on events that had happened and to realise that, unknown to me at the time, they were key milestones along my journey. There were events in which the personal and the political intersected, forever changing who I was and who I wanted to become.

One deeply traumatic and life-altering event was, of course, being taken from my mother at the age of two, along with my sisters Vi and Amy. My brother Geoffrey and eldest sister Eileen had been taken years earlier. Our mother Lily was a housegirl on Granite Downs station, in what is now Aboriginal land. Our father Tom was a station manager of Irish descent. I was not to be reunited with my grief-stricken mother for 33 years, and I never again met my father.

I was reared at Colebrook home in Quorn and later Adelaide, where approximately 350 indigenous children were taken between 1944 and 1971. We tji tji tjuta—Colebrook kids—were expected to be grateful for being saved. In a book about Colebrook written in 1937 called *Pearls from the Deep*, Aboriginal children were seen as 'waste material...rescued from the degradation of camp life...brought up from the depths of ignorance, superstition and vice...to be fashioned as gems to adorn God's crown'.

The following comments from a 1936 Adelaide *Advertiser* will give you a further idea of just how patronising and self-congratulatory were many of the so-called 'do-gooders' of the time.

> Those who have seen the Colebrook Home children are surprised at their charm, their intelligence, and the fact that they are 'like ordinary children'. It is only the training of a Christian home that has made them so. When they were brought in from the bush they were wild, frightened, dirty and ignorant. Few of them had known anything of civilised life.

A spokesperson for the home said:

> The home training has two objects—first, to make Christians of these children, and second, to merge them into the white population. As they are half white, it is better to develop in them the instincts of Europeans, and to make useful citizens of them, than to leave them in the camps to *become* [my emphasis] Aborigines.

It is now widely admitted that, *even by the standards of the time*, these actions were contrary to common law and in breach of international human rights obligations.

My most lasting memory of Colebrook is that it was a time of rigid rule-bound discipline, joyless religious observance, lack of privacy and a stultifying denial of autonomy. When I left at the age of 16 I felt I didn't know how to make a personal decision. But, ironically, I had made one momentous decision. Matron had told me that 'I'd get into trouble' (ie. get pregnant) and that 'I'd never make anything of my life'. I decided to prove her wrong.

My years of domestic work and helping with all the babies and little children at Colebrook led to two more decisions—I was never going to get married and I was never going to have children! Many, many years later in my fifties I reneged on the first decision, but I stuck to the second. More than anything I think I felt inadequate—I couldn't remember being mothered myself and I was frightened of doing it badly.

Another critical incident was my attempt to be accepted as a trainee nurse into the Royal Adelaide Hospital. I'd already spent two years training at the South Coast District Hospital at Victor Harbor. Normally two years of country service qualified you to transfer to a city hospital. Their refusal to accept me led to my active involvement with the Aboriginal Advancement League, joining with other Aboriginal people, trade unions and churches to agitate for the eligibility of Aboriginal people to enter professions and take up apprenticeships.

I was finally accepted at the Royal Adelaide, but denied credit for my two years at Victor Harbor. It was therefore after almost seven years of training that I finally graduated as a registered nurse! But my political initiation was well underway.

Many years later after a stint as a relief nurse in Assam, India, where I worked among people who lived in poverty and suffered all the negative effects of an imposed colonial culture, I decided to work as a welfare officer/nurse in Coober Pedy with my own people. I chose Coober Pedy because I knew that was my best chance of finding my mother, whom I did eventually find in Oodnadatta.

During these years the protector of Aborigines was urging 'half-caste' women like myself to seek exemption from the protection laws, so we could fraternise with whites and possibly marry a white man. Many of us saw it as a blatant attempt to 'make us white'—to get our 'dog medals' as we called the exemption certificates. For me, there was no choice. I knew then that I had to fight the injustice of the laws, rather than find a loophole for my own personal advancement.

A few years after the last protector became the director of the newly formed Commonwealth Department of Aboriginal Affairs, I became the first Aboriginal regional director of the department. In 1976 I chaired the National Aboriginal Conference, and for four years I was the chair of the Aboriginal Hostels board. There was now no turning back—my political pathway was mapped, leading me firstly to the chair of the Aboriginal Development Commission in 1989, and then to the inaugural chair of ATSIC (the Aboriginal and Torres Strait Islander Commission) from 1990–1996.

I plot this personal journey because it highlights some of the many dilemmas I feel. On the one hand I personally have had a successful career in which I have been able to remain focused on the big picture. I have been privileged, enjoying (by-and-large) good health, close ties with my siblings and extended family, and the love and support of a small circle of close friends. I have been honoured by some prestigious awards and my work has brought me into contact with many powerful and inspirational political leaders and thinkers, both in Australia and overseas. I feel as if my journey has been both personally fulfilling and publicly useful.

On the other hand I am acutely aware that most of my people have not had my opportunities and that their lives stand in stark contrast to my privileged lifestyle. And so I wonder what have I really achieved for my people? Has my journey been one step forward, two steps back?

In my recent Australia Day address (January 2000), I made the point that Australia is both an ancient land, and at the same time in its infancy in terms of its identity. This idea is a particularly powerful one for me. My Aboriginal heritage connects me with a rich and complex culture reaching back thousands of years. There are many threads linked to this culture which I feel strongly and tangibly. It is quite central to me and yet there are some aspects of it which cannot always be grasped or understood.

At the same time, my work and public role takes place in times of unimagined change, within whitefella rules and in a climate where often, political posturing is the only game in town. Again, I feel strongly about what I know at the core of my being—that human dignity and social justice are fundamental to a decent society. And I cannot entirely understand why working towards these ends is so challenging and so resisted.

Perhaps it is these big background questions that make it difficult sometimes to know whether we are making progress or not. On the other hand, perhaps it depends on what mood I'm in on any given day or who I have recently been speaking to!

I feel an enormous sense of optimism and pride when I see the tremendous work that Aboriginal doctors and health workers are doing, for example at Danila Dilba in Darwin, or at the Cooperative Research Centre for Aboriginal and Tropical Health or at the Koori Health Research and Community Development Unit. Excellent dedicated staff who understand the importance of collaboration, are the key to the success of these organisations. Their work signals a turning point for Aboriginal health in this country.

In October 1999 I was fortunate to attend and speak at the tenth anniversary celebration dinner of the Bangarra Dance Theatre. These dancers embody creativity, vibrancy and optimism for our future. They represent role models of health, beauty, athleticism, artistry and discipline for young indigenous Australians. They are proud of their cultural identity and their social agenda defines their work. This is not only significant in Australia but for the world stage as well.

Similarly there are many inspiring examples of wonderful achievement in the sporting arena. No doubt as I write, Cathy Freeman and Nova Peris-Kneebone and other Aboriginal athletes are training hard for their Olympic events later this year. I wish them luck and success and I know whatever the result in Sydney, they have already won in the most important way—by demonstrating that excellence and Aboriginality are not mutually exclusive concepts.

In fact in a whole range of fields we can see progress in the representation and contribution of Aboriginal people. And this is not to mention the enormous amount of work and support that goes on, often unrecognised, in the wider Australian context. The people's movement for reconciliation has brought hundreds of thousands of Australian people from all walks of life together in acknowledging the wrongs of the past and working towards a reconciled future. These efforts take place in all kinds of settings; for example community groups, in businesses, in churches, in schools, workplaces and in local government. These people are united not because they are all the same, or because they have the same opinions about every issue. What they do have in common is the commitment to creating a nation which is based on the unifying principle of respect for differences.

So, on a positive day there is much to celebrate and good reason to look to the future with courage and optimism. But of course there is another story to be told. It is a story which I believe must not be silenced or masked by our successes and achievements. Unfortunately, I fear that this silencing is often encouraged by our politicians and opinion leaders. It is no coincidence, for example, that to raise the problems of indigenous people, or to analyse our history, is sure to bring the cry of the 'black armband view of history', or—God forbid—allegations of political correctness. It seems that white-washing, looking on the bright side and being politically incorrect are the order of the day!

However, I cannot write of reconciliation without talking about some of the ongoing realities that are a result of dispossession. The effects of white settlement in Australia have been devastating for Aboriginal people. Our way of life and our culture have been ravaged by cruel indifference and by violence. Aboriginal people who survived it were still vulnerable to introduced diseases, alcohol, the theft of their children and the terrible attitudes of hostility and disrespect for anything other than colonial culture and values.

In real terms this has meant not only that Aboriginal people have had a different and alien culture imposed upon them. But, significantly as well, they have been excluded or marginalised from that prevailing culture. It is not hard to understand that if you are regarded and treated as an outsider in your own land—not only as different but also as subhuman—there will be profound social and emotional consequences. These consequences are identifiable in every aspect of life for indigenous peoples—for example in health, law and justice, housing, education, employment and economic status. They are all interconnected.

At the same time as there have been improvements in the health of white Australians, Aboriginal health is more like the health profile of third-world countries. One staggering statistic alone is that the average life expectancy of Aboriginal people is 20 years less than for non-

Aboriginal Australians. And this tells us nothing of the impact of such loss on families and communities.

Only approximately nine percent of Aboriginal students go on to complete further education or training, compared to 25 percent in the non-Aboriginal population. Unemployment is four times higher and of those adults employed (including CDEP) the median income is only about $16,000 a year.

Aboriginal people are over-represented in custody and arrest statistics. The number of indigenous people who are detained in custody is about 18 times higher than their white counterparts—and imprisonment rates are increasing, not decreasing. The figure is even higher in juvenile detention. In some states, for example Western Australia, Aboriginal youth are 48 times more likely to be locked up.

Each of these examples is a story in itself and behind each statistic are real lives, real tragedies and ongoing struggles. It is for all of these reasons that I think people miss the point when they think of the impact of white settlement only in terms of what happened 200 years ago. I think this is a major gap in some people's understanding of the issues and it reflects what they have been taught, or rather *not* taught, in school. If Aboriginal history was mentioned at all it was likely to have been exotic, romantic aspects like corroborees or the Dreaming that were represented, rather than the political realities of what our people experienced.

These thoughts bring me again to the point of asking, 'Why is this?' Surely such silence, and even lies, about our past is not mere oversight? Embarrassment perhaps? Yet when I think of the attitudes of our political leaders at the moment, it feels more sinister than this. There is, I believe, a vested interest in peddling the view that non-Aboriginal Australians need to be suspicious of Aboriginal people. A view that, even though we constitute only 1.6 percent of the total population, we are a threat; a view that equal opportunities exist for everyone; that the winners deserve to win and that those in trouble have brought it upon themselves. Such themes are enthusiastically embraced in talkback radio too, and I just cannot understand it.

Perhaps my sorts of questions are not the right ones to be asking in this new century. Ideas about trust and human connection don't seem relevant to our current leaders. Maybe it is time to focus more on their frameworks of economic rationalism, of bottom lines, and of performance indicators. I can do this—I can identify performance indicators for a reconciled Australia. They would be things like this: indigenous people will share more equitably in Australia's wealth; indigenous people will enjoy the same good health and live as long as other Australians; indigenous people will have equal access to education and training, and have similar success educationally; employment figures for indigenous and non-indigenous Australians will be similar; indigenous people will have widespread access to good quality and affordable housing; the imprisonment and juvenile detention rates for indigenous Australians will be proportionate to their numbers in the population; indigenous people will be proportionately represented in the professions, in politics, on the boards of corporations.

I could go on endlessly. Perhaps, though, we need only one: indigenous people will feel the same sense of pride, belonging and ownership in this country as other Australians.

And so my dilemmas continue—the question I pose in my title is still unanswered. In terms of both deeds and words, we fall well short of being a reconciled nation. We are a long way from seeing the performance indicators I have outlined above. I am not so naive as to expect overnight change; to think we can turn back the clock on 200 years of oppression with a few documents, or even a few buckets of money. Royal commissions and major government inquiries are not a panacea either. Many of the recommendations of both the Royal Commission into Aboriginal Deaths in Custody and the *Bringing Them Home* report on the stolen generations have not been implemented.

We lost the battle for a treaty many years ago and that is now our biggest problem. We can never expect to be a sovereign national state and to have the negotiating rights that go with that. But we can aim for self-determination and we can aim for agreement on the four national strategies outlined in the draft document for reconciliation: a national strategy for economic independence; a national strategy to address disadvantage; a national strategy to promote recognition of rights; and a national strategy to sustain the reconciliation process.

You don't have to be a genius to know that the actions and outcomes identified in the draft documents will take many years to implement and many generations to have a really significant impact across the board.

But we are morally and ethically bankrupt as a nation if we do not espouse these as ideals and ratify them in some words (maybe imperfect) of collective goodwill and mutual generosity. It is probably misguided to ever expect a heartfelt apology from the prime minister, and probably counter-productive to focus our energies on this.

This is another of my dilemmas. On the one hand I know how important it is for many of my people to hear the word 'sorry'. I share their sense of hurt and disappointment. For this reason I have agreed again to be joint patron, with Malcolm Fraser, of the Journey of Healing. But I no longer believe that an apology is a genuine or realistic possibility with our present leadership. I also personally have some doubts about whether the documents will be worded to the absolute satisfaction of all key stakeholders by May or even December 2000. I wonder whether our search for the perfect words may become an end in itself, distracting us from setting our sights on what is possible and achievable and workable. And it is with a heavy heart that I even voice such doubts.

But I also know that I cannot abandon the cause. We *must* work to the December 2000 deadline. We're committed to that pathway now. We must aspire to keep reconciliation alive. We must maintain the energies of the people's movement for reconciliation and continue the momentum of nine years of hard work. We must have faith in the fundamental decency of the Australian people. This faith and trust must be our bottom line. And that is what makes me believe that my journey, our journey, *will* ultimately be a journey of healing.

Symbolism and Substance in the Surge Towards Reconciliation

Gustav Nossal

At the time this anthology is published, the eyes of the nation and the world will turn to Australia to watch the Council for Aboriginal Reconciliation hand over its final proposals about a national reconciliation document to the Australian people.

This event, Corroboree 2000, will give all Australians the chance to show their support for reconciliation and commit to a set of plans to improve the way Aboriginal and Torres Strait Islander peoples and the wider community work together as a nation.

Though supporters of reconciliation agree that it will take a long time to become a 'reconciled' nation, I believe we also agree that there should be definite reconciliation outcomes by the end of this year. The outcome that the Council for Aboriginal Reconciliation is pushing for is broad national agreement on a national reconciliation document.

By the time we celebrate the centenary of federation in 2001, and before the eyes of the world turn to us for the Sydney 2000 Olympics, we should have agreed on real steps to advance reconciliation and a framework to continue reconciliation in the years to come.

In this article I would like to explain some of the reasons behind the national document, what it will do, and what happens to the reconciliation process when the council ends on 31 December this year. First I would like to explain some of the history to my involvement in this important national process, and some of the lessons I have drawn from it.

It may well be that, among the distinguished contributors to this volume of essays, I am the least experienced person in Aboriginal affairs. This deserves some introductory comment about how I came to be deputy chairman of the Council for Aboriginal Reconciliation.

As an immunologist whose whole working life has been spent in medical research, I was introduced in 1964 to the great problems arising in developing countries through the persistence of communicable diseases and also to the notion that vaccines represented a powerful and cost-effective tool for the reduction of the abysmally high infant and childhood mortality rates in many countries. Down the years, a commitment to contributing to the World Health Organization's efforts at disease control deepened; so much so that I spent 1976 on sabbatical leave working for a full year for WHO. Following my retirement as director of The Walter and Eliza Hall Institute of Medical Research in 1996, global immunisation has in fact become my main preoccupation.

Against this background, dear Australian colleagues including Professor Fiona Stanley in Perth and Professor John Mathews, then in Darwin, persuaded me that it was time I realised the existence of a sub-population experiencing essentially third-world standards of health right here within our own country. I refer, of course, to the Aboriginal and Torres Strait Islander peoples.

Consequently, I joined the so-called Eminent Persons Group of the Australian Medical Association and the Public Health Association of Australia, essentially a lobby group seeking to influence government for greater investment in Aboriginal health. As part of this group's work, we met with the prime minister, with Dr Michael Wooldridge, minister for health, and with senator John Herron, minister for Aboriginal affairs. Subsequent to these meetings, Mr Herron was kind enough to ask me to assume the deputy chairman role and I was thrown headlong into an exciting, complex, difficult but very promising field. I have now been on a very fast learning curve for two and a half years!

My analysis of the problem so far has convinced me that reconciliation has two conceptually separable aspects which, however, are intricately and importantly linked. There is an eminently practical aspect: the poor state of Aboriginal health, the lower standard to which indigenous people are educated, the limited employment opportunities, the frequently poor housing, the inadequate infrastructure in many remote communities—all of these represent areas of disadvantage that clearly must be addressed and progressively fixed in the so-called 'lucky country'. To the extent that reconciliation involves a sincere desire to make progress on these issues, a wide majority of the Australian public will support the concept.

On the other hand, there is also a very important symbolic aspect to reconciliation. Indigenous peoples wish to be recognised and valued as the first Australians, the original owners and custodians of traditional lands and waters. They wish to have their laws, beliefs and traditions respected and recognised. They wish mainstream Australians to gain a greater appreciation of their spiritual affiliation with the land and their historic achievements in living in ecological balance with it while able to exercise their traditional lifestyles. They wish more Australians to know the truth of colonisation without the consent of the original inhabitants, and acknowledge the abject treatment of indigenous peoples by the early settlers which resulted in the dispossession and alienation of many of their descendants.

While many well-intentioned Australians—including myself before an involvement with the council—sought sincerely to work on the practical side, the close linkage between practical and symbolic only becomes apparent on closer examination of the issues.

Reconciliation Convention and beyond

The moving Reconciliation Convention held in Melbourne starting on 26 May 1997 was a major and successful exercise in raising the national consciousness about reconciliation; in showcasing the multi-faceted nature of indigenous talent, both with respect to art and culture and in terms of articulate and vigorous leadership. It really placed reconciliation squarely onto the national agenda and I believe tremendous progress has been made since 1997. This has been evidenced by the hundreds of thousands of Australians who signed Sorry Books following the report of the Human Rights and Equal Opportunity Commission (HREOC) on the stolen generations; the many study circles taking place at community grassroots levels where issues in Aboriginal and Torres Strait Islander affairs are discussed; the successful work of the state reconciliation committees helped by the indefatigable Australians for Reconciliation (AFR) coordinators. Through the council's communications strategies, and particularly through its magazine, *Walking Together*, a real groundswell of positive opinion has been generated.

However, we must be aware that Aboriginal affairs are multi-faceted and complex. We must avoid simplistic approaches to the problems and recognise that true and lasting solutions will require not months but actually decades of effort. The aim of the reconciliation movement is to promote the attitude that it is better to link arms and attack specific issues in a collegial manner—in other words, as friends rather than opponents facing each other across the table with clenched jaws. From that point of view, we hope that at the conclusion of the council's work, a giant step towards reconciliation will have been taken, fully recognising that the completion of the reconciliation process will require further effort, discourse and sacrifice.

This brings me to the major exclamation mark along the road, namely Corroboree 2000. The date and place for Corroboree 2000 were carefully chosen. 27 May 2000 is exactly three years after the Melbourne

Reconciliation Convention and exactly 33 years after the 1967 referendum overwhelmingly supported by the Australian people, which gave Aboriginal and Torres Strait Islander peoples full citizenship rights. The place, the Sydney Opera House, was the place where, 212 years earlier, captain Arthur Phillip began the process of colonisation. The main purpose of Corroboree 2000 is for the council to hand its proposed document towards reconciliation to the Australian people.

A stapled document of reconciliation
The document, finalised only a few weeks ago, has been carefully crafted and in a sense represents the peak result of nearly nine years work of the council. To illustrate how strongly we feel about the linkage between symbolism and substance, it is really two integrated documents, each supporting and dependent on the other.

Firstly there is a brief declaration towards reconciliation which lays down the principle in poetic but strong terms, making the commitment to reconciliation contingent on a recognition of the truth of Australia's past, a sincere desire to heal the wounds and a determination to move on together. The declaration acknowledges that post-Corroboree 2000, a new and difficult journey begins—indigenous and other Australians walking together towards a future where all enjoy equal rights, opportunities and responsibilities. The declaration will be in a form where it can be used in schools, in citizenship ceremonies, on high occasions of state and in other appropriate aspects of public life.

National strategies or action plans
Attached to the declaration will be more detailed national strategies to advance reconciliation. These four strategies arise from the principles of the declaration but map out the detailed steps that need to be taken by governments, organisations and individuals from both indigenous and wider communities to solidify a real practical commitment to reconciliation.

These strategies or action plans are, in the main, non-controversial except to the degree that they will stress targets to be met within specific timeframes. In other words, they will include benchmarks against which governments, organisations and interested parties can measure themselves. To our knowledge this has not been done before in this field.

Obviously, in many areas there will be separate tasks for Commonwealth, state, territory and local governments, and in some areas for the Aboriginal and Torres Strait Islander Commission (ATSIC) as well. It will be tough for the council to be absolutely precise about these respective responsibilities but all parties concerned must resist the temptation of 'passing the buck' from one level of government to the other—this has held back indigenous programs in the past.

Before describing the strategies more closely, it is important to look at the process which created the strategies to be launched at Corroboree

2000. Skeletal outlines of the strategies as well as an advanced draft of the declaration went out for very wide community consultation in the second half of 1999. While the council itself sponsored about 100 community consultation meetings, a total of at least 200 actually took place involving some 10,000 individuals. As well as that, the draft document went to a large number of organisations and individuals.

Over the period, thousands of comments have reached the council secretariat, mostly in accordance with a structured form available to be filled in. Professional research help was sought both to correlate and summarise these responses, and to conduct further independent social research focus groups in both the indigenous and wider communities and a major quantitative survey of wider community attitudes.

The qualitative and quantitative research commissioned by the council contained some mixed signals, but showed that 74 percent of people who read our draft document agreed with at least most of its content. Armed with the responses of the Australian people, the council will revisit both the strategies and the declaration and modify the document to ensure it reflects as closely as possible a majority Australian view. We want to remain faithful to the consultation process but at the same time not to adopt views that the majority would consider extreme.

In the end, the council has the responsibility, under the federal legislation which established it, of preparing the document. While due regard will be paid to all opinions expressed, the council takes final responsibility and signs off on the actual words which will go to the Australian people.

What are the strategies which the council deems to be the most important? They fall into four headings—greater economic independence and self-reliance in the lives of Aboriginal and Torres Strait Islander peoples; addressing indigenous disadvantage and aiming for better outcomes in health, education, employment, housing, law and justice; promoting recognition of Aboriginal and Torres Strait Islander rights from the principle that all Australians should share equal rights and responsibilities as citizens; and sustaining the reconciliation process so that, when the council comes to the end of its life on 31 December 2000, the existing people's movement for reconciliation can continue, probably under the auspices of a reconciliation foundation.

Legislative framework for reconciliation
If the broad thrust of the document receives wide approval, as I sincerely trust it will, there is still a great deal of work to be done in the last seven months of the council's term.

We hope the principles of the document can be enshrined in legislation, though we do not expect agreement will be reached on every last point within such a comprehensive set of documents and recommendations. Rather, we are hoping that it will be possible to legislate a framework agreement, which spells out those areas on which consensus has been reached and which can then be addressed in a practical way. We hope that mention will also be made of areas that are best left for future discussion and eventual solution.

Such legislation would not be a treaty, but rather would provide a framework to be referred back to again and again, as particular issues move more feasibly into the debate and edge closer to final resolution. We consider it possible that draft legislation may actually form a part of the council's final report to parliament towards the very end of this year.

Some of us hope that the passage of such legislation might be a very early event for legislatures in 2001, the centenary of federation year. It is the longer range hope of council that the key principles of the document could eventually find their way into the Australian Constitution either by way of a preamble or into its substance. However, we recognise that this is a longer-range goal which will not be accomplished during the life of the council itself, but rather will belong as part of the task of any successor body.

A foundation for reconciliation

At Corroboree 2000, the council will launch a foundation that might take over the council's work from 1 January 2001. This foundation should capitalise on the people's movement and strengthen it. Although it might require some initial seeding funds from government, it should be free-standing from government, voluntary in nature, gaining much of its funding through sponsorships and donations. It should have a significant input from the currently independent state reconciliation committees, and to the greatest extent possible, should continue the education and community outreach work of the AFR coordinators.

Somewhere in the whole spectrum of endeavour there should be a continuous monitoring of progress towards full reconciliation, but perhaps the main burden of this should be borne not by the foundation but by the appropriate regulatory body within the Commonwealth bureaucracy. We certainly see the HREOC Social Justice commissioner as having a very important role. The foundation should most certainly not be a continuation of the council under another guise. The council was convened to do a particular job, namely to bring the reconciliation process as far as it possibly could by the centenary of federation. For the long haul, a different kind of body is needed within the voluntary sector.

Challenges in Aboriginal health

Having mentioned my entry into Aboriginal affairs via the health field, let me close on some health issues. Aboriginal and Torres Strait Islander people in northern, central and western Australia have a lower life expectancy than any other indigenous minority within a first-world country. Comparisons have been drawn between indigenous Australians and the indigenous populations of New Zealand, the United States and Canada and these do not show Australia in a flattering light. Our indigenous mortality rates from all causes are twice as high as the Maori rate, 2.5 times the United States indigenous rate and over three times the total Australian rate. Moreover, there has been no significant reduction in the death rate for our indigenous peoples between 1985 and 1995.

In contrast, the situation in Canada and the United States as well as in New Zealand has been improving substantially and continuously. This shows that indigenous health problems can be solved, and over a comparatively short period of time.

Some of the particular statistics are frightening. Despite some improvements in this area, the indigenous infant mortality rate is about three times higher than the national average. Life expectancy at birth is about 18 years lower than for other Australians. Heart and arterial disease, respiratory conditions, diabetes, suicide rates, injury, poisoning, and kidney ailments are all far higher in indigenous people.

It is important to explode the myth that tons of money has been thrown at the problem of Aboriginal health but has all been wasted. In fact, for every man, woman and child in the country, we spend a total of $1.08 on indigenous Australians for every $1 spent on other Australians. Given a difference in health status of a factor of at least three, this eight percent differential is actually tiny. When one further considers that many Aboriginal people live in remote locations, where it costs more to do almost anything and in particular to provide services, then the difference from a statistical point of view disappears altogether. In relation to need, this equivalence can only be considered unjust towards indigenous people.

Approximately two percent of the population are identified as Aboriginal and Torres Strait Islander people. Yet total Medicare and Pharmaceutical Benefits Scheme outlays for indigenous peoples are only 0.5 percent of total Australian benefits. Admittedly, because of the severe ill-health of many indigenous people, hospitalisation rates are considerably higher, thus state expenditure on their health is higher.

The Australian Medical Association-Public Health Association working group believes that considerable additional funding is required and should be directed via specific national programs including community-controlled health services, programs directed to specific disease areas, training of indigenous people in all sectors of health care, and further applied research, particularly in the area of improved methods of health service delivery. These are just some of the urgent requirements which should be addressed in the upcoming Commonwealth budget.

Summary and conclusions

Part of the problem in coming to grips with indigenous disadvantage arises from the small size of the indigenous population and from their general remoteness from the main population centres. In other words, 98 percent find it relatively easy to ignore two percent, at least most of the time.

Yet, as the governor-general has said, if we do not achieve substantial progress towards reconciliation, Australia will be a diminished nation as we celebrate the centenary of federation. Corroboree 2000 could be a major step towards reconciliation.

As I mentioned earlier, there are three major occasions this year when the eyes of the world turn to Australia, and when indigenous issues and reconciliation will be in the international spotlight. Corroboree 2000 will be a major event both because of the ceremony in the Opera House and because of the up to 250,000-strong People's Walk for Reconciliation across the Sydney Harbour Bridge on 28 May.

Next of course, in September 2000 we have the Olympic Games, which will be a marvellous opportunity to showcase Aboriginal art, dance, culture and ceremonies. The council has been delighted to be working closely with the Sydney Organising Committee of the Olympic Games to ensure that both the Games themselves and the 27,000 kilometre-long Torch Relay will be outstanding tools for reconciliation.

Great success at Corroboree 2000 would set the scene for a positive flow-on to this aspect of the Games which will be closely watched by the entire world. Finally, the centenary of federation should be a joyous and celebratory occasion for all Australians and will be so for the indigenous community if the document of reconciliation and its spirit resonates widely throughout Australia.

Draft Declaration of Reconciliation
Council for Aboriginal Reconciliation

This is the draft declaration released in 1999. The final version was not available at the time of publication.

Speaking with one voice, we the people of Australia, of many origins as we are, make a commitment to go on together recognising the gift of one another's presence.

We value the unique status of Aboriginal and Torres Strait Islander peoples as the original owners and custodians of traditional lands and waters.

We respect and recognise continuing customary laws, beliefs and traditions.

And through the land and its first peoples, we may taste this spirituality and rejoice in its grandeur.

We acknowledge this land was colonised without the consent of the original inhabitants.

Our nation must have the courage to own the truth, to heal the wounds of its past so that we can move on together at peace with ourselves.

And so we take this step: as one part of the nation expresses its sorrow and profoundly regrets the injustices of the past, so the other part accepts the apology and forgives.

Our new journey then begins. We must learn our shared history, walk together and grow together to enrich our understanding.

We desire a future where all Australians enjoy equal rights and share opportunities and responsibilities according to their aspirations.

And so, we pledge ourselves to stop injustice, address disadvantage and respect the right of Aboriginal and Torres Strait Islander peoples to determine their own destinies.

Therefore, we stand proud as a united Australia that respects this land of ours, values the Aboriginal and Torres Strait Islander heritage, and provides justice and equity for all.

The Dawn is at Hand
Oodgeroo, from the tribe Noonuccal

Dark brothers, first Australian race,
Soon you will take your rightful place
In the brotherhood long waited for,
Fringe-dwellers no more.

Sore, sore the tears you shed
When hope seemed folly and justice dead.
Was the long night weary? Look up, dark band,
The dawn is at hand.

Go forward proudly and unafraid
To your birthright all too long delayed,
For soon now the shame of the past
Will be over at last.

You will be welcomed mateship-wise
In industry and in enterprise;
No profession will bar the door,
Fringe dwellers no more.

Dark and white upon common ground
In club and office and social round,
Yours the feel of a friendly land,
The grip of the hand.

Sharing the same equality
In college and university,
All ambitions of hand or brain
Yours to attain.

For ban and bias will soon be gone,
The future beckons you bravely on
To art and letters and nation lore,
Fringe-dwellers no more.

Notes on Contributors

Bain Attwood is a senior lecturer in history at Monash University and the author and editor of several books on Aboriginal history, including *In the Age of Mabo: History, Aborigines and Australia*, and (with Andrew Markus) *The Struggle for Aboriginal Rights: A Documentary History*. He is currently writing a history of Aboriginal rights in Australia.

Kim Beazley has been leader of the federal Labor Party since 19 March 1996.

Frank Brennan, a Jesuit priest and lawyer, is an adjunct fellow at the Australian National University; honorary visiting fellow at the University of New South Wales; the director of Uniya, the Jesuit Social Justice Centre in Sydney; and a member of the Council of the Constitutional Centenary Foundation. His books include *The Wik Debate*, *One Land One Nation* and *Reconciling our Differences*. In 1998, the Council for Aboriginal Reconciliation appointed him as an ambassador for reconciliation.

Linda Burney is deputy director general of the NSW Department of Aboriginal Affairs; chair of the NSW State Reconciliation Committee; chair NSW Juvenile Justice Advisory Council; member of NSW Board of Vocational Education and Training; NSW Historic Houses Trust; NSW Centenary of Federation Council; University of Canberra Council; the

Sydney Institute Council of NSW TAFE; and a trustee of the Mick Young Scholarship Trust. The piece published here is based on an address to the 50th Anniversary of Australian Citizenship conference in July 1999.

Melissa Castan is a lecturer in the law faculty at Monash University, Victoria. She has a BA/LLB (Hons) from Monash, and an LLM from Melbourne University. She currently teaches constitutional law and indigenous legal issues, and is editor of the *Alternative Law Journal*.

Geoff Clark, from the Tjapwuurong tribe of western Victoria, became ATSIC's first elected national chairman in December 1999 after being re-elected as ATSIC commissioner for Victoria two months earlier. He lives at the Framlingham Aboriginal community near Warrnambool, where he was administrator of the community trust for 17 years prior to election to the ATSIC board in 1996. He is vice-president of the Aboriginal Provisional Government.

Inga Clendinnen, historian and essayist, is an internationally acclaimed scholar of the Aztec and the Maya peoples of Mexico and the process of their conquest and colonisation by Spaniards in the sixteenth century. Her most recent book, *Tiger's Eye: A Memoir* is published by Text. The piece extracted here is from *True Stories: The 1999 Boyer Lectures* published by ABC Books.

Aban Contractor is a reporter for the *Canberra Times* in the federal parliamentary press gallery, specialising in indigenous affairs.

Tim Costello, lawyer and Baptist minister, is the director of the Urban Mission Unit for the Collins Street Baptist Church in Melbourne, a spokesperson for the Interchurch Gambling Taskforce, a member of the Australian Earth Charter Committee, a council member of the Australian Centre for Christianity and Culture, and an ambassador for the Council for Aboriginal Reconciliation. He is the author of *Streets of Hope: Finding God in St Kilda* and *Tips From a Travelling Soul Searcher*.

Mary Darkie belongs to the Jaru tribe. She attended the Reconciliation Convention in Melbourne in 1997 and helped organise reconciliation meetings in her local communities.

Patrick Dodson is a Yawuru man from Broome in Western Australia. He is a former director of the Central Land Council and the Kimberley Land Council, a former royal commissioner into the Aboriginal Deaths in Custody and for six years the chairman of the Council for Aboriginal Reconciliation. The piece published here is based on Dodson's Vincent Lingiari memorial lecture delivered in August 1999.

Rick Farley is the managing director of the Farley Consulting Group, which specialises in land use agreements. He is chairman of the NSW Resources and Conservation Assessment Council, chairman of the Lake Victoria Advisory Committee, an ambassador for reconciliation and a member of the NSW State Reconciliation Committee.

Raimond Gaita teaches philosophy at the Australian Catholic University and at King's College London, University of London. His books include *Good and Evil: An Absolute Conception*; *Value and Understanding* (ed.); *Romulus, My Father*; and most recently, *A Common Humanity: Thinking About Love &Truth &Justice*. The piece extracted here is based on a chapter in *A Common Humanity*.

Peter Garrett is president of the Australian Conservation Foundation as well as being lead singer of the Australian music group Midnight Oil, which is renowned for its active support of a range of contemporary issues including the plight of homeless youth, indigenous peoples rights and protection of the environment.

Petro Georgiou is the federal member for Kooyong. Between 1985–89 he was director of the Liberal Party Policy Unit and in 1989 appointed state director of the Victorian Liberal Party until his preselection for the federal seat of Kooyong in 1994. The article published here first appeared in the *Canberra Times* on 26 February 2000 and the *Age*, 29 February.

Lillian Holt works in Aboriginal education and was the first Aboriginal executive officer for the National Aboriginal Education Committee and the first Aboriginal principal of the Aboriginal Community College, Port Adelaide. She is currently director of the Centre for Indigenous Education at the University of Melbourne. Her essay is based on a paper delivered at the Race, Culture and Democracy conference in August 1999.

John Howard is prime minister of Australia, an office he has held since 1996.

Peter Jull worked for Canadian territorial, provincial, and federal governments on indigenous issues, and has worked with Aboriginal organisations and Torres Strait Islanders in Australia as well as publishing widely on indigenous constitutional reform. He is adjunct associate professor of government at the University of Queensland.

Paul Keating was prime minister of Australia from 1991 to 1996. The speech published here was delivered in Sydney in 1992 at the launch of the International Year for the World's Indigenous People.

Hugh Mackay is a psychologist whose social research project, *The Mackay Report*, has been tracking the mood of Australian society for the past 21 years. He is the author of four bestselling books in social psychology, the most recent being *Turning Point: Australians Choosing their Future*.

Robert Manne is associate professor of politics at La Trobe University and a well-known commentator on political issues. His latest book is *The Australian Century: Political Struggle in the Building of the Nation* published by Text. A part of his essay was published in the *Age* and the *Sydney Morning Herald* on 27 February 1999.

Hannah McGlade is a Nyungar lawyer, teacher and social justice activist. Her areas of interest include human rights with special emphasis on race and race discrimination, Aboriginal women and access to justice.

Padraic Pearse McGuinness is a journalist with the *Sydney Morning Herald* and editor of *Quadrant* magazine. A shorter version of his essay was published in the April 1999 issue of *Quadrant*.

Robert Milliken is a Sydney journalist and author who writes for *The Economist* and *The Eye* magazine.

Drusilla Modjeska's books include *Exiles at Home*, *Poppy* (which won the Banjo and NSW Premier's Awards) and *The Orchard* (winner of the NSW Premier's Award for Non-fiction, Kibble Literary Prize and Australian Booksellers Award). Her latest book is *Stravinsky's Lunch*. 'A Bitter Wind' was the 1997 NSW Premier's Literary Awards Address.

Denis Muller is a senior research associate in the Centre for Public Policy at the University of Melbourne and former senior journalist at the *Age* and the *Sydney Morning Herald*.

Djon Mundine was senior curator of the Gallery of Aboriginal Australia at the National Museum of Australia from 1997–1999. From 1996–97 he was senior curator of Aboriginal and Torres Strait Islander Programs at the Museum of Contemporary Art, Sydney. He is a member of the Bandjalung People, NSW.

Gustav Nossal is deputy chairman of the Council for Aboriginal Reconciliation. He currently chairs the committee overseeing the World Health Organization's Global Programme for Vaccines and Immunisation (1993–) and is chairman of the Strategic Advisory Council of the Bill and Melinda Gates Children's Vaccine Program (1988–). Nossal was knighted in 1977, made a Companion of the Order of Australia in 1989 and appointed Australian of the Year in 2000.

Lowitja O'Donoghue was appointed as the inaugural chairperson of the Aboriginal and Torres Strait Islander Commission and acted in this role from the inception of the commission in 1990 until her retirement in December 1996. This year she was awarded the Companion of the Order of Australia for her work in Aboriginal human rights.

Formerly known as Kath Walker, **Oodgeroo of the tribe Noonuccal** was a writer, artist, teacher and activist. The poems published here are taken from *My People*, which was first published in 1970. The book is now in its third edition. Oodgeroo died in September 1993.

Christopher Pearson has been the editor of the *Adelaide Review* since 1984. He has been publishing on Aboriginal affairs policy regularly since 1981. He is also a former publisher of the Wakefield Press. He serves on the Board of the National Museum of Australia and is a member of the Australia Council.

Noel Pearson is currently an adviser to the Cape York Land Council, of which he was executive director from its inception until July 1996, when he was elected chairman, a position from which he resigned at the end of 1997. His essay is based on an address to the Brisbane Institute in July 1999.

Boori Monty Pryor is a performer and storyteller who has worked in film, television, music, modelling, sport and theatre. His book *Maybe Tomorrow* (1998) which is co-authored by Meme McDonald received the Human Rights and Equal Opportunity Commission Honourable Mention and was shortlisted for the CBC Eve Pownall Information Award in 1999. Other books by Meme and Boori include *My Girragundji* and *The Binna Binna Man*.

Henry Reynolds is a well-known historian, academic and writer. Author of numerous books on indigenous affairs, his latest is *Why Weren't We Told?* A version of his essay first appeared in the *Alternative Law Journal*, December 1999.

Aden Ridgeway is an Australian Democrats senator for NSW and is spokesperson for reconciliation, industry, arts, tourism, financial services and centenary of federation. He was born in Macksville and is a member of the Gumbayyngirr people.

Irving Saulwick is one of Australia's leading social researchers. He has published the Saulwick Poll in the *Age* since 1971.

Evelyn Scott, chairperson of the Council for Aboriginal Reconciliation, is of Aboriginal and South Sea Islander heritage. A member of the former Federal Council for the Advancement of Aborigines and Torres Strait Islanders, she campaigned for the 1967 referendum.

Colin Tatz is director of the Centre for Comparative Genocide Studies at Macquarie University and professor of politics at the University of Western Sydney, Macarthur. He has been a student of Aboriginal affairs since migrating from South Africa in 1961.

Paul D. Wand was the initial vice president Aboriginal Relations Rio Tinto Ltd., Australia from 1995–2000. Now retired from this position, he maintains the chairmanship of the Rio Tinto Aboriginal Foundation. His essay first appeared in *International Policy Review*, Volume 8, Spring 1998–99.

Pera Wells is the director of the consultancy, Cross-Cultural Connections and a former Australian diplomat, head of the first Human Rights Section in the Department of Foreign Affairs (1984).

Indigenous Issues on the Net: A List of Websites

http://www.atsic.gov.au
The Aboriginal and Torres Strait Islander Commission (ATSIC) is the peak indigenous body in Australia.

http://www.vicnet.net.au/vicnet/COUNTRY/ABORIG.HTM
Vicnet includes many Aboriginal resources and links.

http://www.lib.latrobe.edu.au/AHR/emuse/wik/read.html
Belonging, sharing and Wik article by Peter Read, links.

http://www.caa.org.au/publications/briefing/wik/index.html
Community Aid Abroad. Commentary on Wik developments.

Arts and Music
http://www.ozco.gov.au/whatsnew/Atsi-pol.htm
The Australia Council's Aboriginal and Torres Strait Islander arts policy history.

http://www.yothuyindi.com
Yothu Yindi's site—read about the band, hear music clips.

http://www.crt.nt.au/~lewis/index.html
Indidjinart-Aboriginal Art and Craft. Wiradjuri artist Lewis Burns.

http://www.pegasus.oz.au/~firehorse/art/firework.html
Commercial art gallery with emphasis on Australian indigenous artists.

http://www.acay.com.au~cmr/gsl.html
A school resource kit of songs, literature, drama, and essential Australian historical information.

http://www.abc.net.au/rn/talks/8.30/edurpt/estories/er061201.htm
ABC Education report transcript—A new blueprint for improving Aboriginal education, interview with Dr Paul Hughes.

http://www.bushnet.qld.edu.au/schools/mareeba_primary/asspa
Mareeba Aboriginal and Torres Strait Islander page.

Education
http://www.koori.usyd.edu.au
Koori Centre, University of Sydney.

http://www.koori.usyd.edu.au/FIAEP
Federation of Independent Aboriginal Education Providers.

http://www.ntu.edu.au/fatsis
Northern Territory University, faculty of Aboriginal and Torres Strait Islander studies.

Health
http://www.cowan.edu.au/chs/nh/clearinghouse/index.htm
The Aboriginal and Torres Strait Islander Health Research homepage. Indigenous health research, clearing house, online Aboriginal and Torres Strait Islander health bulletin, health bibliography database, reports.

http://www.midcoast.com.au/users/biriamc
Biripi Aboriginal Corporation Medical Centre.

http://www.medicineau.net.au/AbHealth
Aboriginal Culture for Health Workers' Training Manual. Gordon O'Brien and Daniel Plooij, Flinders University, SA.

http://www.alga.com.au/indig.htm
Australian Local Government Association—Indigenous issues, including quarterly indigenous newsletters.

http://www.abc.net.au/rn/#trans
Background Briefing and the Media Report contain talks on racism, removal of children, and Hindmarsh Island; the Law Report, the Health Report, and the Education Report refer to Aboriginal and Torres Strait Islander issues.

History
http://www.abc.net.au/frontier
Website companion to the ABC-TV documentary *Frontier*. Includes new interactive material specially prepared for the web; online discussion.

http://www.ozemail.com.au/~nlc95/index.html
Northern Land Council, describes the history and activities of the organisation, and some of the history of the Top End of the Northern Territory.

Human Rights
http://www.austlii.edu.au/au/special/rsjproject/rsjlibrary/hreoc/stolen/
The full text of the *Bringing Them Home* report.

http://hna.ffh.vic.gov.au/phb/hdev/koori/overview.html
Victorian Government's Koori Health Unit-policy and online publications.

Landrights and Native Title
http://law.agps.gov.au
Text of Wik judgement, from attorney general's database site. Enter 'Wik' on the front page to get to the text.

http://www.nntt.gov.au
National Native Title Tribunal.

http://www.faira.org.au/niwg
National indigenous working group on native title activities, contacts, online resources.

http://www.slq.qld.gov.au/atsi.htm
John Oxley Library, Queensland, Australia. Describes newspaper clippings available and other catalogued resources, including photographs.

http://www.nla.gov.au/nla/staffpaper/thomp.html
'White Australia has a Black History': sources for Aboriginal and Torres Strait Islander studies in the National Library of Australia.

Note: several native title resources are also available online from
http://www.aiatsis.gov.au/ntru_abt.htm

Languages
http://www.dnathan.com/VL/austLang.htm
Virtual Library for Australian indigenous languages.

Law
http://www.austlii.edu.au
Australian Legal Information Institute, includes searchable national native title tribunal database.

http://www.icip.lawnet.com.au
'Our Culture Our Future': Indigenous and intellectual property rights. Proposals for the recognition of indigenous cultural and intellectual property.

http://www.ntu.edu.au/faculties/law/martin/indig.htm
Martin Flynn's web pages to help locate useful legal material on the web.

Media
http://www.nor.com.au/media/kmail/
Koori Mail—national Aboriginal and Torres Strait Islander newspaper.

http://pymedia.in-sa.com.au
Pitjantjatjara Yankunytjatjara Media. Broadcasting on the Anangu Lands; includes a map of the lands.

http://kali.murdoch.edu.au/~cntinuum/dreamtime/dreamtpt2.html
Indigenous issues site in the Culture and Communication Reading Room, Centre for Research in Culture and Communication at Murdoch University. WA access to useful online articles and reports.

http://www.austlii.edu.au/car
Council for Aboriginal Reconciliation site, includes texts of the state and national reports of the Royal Commission into Aboriginal Deaths in Custody.

http://www.cwis.org
Includes Draft Declaration on the Rights of the Indigenous Peoples Law.